THE EFFECTS OF MASS COMMUNICATION ON POLITICAL BEHAVIOR

the EFFECTS of
MASS COMMUNICATION
on
POLITICAL BEHAVIOR

Sidney Kraus
and
Dennis Davis

The Pennsylvania State University Press

University Park and London

For Cecile and Nancy

Library of Congress Cataloging in Publication Data

Kraus, Sidney.
  The effects of mass communication on political
behavior.

  Includes bibliographies and indexes.
    1. Communication in politics.   2. Mass media—
Political aspects.   3. Political socialization.
I. Davis, Dennis, joint author.   II. Title.
JA76.K72   301.5′92   76-3480
ISBN 0-271-01226-9 cloth
ISBN 0-271-00501-7 paperback

Designed by Joe Kredlow

Printed in the United States of America

Contents

1
INTRODUCTION 1

2
MASS COMMUNICATION
AND
POLITICAL SOCIALIZATION 8

3
MASS COMMUNICATION
AND THE
ELECTORAL PROCESS 48

4

MASS COMMUNICATION
AND
POLITICAL INFORMATION 110

5

MEDIA USE
AND
POLITICAL PROCESSES 174

6

CONSTRUCTION OF
POLITICAL REALITY
IN SOCIETY 209

7

METHODS OF POLITICAL COMMUNICATION RESEARCH 246

8

CONCLUDING REMARKS 281

List of Figures

Preface

The events which brought about this book are in and of themselves a part of the book and are, therefore, worth sharing with our readers. The original idea dates back to when the senior author was terminating his political communication consulting business to accept a professorship at the University of Massachusetts in 1970. Most of his consulting experience suggested a need for the infusion of social and behavioral science approaches in political campaigning, particularly with regard to communication use.

In setting about that task, however, it was immediately apparent that the body of knowledge on mass communication and political behavior was not readily available in a suitable form. Moreover, it became increasingly evident that, for reasons discussed throughout this book, communication variables in many studies purporting to examine effects on political behavior were presumed to have little if any effect and consequently were often not included.

These two conditions—lack of a cogent review of the literature and lack of inclusion of communication variables—prompted the abandonment of the original task in favor of the present one: an inventory and review of the knowledge in the social and behavioral sciences on the effects of mass communication on political behavior.

In 1972, three significant events occurred which ultimately insured the completion of this project. The first of these was the kind invitation from Harold Mendelsohn to the senior author to present in plenary session at the annual meetings of the American Association for Public Opinion Research a paper entitled "Mass Communication and Political Behavior." Upon the conclusion of that session, Hope Klapper suggested that the paper be divided into two sections—one on political socialization and the other on the election process. These two appear in the book as Chapters 2 and 3, which were published in an earlier version in the *Quarterly Journal of Speech* (reprinted in A. Wells, ed., *Mass Media and Society*, Palo Alto, Calif.: Mayfield Publishing Co., 1975, pp. 320–30) and *Speech Monographs*, respectively.

The second and third events combined to provide the necessary man and woman power and competencies to complete this study. The senior author moved to Cleveland State University to chair the Department of Communication in a new direction with social and behavioral science emphases and the John and Mary Markle Foundation awarded him funds to support the review project. Sincere thanks are due to Jack Soules, Dean of Arts and Sciences at Cleveland State, for his continued support of this project. A special note of indebtedness must be accorded to Forrest P. Chisman,

Associate Program Director and Director of the Washington office of the Aspen Institute and formerly Executive Assistant at the Markle Foundation. Not only has he continued to support the project vigorously, he has read the entire manuscript and offered several sage pieces of advice. He, perhaps more than any other individual, is responsible for the continuity of this effort and for recognizing the importance of establishing the relationship between mass communication and political behavior. He and the senior author held several discussions between 1972 and 1973 about the state of research in the field. As a result of these discussions and with the advice of several scholars, Chisman persuaded the Markle Foundation to fund the Social Science Research Council to form an ad hoc Committee on Mass Communication and Political Behavior. Now a recognized committee of SSRC, it is currently seeking funds to study the 1976 presidential election in a multifaceted research effort on mass communication and political behavior.

Several members of The Cleveland State University Department of Communication faculty have consistently been helpful in this project. Jae-won Lee, in the summer of 1973, revamped the bibliographic effort of this project, which in and of itself was a massive task. The authors are grateful for his contribution and for his continued counsel, especially with regard to the organization of Chapter 6, "The Construction of Political Reality." We wish also to recognize the helpful comments on that chapter received from Leslie Armour, Chairman of the Department of Philosophy at Cleveland State.

Dennis Davis, the junior author, joined this project in 1974 and contributed to this volume with the preparation of Chapters 4, 5, and 7. Several drafts of all chapters were reviewed by both authors and various editing chores were shared.

As is the case with most efforts of this kind, several individuals, scholars, students, and staff employees were responsible for various interdependent tasks in addition to offering their advice and counsel. We now wish to recognize those individuals and their contributions:

Research Staff—Our research staff, which pored through many volumes and thousands of studies, was originally organized by Jae-won Lee and excellently supervised by Chuck Habjan. Linda Levin and John Fusek were library researchers. Dana Karr and Joann Gibson organized sections of early reports on various topics and provided superb integration of materials. Office overseer was Phyllis Barkan, who maintained reference indexing, files, and correspondence with scholars whose studies we sought and otherwise communicated with. Her coordination was invaluable. Ed Kaminski ran several data sets for us and assumed a variety of assignments.

Scholars—It is, of course, difficult to recognize the many contributions of scholars to this project. Obviously, we were dependent upon many researchers whose studies form the heart of this book. We herewith acknowledge our gratitude to them as a group. Highest on our list are three scholars whose work we have admired for some time: Steven H. Chaffee, Harold Mendelsohn, and John Robinson. These three have been with us as consultants since the Markle award. Their contributions, both formal and informal, have been most welcomed. We are grateful for their kind comments and particularly for their differing perspectives, with each other and with us.

Among the other scholars who have given advice, provided data, or read the manuscript are Jack McLeod, Jae-won Lee, Warren Miller, Art Miller, Leo Bogart, Maxwell McCombs, Lee Becker, Samuel L. Becker, Garrett O'Keefe, Elisabeth Noelle-Neumann, M. Kent Jennings, Judith Torney, Herbert Hyman, Edward C. Dreyer, and Timothy Meyer.

Students—We wish to thank the students in our Political Communication class who used early drafts of this manuscript in their studies. Their comments and reactions were most helpful.

Secretaries—The job of typing was handled by Patti Brent and by Sandra Coy. We are most grateful to both for their attention to detail and for their meeting deadlines, which always seemed to be looming before us. Their persistent patient attitude sustained us throughout the preparation of this book.

Finally, having acknowledged all the help, counseling, and advice given to us, we are certain that those contributions enhanced this effort. Hence any success this book enjoys must be shared with our colleagues. We will, of course, be responsible for errors and points of view presented in this book.

Cleveland State University   Sidney Kraus
December 1975
                                                  Dennis Davis

1

Introduction

The American public at large is continuously bombarded with political reports disseminated through various mass media channels. Hardly a day passes without national, state, and local politicians and issues appearing on television, in newspapers and magazines, and over the radio. Political commercials and advertisements, public policy debates, political issues, referenda, party appeals, candidate news conferences, presidential speeches, congressional activities, and the deliberations of state legislatures and city councils combine to form a weekly, if not a daily, diet for mass media consumption in America.

Recently added to this deluge was the inundation of mass media coverage on Watergate. Not only was Watergate a test of our political system's viability, it was also a test of mass media's credibility. At stake was the public's confidence and trust in two democratic institutions—government and mass media—which were, at once, placed under a public scrutiny stronger than ever before in our country's history. While most of Watergate is behind us, its effects on the public's trust in government and media are yet to be fully assessed.[1]

A democratic society relies upon voter decisions to *elect representatives* and upon a mass communication network to *inform the electorate*. What conditions are necessary to insure that these two functions operate to maintain democracy? To answer that complex question it is important to understand the relationship between the mass media and the political system. Moreover, it is imperative that we identify the effects of mass communication on political behavior. That is the task we have undertaken in this book.

We begin our discussion with an overview of how this topic has been approached in the past; then we comment briefly upon the structure and purposes of this book. Finally, we offer some observations about research and researchers in this field.

Background: A Concern with Effects on Voting Behavior

In 1960, Joseph T. Klapper completed his now widely read book, *The Effects of Mass Communication, An Analysis of Research On The Effectiveness and Limitations of Mass Media In Influencing The Opinions, Values, and Behavior of Their Audiences.*[2] Klapper's objective, as his title indicates, was to review a wide range of research on how the mass media affect our lives. He considered published research on a variety of subjects, some of which related to mass media's impact on political behavior. As we will note in subsequent chapters, one of the obvious limitations of such efforts is that they are dependent upon extant literature. Researchers using this approach cannot alter study designs. They cannot investigate empirically certain events and happenings since often the stimuli and attending data are "fugitive," that is, have escaped the researcher's grasp or gone undetected. If they question investigators' findings they must do so on methodological grounds or counter with more persuasive evidence. In a sense, they sit as judge and jury, weighing evidence which may justify an advocate's position—in Klapper's terms, provide for "some provocative conjecture."

Like Klapper, we are confronted with these limitations. Unlike Klapper, we have chosen to investigate mass media's role in influencing political behavior *only*. At least three other distinctions between the two books should be noted.

First, the "library" from which we are drawing in the 1970s is stocked with significantly more materials than that which housed Klapper's investigation in the late 1950s. Compare Klapper's inventory of over 1000 studies, essays and reports to assess mass media's impact on many behaviors, with ours of more than 3000 sources for its impact on political behavior alone.

Second, the research fraternity and the methods of investigation have substantially increased in number and sophistication. The students of Klapper's authors, and their students, have emerged in our inventory, often joining their mentors in a variety of new research models and applications.

Third, in addition to evaluating the *new* data since Klapper's review, we must compare and reassess the *old*, sometimes reaching conclusions different from his.

Students of mass communication and politics are probably familiar with Klapper's pace-setting work. Two of its conclusions are important for us to remember, in considering how tentative his other generalizations really were:

the classic studies of how voters make up their minds ... provide an incomplete picture of the total effects of mass communication. ... (p. 254)

What role mass communication may play in determining voter's decisions before a "critical" election is not yet known. (p.255)

As these conclusions suggest, many people (including several social scientists) consider the "test" of media's influence upon political behavior to be its impact on voting. Clearly, when candidates use the media in campaigns, their ultimate objective is to get elected to office. Conversely, when the mass media cover campaigns, they deem it appropriate along the way to gauge winners and losers. Similarly, polls keep track records of candidates' chances by regularly assessing public opinion with the question, "If the election were held today, for whom would you vote?"

Social scientists and political pundits find all this activity worthy of investigation. The classic study on *nonvoting* by Merriam and Gosnell appeared in the mid-twenties.[3] Frank Kent, a *Baltimore Sun* reporter, published his hilarious and poignant account of how politicians seek and maintain office in 1928.[4] A splendid, classic volume, which we will have cause to come back to throughout this book, is *The People's Choice*, a study of how the electorate in one community made up its mind in the presidential election of 1940.[5] Two excellent reviews on voting behavior with consideration of mass media's effect on the electorate appeared in the early fifties.[6] In the same period, following the tradition set by *The People's Choice*, Berelson et al. examined the influence of the media on the electorate.[7] Also in the fifties, the Survey Research Center at the University of Michigan conducted two major voting studies.[8] Lane's superb book on how people get involved in politics has several sections on electoral behavior and a brief chapter on "Mass Media and Politics."[9]

A central concern in many of these studies and reviews is the impact of various institutions on voting behavior. Communication researchers have also been curious about mass media effects on voting. During the four televised debates between Kennedy and Nixon in 1960, most researchers were more interested in who had *won* the debates than in how they were conducted. Katz and Feldman noted, "In contrast to the paucity of specific questions concerning the format of the debates, it is surely revealing that so many of the studies asked, unabashedly, 'Who won?'—or words to that effect."[10] Lang and Lang and Mendelsohn and Crespi, among others, investigated the effect of reporting early election returns and outcome projections from the East upon those yet to vote in the West.[11] Recently, Robinson looked into the influence of newspaper editorials on voters in their selection of the President.[12]

These are but a few of the many studies on the relationship between the mass media and the voting behavior of the electorate. In subsequent chapters, especially Chapter 3, we will review and comment on the results of these studies.

The Structure of This Book

Voting behavior, though important for our discussion, is but one of several political behaviors influenced by the mass media. We have organized this book by sections which explore all those influences. We begin by following how the mass media interact with the political values, cognitions, and behavior of people as they proceed from childhood through adult life. Thus, we begin with the mass media's role in how young people acquire political beliefs and attitudes (Chapter 2). Since these young people become voters, we next examine media's influence in the election process (Chapter 3), and in the dissemination of political information (Chapter 4). Next, we investigate how people use the media in the political process (Chapter 5), and we apply our conclusions in an assessment of how political reality is constructed in society (Chapter 6). Finally, we examine the methods used in political communication research, and we complete the book with a brief chapter summarizing our conclusions.

A special feature of this book is the "Abstracts and Bibliography" section which is appended to Chapters 2 through 6. These summaries should be a valuable resource to students and researchers.

The Purposes of This Book

Our purpose is to provide students, scholars, and even politicians who study political communication[13] with a review of and commentary on what is known about the field, what is not yet known, what ought to be known, and how we measure, assess, and evaluate the effects of mass communication on political behavior.

We will not be content merely to relate findings, summarize them, and conclude with a statement of need. As we examine the data we will make judgments about mass media effects on political behavior. We recognize that when scholars review these judgments, to put it in public opinion terms, some will "agree," some will "disagree," and others will "not know" or be "undecided." That is as it should be. Lasswell put it succinctly: "Inquiry does not abolish debate; it sharpens the realism of the perspectives of all who discipline conviction by data."[14] We know from the wise counsel and good offices of many of those mentioned in our acknowledgments that we have not abolished debate.

We hope that the reader, and those whose studies we have consulted, will feel that we have stated the case fairly, even when we have elected to look in directions other than those intended by the author of a study. At times, we have deduced conclusions by combining findings from several studies. We have noted carefully when we have engaged in such deductions.

One final explanatory note is addressed to our colleagues in political science and communication. We are writing about a relatively new discipline. It will become obvious as you read that mass communication research is a comparatively recent addition to scholarly endeavors. Additionally, we are in an interdisciplinary area of inquiry. Studies cited are written by political scientists, sociologists, social psychologists, and mass communication researchers.

After a thorough two-year search through the literature, we came to certain conclusions about the treatment of our topic:

1. Many studies by political scientists whose topics were germane to our inquiry relied on conclusions of classic studies in our field instead of empirically re-examining them with their own instruments. Periodically, we comment with some amazement that, by and large, when the political science fraternity investigates what makes the electorate behave in given ways, mass media variables either have not been included or have not been taken seriously.

2. Many communication researchers have only recently given attention to some areas of political communication, such as political socialization. There is also a tendency within this group to avoid theory building and concentrate instead on developing isolated empirical generalizations. Several studies seem to be grounded in empirical generalizations and not in theory.

These observations may not be startling. About the former, the argument may be advanced that political scientists are interested primarily in *political* variables and not in *mass communication* variables. The latter may be defended by those who feel that because of the newness of our field, not much theory is available; we must build up from data to generalizations to theories.

It seems to us, however, that our observations cannot be dismissed so easily. It would be convenient if people behaved in nice neat ways that correspond to and can be parceled out among the disciplines in the social sciences. That would be the ideal experimental condition. At the other extreme, it would be most fortunate were we able to account for a given dependent variable by examining the impact upon it of all possible independent variables. Though we are able to isolate, with a fair degree of validity, voting behavior—that is, the *act* of voting for a candidate or issue—we have all sorts of problems with *attitudes*. Though we can identify several variables which may be "discipline-bound," what single variable *belongs* to a given discipline in the social sciences?

Ultimately we are all concerned with behavior. While some division of labor among political science and communication, for example, is probably necessary, and at times unavoidable, we ought to be more interdisciplinary in our conceptualizations and research in political communication. When we conduct research we need not mimic Mendel's laws, "inheriting" our subject matter immutably like his particulate genes.[15]

Our observations, then, call for more interdisciplinary research. We hope that this book will help to bring social scientists and their students from various disciplines into a collective effort to advance our knowledge about the effects of mass communication on political behavior. There is no end to the creative efforts that such cooperation might engender.

Notes

1. The mass media fared well in the arena of public opinion. Trust in government, however, was probably at its lowest ebb ever; apparently, Watergate convictions failed to halt the downward trend. In a speech to the U.S. Conference of Mayors in Boston on 7 July 1975, Louis Harris reviewed poll results which showed that while 90 percent of the public believed in the system, only 14 percent had confidence in local government leadership, compared to a margin of 51 percent confidence in garbage collectors. While several Watergate studies have been conducted, relatively few have been published as of this writing. See, for example, a special issue devoted to the Ervin Committee hearings and communication research in S. Kraus and S.H. Chaffee, eds., *Communication Research* 1, no. 4 (October 1974); and S.H. Chaffee, ed., *American Politics Quarterly* (October 1975).
2. J.T. Klapper, *The Effects of Mass Communication* (New York: Free Press, 1960).
3. C.E. Merriam and H.F. Gosnell, *Non-Voting* (Chicago: University of Chicago Press, 1924).
4. Frank R. Kent, *Political Behavior* (New York: Morrow, 1928).
5. P.F. Lazarsfeld, B. Berelson, and Hazel Gaudet, *The People's Choice* (New York: Columbia University Press, 1944).
6. S.J. Eldersveld, "Theory and Method in Voting Behavior Research," *Journal of Politics* 13 (1951): 70–87; and S.M. Lipset, P.F. Lazarsfeld, A.H. Barton, and J. Linz, "The Psychology of Voting: An Analysis of Political Behavior," in G. Lindzey, ed., *Handbook of Social Psychology* (Cambridge: Addison-Wesley, 1954), pp. 1124–70.
7. B.R. Berelson, P.F. Lazarsfeld, and W.N. McPhee, *Voting* (Chicago: University of Chicago Press, 1954).
8. A. Campbell, G. Gurin, and W.E. Miller, *The Voter Decides* (Evanston, Ill.: Row, Peterson, 1954); and A. Campbell, P.E. Converse, W.E. Miller, and D.E. Stokes, *The American Voter* (New York: Wiley, 1960).
9. Robert E. Lane, *Political Life* (New York: Free Press, 1959). Two excellent reviews of voting and elections in America are: N.W. Polsby and A.B. Wildavsky, *Presidential Elections*, 2d ed. (New York: Scribner's, 1968); and Gerald M. Pomper, *Elections In America* (New York: Dodd, Mead, 1968).
10. E. Katz and J. Feldman, "The Debates in the Light of Research: A Survey of Surveys," in S. Kraus, ed., *The Great Debates* (Bloomington: Indiana University Press, 1962), p. 195.

11. K. Lang and G.E. Lang, *Politics and Television* (Chicago: Quadrangle Books, 1970), pp. 250–88; H. Mendelsohn and I. Crespi, *Polls, Television and the New Politics* (Scranton, Pa.: Chandler, 1970).
12. John P. Robinson, "The Press as King Maker: What Surveys From Last Five Campaigns Show," *Journalism Quarterly* 51 (Winter 1974): 587–94, 606.
13. This is an abused term. That is, it is used to include different phenomena by different people. We will, unless otherwise obvious by context, use *political communication* as a substitute term for the process of mass communication (including interpersonal communication) and elements within it which may have impact on political behavior.
14. Harold Lasswell, "Introduction," in Kraus, *The Great Debates*, p. 24.
15. We recognize that reward and status-conferral systems are endemic to scholarly activities; we feel that interdisciplinary research can be compatible with that system.

2

Mass Communication and Political Socialization

In an examination of the literature on mass communication effects upon the political socialization process, one cannot help but be struck by the paucity of studies engaging the two variables. Separately, the mass media and political socialization have been investigated by a variety of scholars in many disciplines. Few studies, however, combine both and test hypotheses about children's cognitive or affective political development as a result of their media experiences. Even fewer consider "socialization" beyond childhood into various phases of the adult life cycle. This lack can be partially explained by observing that academic researchers tend to investigate only variables which are considered to be within the "acceptable domain" of their separate disciplines. Yet it is curious, since these variables appear to be connected in many respects, that few interdisciplinary efforts have been made.

Children and the Media Environment

Youngsters in the last two decades have been increasingly surrounded by a "media environment." The mass media are not involucra in which all socialization experiences are wrapped. Nevertheless, the mass media, notably television, occupy a significant portion of children's attention daily. This attention can be expected to have consequences for socialization.

Consider the period from 1954 through 1973. Young voters in 1972—those newly franchised and those eligible to vote for the first time in a presidential election—were all born after 1948. In that year, there were only 190,000 television sets in use in the United States. By 1960, when these young voters

Figure 1

**CONTIGUOUS EXAMINATION OF THE APPEARANCE OF SELECTED
BENCHMARK POLITICAL SOCIALIZATION AND MEDIA STUDIES WITH THE
AVERAGE WEEKDAY VIEWING HOURS FOR CHILDREN**

Political Socialization and Media Studies[1]	Year	Children's Average Weekday Viewing[2]		Year	Sets in Use[3]
		Hours	Age		
Political Socialization (varied) — Hyman	1948	2.9	6 - 19	1948	190,000
	1949	3.4	14 - 17		
The Effects of Mass Communication (varied) — Klapper	1950			1950	10,500,000
	1951				
	1952	3.7	9 - 14		
Television in the Lives of Our Children (western; U.S.; varied) — Schramm	1953			1953	28,000,000
	1954				
	1955				
	1956				
Children and Politics (New Haven, Conn.)	1957	3.0	6 - 14	1957	47,200,000
	1958				
	1959				
Children in the Political System (national)	1960			1960	54,000,000
	1961				
	1962				
The Development of Political Attitudes in Children (national)	1963				
	1964				
	1965	3.5	6 - 17		
	1966				
Survey Research Center Studies (national)	1967				
	1968				
	1969				
The Learning of Political Behavior (varied)	1970			1970	92,900,000
	1971	4.0	6 - 17		
Emergence of Media and Political Socialization Studies[4]	1972				

[1] Parentheses: sample location; dashed line: year data was gathered; solid line: year of publication.

[2] These are estimates from various sources: Schramm, *et. al., Television In The Lives Of Our Children*; Roper data; Greenberg, *et. al., Mass Media And The Urban Poor*; and others.

[3] Sources: Census data.

[4] Since the completion of this paper several studies have come to the author's attention; the reference here relates to the five studies (Johnson, Chaffee, *et. al.*, Hollander, Dominick, and Kraus). It applies, in part, to some of the studies at Michigan's Survey Research Center.

were no more than twelve years old, 54 million sets were in use. In 1970, the number had increased to approximately 93 million.[1] The sheer number of sets offers proof of the exposure of increasingly large portions of the population to mass media (Figure 1).

Studies by Schramm, Lyle, and Parker (1961) and by Lotte Bailyn (1959) pointed to the ever-growing use of media, particularly television, to support the contention that mass media contribute to acquisition and development of political attitudes. If so, it is important to examine their impact on the election of 1972, for 11 million people between eighteen and twenty years old were old enough to vote for President for the first time and 48 percent voted. Together with those between twenty-one and twenty-four years old, they brought the number first voting for President to approximately 13 million.[2]

These youthful voters were bred on television. In 1961, Schramm et al. noted that "a child in his first sixteen years allocates to television's persuaders and entertainers as large a block of time as he allocates to his teachers in school" (p. 75).[3] At about the same time, Bailyn (1959) reported that the average viewing time for children between the ages of six and sixteen was twenty-two hours a week. Bronfenbrenner (1970), studying changing patterns of childhood, likewise concluded: "By the time the average child is sixteen, he has watched from 12,000 to 15,000 hours of television. In other words, he has spent the equivalent of 15 to 20 solid months, 24 hours a day, before a television screen" (p. 103).

It is difficult to draw conclusions about television effects with which all would agree. The perennial controversy over television and violence is a case in point (see Murray et al., 1972). Nevertheless, only those with tenacious biases would not concede that spending as much or more time with television than with school for twelve years is bound to influence some behavior. We shall argue in favor of the view that television contributes to learning about politics and government, and that political behavior may be formed as a result of systematic television viewing.

The television experience of youthful voters in 1972 undoubtedly included seeing an unprecedented amount of foreign and domestic strife; other media elaborated upon these themes. Hollander (1971) begins his study, "Adolescents and the War," by reflecting that "it is not difficult to conclude that the 'stories' to which the young of this country have listened are different from those of the generation before them" (p. 472). When they went to the polls, some of the political "stories" they brought with them were undoubtedly television "stories." In the previous decade television had given the viewer a running, visual history of a tragic war. It had recorded the killing of a campaigner seeking the presidential nomination of the Democratic Party. Four years later, another campaigner seeking a third-party Presidential nomination was gunned down and television showed the sequence within hours of the shooting. Television showed these same voters the killing of a civil rights leader who had won a Nobel Peace Prize. With each of these tragic shootings and killings, television covered the funeral and mourning and subsequent interpretations of the meaning these events have on our national and international lives.

When these young voters went to the polls they also brought "stories" about other political institutions. For they had seen the killing of students by a state contingent of the National Guard, the destruction of government property by protestors against the draft, and rioting at a political convention with a mayor of one of our largest cities swearing at a U.S. Senator from one of our smallest states. Their television viewing also had included protest speeches at the Supreme Court, civil rights demonstrations at the Lincoln Memorial, the poor in tents before the White House, presidents of universities meeting or not meeting demands and getting arrested, and the unbelievable conquest of the moon.

Thus in the previous decade alone these new voters had been involved with the "Screening of America." The amount and kind of this screening have escaped researchers as an important determinant in the formation of political attitudes and in voting behavior.

These screenings, of course, are of news events. They do not form part of television entertainment fare. Had these new voters seen "Victory at Sea"? Army comedies? Political allegories on distant planets on "Star Trek"? We sorely lack any empirical evidence which gets at the effect a diet of television prime time or a diet of late afternoon programming has on the development of attitudes and values in children and adolescents, or in adults for that matter. In 1960, Klapper concluded his widely used book on mass communication with this notion:

> The role and effects of the media in the socialization of the child can perhaps no longer be accurately assessed, but some concept of its possible scope may be obtained by performing the mental experiment of imagining the process of socialization occurring in a society in which mass media did not exist. Our knowledge of primitive cultures and of pre-media years suggests that the present cultures are at least in part a product of the existence of mass communication, and may be dependent upon such communication for their continued existence. (p. 255)

Thus plausible reasons exist for assuming that mass media, particularly television, play decisive roles in political socialization. Today, children grow up in a world transformed by mass communication. This transformation can be expected to continue as new media, for example, cable television and videodiscs, develop and provide services of increasing importance in the everyday lives of children.

Early Political Socialization Research

During the past two decades, scholars in political science, sociology, and recently in fields more directly concerned with mass communication, such as journalism and radio and television, have begun to examine political socialization. They have studied:

all political learning, formal and informal, deliberate and unplanned, at every stage of the life cycle, including not only explicitly political learning which affects political behavior, such as the learning of politically relevant social attitudes and the acquisition of politically relevant personality characteristics. (Greenstein, 1968, p. 551)

In short, political socialization includes how we come to learn about politics, how we obtain our attitudes and values about political institutions, and how we ultimately behave politically. Six comprehensive reviews of political socialization research have been published since 1959.[4] Other reviews dealing with the same subject have appeared by Greenstein (1968) in an encyclopedia, by Dawson (1966) in an international political review, and by Wasby (1966) in the *Family Life Coordinator*. Four major studies have been reported in the same time period (Greenstein, 1968; Hess and Torney, 1967; Easton and Dennis, 1969; Langton, 1969).[5] In these reviews and studies and others reported in a 1967 fifty-five-page bibliography by Jack Dennis, mass communication and television were totally ignored, dismissed as relatively unimportant, or barely noted.

In the face of the growing television audience, the increased domestic and foreign news coverage, and the amount of time children spend with television, it appears incredible that legions of researchers have avoided considering television as a significant source of political socialization. Yet television and mass communication variables, for the most part, did not figure in socialization studies before the seventies (Figure 1).

Hyman (1959), in the first review of socialization studies, could have pleaded (but did not) that no one had set out to study the influence of television because it was just getting started. Television and the growth of political socialization as a research interest coincided in their development. It is curious, however, that Hyman used mass media findings from the classical voting studies of Elmira, New York, and Erie County, Ohio, to support the view that parental influence dominates siblings' views on political matters without inquiring about what siblings in the fifties were doing with media. The fact was that Hyman did not know, at least not empirically, what children were doing with television when he reviewed the literature on political socialization in 1959. Klapper completed the first systematic review of mass communication effects in 1959. Schramm and his associates produced the first comprehensive study of North American children and their use of television in 1961. Even in these pace-setting works, mass media's contribution to political socialization was barely and inferentially considered, for what was not available to Hyman was still not available to Klapper and Schramm. So we emerge from the fifties with Hyman's conclusion that "foremost among agencies of socialization is the family" (Hyman, 1959, p. 69).

In the review of the political socialization literature which follows, this neglect of mass communication variables continues in study after study. Three reasons for this neglect can be documented by examining these studies.

1. In conceptualizing political socialization, researchers defined dependent variables so as to exclude the mass media as possible primary influences. For example, the media were not expected to initiate attitudes like party identification which were by definition the province of the family. There was a tendency to view the family as the logical center of influence which all other socialization agents more or less reinforce. Research findings may have been preordained partly by such tautological reasoning.

2. Early studies of the mass media concerned with the effects of exposure to radio or newspapers upon adults concluded that the media served only to reinforce existing attitudes, values, or behaviors. Political socialization researchers cited these findings as a basis for excluding the media from their analyses. The fact that these studies used adult respondents did not prevent socialization researchers from generalizing these findings to children.

3. Socialization researchers tended to regard the mass media as little more than simple conveyors of information. Thus, they did not differentiate communication channels from one another or attempt to ascertain differences in children's patterns of media use. Children's orientations toward the various media were ignored. These researchers may have erroneously assumed that all children were equally exposed to the same mass media messages, so that no differences in effects could be ascertained (because no control group existed).

Nonmedia Studies

The Family

In the study of political socialization, the development and progression of political attitudes and values are examined from their inception to their evolution into political behavior. The nonmedia studies and research by Wasby (1966), Bell (1969), Connell (1972), and Searing et al. (1973) center on familial influence as the primary source of political socialization; other studies consider the impact of peer groups, education, socioeconomic factors, and perceptions of authority. The psychological connections between family influences and perceptions of authority create a circular pattern in the study of nonmedia variables: family exists at the center of all other socializing agents and accordingly affects their influence upon political behavior.

Nonmedia political socialization studies are unified by two major concepts: cognitive development and developing perceptions of authority. Elliot White (1969) postulates that cognitive development depends upon both the genetic intelligence potential of an individual and the desire to develop new learning processes. Cognitive development and authority perceptions apparently work hand-in-hand in the learning process; it is Froman's (1961) contention that a child's perception of authority becomes the foundation for the construction of values, beliefs, and attitudes which, in turn, evolve into the principles ultimately governing consistent political behavior. In agreement with Froman's contention are the findings of Adelson and O'Neil (1966), which correlate adolescents' political consistency with the development of a sense of community. Over a period of time, the evolution of a political idea stops and an individual adopts a fairly permanent attitude or form of behavior.

According to Froman, many scholars postulate that the "images" or "perceptions" of political roles are based on an individual's reaction to parental authority. This conceptualization implicitly assumes that the family is the prime source of influence. Froman challenges this theory by emphasizing its limitations: it draws attention away from possible agents of learning other than parents, such as peer groups, mass media, and school sources, including the teacher and reading material; and it has not been adequately tested. It is interesting to note that Froman concedes the possibility that mass media constitute a socializing agent and warns against taking them too lightly as a result of the seemingly dominant family influence.

By contrast, an "environmental" or "multistep" approach shows the balance among agents of political socialization and considers both their individual and collective impact. This approach implies the fragility of the family primacy hypothesis. In an "environment" of political socialization agents, all agents are assumed to have nearly equal status and similar potential for impact upon an individual's political behavior.

It is difficult to isolate an individual socializing agent. The variables are intricately interwoven and it is a complex task to disentangle one from another. The literature on socialization suggests that the family is the nucleus which spirals outward to encompass all other variables: peer groups, education, socioeconomic status, subculture factors, authority perceptions, and the mass media. This idea appears logical on the surface. The family unit is the first observable phenomenon with which an individual has contact, and parents, particularly mothers, generally provide the closest and, in some cases, only early contact with the "outside world." Parents become the child's bridge between consciousness and environment. According to Sigel (1965) and Connell (1972), the family becomes an organ of transmission of ideas, feelings, attitudes, and beliefs on a variety of subjects. Yet this early contact does not constitute conclusive proof of the exclusivity of family influence in the political socialization process. The family does indeed create an environment of a specific type for a child but the other socialization agents integrate themselves into this environment very early. In certain types of families (for example, where both parents work) other agents of socialization may take over to shape much of the child's world. This is particularly true in the case of mass media. Parents provide the accessibility of media and may influence the extent and degree of its use, yet media's own impact is often independent of the parents.

The transmission of attitudes and beliefs appears to be associated with the child's perception of his or her own family. Greenberg (1970) has found that authority within the family becomes the basis for observations concerning governmental authority and authority figures. These images circumscribe and refine an individual's political attitudes and behavior according to childhood discernments. Family-developed and influenced perceptions tend to color the individual's consideration of, and associations with, all other "outside" or "environmental" influences such as education, peer groups, and class subculture. Thus, Greenberg confirms Froman's argument that the family becomes the first learning mechanism of the child, being both affective and cognitive. Again, although the family may be the initial socializing agent, it may not have the greatest long-term impact. The significance of the family influence should be kept in perspective. Other political socialization agents make at least some independent contributions to a socializing "environment."

Several researchers, including Warren Blumenfeld (1964) and Stephen Wasby (1966), have concluded that the family's most obvious political socializing role is the transmission of political preference, that is, political party affiliation and outlook (Maccoby et al., 1954–55; Sears, 1968; Braungart, 1971; and Searing et al., 1973). Parents transfer feelings of party identity and loyalty to their children; this strong association develops into attitudes concerning political involvement and it colors an individual's political viewpoint according to the information passed on by the parents. The child's imitation and ready acceptance of parent's politics is construed as a prime example of the depth and power of parental influence—to the exclusion of influences from other agents. Hyman (1959) and Greenstein (1965) both conclude that American children learn their party identity at an early age and that it persists over time for the majority of the population. This conclusion is another testament to the enduring impact of the family as a political socialization agent.

Political party preference and identification seem to be implicitly bound to an image of a benign president. When this positive image is presented to children by their parents, the rudiments of political attitudes and behavior almost immediately assume positive connotations. The creation of a primarily positive political outlook, as discovered by Hawkins et al. (1971), has its effect on both attitudes and behavior; the degree of an individual's belief in his or her political efficacy acts as an index of his or her participation.

Again neglected in this type of research is any consideration of other socializing variables that aid in creating and sustaining a positive political viewpoint. No mention is made of the influence of the mass media in the presentation of both political leaders and institutions. As we shall see later in this chapter, the images of the political system and its leaders evoked by the mass media appear to be as enduring as or more enduring than those taught by the family.

The Schools and Peers

Fred Greenstein's pioneering study of New Haven school children in grades four through eight was based on data collected in 1958. Greenstein, confirming earlier findings that the family is the important socializing agent, briefly noted that media are a part of the child's environment, but failed to consider them seriously in his analysis.

What is most baffling about the Greenstein study is that the recognition accorded media while developing a *Gestalt* for the study of political socialization,[6] the inclusion of relevant media items in the questionnaire,[7] the empirical verification of television ownership,[8] and the conclusion that television provides models for children[9] were not followed up with some form of multivariate analysis or in-depth analysis to provide a more substantial discourse about mass communication and socialization interaction among the 659 children in the sample.[10]

Instead, Greenstein reverts to earlier works, such as that by Herbert Hyman and Paul Sheatsley,[11] which were deficient in socialization data, to propose that

"across the board" programs of [political] exhortation [designed to increase political involvement] are subject to all of the factors which make propaganda by mass communication an inefficient technique for changing beliefs and behavior. To begin with, the message tends largely to be received by those who are already sympathetic to it and therefore least in need of change. For the remainder of the population, the message is ignored, "crowded out" by other more potent communications, or even misperceived. When it is taken in, it is not reinforced at the face-to-face level and nothing is done to change the individual's actual life situation in order to facilitate acting on the message. (p. 185)

It is unfortunate that in this precursory study about children's political socialization, earlier findings about adult populations and mass communication variables are taken as conclusive. Greenstein's discussion of mass communication's effects upon children's political learning erroneously passes off their television viewing behavior as insignificant.

It is interesting to note that M. Kent Jennings (1966) in his review of Greenstein's *Children and Politics* suggests that there is a "paucity of attention devoted to peer group relationships, formal instruction, feelings of self-esteem and competence, and intra-familial relationships." Again, the mass media are overlooked.

In the first national study, Hess and Torney (1967) obtained some 12,000 school children's responses to political socialization items and concluded that "the effectiveness of the family in transmitting attitudes has been over-estimated in previous research." Instead they found "that the school stands out as the central, salient, and dominant force in the political socialization of the young child." The only item on mass media, which was subsumed under an index of political activity, was the statement-question, "I have read about a candidate in newspapers or magazines."[12] Yet in 1961 and 1962, when these data were collected, children were spending as much or more time viewing television as they were spending in school!

As McClosky and Dahlgren (1959) show, peer group influence on attitudes and behavior appears to be an extension of the influence patterns exerted by the family; there seems to be a relationship between affection and esteem for loved ones which is easily transferred from family members to friends. The influence of peers is less persuasive than that of parents. The individual's attitudes and beliefs have already, to a large extent, taken firm root by the time he is consciously aware of politics. With familial influence established, the peer group generally substantiates or modifies it slightly. However, the peer group may function like the family in the socialization process. Langton (1967) has shown that peer groups also are transmitters of class, religious, and ethnic subcultures. The outcome of the influence of peers and friends is to perpetuate the society or culture of which they are members. Although students, children, and adolescents form subcultures of their own, Havig-hurst and Neugarten[13] have found that these are generally mirror images of the adult society into which they are ultimately integrated.

The influence of contemporaries upon an individual includes the transmission and reinforcement of the political norms of any given society. It is part of a system through which individuals in the society acquire and learn when and how to modify their attitudes and beliefs. Socioeconomic status appears to play an integral part in the impact of peer groups on political behavior and attitudes. Family, too, becomes an interwoven aspect of the peer-related influence: the status of one's family, as determined by socio-economic standing, determines one's social environment, which in turn shapes images that promote a particular class-related attitude. The class structure itself is perpetuated by this circular concatenation. Thus, both family and social status are constant, if unconscious, underlying factors in peer group influence upon the development of political attitudes and behavior.

Education is also related to peer group since the school community acts as a transmitter of social and political attitudes. Social class is often considered a dependent variable in regard to education. Langton (1967) found that most schools perpetuate class differences through the social and political homogeneity of their students. Even in large schools with a wide variation in economic and social status, students have a tendency to observe the political attitudes of their own subculture group—particularly the working class, which has the strongest familial bonds. Nevertheless, education and peer group influences provide an arena of interaction among similar groups of people and thus prevent an opportunity for exposure to differing political attitudes and behavior.

Socialization has been formally defined by Hess, Newmann, et al. (1968) as the process of transmitting stable patterns of behavior and values, and of grooming the young for fulfilling established adult roles in the society. The school has usually been thought of as an important instrument in this process. Classroom education has traditionally assumed the trappings of indoctrination in its perpetuation of dominant societal values. Several researchers (Greenberg, 1970; Hess and Easton, 1962) have revealed that this indoctrination process is usually achieved through the presentation of positive images of government agencies, representatives of power, and national identity. The educational system appears to be concerned with political attitudes only in their relationship to supporting the existing form of government and in equating political stability with political passivity and inertia. As in the majority of family studies, mass media are ignored or glossed over in connection with peer group- and education-related studies. Little research has concerned itself with media's effects upon children either in school or in their own circle of friends. Research has also largely disregarded the uses schools make of the media in the perpetuation of selected societal and political values.

The primary failure of the schools in regard to the development of political attitudes has been their inability to enrich and supplement what students have already acquired from their parents and peers. The school seems to abnegate its responsibility; education should teach an individual how to exercise power effectively within the political system in areas which directly affect his life, rather than just repeat the established virtues of the existing system. Compare the television fare and the political "stories" of the early 1960s with the "pro-system" approach used in many high school civics classes during the same period. Would not the inconsistency lend some explanation for the protests and disorder of the last decade?[14]

Formal education is currently limited in its ability to form political attitudes independently of other agents. A behavioristic approach should be incorporated into the existing system in order to develop an expanded curriculum that takes into account other relevant influences. Diversification of curriculum would allow for a greater sensitivity to individual differences to be developed and utilized in presenting a broader attitudinal perspective.

To sum up, education and peer groups remain riveted around the family. It is logical to assume that the perceptions of authority originating with the family remain generally salient despite the modifications and refinements brought about by peer experience and exposure to the media. The dominance of family influence, suggested in the literature, sets up the criteria for making judgments and creating values by which an individual's political ideas and attitudes are evaluated. The absence of media or the peripheral references to it in classical research suggest two things: either the media were still too new to have any impact, or the media, rapidly saturating the home, functioned in a supplementary fashion, as did peer groups and education.

Conceptualizations of Political Socialization

Linear Progression Models

The political attitudes one develops and sustains may be so ingrained that any new opinions or views are selected out or made to conform to the early image-attitude training from the family. To researchers with this viewpoint, the interwoven structure of the nonmedia socializing agents suggests a layered effect in attitudinal development. One agent creates the beginning of an attitude, idea, or value, and the influence of each successive agent attaches itself to the existing thought and builds upon it.

Such models have been created to explain the development of political attitudes, roles, and behavior. It is assumed that political attitudes generally dictate political behavior, so that the socialization process behind both remains essentially the same. Political behavior is considered the end-product of attitude formation, absorbing impact from the same variables: family, peer group, education, socioeconomic status, perceptions of authority, and mass media. Linear progression models are too simplistic to explain the development of political attitudes and their ultimate impact on political behavior.

ROLE MODEL.   According to this model, political behavior is developed from exposure to political roles. Whatever political roles an individual is exposed to and learns will become the basis for later political activity. The family, as in the development of political attitudes, plays the dominant part in teaching roles, though it has not been established to what extent each agent is responsible for political maturation and subsequent behavior. In support of this view is the fact that family influence is the earliest form of learning and persuasion in the socialization process. Peers and education, coupled with underlying socioeconomic, racial, and religious factors, are experienced much later in an individual's social and political development. Just as the early influences shape attitudes, it is suggested that the family as an agent also begins the formation of political behavior.

POLITICAL BEHAVIOR MODEL.   Several researchers from Maccoby et al. (1954–55) to Braungart (1971) found that attitude and behavior appear to go hand-in-hand. They argued that most children adopt political views similar to those held by their parents. The model posits that parents "indoctrinate" children and subsequently adolescents into the political system. The family, the argument continues, serves as a model for loyalties, beliefs, and values which a child imitates. This model portrays the transmission of "acceptable" political behavior from parents to children, reinforced by family political attitudes and party preferences, forming a shared family value system.

POLITICAL ATTITUDE MODEL.   This model oversimplifies parental influence. Hyman (1959) points to the danger of correlating parental influence with children's attitude as if attitude could be measured on a *discrete* scale. Many attitudes are learned over time and it is unrealistic to suggest that the passing of a particular attitude directly from parent to child can account for the correspondence of relevant political attitudes among parents and children. Further, parents may disagree and children may be subject "to a variety of influences *within* the one family unit. And even where parents agree, the child may still receive *separate*, although cumulative, influences from each parent. [Evidence] clearly shows that where the family influences are not solidified, the consequences are different from those instances where both parents reinforce one another."[15]

Finally, we ought to consider the possibility of *little* influence flowing from parents to children in the formation of political attitudes. Some studies have suggested practically no correspondence on several dimensions between parent and child in the political socialization process (Jennings and Niemi, 1968; Connell, 1972).

Family Primacy Model

Throughout the 1950s and early 1960s, the majority of studies on political socialization indicated that the family influence pervades all other aspects of this process: peer group, education, social status, sex, age, and perceptions of authority appear as circles radiating out from the family nucleus. The other socializing agents modify political behavior only up to a certain point. Studies propose that among the political socialization agents, the family remains a submerged, but dominant, factor in determining the direction and degree of impact of any experience on political behavior. This assumed dominance of the family may be part of the reason for the ancillary treatment accorded media by Greenstein and by Hess and Torney.

Subordination of Media Variables in Socialization Models

Hess and Torney treated media variables inferentially, linking previous media findings to the children's behavior in their sample. What little insight is provided about mass communication's role in the political socialization schema is sketchy and unclear. Throughout their report, Hess and Torney (1967) offer interview dialogues such as this one with a third-grade boy:

"Have you ever seen the President?"
"I've seen him on television, and heard him on the radio, and seen him in newspapers." (p. 42)

and this with a fourth-grade boy:

"Bobby, have you seen the President on TV?"
"Yes. . . ."
"Have you seen him make speeches on TV?"
"Yes." (p. 44)

Another child's interview provides the following:

"Wally, did you see the TV debates [between Nixon and Kennedy]?"
"Some of them. I thought they were very good. It gave you a chance to see what's going on while they're running for President."
"Were you interested before?"
"No, but after the debates I just wanted to see if Kennedy wins." (p. 85)

Wally's comments, among others, suggest that it might have been fruitful to probe for direct and indirect television and media effects upon the political socialization process as a result of viewing, listening, reading, or hearing about the Kennedy-Nixon debates. There was ample evidence to show that the televised debates permeated the 1960 campaign and dominated television viewing in American households on at least four evenings.[16] Hess and Torney acknowledge the occasion by declaring that since "the field testing of the national study took place a year and a half after the 1960 Presidential election, it provided an opportunity to examine the responses of the group to the partisan aspects of this content. Television coverage of the campaign, particularly the debates between Kennedy and Nixon, made the campaign and election struggle a uniquely visible one." But they avoid television by discussing the election outcome and concluding "that the election itself had a strong impact on many children and may in itself have been a socializing experience" (p. 101).

A review of Hess and Torney's work by Sigel (1968) fails to note their lack of concern with television and other media in the development of political attitudes in children. Nor does Sears' (1968) detailed review essay mention mass media. Interestingly, both Sigel and Sears, whose reviews appeared in 1968, fault the Hess-Torney study because no Negro children were included in that study. That neglect is striking since a recent study found that television viewing for black children occupied six hours per day on the average. For white children it took up four and one-half hours per day. Greenberg et al. (1970) concluded that "the mass medium of the poor is television. It is a preferred and almost exclusive source of information about the outside world" (p. 80).

Complementing the Hess-Torney study is the impressive work of Easton and Dennis (1969). Largely derived from the same data as the previously mentioned study, media and television were once again ignored. Since the same data were being evaluated, it was no surprise to find that, like Hess and Torney, Easton and Dennis minimize television in their assessment of children's political orientations.[17] Both efforts "place" media as a utility, conveying information like a telephone or a street sign. Neither study seriously treats mass communication channels such as television, newspapers, magazines, radio, film, records, and books as independent variables. Institutions of family, school, peer groups, and church receive independent treatments; the mass media receive inferential or indirect treatments.

Inherent in this "transmission" or "vehicle" categorization of media is a concern with *what* is conveyed rather than with *how* it is conveyed.[18] Consider Easton and Dennis' (1969) deduction from both events and data:

> *Empirically the prominence of the Presidency is reflected in the attention it obtains from the mass media. Children may sense this current of interest among adults if only by overhearing the conversation of their own parents.*
>
> *The drama of presidential-election compaigns undoubtedly also impresses the office on children.* If we take five years of age as the earliest point at which a presidential campaign might leave some imprint on the child, all our children had undergone one campaign, at least, by the time of our testing in 1960.... It seems plausible to assume that few children could pass through recurrent presidential contests without their curiosity being piqued....
>
> *One indirect indicator of the child's exposure to the phenomenon of the election* and its psychological importance to him is the response to the following question: "How much did you learn from the last election for President?" [Responses: lot, some, little]....
>
> *If this question is an indicator of the degree of sensitization of the child to politics through presidential elections,* we can ask whether responses to the item are associated with the child's perceptions of the President in any way, and more particularly, whether the child who says he has learned a substantial amount from the election is also likely to regard the President

more highly. [At this point, S. Kraus, ed., *The Great Debates*, is cited to suggest that since adults' hostility toward the opposition candidate decreased and favorable feelings increased as a result of simple television exposure it is likely that similar effects occur for children.] . . .

There is at least a prima facie case for the hypothesis that the election has socializing effects . . . even though such effects may be confounded by other *factors which predispose the child to pay attention to the election or to regard the President more favorably.*[19] (Italics added)

Though Easton and Dennis allude to mass media, the television debates, and "the drama of presidential-election campaigns," they did not test for television exposure, television content, or viewing behavior generally. Instead, they relied on a gross measure of learning about campaigns to suggest a positive correlation between that and the child's positive feelings toward the President. They buttress this reasoning with exposure to the Presidency in school: "Furthermore, the classroom itself would seem to generate additional awareness and to provide historical continuity for the role of the President. It is the unusual school that does not have busts or pictures of past Presidents in the corridor and classrooms. Few curricula, even in the early grades, would fail to give some special attention to the office" (p. 158).

The senior authors of these two fine volumes—Easton and Hess, a political scientist and a development psychologist—put together an interdisciplinary approach to study political attitudes of a national sample of elementary school children in grades two through eight in 1957 at the University of Chicago. In 1962, with United States Education Office funding, they collected the data. With all due respect for their pioneering efforts and the contributions made to their respective disciplines, it is difficult to understand why they so obviously avoided television as a source variable for political socialization. During their five-year period of conceptualization and data collection, research on children's viewing patterns was being published. By their own observations, significant political stimuli from the mass media confronted their subjects. To complete the pattern, Greenstein (1972), in his review of the Hess-Torney and Easton-Dennis studies, failed to note their omission of mass media and television.

Media Studies

Recently, several studies have considered the role of the media in political socialization. These studies are reviewed below. They provide insight into how future political socialization research might be designed to provide more complete and useful analyses.

The Effects of Media Use

When data gathered in the mid-sixties by the Survey Research Center at the University of Michigan raised doubts about family and school as primary agents of political socialization, some measures of media began to appear. Using a national probability sample of 1969 high school seniors, M. Kent Jennings and his colleagues found that:

1. Compared with parents, students are more cosmopolitan in their interest in public affairs, knowledge and discourse about political domains, tolerance of political diversity, and evaluations of politics at multiple levels.[20]

2. "If the eighteen-year old is no simple carbon copy of his parents—as the results clearly indicate—then it seems most likely that other socializing agents have ample opportunity to exert their impact.... Not the least of these are the transformation in the content and form of the mass media and communication channels, phenomena over which the family and the school have relatively little control."[21]

3. "Findings certainly do not support the thinking of those who look to the civics curriculum in American high schools as even a minor source of political socialization."[22]

4. Political media use was about the same for both blacks and whites, "but Negro students use television more often than do Whites, and at all levels of parental education."[23]

5. "Regular usage of the mass media for political news rises substantially after high school. A comparison of seniors and their parents shows that parents pay more attention to each of the four media ... although students watch a good deal of television, they pay attention to its news broadcasts much less regularly than parents." Attention to newspapers, radio, and magazines is also less frequent among students.[24]

Despite these and other findings (see the Abstracts at the end of the chapter), well-intentioned scholars cling to the concept that the media act as reinforcers of individuals' predispositions. Dawson and Prewitt (1969) sum up the mass media as an agent in the process of political socialization:

In evaluating mass media as a political socialization agency, four observations are relevant. First, more often than not the media acts [sic] as transmitters of political cues which are originated by other agencies. Second, the information carried by mass media goes through a two-step flow. Third, the media tend to reinforce existing political orientations rather than create new ones. Fourth, the messages of the mass media are received and interpreted in a social setting, and in the context of socially conditioned predispositions. (p. 197)

Incidental Political Learning

Typically, the introduction of media in political socialization research takes its cue from the word *political* and the variables measured are public affairs programs watched, political items read, attention to news and politics in media, and the like. Nowhere do we find data about political socialization as a result of the regular media programming that children and adolescents view daily. Cartoons on television and in newspapers, policemen and authorities portrayed in films and television, contests of power by labor unions and big business, dramas of "making it" against all odds, issues in fictional dramas—all are part of the daily media diet which may be more substantially related to socialization than any other single societal force. At the present time we can only guess the impact of these stimuli on political socialization, but certain indicators are emerging.[25] Evidence today suggests that mass media, particularly television, may be responsible for much of the child's political learning.

Media as an Agent of Socialization

Norris Johnson, in 1967, found that Kentucky high school seniors in economically depressed rural areas obtained most of their political information from television.

Chaffee, Ward, and Tipton (1970)[26] went into schools located in five Wisconsin cities during the months of May and November 1968. Their purpose was to investigate mass media use, political knowledge, and campaigning activity among adolescents. These three variables were measured by a self-administered questionnaire. Adolescents were tested directly to obtain their political knowledge (22 items in May and 29 items in November). Media use and campaigning activity were estimated from the adolescents' self-reports.

The researchers, comparing agents of political socialization (parents, teachers, peers, and mass media), hypothesized that public affairs media consumption effects changes in political cognitions and behavior. Specifically, adolescents' political understanding and subsequent political behaviors were found to be causally influenced by their use of the mass media. With this twice-reached panel of 1291 Wisconsin junior and senior high school students, Chaffee et al. (1970) found that the relationship between media public affairs use and political knowledge is such that over time media use "should be considered as an independent (or intervening) variable in the political socialization process, not merely as one of many dependent variables."

Further, among junior high school students, television entertainment viewing resulted in greater political knowledge; in fact, "*any* use of the mass media tends to expose them to sources of increased political knowledge" (p. 655). This finding is the first attempt to assess nonpolitical public affairs news content impact upon young viewers and media users.

Neil Hollander (1971) studied the way in which adolescents in Everett, Washington, viewed the Viet Nam war and concluded: "The major substantive finding . . . is the importance of mass media as a source of learning about an important political object, war. This finding casts considerable doubt on the present utility of much of the previous research on the sources of political socialization and indicates that researchers have, perhaps, been passing over the major sources of political learning. The new 'parent' is the mass media" (p. 479).

Joseph Dominick (1972), with a sample of sixth and seventh graders in New York City schools, looked at the role of television in political socialization and found that "the mass media are clearly the primary sources of information about the government" and political information generally for youngsters in this age group (p. 51).

Recently, several items in socialization studies were replicated with a statewide probability sample of graduating high school classes in New Hampshire. The preliminary results confirm Johnson's, Chaffee, Ward, and Tipton's, Hollander's, and Dominick's conclusions. When presented with fifteen political topics and asked which sources—among eighteen sources within categories of church, family and friends, mass media, and school— were most responsible for their attitude about the topics, students reported mass media for ten of them; four topics found mass media in second place amoung sources and only for one topic were they in third place (Kraus and Lee, unpublished manuscript).

The Need for Media Variables in Research

To ignore media in empirical political socialization research is to promote less rigor in our efforts to gain knowledge. It may impair meaningful change in today's education process, for it ultimately affects a wide spectrum of pedagogy, at least in America. For example, high school curricula, at least in part, have been and will continue to be influenced by the earlier research reported here. A review of the research presently being diffused in secondary education throughout the country asserts: "These conclusions should not be interpreted as meaning that the influence of mass media upon the process of political socialization is unimportant. Rather, the impact of the mass media should be viewed in terms of the complex social setting in which the media function" (Patrick, 1967; see also Langton and Jennings, 1968).

Like other assertions on media's role in the political process found in the literature of political socialization, these general comments are part of the "daisy-chain" of findings that have been cited by researchers since the late forties. Since they stem from "classic" studies, they are adopted without further empirical verification with the variables being considered at a given time. This brings about an inferential linkage of mass communication and political socialization which is quite suspect.

Roberta Sigel (1965) described researchers' tendency to "label their evidence as 'indirect,' 'inferential,' and the like" as reflecting "the fact that the state of the discipline has not yet progressed enough to offer us much empirical data which lays bare the causal relationship of certain socialization experiences to subsequent political behavior" (p. 129).

The condition may be explainable, but the consequences are not acceptable. Mass media, and television in particular, need to be included in political socialization research whenever sources of learning and elements of influence are being evaluated.

Parameters for Future Research

Although the need is clear for more comprehensive, better conceptualized research designs to study political socialization, it will be difficult to produce theoretical frameworks which can guide such research.

Turning to the studies that are reviewed here and abstracted later in this chapter, the reader will find that the authors come from many disciplines, that the studies are varied in theories, and that they utilize diverse methodologies. Some have empirical bases from which generalizations are made; others are couched in limited, "subjective" experiences. Still other studies review the literature and often incorporate contradictory findings.

The state of political socialization research is far from the ideal, where one might expect to find systematic contributions elaborating and supporting a single, clear theory. Although we cannot derive such a theory from this review of research, it is possible to indicate some parameters for future theory construction. In a later chapter, an effort will be made to construct a conceptual framework which falls within the following parameters:

1. A model of the political socialization process should be constructed which accounts for all agent influences and includes communication patterns among parents, teachers, peers, and children. The model, or models, should consider the mass media as one of the significant agents in the process. Attention should be given to how patterns of media use which affect the political socialization process are developed and maintained.

2. Political socialization studies should go beyond the notion that mass

communication merely reinforces attitudes by exposure. Evidence to date suggests the importance of mass media portrayals of specific events, and of characteristic patterns of media use. Influence cannot be accurately predicted by simple media exposure indices.

3. Information-seeking behavior of children may be more of a catalyst in the political socialization process than any one agent. It would be helpful to know under what conditions children seek out political information and which agents or combination of agents encourage such information seeking.

4. The linear model of parent to child, teacher to child, peer to peer, and media to child is too simplistic an approach for understanding the complex phenomena inherent in the political socialization process. This model places too much emphasis on determining the unique role of discrete agents. Future models should focus on the interrelationships among various socialization agents and, in particular, identify the relationship between media and other socialization agents.

5. Both short-term and longitudinal studies are needed for two reasons: to specify causal relationships between variables in political socialization processes for particular age groups; and to determine how causal relationships between variables in political socialization processes change over time for particular groups of children and ultimately influence political behavior.

Notes

1. Figures based on Census and Electronic Industries Association data.
2. These figures are based on Census Bureau estimates contained in "Population Characteristics, Voter Participation in November, 1972," Series P-20, No. 244, December 1972.
3. See also Schramm, 1960, pp. 214–25.
4. Hyman, 1959; Sigel, 1965, 1970; Patrick, 1967; Dawson and Prewitt, 1969; and *Harvard Educational Review* 38 (Summer 1968).
5. The first three studies report data from American children; Langton's study is derived primarily from Jamaican school children.
6. Following Lasswell's paradigm of the general process of communication, Greenstein delineates five elements for study of political socialization. The third element reads: "*The Agents of Political Socialization.* Among the most obvious sources of political learning in the United States are parents, teachers, neighbors, members of the extended family, peers, and the media of communication and those whose views are transmitted through the media" (p. 13).
7. Seven mass media communication questions were included. These were indices of television viewing, media preference, comic book reading, media content, and media gratification. No tabulation of responses was given. Ibid., pp. 192–93.
8. "By the date of the New Haven Study, possession of a family television set evidently

was close to universal. Only a handful of children reported that their family had no television set." Ibid., p. 147.

9. Ibid., pp. 147–52. Greenstein records the changes in children's exemplars (models) from patriotic figures like George Washington to popular entertainers from 1902 to 1958. Also, he notes that in a 1944 study, almost 45 percent chose exemplars from "Immediate environment figures" with only 8 percent selecting "entertainers"; conversely, Greenstein's 1958 data display 2 percent for environment figures. Extending DeFleur's interesting research on children's learning of occupational roles and knowledge suggests that television exemplars may be stereotyped and distorted. See DeFleur, 1964; DeFleur and DeFleur, 1967.

10. These children were not randomly selected and Greenstein did not use statistical inference, though he did generate some contingency analyses for class and sex. Greenstein, 1965, p. 200.

11. Herbert Hyman and Paul Sheatsley, "Some Reasons Why Information Campaigns Fail," *Public Opinion Quarterly* 11 (Fall 1947): 412–23; and Klapper, 1960.

12. Hess and Torney, 1967, p. 296. "Reading about candidates in the mass media showed the sharpest increase with age (probably as children's reading skills improve). Exposure to the image of candidates in these publications was reported by more than 90 per cent of the students in grade six through eight . . . " (p. 100).

13. Robert J. Havighurst and Bernice L. Neugarten, *Society and Education*, 2d ed. (Boston: Allyn and Bacon, 1962), Chapter 5.

14. The question of "pro-system" pedagogy has been discussed in the literature (see Greenstein, 1970). In a later paper (1975), Greenstein suggests that "more than one commentator has noted that some of the very same preadolescents who blithely described Eisenhower and Kennedy in such benign terms in the early studies may well have been adolescent and postadolescent leaders of protest against 'the system' a few years later" (p. 8).

15. For a discussion of parent-child patterns see Hyman (1959), Chapter 4, "Agencies of Socialization in Politics," pp. 51–70. The reader should weigh Hyman's discussion against a later piece (Connell, 1972) offering evidence suggesting that rank-order correlations used in some studies quoted by Hyman were misconstrued as measures of *pair* correspondence.

16. For a review of the televised debates, audience reactions, and positioning in the campaign, see Sidney Kraus, ed., *The Great Debates: Background, Perspective and Effects* (Bloomington: Indiana University Press, 1962).

17. The Easton-Dennis book differed from the Hess-Torney effort by linking the data to a theoretical framework, largely gleaned from Easton's superb earlier works, *A Framework for Political Analysis* (Englewood Cliffs, N. J.: Prentice-Hall, 1965), and *A System Analysis of Political Life* (New York: Wiley, 1965). Theirs is a political systems approach while Hess and Torney's is one of psychological development.

18. Attention to *how* may, for example, center an investigation on television and the child's behavior using operant learning theory. Television, the independent variable (child's viewing considered as a reinforcing agent), would be assessed by dependent measures of the child's political beliefs and behaviors. Learning, in this approach, is an intervening variable. For an excellent discussion of the concept of learning in this context see Cook and Scioli, 1972. They posit that political socialization research contains "a body of research which provides a description of *what* people have learned up to a certain point in time rather than an explanation of *how* they learned their political preferences" (p. 953).

19. Easton and Dennis, 1969, pp. 151–58. This excerpt is part of a larger discussion on

the child's visibility and salience of political authorities such as the President and policemen.

20. Jennings, 1967, pp. 291–317.
21. Jennings and Niemi, 1968, p. 183. For political influence of mother and father on daughters and sons and for a discussion of symbolic interactionist theory in political socialization research, see L. Eugene Thomas, 1971.
22. Langton and Jennings, 1968, p. 865.
23. Ibid., p. 862.
24. Jennings and Niemi, 1968, p. 450.
25. The work of Schramm et al., 1961 and Himmelweit, 1958 and DeFleur's studies have been early attempts to assess television's impact on children. For a more thorough bibliography, see Abel 1968–69, pp. 101–5; Murray et al., 1972, pp. 3–20. See also Elihu Katz and David Foulkes, "On the Use of Mass Media as 'Escape': Clarification of a Concept," *Public Opinion Quarterly* 26 (Fall 1962): 377–88; Young, 1969–70, pp. 37–46; Greenberg and Dominick, 1969, pp. 331–44; and Smith, 1971–72, pp. 37–50. The studies reviewed under "mass communications" in the *Annual Review of Psychology* 19 (1968) and 22 (1971) are helpful.
26. This study by Chaffee, Ward and Tipton is one of a series of studies by researchers at the University of Wisconsin Mass Communication Research Center. Together these studies provide comprehensive insight into the role families play in the development of communication patterns, including media use patterns. These patterns have been linked to particular uses of media during campaigns, levels of political knowledge and to political activity. These studies are abstracted in this chapter and discussed in several other chapters.

Abstracts and Bibliography*

Abel, John D. "Television and Children: A Selective Bibliography of Use and Effects." *J. Broadcast.* 13 (Winter 1968–69).

Abramson, Paul. "The Differential Political Socialization of English Secondary School Students." *Sociol. Educ.* 40 (Summer 1967): 246–69.

Adelson, Joseph and Robert P. O'Neil. "Growth of Political Ideas in Adolescence." *J. Pers. Soc. Psychol.* 4 (September 1966): 295–306.

Adler, Kenneth P. and Davis Bobrow. "Interest and Influence in Foreign Affairs," in David Riesman, ed., "Political Communication and Social Structure in the U.S." *Pub. Opin. Q.* 20 (Spring 1956): 89–101.

"This paper is a preliminary and partial report on a study which concentrated specifically on persons influential in the making of foreign policy. Persons who influence foreign-policy decisions have been shown to differ in socio-economic status, communication exposure, and communications activity from those who are interested but not influential."

Method: survey; interviewed 99 "interested" and 39 "influentials" in the making of foreign policy. *Statistics*: frequencies. *Pop. (N)*: 138 total subjects.

Findings: Their data on organizational memberships and activity indicate that the

*All periodical abbreviations follow the *American National Standard for Abbreviation of Titles of Periodicals: ANSI Z39.5–1969* (New York: American National Standards Institute, 1970).

"influentials" tend to shun nonpartisan, policy-oriented groups. The top "influentials" use interpersonal rather than organizational channels of communication. The "influentials" aversion to policy-oriented organizations does not, however, extend to the political party; 87% of the "influentials" compared with 62% of the "interested" identify with one of the major parties.

Appell, Clara T. "Television Viewing and the Preschool Child." *Marriage Fam. Living* 26 (August 1963): 311–18.

Bailyn, Lotte. "Mass Media and Children: A Study of Exposure Habits and Cognitive Effects." *Psychol. Monogr.* 73, 1 (1959): 1–48.

Bell, Richard Q. "A Reinterpretation of the Direction of Effects in Studies of Socialization." *Psychol. Rev.* 75 (March 1968): 81–95.

"This paper summarized data indicating that a unidirectional approach is too imprecise and that another formulation is possible which would accommodate our social philosophy as well as new data from studies of man and other animals" (p. 82). Designs are briefly recapitulated to emphasize the fact that offspring and parent effects can be separately identified and experimentally manipulated. This will require less reliance on correlation studies of parent and child behaviors from longitudinal studies but offers no means of ascertaining the direction of effects, unless specifically designed for that purpose. This study tries to develop an alternative to existing socialization theory; many research studies can be plausibly reinterpreted as indicating effects of children or parents. Not an empirical study.

Bell, Roderick. "The Determinants of Psychological Involvement in Politics: A Causal Analysis." *Midwest J. Polit. Sci.* 13 (May 1969): 237–53.

Bishop, Robert L., Mary Boersma, and John Williams. "Teenagers and News Media: Credibility Canyon." *Journalism Q.* 46 (Autumn 1969): 597–99.

According to the authors, news media are becoming a low-credibility source of information for teenagers. The results of a survey they conducted with high school students in a Michigan suburb indicate that news from media, especially print media, was considered untrustworthy, censored, and representative of "the establishment." The particular topics chosen for the survey were the Viet Nam war and race relations. *Method*: survey; questionnaire. *Statistics*: frequencies. *Pop. (N)*: not stated, high school students, 15% black.

Findings: (1) Only 19% consistently believe news reports—whether on radio, television, or in newspapers—on racial affairs. While 30% believe reports about Viet Nam, 27% seldom do (p.599). (2) The students were more skeptical of news about Viet Nam than racial news (p.599). (3) Students are apparently skeptical because they have a strong belief in censorship and in favoritism toward the government. Two questions on censorship reveal that 56% believe that newsmen are very often told what not to say about Viet Nam while 29% believe that racial news is very often censored. (4) 68–70% of the students chose one of the electronic media as the most important source of information; 17–20% chose newspapers as their least important source (p.599). (5) Overall, there was a low level of belief in any kind of news.

Blumenfeld, Warren S. "Note on the Relationship of Political Preference Between Generations Within a Household." *Psychol. Rep.* 15 (December 1964): 976.

Braungart, Richard G. "Family Status, Socialization, and Student Politics: A Multivariate Analysis." *Am. J. Sociol.* 77 (July 1971): 108–30.

Bronfenbrenner, Urie. *Two Worlds of Children—U.S. and U.S.S.R.* New York: Russell Sage Foundation, 1970, p. 103.

Byrne, Gary C. "Mass Media and Political Socialization of Children and Pre-Adults." *Journalism Q.* 46 (Spring 1969): 140–44.

The type of mass media exposure of children and pre-adults is related to certain attitudes toward political authority. Those with primarily TV news exposure were inclined to think favorably about government and feel that government is effective. Newspaper exposure was closely related to more critical assessment of government. *Question*: What is the relationship between the TV and newspaper exposure of children and their attitudes toward the government?

Method: survey; questionnaire. *Statistics*: percentages, chi-square. *Pop. (N)*: 387 sixth, tenth, eleventh graders (184 blacks, 203 whites).

Findings: (1) Black children are exposed to news on TV as often as whites, but black children have less exposure to newspapers. (2) Families of urban children take newspapers more often than families of rural children; there was no significant difference between urban and rural children in their claim to be watchers of TV news programs. (3) Lower SES children have newspaper exposure less than higher SES children; lower SES children see news on TV less than upper SES children (significant at .06 level). (4) Black children, rural children, and lower SES children (those with primarily TV news exposure) have more positive perceptions of governmental effectiveness than do white children, urban children, and upper SES children.

Cameron, David R. and Laura Summers. "Non-Family Agents of Political Socialization: A Reassessment of Converse and Dupeux." *Can. J. Polit. Sci.* 5 (September 1972): 418–32.

Chaffee, Steven, Jack McLeod, and Charles Atkin. "Parental Influences on Adolescent Media Use." *Am. Behav. Sci.* 14 (January-February 1971): 323–40.

Although the modeling correlations based on comparisons within each family are not very supportive of a direct influence modeling interpretation, it appears that families with similar parent-child communication structures indirectly produce characteristic media use patterns that are shared by parent and adolescent.

Method: survey; parent interview, student questionnaire. *Statistics*: Pearson correlation coefficient. *Pop. (N)*: 1300 parents, 1300 students.

Findings: (1) The parents' general entertainment television use is associated with the youngsters' general television use, but not with specific attention to television news. (2) Strong negative correlations are shown between parents' news reading and adolescents' TV time. This suggests that parents may influence their youngsters more by what they do not do than by what they do. (3) If the parent reads news materials a great deal, the adolescent is somewhat more likely to either read or watch news presentations but is definitely less likely to devote much time to television. (4) Analyses by sex of parent and of adolescent showed stronger correlations with the mother, regardless of the youngster's sex. (5) In two-set homes, the second set functions to provide privacy and convenience rather than to resolve program-selection differences. (6) Adolescents report viewing with siblings more often than with parents; they view alone as often as with parents. (7) Media use norms during adolescence shift toward less entertainment and more news consumption.

Chaffee, Steven H., Jack M. McLeod, and Daniel B. Wackman. "Family Communication Patterns and Adolescent Political Participation," in Jack Dennis, ed., *Socialization to Politics*. New York: Wiley, 1973, pp. 349–64.

The study presents the results of a series of studies of family communication structures as they relate to a variety of indicators of the political socialization levels of adolescents which show considerable evidence that parental constraints on the child's interpersonal communication in the home influence the process of political socialization.

Hypothesis: Competent participation in public affairs is stimulated by a family communication environment that combines a relatively weak socio-orientation with a relatively strong concept-orientation, i.e., the pluralistic home.

Method: survey; parent interview, child questionnaire. *Statistics*: Cross-tabulation. *Pop. (N)*: 208 parents, 208 ninth graders.

Findings: (1) Children from pluralistic homes rank consistently above the mean on all measures of political socialization; particularly, they stand out in their degree of knowledge about current political matters. The protectives are at or below the mean in all respects. The laissez-faire are well below the mean in interest, activity, and knowledge. The children from consensual homes are interested and active in political affairs, but deficient in knowledge. (2) The pluralistics indicate the highest preference for public affairs programming. (3) The pluralistic children make better use of their newspaper time. (4) Pluralistic children stand out in the activities of student government, forensics, and news publications. The products of laissez-faire homes appear to avoid student government, and the protectives are notably outside student communication activities. (5) The pluralistic parent is far above the mean in interests, knowledge, activity, and voting. (6) Communication about public affairs is a common behavior among consensual parents, whereas political participation is not. (7) "In laissez-faire families, there is rather little parental influence on the child's political participation—which tends to be low. In protective families, socio-oriented constraints produce moderate to low participation by the child. In consensual families, the combination of socio- and concept-oriented constraints leads to modeling of parental values and political behavior, but the child tends to rank low in knowledge and informational media use. Only in the concept-oriented pluralistic family is the child stimulated to high levels of political participation" (p. 364). (8) "In summary, the pluralistic children (and their parents) stand out as the most politicized; this is in accord with the basic hypothesis. The consensual parents communicate more and are more knowledgeable about politics than their children; the consensual children are comparatively more politically active than their parents. Protective parents tend to be comparatively lower in politicization and related media use than their children.

Chaffee, Steven H., Jack M. McLeod, and Daniel B. Wackman. "Family Communication and Political Socialization." Paper presented at annual meeting of the Association for Education in Journalism, Iowa City, Iowa, August 1966.

This paper limits itself to a brief review of the theory and method concerning family communication and political socialization and presents data from two related surveys. The mass media do not play a straightforward role in political socialization. Instead of providing an alternative to family stimulation of the child, it appears that media use is shaped according to the family communication patterns.

Method: survey. *Statistics*: percentages. *Pop. (N)*: 200 families with children in ninth grade.

Findings: (1) Political socialization is already following predictable patterns when the child is in his mid-teens. (2) Unidimensional conceptions of family structure and personality do not adequately account for differences in political socialization.

Chaffee, Steven H., L. Scott Ward, and Leonard P. Tipton. "Mass Communication and Political Socialization." *Journalism Q*. 47 (Winter 1970): 647–59.

A review of the literature on mass communication and political socialization indicates that there has been little study and evidence of mass media having any direct effects on political socialization. In order to fill the gaps in this area, the authors conducted a time-variated study of adolescents' political socialization. Media use was compared with other independent agents of political socialization: peer groups, parents, and teachers. The results of the study tend to indicate that there are causal effects between mass media and political knowledge. Mass media were a main source of information.

Hypothesis: Public affairs media consumption accounts for some change in political cognitions and behavior by comparison with three other agencies of political socialization: parents, peers, and teachers.

Method: survey; questionnaire. *Statistics*: Partial correlation. *Pop. (N)*: 1291 students in seventh, eighth, and ninth grades in Wisconsin.

Findings: (1) "For the junior high group there are significant partial correlations between entertainment use via both media and political knowledge. For junior high groups any use of the mass media tends to expose them to sources of increased political knowledge" (p. 655). (2) "For senior high students there seems to be a negative effect with TV entertainment viewing and political knowledge, as well as a mild negative effect with campaigning activities" (p. 655). (3) "We could tentatively infer that newspaper public affairs reading leads to greater campaigning activity regardless of grade level" (p. 656). (4) "Use of newspapers for public affairs news inputs emerges as an important functional variable in the process of political socialization" (pp. 656–57). (5) "Television has a more mixed effect and may even deter active campaigning behavior. But specific viewing of public affairs programming does lead to knowledge gain" (p. 657). (6) "Comparing the sources, the mass media are clearly rated as the most important source of information and personal opinions. Friends are the least important source. Teachers appear to be more a source of information than of opinion" (pp. 657–58). (7) "In all, our data point to the inference that mass communication plays a role in political socialization insofar as political knowledge is concerned, but its influence does not extend to overt behavior such as campaigning activity" (p. 658). (8) "We should consider the attitudinal effects of the mass media on political socialization as an open question" (p. 666).

Clarke, Peter. "Parental Socialization Values and Children's Newspaper Reading." *Journalism Q.* 42 (Autumn 1965): 539–46.

"This study suggests a new set of explanatory variables for studying changes in children's media behavior. The findings presented here only hint at the impact of parental reinforcement patterns on the development of children's newspaper reading tastes." Four independent variables are parental socialization values, public affairs opinion leadership, the extent to which parents say they like to read newspaper stories about federal government activities, and how often parents interact socially with the 15-year-olds.

Method: field experiment; questionnaire, interview. *Statistics*: chi-square and percentages. *Pop. (N)*: 445 tenth graders and parents.

Findings: (1) Differences in newspaper reading or looking are associated with parental socialization values (chi-square equals 7.9, 3 d.f. $p < .05$). (2) High-status parents are more likely to have value profiles described here as child-centered or high intellectual concern ($p < .01$) and family status alone is more highly predictive of childrens' newspaper attention than the value variable ($p > .005$). (3) Children in nonleader families are more likely to read and like information content if either parent is child-centered or expresses high intellectual concern (15.07 d.f. $p < .05$). (4) Parents' interest in topics on federal government is not directly correlated with their childrens' interest at this age level.

Clarke, Peter. "Some Proposals for Continuing Research on Youth and the Mass Media." *Am. Behav. Sci.* 14 (January-February 1971): 313–22.

Clausen, John A., ed. *Socialization and Society Symposium, 1968.* Special Science Research Council, Committee on Socialization and Social Structure. Boston: Little, Brown, 1968.

Findings: (1) "The mass media research shows that adults routinely select confirming evidence from the mass media to substantiate their existing attitudes and beliefs" (p. 193). (2) "The mass media may become a source for the acquisition of behavior through observational learning. Bandura and Walters (1963) argue convincingly that they do indeed function in this way" (p. 242).

Coldevin, Gary O. "Internationalism and Mass Communications." *Journalism Q.* 49 (Summer 1972): 365–68.

This study concerned high school students' socialization to international information. From the results of the author's survey it was apparent that TV was an important factor in supplying information. Specific international information was obtained from the mass media, general international information from school, and minimal information from the family. These findings implicated the importance of TV in political information.

Method: content analysis, survey; questionnaire. *Statistics*: percentages, correlation.
Pop. (N): 200 eleventh graders in urban Seattle high schools.
Findings: (1) "Interestingly the data reveal that the majority of attributes (of internationalism) are primarily derivatives of mass media sources. Television is the dominant single medium within this grouping with the majority of program content allotted to newscasts" (p. 367). (2) Newspapers were the second most important medium source. (3) "The fact that television has, in less than two decades, emerged as a primary medium of socialization underscores the present finding that much of its content is considered irrelevant" (p. 367). (4) "If internationalism is considered a desirable objective for American pre-adults, it would appear that the potential for mass communication is only being partially realized" (p. 367). (5) "Given the assertion that the news presented in the mass media 'constitutes a sampling of negative events and a systematic undersampling of positive events,' the overwhelming dominance of the attribute category, cooperation and peace, is reflective of the increasingly negative youth reaction to the highly salient war in Vietnam" (p. 367).

Connell, Robert William. *The Child's Construction of Politics*. Victoria, Australia: Melbourne University Press, 1971.
The author relates to the reader a series of case studies of Australian children's political views. He charts the children's stages in the development of political beliefs. In various interviews, children revealed TV as a source of information. Children often exposed themselves to news programs and were able to relate national stories such as the Kennedy assassination and the Viet Nam war clearly. According to the author, television plays an important part in the political socialization of the child.
Question: How do children construct interpretations of the political world as they grow up and how do they come to adopt stances toward it?
Method: panel study; questionnaire, interviews.
Findings: (1) Children of five or six are at the stage of "intuitive" thought about political consciousness. (2) At the age of seven, fantasy elements disappear; they are able to distinguish a political and governmental world from other areas of life. (3) "Of the 112 children in the main sample asked about the matter, 108 said they saw television news and gave corroborating details. Many saw it three or four times a week, some every night" (pp. 118–19). (4) "Television news is in fact the main source of the children's knowledge of politics" (p. 119). (5) In these interviews a majority of the children indicated that TV was their news source in knowledge of the president of the United States, Viet Nam, the prime minister's task, the queen, and the leader of the Federal opposition. The ages vary from seven to sixteen. (6) "Under the influence of mass media, and particularly under the influence of television, the political communication is indeed breaking down parochial tradition" (p. 128).

Connell, Robert William. "Political Socialization in the American Family: The Evidence Re-examined." *Pub. Opin. Q.* 36 (Fall 1972): 323–33.
The author re-examines the evidence leading to the conclusion that the family is the major agent of political socialization. His major statement is: "It appears from a substantial body of evidence that processes within the family have been largely irrelevant to the formulation of specific opinions. It appears that older and younger generations have developed their opinions in parallel rather than in series, by similar experiences in a common way of life" (p. 330).

Cook, Thomas J. and Frank P. Scioli, Jr. "A Critique of the Learning Concept in

Political Socialization Research." *Soc. Sci. Q.* 52 (March 1972): 949–62.

Cushing, William G. and James B. Lemert. "Has TV Altered Students' News Preferences?" *Journalism Q.* 50 (Spring 1973): 138–41.

Study tests whether students have altered news media preferences given that adults have changed their preferences from newspapers to television, and each network had doubled the length of its evening newscasts. "These results suggest that little has changed since the last comparative studies (1962) of students' choices were done despite the recent emergence of a generation of students who have had TV at hand all their lives."

Method: attitude survey. *Statistics*: percentages, chi-square. *Pop. (N)*: 150 University of Oregon students.

Davies, James C. "The Family's Role in Political Socialization." *Ann. Am. Acad. Polit. Soc. Sci.* 361 (September 1965): 10–19.

Davis, Richard H. "Television and the Older Adult." *J. Broadcast.* 15 (Spring 1971): 153–59.

Dawson, Richard E. "Political Socialization," in James A. Robinson, ed., *Political Science Annual: An International Review*, vol. 1. Indianapolis: Bobbs-Merrill, 1966, pp. 1–84.

This article gives a brief history of the concept "political socialization," an outline of its relation to contemporary political science, and a discussion of definition and foci of research in political socialization. "Research on the mass media suggests three important ideas about their impact on political socialization: (1) the hypothesis of a two-step flow model of communication; (2) the idea that mass media play more of a reinforcing role than a conversion role; and (3) the proposition that mass media content is received and interpreted in a social setting and in the context of socially conditioned individual predispositions" (p. 372).

Dawson, Richard and Kenneth Prewitt. *Political Socialization*. Boston: Little, Brown, 1969.

DeFleur, Melvin L. "Occupational Roles as Portrayed on Television." *Pub. Opin. Q.* 28 (Spring 1964): 57–74.

This study looked at 436 occupations displayed on 250 half-hour shows. The shows were chosen at times when children were most likely to watch TV. This study looked at occupational roles as portrayed on TV over a six-month period. It compared the realism of the frequency of various occupations portrayed with 1960 census data.

This study wished to examine the occupational roles portrayed on TV to see what kinds of occupations were being presented to children.

Method: content analysis. *Statistics*: frequencies.

Findings: (1) There is an over-representation of managerial and professional roles. (2) There is an under-representation of jobs of less prestige. (3) Television portrays a labor force that was heavily preoccupied with enforcement and administration of law. "As a learning source, then, television content that deals with occupational roles can be characterized as selective, unreal, stereotyped and misleading" (p. 74).

DeFleur, Melvin, L. and Lois B. DeFleur. "The Relative Contribution of Television as a Learning Source for Children's Occupational Knowledge." *Am. Sociol. Rev.* 32 (October 1967): 777–89.

"The data reported here concern children's knowledge of selected occupational roles and the relative contribution of television as a learning source in shaping that knowledge" (p. 778). Vicarious contact via television is a potent source of "incidental" learning for children concerning adult occupational roles. Three learning sources of occupational knowledge were assessed.

Method: survey; interviews using occupation test. *Statistics*: means, coefficient of concordance (rank order correlation). *Pop. (N)*: 237 children and their mothers, measured differences in age, status, and sex of child.

Findings: (1) Role knowledge increases linearly with age. (2) Children become more consistent with status rankings of occupation with age. (3) Boys knew significantly more about less visible occupations in the community. (4) Children at the bottom of the class hierarchy know less about each set of occupational roles. The authors' major conclusion concerning TV is that "a substantial homogenization effect was noted regarding children's knowledge of the world of work, apparently resulting from the stereotyped ways in which TV portrays occupation" (p. 777).

Dennis, Jack. "Major Problems of Political Socialization Research." *Midwest J. Polit. Sci.* 12 (February 1968): 85–114.

Dennis, Jack. A Survey and Bibliography of Contemporary Research on Political Learning and Socialization (Occasional Paper No. 8). Madison: Center for Cognitive Learning, University of Wisconsin.

Dennis, Jack, ed. *Socialization to Politics: A Reader*. New York: Wiley, 1973.

Dennis, J., L. Lindberg, and D. McCrone. "Support for Nation and Government Among English Children." *Br. J. Polit. Sci.* 1 (January 1971): 25–48.

Denver, D.T. and J.M. Bochel. "The Political Socialization of Activists in the British Communist Party." *Br. J. Polit. Sci.* 3 (January 1973): 53–72.

This paper examines three main areas of interest: the extent to which the socialization of Communists predisposed them to support the Communist Party; how far the initial recruitment of our respondents into activity is similarly connected with socialization; and why people stay in the party and support it. The study points to family, school, and peer groups and especially to experiences of individuals as extremely relevant factors.

Method: survey; interviews, questionnaire. *Type*: percentages. *Pop. (N)*: 279 Labour members, 43 Communists.

Findings: Communists watch television and listen to the radio as much as other groups. They regarded media as unreliable sources of information. Communists seek to immunize themselves from hostile media. They seek political sustenance by reading party literature; therefore they minimize the effects of mass media.

Dominick, Joseph R. "Television and Political Socialization." *Educ. Broadcast. Rev.* 6 (February 1972): 48–57.

Explores the role of television as a teacher of political facts and attitudes to children in grades 6 and 7.

Hypotheses: (1) There will be more reliance on TV as source of political information among low-income children. (2) Children who use TV as a primary information source show lower levels of political activity, knowledge, and cynicism and more positive evaluation of government and political institutions.

Method: survey; questionnaires. *Statistics*: percentages. *Pop. (N)*: 313 sixth and seventh graders from one middle- and one low-income school.

Findings: (1) 80% of the sample named one of mass media as source of most information about president and vice president. (2) 60% named media as source of information about Congress. (3) 50% named media as source of information about the Supreme Court. (4) Differences in attitudes among children who do and do not use the media as chief political information sources were inconsistent. (5) Children showing high TV usage for political information were more likely to believe that TV commercials for candidates would help make up their minds about how they should vote.

Easton, David and Jack Dennis. *Children in the Political System: Origins of Political Legitimacy*. New York: McGraw-Hill, 1969.

Easton, David and Jack Dennis. "The Child's Image of Government." *Ann. Am. Acad.*

Polit. Soc. Sci. 361 (September 1965): 40–57.

Easton, David and Robert D. Hess. "The Child's Political World." *Midwest J. Polit. Sci.* 6 (August 1962): 229–46.

Froman, Lewis A. "Learning Political Attitudes." *West. Polit. Q.* 15 (June 1962): 304–13.

Froman, L. "Personality and Political Socialization." *J. Polit.* 23 (May 1961): 341–52.

Gerson, Walter M. "Mass Media Socialization Behavior: Negro-White Differences." *Soc. Forces* 45 (September 1966): 40–50.

A comparative analysis of differences between Negro and white adolescents in their use of mass media as an agency of socialization (relative to the premarital socialization of Negro and white adolescents) indicates more Negro than white adolescents were media socializees.

Questions: How do persons of different status in different social structures use the media and what are the resulting consequences?

Method: survey; questionnaire. *Statistics*: frequencies. *Pop. (N)*: 351 black, 272 white adolescents.

Findings: (1) More black than white adolescents used the media for each of the socialization behaviors (reinforcing existing attitudes and values, and as a source of norms and values which affect solutions to personal problems). (2) About 3/5 of the study population (60.4%) used the media as an agency of socialization in cross-sex behavior. (3) Almost 2/3 (66.0%) of the blacks were media socializees compared to 53.3% of the white teenagers. (4) Overall, age within the limited range studied here (respondents from 13 years to 17 years) does not significantly change black-white differences in media behavior. However, the data suggest that among white adolescents, media reinforcement increases with age. (5) In general, among both white and black adolescents, working-class persons tend to use the media as a socializing agency more than do middle-class individuals. (6) Among the whites, those who are integrated in a peer culture are more likely to be media socializees. Among the blacks, the nonpeer integrated individuals are the most likely to be media socializees.

Greenberg, Bradley, B. Dervin, J.R. Dominick, and J. Bowes. *Use of the Mass Media by the Urban Poor*. New York: Praeger, 1970.

Greenberg, Bradley and Joseph Dominick. "Racial and Social Class Differences in Teen-Agers' Use of Television." *J. Broadcast.* 13 (Fall 1969): 331–44.

Greenberg, Edward S. "Orientations of Black and White Children to Political Authority Figures." *Soc. Sci. Q.* 51 (December 1970): 561–71.

Greenstein, Fred I. "The Benevolent Leader: Children's Images of Political Authority." *Am. Polit. Sci. Rev.* 54 (December 1960): 934–43.

The author studied the development of children's awareness of political leaders. The results indicate that children are similar to adults in their ranking of high political roles at an early age, but generally are less critical and more idealistic than adults. The family is considered the most important political socializing agent, followed by schools and mass media. The author calls for more research in childhood development of political images, for more significant findings in how political behavior is developed.

Questions: What are the child's attitudes toward political leaders, and how may this developmental process affect his adult responses?

Method: survey; questionnaire. *Pop. (N)*: 659 New Haven public and private school children, nine to thirteen years of age.

Greenstein, Fred I. "The Benevolent Leader Revisited: Children's Images of Political Leaders in Three Democracies." *Am. Polit. Sci. Rev.* (September 1975).

Greenstein, Fred I. *Children and Politics*. New Haven: Yale University Press, 1965.

Greenstein, Fred I. "More on Children's Images of the President." *Pub. Opin. Q.* 25 (Winter 1961): 648–54.

Greenstein, Fred I. "Personality and Political Socialization: The Theories of Authoritarian and Democratic Character." *Ann. Am. Acad. Polit. Soc. Sci.* 361 (September 1965): 81–95.

Greenstein, Fred I. *Personality and Politics.* Chicago: Markham, 1969.

Greenstein, Fred I. "Political Socialization," in *International Encyclopedia of the Social Sciences*, vol. 14. New York: Macmillan, 1968, pp. 551–55.

In this article, Greenstein focuses on generalizations concerning the processes of political socialization agents and circumstances and effects. He states that media variables are important agents of political socialization, but the research points to the fact that face-to-face communication is more persuasive than the mass media.

Findings: In his short paragraph on mass media, Greenstein states: "Many of the communications thus received are without specific political content, but some contact with political information is unavoidable, and children deliberately seek information about certain democratic political events. The long-run effect of media attention is probably to build up, gradually, and inadvertently, an awareness of basic elements in the political system" (p. 554).

Greenstein, Fred I. "Popular Images of the President." *Am. J. Psychiat.* 122 (November 1965): 523–29.

Greenstein, Fred I. "Research Notes: A Note on the Ambiguity of 'Political Socialization': Definitions, Criticisms, and Strategies of Inquiry." *J. Polit.* 32 (November 1970): 969–78.

Greenstein, Fred I. "Review of Easton and Dennis' *Children in the Political System: Origins of Political Legitimacy.*" *Polit. Sci. Q.* 87 (March 1972): 98–102.

Greenstein, Fred I. "Sex-Related Political Differences in Childhood." *J. Polit.* 23 (May 1961): 353–71.

Greenstein, Fred I. and Sidney Tarrow. *Political Orientations of Children; The Use of a Semi-Projective Technique in Three Nations.* Beverly Hills, Calif.: Sage, 1970.

Harvard Educ. Rev. 38 (Summer 1968). Special issue on political socialization.

Hawkins, Brett W., Vincent L. Marando, and George A. Taylor. "Efficacy, Mistrust, and Political Participation: Findings from Additional Data and Indicators." *J. Polit.* 33 (November 1971): 1130–36.

Hess, Robert D. and David Easton. "The Child's Changing Image of the President." *Pub. Opin. Q.* 24 (Winter 1960): 632–44.

The article explores the influence of parents and institutions on the political socialization of children. The results of the study indicated that the "attitude toward figures such as the President are initially attitudes that have been held toward other authority figures" (p. 643). These initial attitudes are likely to develop from the adult family members. The child's concept of authority figures is also derived from other sources: children's books, television, and comics.

Method: survey; questionnaire. *Pop. (N)*: approximately 350 elementary school students in a middle-class suburb of Chicago.

Findings: (1) Most of the children had seen, or claimed to have seen, the President of the United States on television (p. 635). (2) Data indicated the importance of the pre-high school period as a time during which the process of political socialization proceeds. (3) "The level of response at the second grade supports an argument advanced in another article: that political attitudes, at least toward authority figures, represent an area of considerable salience in the socializing process of children in our society" (p. 639). (4) "The child's concept of authority figures is derived from a variety of sources. His experience with his own parents may be assumed to play a prominent role in this type of learning, but other experiences undoubtedly contribute to it. The concept of a king or prince is presented through children's books, television, and comics, and the superior position of such persons as well as the respect they receive is evident" (p. 643). (5) Television is mentioned as a source for the child's image of the president but not considered as a variable.

Hess, Robert D. and David Easton. "The Role of Elementary School in Political Socialization." *School Rev.* 70 (Autumn 1962): 257–65.

Hess, Robert D., Fred M. Newmann et al. "Political Socialization in the Schools." *Harvard Educ. Rev.* 38 (Summer 1968): 528–57.

Hess, Robert D. and Judith Torney. *The Development of Basic Attitudes and Values Towards Government and Citizenship During the Elementary School Years, Part I.* Cooperative Education Project No. 1078. U.S. Office of Education. Chicago: University of Chicago Press, 1965.

Hess, Robert D. and Judith Torney. *The Development of Political Attitudes in Children.* Chicago: Aldine, 1967.

Himmelweit, Hilde, A.N. Oppenheim, and Pamela Vince. *Television and the Child: An Empirical Study of the Effects of Television on the Young.* London and New York: Published for Nuffield Foundation by the Oxford University Press, 1958.

Hirsch, H. *Poverty and Politicization.* New York: Free Press, 1971, pp. 118–35.

Radio, television, and newspapers are the top three ranked agents of information transmission for the Appalachian child and these rankings are not affected by the respondent's age or by the status of the intrafamilial relationships in his primary environment.

Method: survey; questionnaire. *Statistics*: rank orders, gamma correlation, chi-square. *Pop. (N)*: 2544 students, grades 5–12, Knox County, Kentucky.

Findings: (1) "The media are generally more salient agents of information transmission than the parents, peers, or school" (p. 120). (2) There is no relationship between age and the rank of the media as agents of information transmission. Generally, as age increases, the ranking of the media remains the same. (3) There are no significant differences between the sexes in attention paid to news in the media among Appalachian children. (4) The following hypothesis was not supported: as the child's relationship with his father deteriorates, the media increase in rank. (5) Though the rankings of the media are universally high, father-absence does produce significant differences on the local level for radio and on the local level and national level for television. Father-absent children rank radio and TV higher than their father-present counterparts. (6) The rate of exposure to the media does relate to the rank of the media, while the distribution or content of this exposure does not. (7) There is a relationship between the rate of exposure to the media and political knowledge. Those who do watch TV and listen to radio are slightly higher in knowledge than those who do not. Those who read newspapers are significantly higher on political knowledge than those who do not; those who read news stories in the paper most often are higher than those who read them less. (8) There is no relationship between content exposed to and political knowledge. (9) Since the rate of exposure does have a relationship to knowledge and content does not, merely being exposed to the media is the most salient variable.

Hollander, Neil. "Adolescents and the War: The Sources of Socialization." *Journalism Q.* 48 (Autumn 1971): 472–79.

Hollander discusses the sources of learning and socialization of high school seniors with respect to war in general and the war in Viet Nam. Five classifications were offered: church, family, friends, media, and schools.

Question: What was the major source of socialization and learning about war? *Method*: survey; questionnaire. *Statistics*: percentages. *Pop. (N)*: not given.

Findings: Media was found to be the dominant source. Television was being highest in the media class, newspapers and magazines were second highest. Salience—war in Viet Nam and war in general.

Hyman, Herbert. "Mass Communication and Socialization." *Pub. Opin. Q.* 37 (Winter 1973–74): 524–40.

Hyman, Herbert. "Mass Media and Political Socialization: The Role of Patterns of Communication," in Lucian Pye, ed., *Communication and Political Development.* Princeton, N.J.: Princeton University Press, 1963, pp. 128–48.
Nonpolitical communication content may make an independent contribution to political socialization and modernization.
Question: Does political communication have different outcomes for political socialization depending on its context?
Findings: (1) "The non-political content mediates and modifies the response to political communication by acting not merely as a filter but also as a buffer between the audience and the political world, insulating them from the undesirable effects of an overdose of politics. . . . The buffer provided by the non-political content may thus produce a responsive audience for political news, and one that reacts in less extreme fashion" (p. 132). (2) "Selective exposure, attention and memory, by which individuals defend themselves against hostile information, is less operative when the first part of a medium or communication to which they are exposed is pleasurable or congenial" (p. 133). (3) "Non-serious content in the media package mediates the exposure of the audience to serious content by keeping them captive; and it mediates the response by preventing too much anxiety from accompanying exposure to what would be otherwise unmitigatedly threatening" (p. 137). (4) The media contents, within which a communication is framed, provide a frame of reference and somehow modify the meaning we give something, the weight we assign it, and the judgment we make of it. "Prior exposure to a particular train of media experiences has a directive influence in organizing the way we perceive and define and interpret some ambiguous item of information" (pp. 140–41). (5) For a transitional society, the properties of the media as socializers may be appropriate, but there are barriers to their effectiveness (such as limitation in the supply of the mass media in poorer countries). (6) The media have become so common in Western society that their vitality is lost; their dynamics for changing our opinions is reduced. "The Western public doesn't suddenly change many of its topical opinions as a result of particular exposure, but, at the same time, the media do mold the rather odd way some see the political world and relate to it" (p. 147).

Hyman, Herbert. *Political Socialization.* Glencoe, Ill.: Free Press, 1959.

Jaros, Dean. *Socialization to Politics.* Basic Concepts in Political Science Series. New York: Praeger, 1973.

Jaros, Dean, H. Hirsch, and F.J. Fleron, Jr. "The Malevolent Leader: Political Socialization in an American Subculture." *Am. Polit. Sci. Rev.* 62 (June 1968): 564–75.

Jennings, M. Kent. "Observations on the Study of Political Values Among Pre-Adults." Prepared for The Center for Research and Education in American Liberties, Columbia University and Teachers College in connection with its "Conference to Explore the Factors Involved in Conducting a Depth Survey of Young People's Attitudes and Self-Concepts Regarding American Liberties. . . ." 21–23 October 1966, Suffern, N.Y.

Jennings, M. Kent. "Pre-Adult Orientations to Multiple Systems of Government." *Midwest J. Polit. Sci.* 11 (August 1967): 291–317.

Jennings, M. Kent. "Review of Fred I. Greenstein's *Children and Politics.*" *Pub. Opin. Q.* 30 (Summer 1966): 322–23.

Jennings, M. Kent and Richard G. Niemi. "Media Exposure and Political Discourse." Unpublished paper, 1973. This study was conducted to evaluate the political involvement of high school students and the importance of media use for their information. The authors indicate that the family influence is one of the determinants of political influence for the child, but that equally important to political socialization is the media exposure. Youth today are being exposed to various aspects of political issues, parties, and interests outside of the family. As expressed in this study, students too young to vote do have access to political views through mass media, so that they can engage in meaningful discussions and participate in various political activities. *Questions*: What is the extent of students' political interests and what are their sources of information?

Method: survey; questionnaire. *Pop. (N)*: 2062 students and 1922 parents.

Findings: (1) The political interest of students is very nearly independent of the levels of interest expressed by their parents (p. 5). (2) Among high school seniors there is a considerable amount of regular exposure to political and public affairs via the mass media (p. 9). Students' ranking of use of media for political news was (1) newspaper, (2) television, and (3) radio and magazines. (3) The use of television is somewhat more highly related to political interest than the radio (p. 12). (4) Television is the prime source of political information for nearly half of the student population (p. 13). Television viewing is so pervasive that only the most uninterested can avoid seeing news or public affairs programs at least occasionally (p. 13). (5) The agents that increase the political interest of students are likely to have an indirect impact on only some media usage. Specifically, they will increase regular use of the print media, but not necessarily decrease attention paid to the broadcast media (p. 16). (6) Instead of being restricted to the family and school, the student is bombarded with a wide variety of ideas and activities made available in the media and in discussions with other people (p. 44). Both the media and political discussions convey to the child information and ideas that he might not otherwise receive (p. 45). Information on global matters such as war, and on local matters such as schools, are brought to him by the media (p. 45).

Jennings, M. Kent and Richard G. Niemi. "Patterns of Political Learning." *Harvard Educ. Rev.* 38 (Summer 1968): 443–67.

Jennings, M. Kent and Richard G. Niemi. "The Transmission of Political Values from Parent to Child." *Am. Polit. Sci. Rev.* 62 (1968): 169–84.

The primary objective of the article is "to assay the flow of certain political values from parent to child" (p. 170). The data are taken from a study conducted by the Survey Research Center.

Method: survey. *Pop. (N)*: 1669 high school seniors, 1992 parents of these seniors. The procedure employed in the study was to match parent and student samples, thereby forming parent-student pairs.

Findings: There is a direct correlation of attitudes in only one area, that of party identification. In all other areas, the results show little or no support for the theory that political values are transmitted from parents to children. Among the socializing agents mentioned in the article as being at least partially responsible for the differences in the political values of the parents and children are the rapid sociotechnical changes occurring in modern society. The transformations in the content and form of the mass media and communications channels are "phenomena over which the family and the school have relatively little control" (p. 183).

Johnson, Norris R. "Television and Politicization: A Test of Competing Models." *Journalism Q.* 50 (Autumn 1973): 447–55, 474.

Data from a study on television availability and its effects on politicization indicate "that the family's involvement in politics is the primary determinant of politicization, that the family's effect is initially on political interest, which in turn is the determinant of other aspects of politicization, and that television availability in the community affects only political information" (pp. 455–56).

Method: survey; questionnaire. *Statistics*: Goodman and Kruskal's gamma. *Pop. (N)*: 472 high school seniors.

Findings: (1) There is only a slight relationship between the extent to which TV is available in an area and the political information of its high school seniors. (2) Media availability does not affect the indices of political interest or political participation. (3) "It appears that political participation lies outside the process which includes political interest, mass media usage, and political information, and that the relationship of political participation with political information is a spurious one" (p. 454).

Klapper, Joseph T. *The Effects of Mass Communication*. Glencoe, Ill.: Free Press, 1960.

Klecka, William R. "Applying Political Generations to the Study of Political Behavior: A Cohort Analysis." *Pub. Opin. Q.* 35 (Fall 1971): 358–73.

Kline, F. Gerald. "Youth and Political Activism." *Politera* 1 (Autumn 1971): 22–24.
Kline discusses the works of popular and academic writers concerned with the now and future political socialization of the nation's youth. What is seen and heard on television is useful, real, and helps organize everyday behavior. TV influence rises and falls in relation to adolescents' dependency on peer groups. Life cycle determinants influence an individual's political involvement.

Kline, F. Gerald, Niels Christiansen, Dennis K. Davis, Ron Ostman, Lea Vuori, and Shelton Gunaratne. "Family Communication Patterns, Family Autonomy and Peer Autonomy: A Theoretical Model of Socialization." Paper presented to the International Sociological Association, Varna, Bulgaria, September 1970.
"A review of the literature and a previous descriptive study by the authors provide the basis for the formulation of a theoretical model of socialization for adolescents." Dependent variables include radical political activism, mass institution evaluation, and mass media time budgeting. Independent variables are family communication patterns and autonomy from family and peers.
Method: path and dummy variable cohort analysis. *Pop. (N)*: random sample of 200 13–20-year-olds and nonrandom sample of sociology class.
Findings: "The findings provide evidence that family communication patterns have an effect on the youth's autonomy from family and peers with reasonably predictive capability for political behavior and mass institution evaluation, but less for media time budgeting."

Kraus, Sidney and Jae-won Lee. "Mass Communication and Political Socialization Among Adolescents in a Presidential Primary." Unpublished manuscript, 1973.

Krause, Merton S., Kevin Houlihan, Mark I. Oberlander, and Lawrence Carson. "Some Motivational Correlates of Attitudes Toward Political Participation." *Midwest J. Polit. Sci.* 14 (August 1970): 383–91.

Kuroda, Yasumasa. "Agencies of Political Socialization and Political Change: Political Orientation of Japanese Law Students." *Hum. Organ.* 24 (Winter 1965): 328–31.

Lane, Robert E. "Political Education in the Midst of Life's Struggles." *Harvard Educ. Rev.* 38 (Summer 1968): 468–94.

Langton, Kenneth P. "Peer Group and School and the Political Socialization Process." *Am. Polit. Sci. Rev.* 61 (September 1967): 751–58.

Langton, Kenneth P. *Political Socialization*. New York: Oxford University Press, 1969, pp. 106–9.
The overall results show a lack of effect of the curriculum of high school civics courses upon the political evaluation variables. The direction of the findings are consistent with the study's idea that civics courses are effective. The more civics courses that a person has the more interested and active in political affairs he is.
Method: survey; interview. *Statistics*: correlation coefficients. *Pop. (N)*: 1669 high school seniors.
Findings: (1) "Students from each racial grouping employ newspapers and magazines at about the same rate; but Negro students at all levels of parental education look at television more often than whites" (p. 108). (2) "For white students there is a

consistent but very weak association between taking civics courses and using media as an access point to political information, while among Negroes a consistently negative but somewhat stronger association exists" (p. 108). Possible explanation for negative correlations among Negroes is that a civics course may increase a student's political interest, while at the same time acting as a substitute for political information-gathering in the media. (3) "There is a significant increase in political interest among lower-status Negroes as they take more civics courses" (p. 109). (4) The more courses higher-status Negroes take, the less likely they are to seek political information in newspapers, magazines, and television.

Langton, Kenneth P. and M. Kent Jennings. "Political Socialization and the High School Civics Curriculum in the U.S." *Am. Polit. Sci. Rev.* 62 (September 1968): 852–67.

Leiserson, A. "Notes on the Theory of Political Opinion Formation." *Am. Polit. Sci. Rev.* 47 (March 1953): 171–77.

The present formulation of public opinion, particularly political opinion during this period, is discussed in this article. The author keys in on Lasswell's conceptual model of the political process as a determinant hierarchy of authority. The author discusses the use of mass media on political opinion formation by relating some of the propositions that evolved from research in the area. The importance of a nonpartisan, independent media is emphasized. As Lowell and Lippmann pointed out, the significance of the mass media lies in their strategic function of formulating the content and emphasis of issues brought to public attention (p. 175). The leadership role of the media in "structuring the situation" for their reader or listener is of inestimable political importance (p. 175). There is already considerable evidence upon which to build further research into the politics of the mass media—the relations of its controlling values to those of the society of which they are a part, the internal and external pressures to which policy-makers at operating levels are institutionally exposed, and the professional and social standards of decision that are applied by administrative personnel in determining content (pp. 175–76). In short, the task for political research into the mass media in the community is to show how public policies affecting the mass media are related to the character of political organization within the opinion industries, the impact of proposed public policies upon the various control groups within the media, and the type of arrangements provided by the media managers for leaders of both governmental and nongovernmental opinion seeking public expression of their political views (p. 177).

Lyness, Paul I. "The Place of the Mass Media in the Lives of Boys and Girls." *Journalism Q.* 29 (Winter 1952): 43–54.

This article is a survey of media use of children. Mass media were heavily used by the children during leisure time; use increased with age and was a main source of political information. The area of study included all media except TV, which was still in its formative stages.

Method: survey; questionnaire. *Pop. (N)*: 1418 boys and girls in grades 3, 5, 7, and 11. *Findings*: (1) The mass media dominated the respondents' leisure time at home in the evening. Moviegoing was the most popular activity away from home (p. 54). (2) Attention given newspapers, radio, and magazines increased to some extent with age (p. 54). (3) Most respondents thought radio more reliable than newspapers in reporting an event.

Lyons, Schley R. "The Political Socialization of Ghetto Children: Efficacy and Cynicism." *J. Polit.* 32 (May 1970): 288–304.

Maccoby, Eleanor E. "The Effects of Television on Children," in Wilbur Schramm, ed., *The Science of Human Communication.* New York: Basic Books, 1963, pp. 116–27.

The author summarized studies conducted on the effects of TV on children. She cites such authors as Schramm, Bandura, and Himmelweit. She indicates that TV does have some effects on children by providing them with models for imitation, transmitting certain attitudes and feelings about people and events, and arousing an emotional defense. However, the author cautions researchers not to assume direct causal effects of TV on children without considering many variables, including pre-existing attitudes of children, parental attitudes, variety of entertainment exposure, and limited effects. Nevertheless, potential for effects exists. The greatest impact on attitudes ought to occur in those areas where television programs present the same themes repeatedly with only slight variations (p. 124). Television is not the only, and not even the major, influence upon children's attitudes and values in most spheres of life. When TV presents values and models for behavior which are not consistent with the values parents hold for their children, there is no reason to believe that the influence of television will be paramount (p. 125).

Maccoby, Eleanor E. "Why Do Children Watch Television." *Pub. Opin. Q.* 18 (Fall 1954): 239–44.

Maccoby, Eleanor E., Richard E. Matthews, and Anton S. Morton. "Youth and Political Change." *Pub. Opin. Q.* 18 (Winter 1954–55): 23–39.

McClosky, Herbert and Harold E. Dahlgren. "Primary Group Influence on Party Loyalty." *Am. Polit. Sci. Rev.* 53, 3 (1959): 757–76.

McCombs, M.E. and L.E. Mullins. "Consequences of Education: Media Exposure, Political Interest and Information-Seeking Orientations." *Mass. Comm. Rev.*, August 1973, pp. 27–31.

Merrill, Irving R. "Broadcast Viewing and Listening by Children." *Pub. Opin. Q.* 25 (Summer 1961): 263–76.

Murray, John P., Eli A. Rubenstein, and George A. Comstock, eds. Television and Social Behavior; Reports and Papers, volume 2: Television and Social Learning. Washington, D.C.: U.S. Government Printing Office, 1972.

Musgrave, P. "Aspects of Political Socialization of Some Aberdeen Adolescents and Their Educational Implications." *Res. Educ.* 6 (November 1971): 39–51.

Nogee, Philip and Murray B. Levin. "Some Determinants of Political Attitudes among College Voters." *Pub. Opin. Q.* 22 (Winter 1958): 449–63.

O'Neil, Robert Paul. "The Development of Political Thinking During Adolescence." Doctoral dissertation, University of Michigan, 1964.

Orren, Karen and Paul Peterson. "Presidential Assassination: A Case Study in the Dynamics of Political Socialization." *J. Polit.* 29 (May 1967): 388–404.

This study examines how and why parents verbally interpret a political event (the assassination of President Kennedy) to their children. No media variables were directly employed.

Method: survey; interview. *Statistics*: percentages. *Pop. (N)*: parents of children ages 4–12.

Findings: (1) Emotionally involved parents were more likely to explain the assassination than were those who were less emotionally involved. (2) 40% of the parents who scored high on the current event information index explained the assassination of Kennedy, whereas 29% of those less explained. (3) The political information of the parent was the factor most closely associated with giving a historical or political explanation of the assassination.

Orum, Anthony M. and Robert S. Cohen. "The Development of Political Orientations among Black and White Children." *Am. Sociol. Rev.* 38 (February 1973): 62–74.

Pammett, John H. "Development of Political Orientations in Canadian School Children." *Can. J. Polit. Sci.* 4 (March 1971): 132–41.

Patrick, John J. *Political Socialization of American Youth: Implications for Secondary*

School Social Studies. Research Bulletin No. 3. Washington, D.C.: National Council for the Social Studies, 1967.

Prewitt, Kenneth, Heinz Eulau, and Betty H. Zisk. "Political Socialization and Political Roles." *Pub. Opin. Q.* 30 (Winter 1966–67): 569–82.

Richert, Jean Pierre. "Political Socialization in Quebec: Young People's Attitudes Toward Government." *Can. J. Polit. Sci.* 6 (June 1973): 303–13.

Schramm, Wilbur, ed. *The Impact of Educational Television*. Urbana: University of Illinois Press, 1960.

Schramm, Wilbur, Jack Lyle, and Edwin B. Parker. *Television in the Lives of our Children*. Stanford: Stanford University Press, 1961.

Scott, Lloyd. "Social Attitudes of Children Revealed by Responses to Television Programs." *Calif. J. Elem. Educ.* 22 (September 1954): 176–79.

Searing, Donald R., Joel J. Schwartz, and Alden E. Lind. "The Structuring Principle: Political Socialization and Belief Systems." *Am. Polit. Sci. Rev.* 67 (June 1973): 415–32.

Sears, David O. "Review of Robert D. Hess and Judith V. Torney's *The Development of Political Attitudes in Children*." *Harvard Educ. Rev.* 38 (Summer 1968): 571–77.

Sheinkopf, Kenneth G. "Family Communication Patterns and Anticipatory Socialization." *Journalism Q.* 50 (Spring 1973): 24–30.
Many of the norms and orientations a child learns cannot be applied until later life. In terms of political socialization, the author studied the communication pattern of the family and how it affects the child's future political orientations. Results indicate the tendency that a pluralistic family orientation (one which stresses concept formation in the child) is conducive to high levels of political participation during adulthood.
Method: survey; questionnaire. *Pop. (N)*: 1300 children from five eastern Wisconsin cities (grades 7, 8, 10, and 11).
Findings: The evidence lends support to the hypothesis that students with a strong concept-orientation expect that social norms will involve a high level of political participation during adulthood (p. 133). The pluralistic families emphasize the development of strong and varied relations in an environment comparatively free of social restraints. The child is encouraged to explore new ideas and often is exposed to controversial material; he can make up his own mind without fear that reaching a different conclusion from that of his parents will endanger family relations.

Shonfeld, William R. "The Focus of Political Socialization Research: An Evaluation." *World Polit.* 23 (April 1971): 544–75.

Sigel, Roberta S. "Assumptions about the Learning of Political Values." *Ann. Am. Acad. Polit. Soc. Sci.* 361 (September 1965): 1–9.

Sigel, Roberta S. "An Exploration into Some Aspects of Political Socialization: School Children's Reactions to the Death of a President," in Martha Wolfenstein and Gilbert Kliman, eds., *Children and the Death of a President*. Garden City, N.Y.: Doubleday, 1965, pp. 30–61.

Sigel, Roberta S. "Image of a President: Some Insights into the Political Views of School Children." *Am. Polit. Sci. Rev.* 62 (March 1968): 216–26.

Sigel, Roberta S. *Learning About Politics, A Reader in Political Socialization*, New York: Random House, 1970.

Sigel, Roberta S. "Political Socialization: Some Reflections on Current Approaches and Conceptualization." Paper delivered at annual meeting of the American Political Science Association, New York City, 6–10 September 1966.

Sigel, Roberta S. "Review of Robert D. Hess and Judith V. Torney's *The Development of Political Attitudes in Children*." *Pub. Opin. Q.* 32 (Fall 1968): 534.

Sigel, Roberta, ed. "Political Socialization: Its Role in the Political Process." *Ann.*

Am. Acad. Polit. Soc. Sci. 361 (September 1965).

Sigelman, Lee and Jonathan Hantke. "The Relative Impact of Socialization Agents: An Exploratory Study." Unpublished manuscript.

Smith, David M. "Some Uses of Mass Media by 14 Year Olds." *J. Broadcast.* 16 (Winter 1971–72): 37–50.

Stewart, Roger G. "Some Attitudes of College Students Toward Certain Aspects of Social, Political, and Economic Change." *Educ. Psychol. Meas.* 30 (Spring-Summer 1970): 111–18.

In this study, college undergraduates gave their opinions of controversial issues chosen from a "Revolution" symposium and local newspapers. The results indicated that students had a need for personal and social independence in thinking and action for the present and future. The author concludes that through college experience, public programs, and news media, these students can obtain information and make independent decisions.

Method: survey; questionnaire. *Statistics*: Likert scale, attitude scale, frequency, percentages. *Pop. (N)*: 176 undergraduate students from Central Washington State College.

Findings: (1) The author believes that the responses generally suggest a real belief in, a need for, and a justification of personal and social independence in thinking and action for the present and future (p. 117). (2) Through public programs, news media, and perhaps college experiences themselves, students seek information on which they can base some rational decisions independently of the conclusions and often one-sided explanations neatly expressed in capsule form by others (p. 117).

Stone, Vernon A. and Steven H. Chaffee. "Family Communication Patterns and Source-Message Orientation." *Journalism Q.* 47 (Summer 1970): 239–46.

Tapper, E.R. and R.A. Butler. "Continuity and Change in Adolescent Political Party Preferences." *Polit. Stud.* 18 (September 1970): 390–94.

Thomas, L. Eugene. "Political Attitude Congruence Between Politically Active Parents and College Age Children: An Inquiry into Family Political Socialization." *J. Marriage Fam.* 33 (May 1971): 375–86.

Wasburn, Philco C. "Some Political Implications of Students' Acquisition of Social Science Information." *Soc. Forces* 48 (March 1970): 373–83.

Wasby, Stephen L. "The Impact of the Family on Politics: An Essay and Review of the Literature." *Fam. Life Coord.* 15 (January 1966): 3–23.

Weisberg, Robert. "Adolescents' Perceptions of Political Authorities: Another Look at Political Virtue and Power." *Midwest J. Polit. Sci.* 16 (February 1972): 147–68.

Whisler, L. and H.H. Remmers. "The Effect of the Election on High School Pupils' Attitudes Toward the Two Major Parties." *School Soc.* 45 (17 April 1937): 558–60.

White, Elliott. "Intelligence, Individual Differences, and Learning: An Approach to Political Socialization." *Br. J. Sociol.* 20 (March 1969): 50–68.

White, Elliott. "Intelligence and Sense of Political Efficacy in Children." *J. Polit.* 30 (August 1968): 710–31.

Young, Ruth. "Television in the Lives of Our Parents." *J. Broadcast.* 14 (Winter 1969–70): 37–46.

Zimblatt, David. "High School Extracurricular Activities and Political Socialization." *Ann. Am. Acad. Polit. Soc. Sci.* 361 (September 1965): 20–31.

3

Mass Communication and the Electoral Process

Studies of the effects of mass communication on political behavior have persuaded scholars for over two decades that the mass media have minimal influence in the process of political socialization of children and relatively no effect on the voting behavior of adults. In Chapter 2 we noted two compelling reasons for questioning, if not rejecting, these "classical" proclamations:

1. In a substantial amount of research on political socialization the mass media were not included as either independent or dependent variables.
2. In much of the classical research on political socialization or voting behavior influences, television was not included because the medium had not been or was just being introduced. Further, when included, the mass media were not seriously treated as variables as were party identification, group affiliation, and the like.

To support both conclusions, we provided an analysis of the mass media-political socialization research and reviewed current data which offer persuasive evidence of the media's influence upon children's political development.

In this chapter we turn to the electoral process. We will again discuss the classic studies and their shortcomings; then we will examine the new, contrasting research and provide hypotheses which in our view warrant the attention of scholars investigating the relationship of mass communication to the electoral process.

The Classical Studies

Although researchers have largely ignored the roles of mass communication in the process of political socialization, they have given much attention to mass communication's influence in election campaigns.

The classical voting studies of Lazarsfeld (1944), Berelson et al. (1954), Campbell et al. (1954, 1960), and subsequent contributions of Katz and Lazarsfeld (1955), Pool (1959), Key (1961, 1966), Kraus (1962), Lang and Lang (1968), and recently Mendelsohn and Crespi (1970) and DeVries and

Figure 2

**CONTIGUOUS EXAMINATION OF THE APPEARANCE OF SELECTED
BENCHMARK ELECTION, VOTING, AND MASS MEDIA STUDIES WITH THE
GROWTH OF THE POLITICAL USE OF TELEVISION**

Election and Mass Communication Studies[1]	Year	Political Use of Television[2]	Sets in Use[3]	
The People's Choice (Erie County, Ohio)	1940	No Television		
Voting (Elmira, N.Y.)	1944		'46	10,000
		TV enters elections	'48	190,000
The Voter Decides (national)	1948		'50	10,500,000
		First commercials in political campaigns		
The American Voter	1952	Televised conventions	'60	54,000,000
American Voting Behavior (national)	1956			
		First presidential TV debates	'70	92,900,000
The Great Debates (national)	1960			
		Tandem use of TV and computers		
The Responsible Electorate (national)	1964	Tandem use of TV and polls		
Politics and Television (varied)	1968			
Polls, TV and the New Politics (national with California emphasis)	1972	Voter-viewer per day average TV viewing 3.5 hrs.		
The Ticket-Splitters (national with Michigan and Texas emphasis)	1973	Watergate Senate Hearings		

[1] Parentheses: sample location; dashed line: year data was gathered; solid line: year of publication.

[2] Pertinent to campaigns and elections only, excluded are Army-McCarthy Hearings (1954); Kefauver Crime Hearings (1951); Presidential News Conferences (1953); Ervin Watergate Hearings (1973); etc.

[3] Sources: Census data.

[4] Median hours projected from Roper data; see, *An Extended View of Public Attitudes Toward Television and Other Mass Media*. A Report by the Roper Organization, Inc., Television Information Office, New York, 1971.

Tarrance (1972), have all advanced our knowledge of how voters use mass media in choosing our leaders.

There is no need to detail the major contribution of the Columbia and Michigan groups. Hardly a report on communications and elections exists in which these studies have not been cited. But while they have served to chart research directions and have contributed to our knowledge generally, no one effort, however precocious, could have reflected television's effect on the election process in the fifties and the sixties. Consider the parameters (Figure 2). Television entered the election process in 1948.[1] Data were collected in Erie County in 1940 and reported in *The People's Choice* in 1944; data from Elmira were collected in 1948, the year of television's political debut, and appeared in *Voting* in 1954, but with only three minor references to television.[2] In 1952, Eisenhower employed the first political commercials on television in a presidential campaign. The same year also saw the introduction of televised conventions.[3] It was at this time that the Michigan group, under Angus Campbell, collected the data for the impressive volume *The Voter Decides*, which appeared in 1954. Data collected in 1956 were added to those of 1952 in the sequel, *The American Voter,* available in 1960. These last efforts stemmed in part from 1948 data and therefore did not substantially look into television's role.[4]

Campbell (1962) asserted at this time that television had no discernible relationship to that neat and acceptable barometer of public involvement with politics—voter turnout figures. Radio use, on the other hand, had correlated significantly with voter turnout in the years before television. "Between the elections of 1932 and 1940 [radio's fullest campaign coverage years] ... turnout records jumped more than eight percentage points; the off-year Congressional vote increased even more markedly." It seemed apparent: "The advent of radio was followed by a general and significant increase of turnout ... the arrival of television was not" (p. 11).

The question remained, however, whether television's role in the political process had been adequately measured. "Television, while available only to a minority, led the other media (in 1952) in number of persons who rated it most informative." This was found to be true even of those who had been exposed to other media sources (Campbell et al., 1953, p. 47).

A more recent study (Prisuta, 1973), using 1968 Michigan data from the Survey Research Center at Ann Arbor based on 1400 interviews, examined the relationship between the mass media and political behaviors (voter turnout, voting decision, and interest and information level). Prisuta found that use of newspapers as a source of political information correlated significantly with voter turnout. Those individuals highly exposed to newspaper political content were more likely to vote than those who were not so exposed. This finding did not extend to the other media. Stressing the point that the number of people exposed to the different media varies greatly,

Prisuta suggests that media reach and media impact (effectiveness) must be considered in order to gain insight into media's role in a campaign. While he never undertook this secondary analysis of the data to examine reach versus effectiveness, he offers some evidence that television is "the most important medium; although its impact may be less [than newspapers'], its reach is by far the greatest" (p. 169). Of his sample, 75 percent felt that television provided them with the most information and exposure to the campaign, while 48 percent felt that way about newspapers.

The special role of television—its reach, and its use by the public as a prime source of information—has been well documented. Converse (1962), discussing information flow in campaigns and the differences between "print" and "electronic" media, concludes that

> a majority of those who do notice some political news in the printed media nonetheless feel that they learned more about what is going on politically from the spoken media [radio and television]. Given the sketchy coverage of politics in the spoken media by contrast with the written [newspapers, magazines and books], this is quite a commentary on the relative "reach" and impact of the newer spoken media. (p. 592)

Measurement of television's reach and impact, however, cannot be found in the classical voting studies.

Generalizing from the Classics

These classical studies were undeniably important first attempts to use survey methodology and to gain *some* insight into the impact of media and mass communication on the behavior of voters. Yet they were limited in the extent to which they were able to assess mass media impact.

Often, these studies' findings have been cited in the literature of the social and behavioral sciences as benchmark indicators of mass communication's role in political behavior without recognizing their limitations.[5] Katz, in a 1971 review, writes of the empirical studies which constitute the "classics." His major thesis is that all of the election studies prior to the one conducted in England (Blumler and McQuail, 1969) were "more concerned with the functions of election campaigns for the parties than for the voters" (p. 306). Katz reviews the major media findings, largely from the "classics," and concludes that "it is a fact that mass media campaigns—not just political campaigns—convert very few people."[6] Katz summarizes: 80 percent of the voters have their minds made up (know for whom they will vote) before the campaign; 70 to 80 percent vote for the same party as they did in the previous election; and of the remaining 20 percent (shifters-doubters), one-fifth may return during the campaign to their original party. From the classical studies it became axiomatic to "believe that nearly all the voters make up their minds early in the (election) year . . . and are immoveable thereafter" (Bliven, 1952, p. 29).

Another of Katz's summary points focuses on the shifters-doubters—the crucial "floating voters"—and posits that these voters are the most uninterested, the most unexposed, and the most uninvolved. In a 1962 study once again using The Survey Research Center data, Converse examines two- and four-year longitudinal data which support this floating voter hypothesis. Amending the hypothesis slightly, Converse argues that short-term partisan change may occur if information actually reaches the less politically involved. For instance, in off-year congressional elections, the vote will tend to be highly partisan and stable because information flow is weak and does not reach the uninvolved, unexposed floating voter (pp. 581, 585–86).

The staunch partisan, much of the literature suggests, is not likely to be exposed to equal levels of communication. Because of selective exposure, the partisan will favor and be more exposed to communication which originates from his own side. Schramm and Carter (1959), in their study of Senator William F. Knowland's telethon (devised as a last-minute effort to win votes) argue for selective exposure, as does Greenberg (1965) in a field study of school issues in a local election. Schramm and Carter found evidence that Republicans were twice as likely to watch and were more impressed by Republican Knowland's telethon than were Democrats (pp. 122, 124); and Greenberg found that "consistent" voters (those who thought their side would win) were exposed to more information, mostly to printed material which came from their own side. Greenberg concluded that voters exposed themselves to significantly more campaign information if they thought their side was likely to win than if they thought their side would not win (p. 158).

Two widely held conclusions about mass media effects during the election process emerge from the findings of the "classics" and the studies which followed them: first, that mass media, particularly television, have little direct effect on political behavior; and second, that the media act as reinforcers rather than formers of opinion. These conclusions stem from studies conducted in an era in which the number of television sets in American households was no more than one-quarter of what it is today (Figure 2).

Blumer, referring to the finding in the Erie County and Elmira studies that mass media have restricted and minimal influence, suggests that "considering the wide range possible to media presentation . . . varying sensitivities of people, and the different possibilities in the moving developments in political settings, such a view is indeed pretentious" (Blumer, 1959, p. 201).

Pool's discussion of the limitations of the "classics" is perhaps more to the point. He found that *The People's Choice* contained "much fascinating material on the role of the mass media, but not on their effects." *Voting*, he

said, "adds little to the earlier volume in its treatment of the mass media."
The Voter Decides, he continues, "is much more sketchy in its treatment of
the impact of the campaign messages" (Pool, 1959, p. 238).

In a manner similar to Pool, Swanson pinpoints the limitations of the
"classics." These studies of voting behavior, he points out, were carried on
either as sociological or intervening variable studies, both of which sought
primarily to "establish correlations between distinctive voting patterns and
the sociological or attitudinal characteristics of voters" (Swanson, 1972, p.
36). This is a severely limiting concept, for such studies, then, do not deal
with the communication itself as a variable. We will deal with this point at
length in Chapter 7.

Other statements by Pool in 1959 foreshadow current research and have
a prophetic ring:

> It is possible to speculate on the reasons for the failure of research to shed
> much light on what had always seemed by common sense to be the signifi-
> cant aspect of the campaign [media messages]. (p. 239)

> Most political scientists believe . . . that with the use of radio and television,
> and the decline of party machines and political fervor, the direct impact
> of the media is increasing and that of opinion leaders declining. (p. 239)[7]

> There is little doubt that the effect of television will be profound. To say
> something about the specific quality of its impact is a challenge to students
> of communication. (p. 242)

Summing up television's first presidential campaign, Campbell, Gurin,
and Miller (1953) said that the new medium played an important role but
that no studies had been designed to determine the electorate's thinking as
a result of it.[8] Studies did emerge, however. Most germane, in the light of
Campbell's analysis of voter turnout in the television years (1962), is Glaser's
study of voter turnout in the years 1952 to 1960. This study found television
and newspapers a stunning combination, correlating with high voter turnout, and radio independent of turnout. Glaser concluded that television has
placed "a higher floor under [the] public's interest," and that because of
television there are no low turnouts as there had been in earlier elections
(1965, p. 81).[9] Other studies and reports that record television's notable
impact on politics in the fifties and sixties include Bendiner (1952), Goodman (1955), Salant (1962), Kelley (1962), Kraus (1962), Greenberg and
Parker (1965), O'Donnell (1966), Alexander (1969), and Blumler and
McQuail (1969).

Not all research indicated that the mass media were influential on voting.
Campbell and others at Michigan's Survey Research Center felt that when
it came to voting outcome television played a minimal role. They argued,
persuasively, that *party identification* was "an attachment held widely through

the American electorate with substantial influence on political cognitions, attitudes and behavior." They asserted that voters' group affiliations and loyalties were good indicators of party support and voting. Many advanced the idea that socioeconomic characteristics were variables which could predict voting behavior (Campbell et al., pp. 146, 295–401).[10]

That such a view was widely held is evidenced by reference once again to Katz's review article. He points to an underlying party loyalty among the electorate. Such loyalty is subject to occasional situational pulls. By and large, however, voters remain loyal to their party identification. Other studies view the electorate in the same light as suggested by the "classics." It is a pervasive view and dies hard. A study of a small community *between* elections found that voting activity was just one more factor in a complex of civic activities, correlating in expected ways with one's socioeconomic status (Buchanan, 1956, pp. 286–87). In Britain the electorate views voting as a "norm." The citizen votes to dissipate tension that would arise if he failed to act according to the norms established by his group (Rose and Mossawir, 1967, pp. 189, 199). As late as 1971 a field study of a Texas gubernatorial election concluded that political party identification remained the "single best predictor of voting behavior" (Russell, 1971).

What emerges from the classics, then, is that the voter is bound by his past, is largely uninterested in politics per se, and has a "limited awareness of public affairs." The data were interpreted to suggest that the "voter's pervasive character was his partisan commitment" (Campbell et al., 1960, p. 558).

The New Data

The Image of the Voter

Perhaps the first to draw a somewhat different picture of the voter—that of a rational person making choices—was V.O. Key, Jr. In *The Responsible Electorate*, which was not finished when he died in 1963, Key advanced the opinion that voters are swayed by their own policy views and by their evaluations of performance in government. As Maass interprets Key: "Voters respond most clearly to those events that they have experienced and observed" (Key, 1966, p. xii).[11]

As early as 1948, well before there was television newscasting, Berelson was aware of possible long-term changes being created by the media. The media could have, he suggested, "pervasive, subtle and durable effects" on the political attitudes of the public (Berelson, 1948, p. 182). In the intervening years, with the advent of television, this influence has become even greater. A general shift in the use of news media for political information from newspapers and radio to television has been noted.[12] The day-to-day news coverage by television and newspapers has an impact on cognitive and affective behavior, and voting behavior is affected thereby. But that behavior is not affected solely by campaign activity (Mickelson, 1960, p. 14). As McCombs states: "The influence of the media is seen to be in their long-range ability to shape frames of reference, to create the pseudo-environment to which political behavior is a response" (1967, p. 14). Assuredly, newscasters played an important part in informing voters of the sixties about the development of issues and positions taken by political figures and political candidates. Viewers have come to rely on their daily television news for most of their political information.

Two British investigators, Blumler and McQuail (1969), in their excellent book, *Television in Politics: Its Use and Influence*, point out that the voting public uses television less for guidance and reinforcement and more for their "surveillance" needs. To illustrate, they studied viewer response to party broadcasts in a 1964 general election in England and found that 52 percent used television to keep up with the main issues of the day, 51 percent to judge the leaders of the parties, and 55 percent to see what a particular party would do if it came to power. Blumler and McQuail also indicate that the net shift in party identification during the campaign was only about two-fifths as large as the shift which took place between elections. In other words, the movement toward one party and away from the other was a shift in viewpoint already taking place before the campaign. "One is led to the conclusion that the reporting of political news during periods of normal party activity is a stronger determinant of the climate in which the electoral contest takes place than the oratory and propaganda that constitute electioneering activity" (Lang, 1969–70, p. 647; Bradley, 1962).

In the United States and England we have confirmation of television's pervasive and persuasive role in political campaigns and the reliance upon it by the public for understanding issues and evaluating political leaders. Studies of the 1960 Kennedy-Nixon debates (Kraus, 1962) and the 1964 British election (Blumler and McQuail, 1969), among others, provide evidence of television's impact on the political process.[13] Blumler and McQuail suggest that British voters

> overwhelmingly nominated television when asked which medium was best for helping them to weigh up political leaders. Perhaps the degree of public reliance on television is best indicated by the fact that a half of the sample also found it most helpful in enabling them to understand political issues—compared with only a quarter who preferred the press in this respect. (p. 43)

Voters of the sixties observed much political fare on television.[14] Television coverage of presidential primary races and particularly of both Democratic and Republican nominating conventions reflected the importance of television in the political arena. The voters of the sixties were able to observe and experience, through television, the political process at work. In turn, researchers have learned a great deal about the political process through studying those voters' responses.

Media in the Primaries

Little exists in the way of formal studies of the media's impact in presidential primaries. Hirsch (1972), examining mass communication in the 1972 Illinois primary, found no correlation between media channel use and voting behavior. However, a study of press coverage in the New Hampshire primary found a "dramatic" effect (Churgin, 1970). Pepper (1973), in a content analysis study of the television's primary night coverage in 1972, concluded that it was "important, because it familiarizes the viewer with the candidate and clarifies the issues and trends for him" (p. 160).

In agreement with Pepper, Kelley (1962) also suggests that media coverage has an impact on the primaries. By their thorough coverage of the primaries, the mass media help the public decide which candidates are worthwhile. In fact, Kelly hypothesizes that "the treatment the media give candidates may have even more important consequences than it does in general election campaigns" (p. 311). Writing in reference to a specific primary, a veteran newsman offers support for Kelly and Pepper's assessment. Tom Wicker, commenting on the 1964 New Hampshire primary, noted the saturation coverage by television and remarked that Goldwater seemed unprepared for the camera. To Wicker's eye, the negative impact Goldwater made at this time was one from which he was never to recover: "The first exposure in New Hampshire shaped the whole campaign" (Wicker et al., 1966, p. 16).

Televised Conventions

The literature dealing with the conventions is much more extensive than that of the primaries. It reveals how the conventions were affected directly by television coverage. In television's first big political year, 1952, the conventions were assessed by the public as "an ill-behaved spectacle," and a "prolonged agony" (Bliven, 1952, p. 30). Undoubtedly, in response to such opinion, the conventions adapted to television; our nominating process, by this time, substantially changed in manner of operation and presentation. J. Leonard Reinsch, who was Executive Director of the Democratic National

Convention, contended that "television has altered the form and style of the convention system ... a good yardstick to measure the influence that television began to have on political conventions by 1956 is the noticeable alterations it created in the program. Sessions were scheduled to reach a maximum audience in prime time." Reinsch felt that televising national political conventions "involves the viewer in such a way that it helps him realize that what he thinks can and does often affect public policy" (1968, pp. 221, 223).

However, the view which the public gets from television can be misleading. In their study of television network coverage of the 1952 political conventions, Lang and Lang (1968, pp. 78–144) report that this coverage served to dramatize these conventions and report them from a particular point of view. Observers of these dramatized reports developed views of the conventions which differed sharply from those of persons who were actually present. We will return to this problem in Chapter 6.

A review article by Cranston substantiates Reinsch explicitly. Speaking directly of the change made in the 1956 televised conventions, Cranston details the changes made in time schedule, site, use of visual materials, and in the general behavior of the delegates. Further, he observes that television's reach was greater than ever. Audience growth from 1952 to 1956 had doubled (see Figure 2), and in 1956, people in an unprecedented 99.6 percent of American homes were able to view the conventions live (American Research Bureau Figures, in Cranston, 1960, p. 193). A Roper survey of the 1960 conventions revealed that of the 93 percent following the conventions, 69 percent of the public who followed the conventions did so via television, as opposed to 47 percent via newspapers and 16 percent via radio (Roper, 1960; Salant, 1962).

The experience which television can provide and the direct impact it can achieve upon the convention and the political process are vividly illustrated by Wicker's account of Goldwater's televised acceptance speech at the Republican convention: There was tremendous interest—millions of people watching—at that moment when he had the greatest opportunity to bind up the wounds of the party. Either by design or oversight, he reopened them with his remarks about extremism and by reading out of the party those who he said did not agree with him. Here was a specific instance of how the shape of events can be influenced by one dramatic and climactic episode on television (Wicker et al., 1966, p. 16).

Of the 1968 conventions, the Democratic Convention in Chicago was the subject of media attention. Not only the convention itself, but also the demonstrations, rioting, and police activities surrounding it received extensive coverage. Television provided on-the-spot monitoring of one of the most distasteful and embarrassing events in the history of our political process. Scholars, likewise, gave prominence to the event. One study revealed that televising the conventions did not influence the delegates (the study was drawn from the North Carolina delegation). However, although the delegates were not influenced by the televised coverage, they did feel that the conventions had a negative impact, partially because television dramatized the convention in ways the delegates thought misleading, and that under the guise of news coverage, the networks were taking a stand (Paletz, 1972, p.449). There is evidence that the general viewing public reacted in a similar fashion: "Television found itself facing an apparently hostile majority. Seven out of ten Americans are said by opinion samples to feel that television took the side of the anti-administration demonstrators in Chicago and [that television] was biased against the police who beat them up" (MacNeil, 1968, p. 631). Apparently, this particular televised convention stirred the electorate.

A recent study explains why. In a study of television news coverage and voter behavior, McClure and Patterson (1973) list five criteria necessary to produce television news which will leave the viewer with "a unique and powerful impact": the news coverage should be of real, live events; it should have an exciting visual context; it should have an uncomplicated story line; there should be repeated and/or saturation coverage; and it should be outside the context of a political campaign. As an example of television news which fulfilled these requirements, the authors offered the "violence and brutality of the 1968 Democratic National Convention" (p. 25).

Recent survey data offer the most concrete evidence yet that televised conventions are directly important to voter decision. Data from the years 1948 to 1968 reveal that one-third of the voters reach their voting decision before the nominating convention; *one-third of the voters reach their decision during the convention*; and one-third during the campaign. A look at the findings regarding the 1972 conventions reveals their impact. Fully 50 percent of the Nixon supporters and almost 30 percent of the McGovern supporters listed as their time of decision the period immediately before, during, or immediately after the conventions (Swanson, 1973, p. 133). This seems to suggest that the voters are indeed responding to, as Maass suggests, "those events that they have experienced and observed...."

Televised Debates

During the 1960 presidential campaign a good deal of the electorate was observing the Kennedy-Nixon debates. According to the president of CBS News, an unprecedented 115 million people saw the debates. Even paid political broadcasts, he said, averaged audiences well over 20 million, which was better than Nixon did in all of his grueling fifty-state tours (Salant, 1962, p. 338). Even a conservative estimate of the audience for all four debates claimed that it constituted about 55 percent of the 1960 adult population, with more than 80 percent of the population attending to at least one debate (Katz and Feldman, 1962, p. 190).

Kraus (1964) suggested that television's effect is "phenomenistic." As Kraus states, "a substantial amount of behavioral and social factors serve as mediating influences" when a voter watches a campaign on television, because the media are, and here he quotes Klapper, "working amid other influences, in a total situation" (pp. 219, 223).

The "phenomenistic" effect of the televised debates is borne out by reference to other studies. Kraus and Smith (1962) suggest that there was little alteration of basic thought toward the candidates, and "though each debate tended to alter the bias of viewers, other factors seemed to counterbalance this effect." Issues in the debates, they found, came to be strongly linked with viewer's perception of the candidate's image (pp. 307, 311). Additional evidence indicates that through the debates the audience came to discern the men more clearly, and came to respond to the image they projected. Issues were not seen as separate from image, but as one and the same (Rider, 1963; Katz and Feldman, 1962). The findings in yet another study are in substantial agreement. The debates helped bring the voter's conception of the image of the candidate and the issues close to the original voting preference. There were some dramatic changes in image perception (with Kennedy rallying the undecided), but there were no substantial changes in vote preference (Lang and Lang, 1961, pp. 277, 287).

Other studies, not dealing directly with the debates, suggested that the debates had a measurable direct influence on the outcome of the election. One investigation asserted that television played a significant role in the campaign, the debates being of major importance to Kennedy's victory (Gilbert, 1967). A second, stemming from research on the civil rights issue, found that although the majority in this particular sample was not affected by the debates (because, as the other studies also suggest, of selective perception), about one-third *was* influenced in their vote decision to some degree by the debates—29 percent of the white respondents and 34 percent of the black respondents. In this study of a sample of Tallahassee, Florida, voters, the debates influenced one out of every eight registered voters in candidate cognition and subsequent voting decision. Middleton (1962, pp. 428–29) concludes that "certainly the mass media can no longer be considered of minor significance in political campaigns."

Despite their inadequacies, the debates did provide a new vehicle which gave the voter-viewer a longer period of time, during and between the four debates, to raise questions and participate in political discussions. And while it may be risky, as Rider phrases it, to argue that the debates had a "hypodermic effect," the studies do indicate they had a "phenomenistic effect" well worth reckoning.

Polls

Polling became an important campaign variable in the last decade. Harris estimated that over two-thirds of all candidates for senator and three-fourths of all candidates for governor had polls conducted for them by professional polling organizations in the 1962 campaign, and that one congressional candidate in ten used survey research in his or her campaign (Harris, 1963, pp. 3–8). These polls, and the published polls of Gallup and Roper, were used in tandem with television during campaigns. Exposure to polls may serve to increase a general interest in voting in the public (Fuchs, 1965), but there is little to demonstrate a change in voter intention—either by an underdog or a bandwagon effect—due to polls (Fleitas, 1970; Mendelsohn and Crespi, 1970).

Television News Programming

Several studies outline the influence of television news programming on voting patterns and political behavior. Danielson (1956) measured the impact of one outstanding news story: Eisenhower's announcement, in February 1956, that he would run again for President. This dramatic news story spread rapidly through the media and through interpersonal contact. The story itself left the American public feeling quite optimistic about the chances for a Republican victory in the fall and left Republicans (but not Democrats) feeling that there were greater chances for peace and prosperity. Although this study did reveal some attitudinal effect, there was no increase in intention to vote for Eisenhower in the respondents as measured after his decision to run. It is not surprising to find that on 29 February 1956 news of Eisenhower's decision first reached Danielson's sample by the following means (in rank order): radio (39 percent), newspaper (27 percent), interpersonal contact (20 percent), and in last place television (14 percent) (p. 437). Again, reference to Figure 2 will make clearer Danielson's findings vis-à-vis media channel selection of his sample. In 1956 the media environment was in flux and it was precarious, at best, to venture hypotheses about media use and political content. Based on his evidence, however, Danielson thought that given a political news story "which was practically complete with the first bulletin" he could hypothesize that

> as communities become more heavily saturated with television sets, and as old habits of the pre-TV era die or change, this single dimension may emerge: if radio is used as a supplementary source of information about an event, then television and the newspaper will be used also; if television is used, then the newspapers will be used also; only the newspaper will be used alone as a supplementary medium by any large number of people,

and if people do not use the newspaper, they will be unlikely to use either radio or television. (p. 438)

The Danielson study makes a convenient starting point for a discussion of the effect of television news programming, with its finding that an isolated news story, dramatically presented, can indeed have a measurable effect on the public's attitudes.

Michael Robinson (n.d.) studied the George Wallace vote in the 1968 presidential election using Survey Research Center data, and explored the information source as a possible critical variable. He reached a startling conclusion. The relationship between reliance on television for political information and support for Wallace was not spurious, but was significant even when controls for education, age, and socioeconomic status were added. Discounting partisan disaffection and Wallace charisma as theories explaining this correlation between television dependency and support of Wallace, Robinson explained that in 1968 television had presented a unique social issue, and by "exacerbating white political frustrations with blacks [television helped]. . . move George Wallace out of the South and into Mid-America. . . . Without video and without the television news format, the Wallace vote would have been smaller" (p. 8).

Three studies of the 1972 presidential campaign directly examine television news coverage as a nonpartisan source of political information. Swanson's (1973) pilot study of a small group of southern Illinois voters reveals that in this campaign 69 percent of the public received most of their political information from the mass media (as opposed to 7.6 percent who used friends and acquaintances, that is, interpersonal communication, as their primary source of political information). Further, 54 percent of the respondents found television news their most *important* source of information, while 23 percent listed newspapers. Also, "most subjects judged the performance of the mass media in covering the campaign favorably. More than two-thirds of the respondents . . . thought that the media they identified as their first and second most important sources of information about the campaign (television and newspapers) had devoted equal attention to both candidates . . . more than half the voters . . . believed that the news coverage generally had presented a fair picture of both Nixon and McGovern . . . " (pp. 140–41).[15] Meadow's (1973) study, a content analysis, cross-media comparison of presidential campaign news coverage in 1972, reveals that such was indeed the case. Despite its time constraints and inflexible deadline, television news and newspapers gave equal coverage to McGovern and Nixon.

Meadow found that "the most striking pattern is the uniformity of coverage across several media sources. For example, newspapers gave McGovern 58 to 63 percent of the total space about the two major candidates while networks gave from 58 to 64 percent, and Nixon received from 37 to

42 percent total space by newspapers, compared with 36 to 42 percent by networks. Coverage for the vice-presidential candidates, however, did differ. It is suggested that Agnew's aggressive criticism of television news programming led the networks to favor their severest critic, for in some cases Agnew received from 62 to 96 percent of the total air time, while Shriver, the Democratic vice-presidential candidate, received as little as 14 percent. Also, Nixon's incumbency gave him an air-time advantage by adding a significant amount of administration news to candidate news. Meadow's findings regarding the incumbency advantage in the 1972 campaign are consistent with an earlier study by Repass and Chaffee (1968) which stressed that during the campaign period the incumbent President has two opportunities for exposure—as President and as candidate. But the significant finding in the Meadow analysis is that television news programming and newspaper coverage of the 1972 presidential campaign were "remarkably similar."

McClure and Patterson's study of the 1972 presidential campaign in the United States assessed the impact of the television news programming during that election. Specifically, they explored whether there was a change in viewer perception on certain issues on which there could be a reasonable expectation of attitude change as a result of exposure to television news programs. In the low-interest political group, 30 percent of those with high exposure to television news changed their belief regarding McGovern's position on the corruption issue, and this change in belief moved in a direction consistent with the news message. The same was true in two out of the five issues explored (McClure and Patterson, 1973, pp. 13–16). There is reason to believe, then, that television news programming has considerable impact both within and between elections.

Television Election Day Coverage

The mass media's role in a campaign culminates with the reporting of election returns on election day. With the growth of television communication, researchers became interested in the effects of election day coverage on voters yet to vote.

In the 1960s, all of the networks began a "contest" to see which could predict the winner first. In doing this, each hired computer experts and political analysts. All the trappings that market research, ·polling, and political research had developed in the forties and fifties found their way into television studios on election day.

It was important to make a prediction as early in the telecast as possible. In 1964 and in 1968 eastern winners were announced before polls were closed in the West. The national broadcast networks, understandably, were concerned about criticism from politicians and various groups that eastern election results and network election predictions broadcast before votes were cast in the West might have influenced voting behavior and even the outcome of the elections. Policy implications were clear. If networks' predictions influenced voters, legislation to inhibit election day radio and television coverage would probably be passed.[16] Two networks and several communication researchers investigated the problem. The Columbia Broadcasting System commissioned a study (Mendelsohn, 1966) and The National Broadcasting Company conducted one of its own (Tuchman and Coffin, 1971). Other studies were conducted by Clausen (1966), Fuchs (1965, 1966), and Lang and Lang (1965, 1968).

These studies tested the effects of such broadcasts on *voting turnout, candidate switching, undecided voters,* and the like. Assessment of the effect of the election return broadcasts in the 1964 race between Johnson and Goldwater indicated there was no change in voter turnout, nor was there vote switching as a result of exposure to the return broadcasts (Mendelsohn, 1966; Fuchs, 1965, 1966; Lang and Lang, 1965, 1968). The 1968 Humphrey-Nixon contest presented a new situation. The race was much closer, without the clear-cut differences apparent in 1964, with its slogan, "A choice, not an echo." It might have been supposed that exposure to early returns in the western states would have had more of an effect than in the 1964 landslide election. Tuchman and Coffin found, however, that "there was no difference between exposed and unexposed voters in terms of changes in voting turnout plans or candidate-switching, as well as no differences between decided and undecided voters in terms of viewing the broadcasts before voting" (p. 325). Their data on voter turnout revealed that no exposure to early returns resulted in a 3 percent change. Exposure to early returns resulted in a 4 percent change. Vote switching occurred 6 percent of the time without such exposure and about 7 percent with exposure. In the "undecided" category, only 16 percent watched the early returns, as opposed to the 18 percent "decided" who watched, and that 16 percent did not use the broadcasts to help make their decision. The authors speculate that television coverage might have effects only in a very unusual election when a race which is expected to be close turns into an obvious landslide.

Authoritative sources on the influence of election day predictions on those who have yet to vote are Lang and Lang's *Voting and Non-Voting: Implications of Broadcasting Returns before Polls are Closed* (1968) and Mendelsohn and Crespi's *Polls, Television and the New Politics* (1970). They present most of the available evidence to support the view that exposure to election day broadcasts and predictions of winners and losers does not have any appreciable effect on those yet to vote. In an aggregation of studies no evidence was uncovered to support the contention that eastern network coverage of election returns was responsible for either a bandwagon or an underdog effect upon voters in the West. Thus the evidence to date suggest that broadcasts of election returns and predictions do not influence voting behavior.

Decline of Party Identification

As Pool noted in 1959 (p. 239), early research did not deal with the effect of media messages during campaigns, despite television's increasing reach and importance to the public, coupled with a decline in the party machine. Early researchers seemed still influenced by and laboring under the generalization proposed by the "classics." But the awareness that there was a change in the profile of the voter began to be articulated. Stanley Kelley, in 1960, while still proposing that long-term stabilizing influences such as party identification and group norm pressures were the most important facts about the electorate, felt that "the decline of the (political) machine and the increasing dependence of politicians on the media . . . has meant a general shift in American political life from the politics of personal favors towards a politics of issues and images" (pp. 310, 316).

Ten years after Pool's and Kelley's prescient statements, Mendelsohn and Crespi (1970) could confidently summarize some of the effects of television on American politics:

Television has spawned four major changes in traditional American politics: 1) It has altered the process of nominating candidates at party conventions; 2) It has altered campaigning; 3) It has altered traditional party structures and functions; and 4) It has helped to encourage questioning of the traditional ways of choosing and electing candidates, and as a consequence, will aid in ushering in the new politics of the future. (pp. 297–98)

Studies from the seventies delineate the change in the voter and suggest a "new politics." Crespi looked at three studies dealing with attitudes about behavior and situations in which those attitudes correlate with the behavior itself. One of the three was a voting study, and like the nonpolitical studies, it revealed that predictive attitudes which correlate with actual behavior must be seen as multidimensional. Voting, a well-defined behavior, is ill-suited to be measured in attitudinal terms because the voter's situation is in flux, and is subject to certain situational dynamics which will be a greater determinant of behavior than so-called predisposing attitudes (Crespi, 1971, pp. 327–34). The suggestion is implicit, but quite clear: Television, as part of the situational dynamics in a campaign, makes it difficult to defend a long-term pull toward stability, such as party identification, as a single positive attitudinal measure from which voting behavior can be accurately predicted.

Three recent studies offer data supportive of such a viewpoint. Under the auspices of The American Institute for Political Communication, a panel study of voter attitudes, behavior, and knowledge of public affairs in the 1970 elections was conducted in York, Pennsylvania, and Zanesville, Ohio. Among the findings related to influences on the voting decision, the mass media were found to be most influential whereas party affiliations played a limited role:

> Television is viewed as the single most influential medium on his voting decision by the man in the street but the newspaper runs a close second. Traditional voting patterns and individual habit and party affiliations are more limited than the image factors, the media and close personal advisers among family and friends.[17]

Rusk and Weisberg (1972) used data from the University of Michigan's Center for Political Studies to analyze the factional lines of American politics. They compared the voter's perceptions of the candidates in the 1968 election to their perceptions two years later. In 1968, issues such as civil rights, the Viet Nam war, the plight of cities, and "law and order" were dominant. In 1970, these same issues were the concern of 63 percent of the respondents, and most remarkably these issues had, in both years, a very low correlation with party identification—.07 in 1968 and .12 in 1970. Rusk and Weisberg also drew some conclusions from the data relating to what they termed the volatility of the electorate. Defining low system volatility as characterizing a time when voters were faithful to their party, and high level volatility as being evidenced by a large number of independent voters and also by sizable deviations from a party vote, Rusk and Weisberg concluded that "evidence from the late 1960's is unequivocal in its indication of increasing volatility of the electorate" (p. 406).

Evidence of increased volatility mounts with a recent study by Dreyer (1971–72), concerned with pinpointing to what degree mass media impact might be greater than that found in Converse's study of the floating voter hypothesis (discussed earlier). Dreyer used Converse's methods, pooled five sets of SRC data (thereby increasing the size of the no-media cells), and examined individual elections in the years 1952 to 1964. He found general electorate stability eroded, with little support for party identification leading to party vote. Such behavior declined with each election, and declined at every level of exposure. Party voting is no longer a significant political fact of life. Dreyer concludes that

> with the growing availability of mass media (primarily television since 1952), and the increased utilization of the media by candidates and parties, the flow of short-term political stimuli—both during campaigns and in the lengthy lulls between them—has effectively penetrated all segments of the electorate. These data also suggest that the more or less

immediate circumstances that surround any given election have eroded and probably will continue to erode the stabilizing influences normally associated with the electorate's partisan loyalties. This weakening of the party identification-party vote relationship will be manifested across the total electorate. . . . Converse's modification of the floating voter hypothesis, while probably applicable to an earlier era of rather weak political communication, no longer seems to apply to the current situation. (p. 553)

Thus Rusk and Weisberg identify an issue-oriented, volatile electorate and Dreyer documents an erosion of party stability due in large part to television's impact on the electorate. Another recent work validates these conclusions, which upsets our notions about the voter and reinforces the importance of television in the election process. In *The Ticket Splitter: A New Force in American Politics* (1972), DeVries and Tarrance present a forceful case to show that party affiliation is relatively unimportant for the person who splits a ticket, and that ticket-splitters have been increasing. They interpret Key's last work, *The Responsible Electorate* (1966), as being in support of this new evidence and cite the "Key Corrective," which was issued by Michigan's Survey Research Center supporting Key's theory of rational voting. David S. Broder's introductory description of DeVries and Tarrance's ticket-splitter shows that he

is slightly younger, somewhat more educated, somewhat more white-collar, and more suburban than the typical middle-class voter. He tends to consume more media output about politics and is more active politically than the straight Democrat, but less than the straight Republican. He bases his decision on his judgment of the candidate's ability, personality, his competence to handle the job and his stand on the issues. Party identification is relatively unimportant to him.

He gets the information on which he bases his judgments primarily from television, particularly television news shows, documentaries and discussion programs, and secondarily from newspaper editorials and family talks. Advertising—even the much-vaunted television spots—rank well down on his list of influential factors. (p. 15)

Broder's last sentence deserves attention, for the role of television political advertising is a special one—about which we have just begun to develop some empirical knowledge.

Political Advertising

Current knowledge about political advertising's impact in elections is at best speculative. Recently researchers have given this area some attention, though much more is needed if we are to assess the effects of political advertisements appearing in newspapers and magazines and political commercials aired on radio and television.

In 1928 a political pundit, Frank Kent, wrote what was perhaps the first effort by a nonacademician to assess how candidates get elected to office. Kent, a reporter covering many campaigns for the *Baltimore Sun,* wrote *Political Behavior—The Heretofore Unwritten Laws, Customs and Principles of Politics as Practiced in The United States.* Writing with wit and candor about politics in the twenties, Kent includes a chapter entitled "Name and Face Stuff." Many of us will disagree with his view of the voter and perhaps even with his impressions of politicians, but his comments on political advertising are worth repeating:

> But getting away from mere "name and face" stuff, vital as it is, there are so many kinds of political publicity, such an infinite variety of ways of getting it, and so wide a range of effect, that it is impossible to catalogue them all. The best that can be done is to set down as concretely as possible the proven facts about publicity. Necessarily these will not be in narrative form. They will be more or less jerky in style but if there is any other way of presenting them I cannot now think of it.
>
> In the first place, the fact which most politicians seem too dumb to grasp is that newspaper political advertisements are a net loss. I am not now referring to advertisements of political meetings. Of course they are both necessary and effective. Nor do I mean advertisements of open letters or of speeches or statements which it is desirable to have fully printed and only parts of which can be got in the news columns. The advertising I mean is the sort that proposes to "sell" the candidate to the people just as is sold any other product—advertisements setting forth the merits of the man, the soundness of his issue, the reasons he should be elected. In recent years the tendency toward full-page advertisements of this character in national campaigns has been greatly increased. In 1924 both Democrats and Republicans spent many thousands of dollars in such advertisements in the metropolitan newspapers.
>
> It of course has a "name and face" value but beyond that practically none and the reasons are clear. One is that the voter instinctively discounts the argument in the political advertisements and disbelieves the facts if any. The second is that they utterly lack the pulling power of the ordinary advertisement. What is equally overlooked by the political managers who pay for these advertisements and by the professional men who prepare them is that "selling" a candidate to the voters is not like selling ordinary merchandise to the consumers. Perhaps it ought to be the same but it just is not. The fundamental mistake of course is in thinking that the voters, like the consumers, make merit the real test. Unless everything previously written in this book has been wasted, it ought not to be necessary to repeat that merit is not the thing that sways the voter, prejudice is. Advertisements must appeal to his reason, invoke his intelligence. Otherwise they would render attack easy and disgust the discriminating but influential few. It being conceded that, politically speaking, the average American is practically devoid of these qualities, the failure of the political advertisement is easy to understand.[18]

Nevertheless, two very early pretelevision studies indicate that partisan advertising ought to be a well-founded campaign tactic. A field experiment in a 1935 local and state election in Pennsylvania tested the appeal of leaflet advertising, and found "emotional" leaflets with sentimental appeal were more impressive and were retained better than were "rational" leaflets (Hartmann, 1936). A study of a 1948 city election in a Detroit judgeship race found that advertising in the form of a motion picture trailer was influential in gaining votes. Specifically, the candidate using the trailer got 4 percent more votes in areas where the trailer was seen than he did in a control area which did not use the trailer (Perentesis, 1948). Over the years, and persisting today, is the belief that all media should be employed in partisan advertising. McBath and Fisher quote a "veteran campaigner: 'all advertising and propaganda devices are used—billboards, radio, television, sound trucks, newspaper ads, letter writing or telephone . . . handbills, bus cards. No one dares omit any approach. Every cartridge must be fired because among the multitude of blanks one may be a bullet'" (McBath and Fisher, 1969, p. 24).

But what of that monolith of partisan advertising, television? In 1952, television's first big election year, Eisenhower commercials were "shown either just before or just after popular programs, in areas deemed crucial to Republican success at the polls" (Worsnop, 1968, p. 369). By 1956, heavy use of radio and television advertising appeared to be the most useful single strategy in campaign activity (Margolis, 1968). The Great Debates in 1960 did not set a precedent for presidential elections (though they did prompt many mini-debates in local and state elections), for in their wake, the frontrunner now avoids them since it is in his or her interest not to provide exposure for the opposition. After the debates, there was a growing use of spot ads (MacNeil, 1968, p. 632). The 1964 campaign was sparked by highly controversial television spots (Worsnop, 1968, p. 375–76) and found Nixon spending $12 million on television ads, Humphrey $6 million, and Wallace $3 million.[19] The 1968 campaign probably best reflected the prevalent idea, then, that a television commercial was the apex of political advertising, and "the 1968 Presidential elections were a series of hermetically sealed advertising packages"(Worsnop, 1968, p. 376). Although the expenditure for television ads is now limited by law, politicians show no signs of forsaking them. The question is, however, "It makes a lot of noise, but does it work?" (Gardner, 1972, p. 10).[20]

From the point of view of the ad "experts," the average American is not skeptical of political commercials, but will accept them. This *may* be true of low-involvement voters, those politically uninvolved but addicted to television (MacNeil, 1968, p. 632). There seems to be some support for this contention, but can we define the "average American" as a low-involvement voter, in the light of present evidence?

One study focuses on Krugman's theory[21] of learning without involvement. This theory is based upon the idea that a person with low salience on a topic can be affected by messages about that topic; because perceptual defenses are low, such a person "stores" such messages, which can then cause an attitude change that affects behavior. Rothschild studied voters with low involvement (that is, they were not seeking information), but a zero-order involvement was experienced (they felt a need to conform to societal norms by voting). Such a voter, Rothschild felt, would let the messages find him. A laboratory experiment involving political advertising and the low-involvement voter found both recall and attitude improvement positive for the presidential race, but no change in voting intention. In the state races there were dramatic results with good recall and change in voting intention (but no concomitant change in attitude). Rothschild's results buttress the theory proposed by Krugman, that low-involvement learning can take place with visual aids. Support for this theory is also offered by Manheim in a study of five Congressional seats in a 1970 election (Rothschild, n.d.; Rothschild and Ray, 1973; Manheim, 1971). Hager's study of the Scott versus Spong Senate race in 1972 assumed a strong relationship between Scott's able use of media and his election to the Senate (1973, p. 20).

But these findings must be balanced against other evidence. The presidential primaries in 1972 found a telegenic Lindsay rejected in Florida and Wisconsin, and saw Muskie flop in a television onslaught in Wisconsin (Zimmerman, 1972, p. 10). Are the voters buying their political candidates —did they buy Wallace, Humphrey, or Nixon in 1968—like so many packaged goods? Do the media manipulate, or has the average American a modicum of discrimination which makes him less susceptible to advertising than has been proposed? Rothschild's study finds the high-involvement voter predictably leery of political advertising. Much of the discussion of the "responsible electorate" in his paper also argues against a view which posits that the electorate as a whole is unarmed and defenseless against a slickly produced, packaged candidate. As McBath puts it, there is "broad public awareness of the use of marketing techniques in campaigns ... [and] as campaigners have sharpened skills in the arts of political advocacy, the voter has kept pace in his appreciation of their craftsmanship" (McBath and Fisher, 1969, p. 23; see also Bradley, 1962).

An excellent study by Patterson and McClure (1973) examined television political advertisements and their impact on the voters in the 1972 presidential campaign. They found that in specific ways, certain voters can be affected. The study centered on three one-minute "Democrats for Nixon" commercials, testing recall and attitude change. Low-interest voters did gather substantially more information from the commercials than did the high-interest voters who, as is to be expected, had more channels open for information flow. Patterson and McClure made an important distinction between beliefs and attitudes: they defined attitudes as how a voter feels about an issue, and beliefs as how a voter perceives a candidate's stand on an issue. Attitudinal defenses are up during a campaign, and not subject to change. Political ads on television which focus on beliefs, however, are wisely so structured, for belief is subject to change in the course of an election. Two of the three one-minute Nixon spots succeeded in changing voter beliefs in the direction of the Nixon message: in one ad, 43 to 44 percent changed, in the second, 32 percent. Possibly even more to the point, the low-interest, frequent television viewers had a higher change in belief (37 to 48 percent) than did the high-interest, frequent television viewer (18 to 35 percent). Patterson and McClure offer a likely middle ground, for they duly demonstrate that television commercials can penetrate the defense mechanisms of viewers and can, under certain conditions, affect a belief change in certain voters. But it would seem that nowhere is there evidence that the bulk of the voting public is heavily swayed by political advertising in typical election campaigns.

The Press

As the reach of television has increased and as its impact and influence on the voting behavior of the public have increased, radio's use and influence in that area have declined. Radio is no longer a medium which affects voting behavior to a significant degree. Newspapers, however, retain a degree of relevance to the voting behavior for some members of the public. Television and newspapers together correlate very highly with the voter turnout (Glaser, 1965, pp. 84–86; Prisuta, 1973, pp. 168–69). Other studies prove that for high-interest voters, those who are open to a heavy information flow, television *and* newspapers are important.

Beyond that concern with the high-interest voter, however, there is a unique role played by the press in the electoral process, a role which affects the general voting public. The bulk of the studies which focus on the special effect of the press indicate that voters place a high reliance on the press for local and nonpartisan issues. This was true in the Chicago of the thirties (Gosnell, 1936), and recent research shows that it is true at the present time. Gregg, in 1965, hypothesized that the press—particularly through its editorial endorsements—has an effect on voting behavior in local elections because there are fewer salient variables affecting the outcome. That is, if party identification, political attitudes, and information flow are not salient variables in a campaign (and often they are not in local elections), the newspaper will surely exert its special power (Gregg cited, explained by McCombs, 1967, pp. 5–6). Other studies support Gregg's hypothesis. The press affected voting preference in a rural village election (Krischak, 1971), in mayoral and councilmanic races (Conway, 1968); in obscenity and 15 other ballot measures (McCombs, 1967), in various local nonpartisan races including the judiciary (Vinyard, 1971), and in local Texas elections spanning the years 1960 to 1971 (McClenghan, 1973).

Early evidence records that print media (and here again, the emphasis is on newspaper campaign coverage and/or editorial endorsements) had no effect in national elections. In 1936 Roosevelt was opposed by 80 to 85 percent of the dailies (Dabney, 1937). In 1944 only 14 percent of the dailies endorsed Roosevelt, while 64 percent endorsed Dewey. In 1948 Truman received virtually no editorial support. Bone seems safe in concluding about that time: "In the matter of the Presidency, the voter apparently does not always follow the press" (1952, p. 134; see also our discussion of editional endorsements in Chapter 6).

Recent evidence suggests that the influence of the press may be felt not just in local elections, where there seems to be no disagreement that the press' effect is considerable, but in state and national elections as well. McCombs found that in the 1966 California election which formed the basis of his study, the impact of editorial endorsements was heavier in the races for Governor (Brown versus Reagan) and for Secretary of State than for State Senator or District Member of the Board of Education. He explains this anomaly in the following way: "if there is disagreement among the variables shaping the ballot decisions . . . [the] greater is the influence of an editorial endorsement" (McCombs, 1967, p. 547). Vinyard's study revealed that in the 1964 national election, voters depended on the press more than had previously been thought. Although both television and the press were accorded a great deal of "trust" in their credibility, 51 percent of the respondents relied on the newspapers "a lot" and/or "somewhat" in making their presidential choice (Vinyard and Sigel, 1971, p. 492). Survey Research Center data gathered at the time of the 1968 presidential election found television the unbiased source of campaign news, but in terms of voting behavior there was about a 6 percent edge in the vote for the candidate endorsed by the press (Robinson, 1972, p. 245). Prisuta's study of the same election also revealed a positive correlation between print media and political behavior: .22 correlation, as opposed to .10 for television. Further, Prisuta suggests that newspapers served as "mobilizers for Nixon" (1973, pp. 168–73).

The Vinyard and Sigel and Robinson studies both suggest why some candidates depend on newspaper endorsements. Robinson suggests that newspapers are traditionally partisan and therefore the public sees it "as legitimate for newspapers to take sides" (p. 246). Vinyard and Sigel's study included an open-ended question in response to which "a majority . . . [did] . . . not hesitate to tell us why they depend on the paper's electoral recommendation 'in helping [them] decide how to vote.' . . . Respondents apparently see nothing inherently wrong or inappropriate in letting their vote be influenced by the newspapers. It must be emphasized that this situation also prevails for presidential elections (although to a much diminished degree), and not just, as we had hypothesized, for non-partisan ones" (1971, pp. 491–92).

Directions for Future Research

This review of the literature cannot permit us to reach unequivocal conclusions about the role of the mass media in election campaigns. However, recent research has tended to support a position which assigns importance to certain media, particularly television, at certain crucial points in the electoral process. It is unwise to continue to use classical studies of the influence of the mass media upon election campaigns as reference points. In the following chapter we will argue that the conceptualizations used in these studies can be questioned. Even if the approaches used in these studies were valid, changes in social conditions and mass media technology would necessitate a renewed effort to assess the role of mass communication in the electoral process.

Future research should be oriented toward specifying those conditions under which mass communication has significant influence. The research reviewed in this and the previous chapters makes it clear that the mass media are influential in certain social situations when they communicate particular types of content which are used by a particular public for specific purposes. For example, newspaper editorials may influence voting decisions when the public has limited access to other information and when they have come to refer to and trust the newspaper as a source of information and opinion. This complex type of finding suggests that the task facing political communication researchers is an enormous one. Some might feel it cannot be accomplished because no useful theoretical conceptualizations can be created to guide and eventually to synthesize the results of a diversity of research conducted in very different politically relevant situations. We believe that such judgments are premature. Although the task is complex and demanding, it is not insurmountable. In the following chapter, we will review the conceptualizations which have guided political communication research. Our focus is on conceptualizations which have used the mass media as important independent or dependent variables. This focus is limited, but we believe it is broad enough to provide a sound basis for interdisciplinary research on political communication.

Some researchers who concede the possibility of conducting research on media effects still question its usefulness. They argue that social conditions which facilitate media influence also act as an effective control mechanism.

In support of this argument, they point to a myriad of findings suggesting that the mass media simply reinforce causal trends which social, structural, or psychological variables initiate. For example, the mass media are not viewed as the prime cause of violent or aggressive behavior by some adolescents. Rather, violent content on television is held to reinforce an individual's "predispositions" toward violence. This school of thought holds that what a child "brings" to the television set is more a determinant of subsequent behavior than what he "receives" from it. These "predispositions" are thought to stem from familial relationships, peer relationships, or psychological states such as anxiety or tension. Similarly, it can be suggested that the mass media do not "significantly" influence an individual's image of political candidates. Rather, the media reinforce "predispositions" toward viewing a candidate in a particular way. Such "predispositions" are initiated by social influence from one's family or by the opinion leaders of the groups to which one belongs. In both of these examples, the significant independent variables are the social or psychological conditions which give rise to the "predispositions" for responding to mass media content in particular ways. The mass media are treated as intervening variables. Typically, the way in which these intervening variables are measured is by obtaining self-reports of an individual's exposure to certain media content (for instance, violent programs or "image" advertising). Then a linear, metric data analysis technique (multiple regression analysis or partial correlation) is applied to determine whether the mass media variables can significantly increase the amount of variance explained in the dependent variables. In subsequent chapters, we will describe reasons why this approach to research on mass communication effects usually results in findings of no significant influence by the mass media. Our two primary objections to it are the way in which mass media variables are conceptualized and the mathematical models which are used to ascertain the effects of the media.

The mass media should not be viewed as simple sources of "stimuli" which reinforce "predispositions." This view fails to take into account the increasing evidence that media use is a highly structured activity. People form habits of media use, involving specific media at specific times. These habits are often formed because an individual consciously decides to use the media to serve certain purposes or desires. Other habits are learned in social situations. While not all of these uses are "rational," neither are they determined solely by unconscious "predispositions." These habits are adjusted to an individual's everyday life routine. Use of the media is best viewed as a social communication activity, not as a simple response to predominant social influences.

Society-wide patterns of media use may develop when people in similar social situations have similar rationales for media use. Such society-wide patterns mean that exposure to and use of certain forms of media content can be predicted and this use can be linked to particular effects. Thus, when political events are given extensive coverage by the mass media, we can expect that these reports will be attended to by a majority of the public. Furthermore, the impact of such reporting on the public may be predicted by a knowledge of the habitual uses which they make of such content. It is possible that certain ways of presenting news about particular events may have more or less immediate consequences for political processes. Certain events may be communicated so that they are perceived as being highly salient by a majority of the public. This saliency may increase the likelihood that the definitions of the event which are communicated by the mass media will ultimately influence certain forms of political action. These arguments can be summarized in the form of hypotheses which should receive attention in future research on election campaigns:

1. Mass media presentation of campaign events will directly influence political behavior and political processes when widely held patterns of media use exist which facilitate exposure to such presentations and which result in the perception of these events as salient.
2. Mass media presentations of campaign events will indirectly influence political behavior and the political process when widely held patterns of media use exist which do not facilitate exposure to such presentations or which result in the perception of these events as nonsalient.

These hypotheses may explain why the Watergate break-in was a "non-event" during the 1972 political campaign but the cover-up of the break-in became a salient event in 1973. McClure and Patterson (1973) suggested that the public's use of the mass media changes drastically during a political campaign. The public expects to be bombarded constantly by partisan political messages. These messages are viewed with suspicion. Reports about the Watergate break-in may have been associated in people's minds with Democratic campaign rhetoric and thus discounted. Meadow (1973, p. 487) points out that network television reports of the break-in generally attempted to be "fair" by devoting as much time to administration denials of the significance of the event as to Democratic views of it. Only CBS gave greater attention to presentation of information about the event than to administration views of it. Thus the way in which the media presented the event may have encouraged the public to view these reports as just part of the campaign. Not surprisingly, in the fall of 1972 the Harris Poll reported that the Watergate charges were seen as "political rhetoric" and only 26 percent felt otherwise (Harris, 1973). In this case, patterns of media use existed which resulted in the perception of the event as nonsalient. The influence of the media on the campaign was indirect. Existing views of campaign rhetoric were reinforced.

Exposure of the Watergate cover-up apparently produced significant shifts in public opinion. By the summer of 1973, 47 percent saw Watergate as "a very serious question involving honesty of the White House" whereas 43 percent concluded that it was "mostly political" (Harris, 1973). These shifts may in part have resulted from two changes: after the campaign the news media no longer felt compelled by fairness to provide balance in stories about Watergate and their stories tended to present only facts about the event; and the public may have begun to use news stories for information rather than viewing them as vehicles for campaign propaganda. Of course, the revelation of the cover-up of the break-in did much to change the public's perception of the event. However, the question remains whether even well-documented stories about the cover-up would have been accepted by the public during the campaign.

Clearly, these are not the only hypotheses worthy of further investigation. They do, however, warrant current consideration since the literature has not resolved the question. Moreover, studies incorporating these hypotheses would be of significant aid in reassessing our knowledge about mass communication effects in the electoral process.[22]

In Chapters 4, 5, and 6 we will develop a conceptual framework which enables hypotheses like these to be studied systematically. This framework draws heavily on two approaches which have recently become prominent in the literature on mass communication: the uses and gratifications approach, and the agenda-setting approach. The historical emergence of these approaches is traced with a focus on models of information flow in Chapter 4. Chapter 5 applies the uses and gratifications approach to political participation and alienation. Chapter 6 discusses agenda-setting and its implications for political communication.

Notes

1. For an historical review, see Becker and Lower, 1962; see also Edward W. Chester, *Radio and Television and American Politics* (New York: Sheed and Ward, 1969).
2. These references are scattered and are textually treated without empirical data; see pages 139, 178, and 234. Chapter 11, "Political Processes, The Role of Mass Media," pp. 234–52 does not provide television data. Additionally, of the 40 findings among the 14 studies tabulated under the heading of "Communication and Contact" (pp. 338–41), none refers to television.
3. See Charles A.H. Thomson, *Television and Presidential Politics* (Washington, D.C.: Brookings Institution, 1956). See also Herbert A. Simon and Frederick Stern, "The Effect of Television upon Voting Behavior in Iowa in the 1952 Presidential Election," *American Political Science Review* 49 (1955): 470–78; Joseph C. Siebert, *The Influence of Television on the 1952 Elections* (Department of Marketing, Miami University (Ohio), 1954); and Herbert R. Craig, "Distinctive Features of

Radio-TV in the 1952 Presidential Campaign" (unpublished master's thesis, State University of Iowa, 1954). For research on television's impact upon Eisenhower and Stevenson images in 1952, see Pool, 1959, pp. 242–61.

4. Thomson notes that in *The Voter Decides* Campbell and his associates "are largely non-commital on the influence of television," and that "no separate attention to television is given at all. Interpretations of the role of mass media are founded on an assumption that they are the chief means whereby a party communicates with its relevant publics, and are restricted to a generalized description of the 'vicarious' participation of voters in the campaign via these media. Campbell is interested in plotting the voting behavior of panel members against the degree of their exposure to one or more of four mass media: television, radio, newspapers and magazines" (p. 63).

5. Two notable exceptions appear in Burdick and Brodbeck, 1959; Pool, 1959; and Blumer, 1959.

6. We take exception to presenting Katz's conclusion as a statement of fact. There is no denying that most *studies* have found little, if any, conversion among respondents as a result of campaign propaganda. Yet we are left in doubt when comparing two well-recognized studies, each conducted by a past president of the American Association of Public Opinion Research, and each offering an opposing view. See B. Berelson, "Some Reasons Why Campaigns Fail" and H. Mendelsohn, "Some Reasons Why Campaigns Succeed," discussed and abstracted in Chapter 4.

7. See also Katz and Lazarsfeld, 1955; Elihu Katz, "The Two-Step Flow of Communication: An Up-to-Date Report on an Hypothesis," *Public Opinion Quarterly* 21 (1957): 61–78; and Verling C. Troldahl, "A Field Test of a Modified 'Two-Step Flow of Communication' Model," *Public Opinion Quarterly* 30 (1966): 609–23.

8. Campbell, Gurin, and Miller, 1953, p. 46. As Pool (1959, p. 239) suggested, studies did appear, but Campbell et al. could not have known about them.

9. The oft-cited Simon and Stern Iowa study of the 1952 presidential election (see footnote 3 above) revealed that television had no effect on voter turnout. Even so, Simon and Stern are in remarkable agreement with Glaser here, for they qualified their study, cautioned against generalizing, and pointed out that since interest in the election was already intense, "there might be little room for further (voter) increase . . ." (p. 477).

10. See also Warren E. Miller, "The Socio-Economic Analysis of Political Behavior," *Midwest Journal of Political Science* 2 (1958): 239–55; Herbert McClosky, "Survey Research in Political Science" in Charles Y. Glock, ed., *Survey Research in the Social Sciences* (New York: Russell Sage Foundation, 1967), pp. 96–104; and Lipset et al., 1954.

11. A forthcoming publication by Forrest Chisman provides significant corroboration for Key's views. Chisman argues that the public is interested in political issues and that their concern has an impact on government. See Forrest P. Chisman, *Attitude Psychology and the Study of Public Opinion* (University Park: Pennsylvania State University Press, 1976).

12. Meadow (1973), a political scientist, noted that "the majority of . . . campaign studies were conducted during the 1950's when newspapers were the dominant source of political information. Since that decade there has been a shift in the relative use of the news media from newspapers to television, but there has been no corresponding shift among communication researchers to study the presentation of campaign news on network television" (p. 482). This shift is discussed further in Chapter 4. The uses of the mass media for political information-seeking varies according to the structure of the various media, perceived need, and demographic characteristics of the voter. Blumler and McQuail (1969) found that "the preference

of an individual for television or the press as a source of political news is a function in part of his demographic traits" (p. 44).

13. It is a sad commentary on mass communication and political behavior research in America and Britain to record the fact that as of this writing we do not have a nation-wide study of political communication in the election process. A recent American effort to mobilize resources to conduct such a study failed. It is hoped, however, that remedies for the problems which accompanied the effort will be found and that the first American political communication-political behavior national study will occur with the advent of the 1976 presidential election. The preface of this book gives an account of the activities and the people associated with them which prompts our optimism for the realization of such a study.

14. See Lawrence W. Lichty, Joseph M. Ripley, and Harrison B. Summers, "Political Programs on National Television Networks: 1960 and 1964," *Journal of Broadcasting* 9 (1965): 217–29; and Topping and Lichty, 1971.

15. Were it not for corroborative evidence we would not generalize Swanson's findings either to media fairness in the 1972 campaign or to the use of media by voters in the campaign because of his extremely small sample size. His paper had another purpose related to an "analytic-evaluative judgment resting on an empirical base" to examine campaign persuasion.

16. At least one congressional committee has discussed the issue. See "Projections-Predictions of Election Results and Political Broadcasting," Hearings before the Subcommittee on Communications of the Committee on Commerce, United States Senate, 18–20 July 1967 (Washington, D.C.: U.S. Government Printing Office, 1967).

17. *Media Monopoly and Politics* (Washington, D.C.: The American Institute for Political Communication, May 1973), p. 5. These studies present several problems in sampling, execution, and analysis. Hence the findings should be carefully considered.

18. Frank Kent, *Political Behavior* (New York: Morrow, 1928), pp. 263–66.

19. In 1972, Congress passed legislation limiting television and radio advertising expenditures to $8.4 million in presidential campaigns.

20. One possible effect of heavy political advertising is suggested by Mendelsohn and Muchnik. The public suffers because "the result in such media usage [as heavy advertising] is a dearth of longer programs that could deal with both substantive and in-depth campaign issues and the qualification of candidates for office" (1970, p. 3).

21. Herbert E. Krugman, "The Impact of Television Advertising: Learning Without Involvement," *Public Opinion Quarterly* (Fall 1965): 349–56.

22. As of this writing, 30 studies on the effects of mass communication on the Watergate "affair" and the 1972 election have been identified. Several of these have been published (Kraus and Chaffee, 1974; Chaffee, 1975).

Abstracts and Bibliography

Abels, Jules. *The Degeneration of Our Presidential Election.* New York: Macmillan, 1968.

Adamany, David W. "The Media in Campaigning." *League of Women Voters Q.* 47 (Autumn 1972): 46–47.

Agranoff, Robert. *Elections and Electoral Behavior: A Bibliography.* DeKalb: Center for Governmental Studies, Northern Illinois University, 1972.

Agranoff, Robert. *Political Campaigns: A Bibliography.* DeKalb: Center for Governmental Studies, Northern Illinois University, 1972.

Agranoff, Robert, ed. *The New Style in Election Campaigns.* Boston: Holbrook Press, 1972.

Alexander, Herbert E. "Communications and Politics: The Media and the Message." *Law Contemp. Probl.* 34 (Spring 1969): 255–77.
Alexander discusses the media's role in politics: how they are used, their effects, their costs. Effective communication is a vital element in the political process.
Conclusions: (1) A Roper 1968 survey concerning the media through which the public gained its clearest understanding of national candidates and issues revealed the following percentages: 65% television; 24% newspaper; 4% magazines (p. 258). (2) In statewide political contests the public gained a clear understanding of candidates and issues through the media according to these percentages: 42% television; 37% newspapers; 6% radio; 1% magazine; 9% "other people" (p. 258). (3) In local elections a clear understanding of candidates and issues was gained through media according to the following figures: 26% television; 40% newspapers; 6% radio; 1% magazines; 23% "other people" (p. 258). (4) Television enlarges political options and helps keep the political system open and flexible. (5) Television provides a soapbox for minority views, thus providing alternatives to party control. (6) Television has bred a feeling of intimacy between voter and public official, an intimacy which has led voters to trust their own impressions of outside commentators. (7) Television may influence citizens' opinion of the electoral process; it may strengthen or undermine the nation's confidence in its institutions and democracy.

Alford, R.R. and E.C. Lee. "Voting Turnout in American Cities." *Am. Polit. Sci. Rev.* 62 (September 1968): 796–813.

Anderson, Totton J. "Politics in the Western States: 1970." *West. Polit. Q.* 24 (June 1971): 225–33.

Anderson, Totton J., and Charles G. Bell. "The 1970 Election in California." *West. Polit. Q.* 24 (June 1971): 252–73.

Andrews, William G. "American Voting Participation." *West. Polit. Q.* 19 (December 1966): 639–52.

Arora, Satish K. and Harold D. Lasswell. *Political Communication: The Public Language of Political Elites in India and the United States.* New York: Holt, Rinehart, and Winston, 1969.

Atkin, Charles. "The Effect of Imbalanced Political Campaign Coverage on Voter Exposure Patterns." Paper presented at Association for Education in Journalism Convention, Washington, D.C., August 1970.

Atkin, Charles K., et al. "Patterns of Voter Reception and Response to Televised Political Advertising in Two Gubernatorial Campaigns." Paper presented at Association for Education in Journalism Convention, Carbondale, Ill., August 1972.

Atkin, Charles K., Wayne W. Crouch, and Verling C. Troldahl. "The Role of the Campus Newspaper in the New Youth Vote." Paper presented at the International Communication Association Convention, Montreal, April 1973.

Atwood, L. Erwin, Adrian Combs, and JoAnne Young. "Multiple Facets of Candidate Image Structure: Effects of the McGovern Television Biography." Paper presented at the annual convention of the Association for Education in Journalism, Fort Collins, Colo., August 1973.

Auer, J. Jeffery. "The Counterfeit Debates," in Sidney Kraus, ed., *The Great Debates.* Bloomington: Indiana University Press, 1962, pp. 142–50.

Baer, Michael A. "Residential Mobility: Some Political Implications for New Towns." *West. Polit. Q.* 26 (March 1973): 83–89.

Barber, James David. *Citizen Politics.* Chicago: Markham, 1972.

Barnes, J.A. *Politics in a Changing Society.* New York: Humanities Press, 1954.

Barney, Ralph D. "Toward a Theory of Mass Media Governance Attitudes in Predicting Direction of Political and/or Economic Development." Paper presented to the annual convention of the Association for Education in Journalism, Fort Collins, Colo., August 1973.

Bartell, Ted and Sandra Bouxsein. "The Chelsea Project: Candidate Preference, Issue Preference, and Turnout Effects of Student Canvassing." *Pub. Opin. Q.* 37 (Summer 1973): 268–75.

Becker, John F. and Eugene E. Heaton, Jr. "The Election of Senator Edward W. Brooke." *Pub. Opin. Q.* 31 (Fall 1967): 346–58.

Becker, Samuel L. and Elmer W. Lower. "Broadcasting in Presidential Campaigns," in Sidney Kraus, ed., *The Great Debates.* Bloomington: Indiana University Press, 1962, pp. 25–55.

Bendiner, Robert. "How Much Has Television Changed Campaigning?" *New York Times Magazine*, 2 November 1952, pp. 31 ff.

Although television functions well in distilling the essentials of a political campaign to a large audience, it will never replace traditional forms of American electioneering or active reporting by the press.

Conclusions: (1) Television can be effective in enabling an unknown to become known in a short time and in promoting high registration throughout the country. (2) Television coverage may be too extensive and too indiscriminate. (3) A televised campaign can present problems for the viewer, who has no opportunity to ask questions or demand clarification. (4) Television helps establish a good rapport between the nation and its leaders. (5) Television gives the viewer a better impression of democracy.

Benewick, R.J., et al. "The Floating Voter and the Liberal View of Representation." *Polit. Stud.* 17 (June 1969): 177–95.

Bennett, Ralph K. "Television and the Candidates." *Nat. Obs.*, 20 May 1968, pp. 1+.

Ben-Zeev, Saul and Irving S. White. "Effects and Implications," in Sidney Kraus, ed., *The Great Debates.* Bloomington: Indiana University Press, 1962, pp. 331–37.

Berelson, Bernard. "Communications and Public Opinion," in Wilbur Schramm, ed., *Communications in Modern Society.* Urbana: University of Illinois Press, 1948, pp. 167–85.

This discussion on communication and public opinion indicates that communication and public opinion have reciprocal effects on each other.

Conclusions: (1) One factor that conditions what the media relates on issues is the desire or expectations of the audience to be told certain things and not others. (2) The effectiveness of communications as an influence on public opinion varies with the nature of the communication. The more personal the medium, the more effective it is in converting opinions. (3) Within the media of communications, the particular channels specialized to the subject's predispositions are more effective in converting his opinion than the generalized channels. (4) Emotional content of the media is more effective in converting opinions than rational content. (5) The effectiveness of communications as an influence upon public opinion varies with the nature of the issue. Communication content is more effective in influencing opinion in peripheral issues than on crucial issues. (6) The effectiveness of communications as an influence on public opinion varies with the nature of the people. Direct effects of the media on public opinion can be exercised only on that part of the public which attends to the different media. The less informed people are on an issue, the more susceptible they are to conversion of opinion through the influence of the communication media. (7) The effectiveness of communications as an influence on public opinion varies with the nature of the conditions. (8) There is some evidence to suggest that nonpurposive reading and listening is more effective in changing opinions than purposive. (9) The media have a major influence in producing an interest in public affairs by constantly bringing them to peoples' attention. The more the media stress a political issue, the less indecision there is on the issue among the general public. At the same time, the media may be promoting a sense of political apathy among some of its audience. This can occur in two ways: the attractive substance and easy accessibility of the entertainment or diversionary content of the media operate to minimize political interest for some groups in the population; and "non-serious" content of the media may divert attention from political affairs directly and also re-create the audience so that it is under less compulsion to "face up to" the general political problems which confront it. (10) The media can increase political apathy simply through presentation of the magnitude, the diversity, and the complexity of political issues on which the responsible citizen is supposed to be informed. Overwhelmed by the presentation of issues and problems, part of the audience may withdraw into the relative security of their private lives.

Berelson, Bernard, Paul F. Lazarsfeld, and William McPhee. *Voting: A Study of Opinion Formation in a Presidential Campaign.* Chicago: University of Chicago Press, 1954.

Berenson, William M., Robert D. Bond, and J. Leiper Freeman. "The Wallace Vote and Political Change in Tennessee." *J. Polit.* 33 (May 1971): 515–20.

Birch, A.H., Peter Cambell, and P.G. Lucas. "The Popular Press in the British General Election of 1955." *Polit. Stud.* 4 (October 1956): 297–306.

Bliven, Bruce. "Politics and TV." *Harper's Magazine* 205 (November 1952): 27–33.

Blumer, Herbert. "Suggestions for the Study of Mass Media Effects," in E. Burdick and A.J. Brodbeck, eds., *American Voting Behavior.* Glencoe, Ill.: Free Press, 1959, pp. 197–208.

Blumler, Jay G. and Jack M. McLeod. "Communication and Voter Turnout in Britain." Paper presented to the annual convention of the Association for Education in Journalism, Fort Collins, Colo., August 1973. Extensively reviewed in Chapter 5.

Blumler, Jay G. and Denis McQuail. *Television in Politics: Its Uses and Influence.* Chicago: University of Chicago Press, 1969.

Blydenburgh, John C. "The Closed Rule and the Paradox of Voting." *J. Polit.* 33 (February 1971): 57–71.

Blydenburgh, John C. "A Controlled Experiment to Measure the Effects of Personal Contact Campaigning." *Midwest J. Polit. Sci.* 15 (August 1971): pp. 365+.

Blydenburgh, John C. "Two Attempts to Measure the Effects of Precinct-level Campaigning Activities." Unpublished doctoral dissertation, University of Rochester, 1969.

Bochel, J.M. and D.T. Denver. "Canvassing, Turnout, and Party Support: An Experiment." *Br. J. Polit. Sci.* 1 (July 1971): 257–70.

Bochel, J.M. and D.T. Denver. "The Impact of the Campaign on the Results of Local Government Elections." *Br. J. Polit. Sci.* 2 (April 1972): 239–43.

Bogart, Leo. *Silent Politics: Polls and the Awareness of Public Opinion.* New York: Wiley-Interscience, 1972.

Bone, Hugh A. "Campaign Methods Today." *Ann. Am. Acad. Polit. Soc. Sci.* 283 (September 1952): 127–40.

Bone, Hugh A. "The 1970 Election in Washington." *West. Polit. Q.* 24 (June 1971): 350–61.

Bone, Hugh A. and Austin Ranney. *Politics and Voters.* New York: McGraw-Hill, 1967.

Boyd, Richard W. "Presidential Elections: An Explanation of Voting Defection." *Am. Polit. Sci. Rev.* 63 (June 1969): 498–514.

Bradley, Rulon LaMar. "The Use of the Mass Media in the 1960 Election." Unpublished doctoral dissertation, University of Utah, 1962.
"The primary purpose of this study was to survey the opinions of some vitally active political workers in both the Democratic and the Republican parties, as well as key individuals within the workings of the mass media, as to the influence of the media upon the American voter in the 1960 election. The national committeemen from both the Democratic and the Republican parties were chosen to participate in the study, as well as news editors from the various media."
Method: survey; questionnaire. *Statistics:* frequencies. *Pop. (N):* 305 national political committeemen and media professionals.
Conclusions: "1. In this study newspapers were considered by both the Democratic and the Republican national committeemen to have been the most important of the four major media in furnishing voters with the bulk of the information on which they base their election choices. 2. Radio is considered to be much less important as an influence of political choices than it was in the 1948 election and others previous to 1948. 3. Magazines are influential and as far as the printed word is concerned they are second only to newspapers. However, compared with the other major media, they wield a comparatively small influence. 4. It is highly desirable that the new challenges and problems of television be most carefully considered and the medium used for the greatest advantage of the American voter in every future major campaign. 5. Personal appearances and speaking engagements around the country are considered to be of 'lesser' importance since the advent of television. TV provides an impressive substitute for the physical personal performance. 6. Most of the Republican national committeemen were of the opinion that the so-called 'great debates' of television should not become a permanent institution. The Democratic committeemen stated that the debates served as a good vehicle this time, but there was some question as to whether this method should become a permanent institution. 7. There is a wide divergence of opinion in the minds of the national committeemen of both parties and the various media newsmen as to the cause of any increase in the popular vote in the 1960 election. 8. Books and articles of learned societies have little influence in determining the political behavior of the American voter en masse. 9. Paid political advertisements carried by all media make a 'lesser' impression upon the American voter than the news and editorial coverage given to candidates by the media. 10. Editorial positions taken by writers for newspapers and popular magazines exercised only 'moderate' influence on the American voter in the 1960 election. 11. The average American is more inclined to be influenced by regular news coverage than he is by columnists and commentators. 12. A substantial majority of all categories answering the questionnaire were of the opinion that Senator Kennedy was treated more sympathetically than any other Democratic candidate since 1932. 13. Media coverage of the candidates' wives had only 'moderate' influence upon the voters' choices."

Brown, Steven R. and John D. Ellithorp. "Emotional Experiences in Political Groups: The Case of the McCarthy Phenomenon." *Am. Polit. Sci. Rev.* 64 (June 1970): 349–66.

Buchanan, William. "An Inquiry into Purposive Voting." *J. Polit.* 18 (May 1956): 281–96.

Burdick, E. and A.J. Brodbeck, eds. *American Voting Behavior.* Glencoe, Ill.: Free Press, 1959.

Burnham, Walter Dean. "American Voting Behavior and the 1964 Election." *Midwest J. Polit. Sci.* 12 (February 1968): 1–40.

Butler, David E. "Book Review of *Television in Politics*, by Jay G. Blumler and Dennis McQuail." *J. Polit.* 32 (August 1970): 737–38.

Butler, David E. and Donald E. Stokes. *Political Change in Britain: Forces Shaping Electoral Choice.* London: Macmillan, 1969.

Campbell, Angus. "A Classification of the Presidential Elections," in Angus Campbell et al., *Elections and the Political Order.* New York: Wiley, 1966, pp. 63–77.

Campbell, Angus. "Has Television Reshaped Politics?" *Columbia Journalism Rev.,* Fall 1962, pp. 10–13.

Comparisons of national elections during the era of television raises doubt as to whether television, despite its vast audience, has greatly altered the relationship of the electorate to the national government.

Conclusions: (1) There has been only a small proportionate increase in the presidential vote during the television era; the off-year congressional elections do not show even this increase. (2) The advent of radio was followed by a significant increase of turnout in national elections; the arrival of television was not, because radio made contact with millions who were beyond the reach of print media, whereas there was little room for further expansion with television, and because television seems largely to have taken over the role of radio. (3) If total volume of comment in the three election years (1952, 1956, 1960) as well as measures of involvement are considered, the following pattern emerges: highest in 1952, lowest in 1956; higher in 1960. (4) "Television has shown a capacity to catch the public eye but it has yet to demonstrate a unique ability to engage the public mind" (p. 13).

Campbell, Angus. "Voters and Elections: Past and Present." *J. Polit.* 26 (November 1964): 745–57.

Campbell, Angus, Philip E. Converse, Warren E. Miller, and Donald E. Stokes. *The American Voter.* New York: Wiley, 1960.

Campbell, Angus, Philip E. Converse, Warren E. Miller, and Donald E. Stokes. *Elections and the Political Order.* New York: Wiley, 1966.

Campbell, Angus and H.C. Cooper. *Group Differences in Attitudes and Votes.* Ann Arbor: University of Michigan, Institute for Social Research, 1956.

Campbell, Angus, Gerald Gurin, and Warren E. Miller. "Television and the Election." *Sci. Am.* 188 (May 1953): 46–48.

The authors compare television to radio, newspapers, and magazines as sources of information in 1952 election.

Method: survey; questionnaire. *Statistics*: frequencies. *Pop. (N)*: 1714 voting-age citizens.

Findings: (1) The percentage of people who "paid attention to campaign" through the media was: television, 53%; radio, 69%; newspapers, 79%; magazines, 40%. (2) The percentage of people who used the media as a source of information about the campaign was: television, 31%; radio, 27%; newspapers, 22%; magazines, 5%; more than one medium, 9%; none of the four, 6% (p. 47). (3) There is no clear evidence of television's effect on the voting itself. (4) Among persons who could afford television sets, a greater impact (of the campaign on television) was made on those with grammar or high school education than on college people. (5) The better educated the respondent to the questionnaire, the more he relied on reading.

Campbell, Angus, Gerald Gurin, and Warren E. Miller. *The Voter Decides.* Evanston, Ill.: Row, Peterson, 1954.

Carney, Francis M. and H. Frank Way, eds. *Politics 1972.* Belmont, Calif.: Wadsworth, 1971.

Chafee, Zechariah, Jr. *Government and Mass Communications*, 2 vols. Chicago: University of Chicago Press, 1947.

Chaffee, Steven H., ed. *American Politics Quarterly* (October 1975).

Chaffee, Steven H., ed. *Political Communication, Issues and Strategies for Research*. Beverly Hills, Calif.: Sage, 1975.

Chartrand, Robert L. *Computers and Political Campaigning*. New York: Spartan Books, 1972.

Chester, Edward W. *Radio, Television and American Politics*. New York: Sheed and Ward, 1969.

Chinn, Ronald E. "The 1970 Election in Alaska." *West. Polit. Q.* 24 (June 1971): 234–42.

"Choosing Sides." *Newsweek* 70 (20 November 1967): 94.

Churgin, Jonah Reuben. "Anatomy of a Presidential Primary: An Analysis of New Hampshire's Impact on American Politics." Unpublished master's thesis, Brown University, 1970.

Clausen, A.R. "Political Predictions and Projections: How Are They Conducted? Do They Influence the Outcome of Elections?" Washington, Conn.: Center for Information on America, 1966.

Cnudde, Charles F. "Elite-Mass Relationships and Democratic Rules of the Game." *Am. Behav. Sci.* 13 (November-December 1969–70): 189–200.

Cole, Stephen G. "Coalition Preference as a Function of Vote Commitment in Some Dictatorial 'Political Convention' Situations." *Behav. Sci.* 16 (September 1971): 436–41.

Colldeweih, Jack Howard. "The Effects of Mass Media Consumption on Accuracy of Beliefs about the Candidates in a Local Congressional Election." Unpublished doctoral dissertation, University of Illinois, 1968.

Comstock, G.A., E.A. Rubinstein, and J.P. Murray, eds. *Television and Social Behavior*, 5 vols. Washington, D.C.: Government Printing Office, 1972. Vol. 1: *Media Content and Control*; Vol. 2: *Television and Social Learning*; Vol. 3: *Television and Adolescent Aggressiveness*; Vol. 4: *Television in Day-to-Day Life—Patterns of Use*; Vol. 5: *Television's Effects—Further Explorations*.

Converse, Philip. "The Concept of a Normal Vote," in Angus Campbell et al., eds. *Elections and the Political Order*. New York: Wiley, 1966.

Converse, Philip E. "Information Flow and the Stability of Partisan Attitudes." *Pub. Opin. Q.* 26 (Winter 1962): 578–99.

Converse discusses and gives examples from current research of a paradox in the findings of public opinion research, that those individuals who shift their political position from one election to another frequently have less information about the political situation and the issues than persons whose attitudes and positions remain relatively unchanged. He considers the low level of public information about politics, and discusses why and how it affects voting behavior, especially in regard to the "floating voter."

Method: survey; questionnaire. *Pop. (N)*: 182.

Findings: (1) Newspapers are the major source of information about the election campaign. (2) Attention to the mass media was positively related to voting and knowledge.

Converse, P.E., A.R. Clausen, and W.E. Miller. "Electoral Myth and Reality: The 1964 Election." *Am. Polit. Sci. Rev.* 59 (June 1965): 321–36.

Conway, M. Margaret. "Voter Information in a Nonpartisan Local Election." *West. Polit. Q.* 21 (March 1968): 69–77. This study examines the relationship between perception of campaign information in the various mass media, alternate sources of information available to and used by the voters, and voter turnout, perception of city problems, and perception of issues in the campaign.

Costigan, James. "Media Exposure, Political Preference, and Candidate Image." Unpublished paper, Speech Department, Southern Illinois University, 1969.

Cranston, Pat. "Political Convention Broadcasts: Their History and Influence." *Journalism Q.* 37 (Spring 1960): 186–94.

This survey of radio and television coverage of the national political conventions indicates that the media have helped shape the manner in which the sessions are done and have influenced the behavior of the delegates.

Conclusions: (1) The broadcast of election returns on the night of 2 November 1920 over station KDKA is often cited as the beginning of political broadcasting. (2) Coverage of national political conventions was initiated in 1924 by broadcast networks as a program amalgamation. (3) The 1928 convention was the first at which a radio plank was introduced into the platform. Both parties turned to radio to argue their planks. Political parties bought time on networks at commercial rates in order to reach the nation. (4) One group of 18 radio stations was utilized in broadcasting the convention in 1924; more than 200 regularly affiliated stations served listeners in 1936. (5) The first telecasting of a national convention was made possible when Republicans met in Philadelphia on 24 June 1940. (6) Television induced a complete change in site for the 1952 conventions—from Chicago Stadium to International Amphitheatre where broadcasters would have more space. (7) In the 1956 convention, attention of the party planners was paid to audience attraction factors of the convention; celebrity entertainment was interspersed with convention business. (8) The 1956 convention was the scene of a CBS-Democratic Party disagreement in which freedom of the press became an issue (pp. 191–92). (9) During the 1956 convention, viewers in 99.6% of the nation's television homes—34,611,000 television sets—were able to see the conventions live on at least one of the networks. (10) "It is evident that the presence of the electronic media has induced changes in the national convention, the convention time schedule, and location, use of visual material in the hall, the behavior of the delegates, and the pacing of proceedings all now bear the mark of planning for electronic coverage" (p. 192).

Crespi, Irving. "1972 and the American Voter." Paper presented at the American Association for Public Opinion Research conference, Asheville, N.C., April 1972.

Crespi, Irving. "What Kinds of Attitude Measures Are Predictive of Behavior?" *Pub. Opin. Q.* 35 (Fall 1971): 327–34.

Crossman, R.H.S. "The Politics of Viewing." *New Statesman* 25 (October 1968): 525–30.

The positive effects of the use of TV in British politics is doubtful to the author: "TV should concentrate its own election coverage on what television does best—outside broadcasts, straight coverage of politicians at work, interviews in depth, and illustrated talks" (p. 529).

Conclusions: (1) The effect of TV on politics has been to strengthen the plebiscitary tendencies and to weaken the participatory tendencies. (2) A danger of TV in politics is that in the competition for the mass audience the discussion of live social and economic issues will come to be treated as an inferior form of entertainment which has to be "gimmicked up" in order to be made palatable to an indifferent audience. (3) Often television trivializes great issues by "snippety treatment" and personalizes politics into a gladiatorial show between combatants.

Cummings, Milton, Jr. "Split-Ticket Voting and the Presidency and Congress," in Milton Cummings, ed., *Congressmen and the Electorate: Elections for the U.S. House and the President, 1920-1964.* New York: Free Press, 1967.

Cunningham and Walsh. *Television and the Political Candidate.* Report by Research Department. New York: Cunningham and Walsh, 1959.

Dabney, Virginius. "The Press and the Election." *Pub. Opin. Q.* 1 (April 1937): 122–25. Dabney examines the influence of the press in the presidential election of 1936; as a basis he used Roosevelt's victory in the face of opposition from 80 to 85% of the nation's daily newspapers.

Hypothesis: The press does not have the ability to mold public opinion.

Conclusions: (1) American publishers are chiefly concerned with the profits of the paper rather than their influence on the public. (2) The average American newspaper is conservative, unimaginative, and avoids controversy; it is therefore unable to mold public opinion.

Dahl, Robert A. *Who Governs?* New Haven: Yale University Press, 1961.

Danielson, Wayne A. "Eisenhower's February Decision: A Study of News Impact." *Journalism Q.* 33 (Fall 1956): 433–41.

This study made at the time of President Eisenhower's decision to run for reelection failed to demonstrate that Eisenhower's decision had any effect on the voting intentions of respondents.

Method: survey; panel interviews. *Statistics:* percentages. *Pop. (N):* 198 California residents.

Findings: (1) Eisenhower's decision to run again markedly increased the chances of the Republican party for victory in the eyes of the respondents regardless of party preference. (2) There was no significant increase in intentions to vote for Eisenhower after he announced his candidacy. (3) The news spread most rapidly during the two hours immediately following Eisenhower's announcement. (4) In terms of the number of persons who received the news first through each of these means, the media ranked in this order: radio, 39%; newspaper, 27%; interpersonal contact, 20%; television, 14%. (5) Rank of the media in terms of speed of getting news to the respondents is as follows: radio was first, interpersonal contact was second, television third, newspaper fourth. (6) Respondents were asked which media they used to get more information about Eisenhower's decision. The newspaper was reported as a supplementary source by 86% of the respondents. TV was reported by 54% and radio by 46%. (7) The following pattern emerged: if radio is used as a supplementary source of information about an event, then TV and the newspaper will also be used; if TV is used, then the newspaper will be used also; only the newspaper will be used alone as a supplementary medium by any large number of people, and if the people do not use the newspaper, they will be unlikely to use either radio or television.

Darcy, Robert. "Communications and Political Attitudes." Unpublished doctoral dissertation, University of Kentucky, 1971.

Darcy, Robert. "Communications and Political Attitudes: An Experimental Investigation." Paper presented at American Political Science Association Convention, Washington, D.C., September 1972.

Daudt, H. *Floating Voters and the Floating Vote: A Critical Analysis of American and English Election Studies.* Leiden, Holland: H.E. Stenfert, Kroese N.V., 1961.

Dawson, Paul A. and James E. Zinser. "Broadcast Expenditures and Electoral Outcomes in the 1970 Congressional Elections." *Pub. Opin. Q.* 35 (Fall 1971): 398–402.

DeGrazia, Sebastian. *The Political Community.* Chicago: University of Chicago Press, 1948.

Dennis, Jack. "Support for the Institution of Elections by the Mass Public." *Am. Polit. Sci. Rev.* 64 (September 1970): 819–35.

Deutschmann, Paul John. *Communication and Social Change in Latin America.* New York: Praeger, 1968.

Deutschmann, Paul John. "Viewing, Conversation, and Voting Intentions," in Sidney Kraus, ed., *The Great Debates*. Bloomington: Indiana University Press, 1962, pp. 232–52.

DeVries, Walter and V. Lance Tarrance. *The Ticket-Splitter: A New Force in American Politics*. Grand Rapids, Mich. : Eerdmans, 1972.

Dexter, Lewis. "Congressmen and the People They Listen To." Unpublished manuscript, Center for International Studies, Massachusetts Institute of Technology, n.d.

Dinerman, Helen. "1948 Votes in the Making." *Pub. Opin. Q.* 12 (Winter 1948–49): 585–98.

Doob, Leonard William. *Public Opinion and Propaganda*. New York: Holt, 1947.

Dreyer, Edward C. "Media Use and Electoral Choices: Some Political Consequences of Information Exposure." *Pub. Opin. Q.* 35 (Winter 1971–72): 544–53.

This study tests the adequacy of two "floating voter" hypotheses: (1) Lazarsfeld hypothesized that changers tend to be people who pay least attention to politics and absorb least amount of political information (changers are people who switch turnout and/or candidate intention); (2) Converse adds the proviso to Lazarsfeld that short-term partisan change is contingent upon whether new political information actually reaches the less politically involved electorate. (For Converse, changers are those who switch in turnout and/or candidate intention.)

Method: survey; questionnaire. *Statistics*: tau-beta correlation. *Pop. (N)*: national samples drawn by Survey Research Center at University of Michigan, 1952–68. *Findings*: (1) The least informed or least exposed voters are also the most changeable in party preferences. (2) There is a lack of consistent support for Converse's modified hypothesis with the exception of 1952 election findings. (3) Strength of the relationship between party identification and party vote not only declines with each passing election but also declines at every level of media exposure.

Dreyer, Edward C. "Political Party Use of Radio and TV in the 1960 Campaign." *J. Broadcast.* 8 (Summer 1964): 211–17.

Dreyer, Edward C. and Walter A. Rosenbaum, ed. *Political Opinion and Electoral Behavior: Essays and Studies*. Belmont, Calif. : Wadsworth, 1970.

Driberg, Tom. "The First Television Election." *New Statesman* 61 (10 March 1961): 374–76.

Driberg discuss the planning and direction of 1959 British election. *Conclusions*: (1) Television and news coverage of the election had two effects on the voters: (a) "Television enlarged political knowledge"; (b) "With some slight exception, no media or source of propaganda ... had any ascertainable effect upon any attitude change" (p. 375). (2) "Uncertainty in voting intention is strongly associated with a genuine difficulty in distinguishing between the merits of the parties" (p. 375).

Driggs, Don W. "The 1970 Election in Nevada." *West. Polit. Q.* 24 (June 1971): 308–15.

Duncan, Hugh D. *Communication and Social Order*. New York: Bedminster Press, 1962.

Duncombe, Herbert S. and Boyd A. Martin. "The 1970 Election in Idaho." *West. Polit. Q.* 24 (June 1971): 292–300.

Dykstrz, Robert R. "Stratification and Community Political Systems." *Am. Behav. Sci.* 16 (May-June 1973): 695–715.

Easton, David. *A Framework for Political Analysis*. Englewood Cliffs, N.J. : Prentice-Hall, 1965.

Easton, David. *A System Analysis of Political Life*. New York: Wiley, 1965.

Edelman, Murray. "Escalation and Ritualization of Political Conflict." *Am. Behav. Sci.* 13 (November-December 1969–70): 231–46.

Edelman, Murray. *The Symbolic Uses of Politics*. Urbana: University of Illinois Press, 1967.

Editorial. "The Press and Politics." *Polit. Q.* 38 (April-June 1967): 113–21.

Eggers, Paul. "The Candidate's Point of View." Report presented to Seminar in Political Campaign Communication, Southern Illinois University, Carbondale, July 1969.

Eldersveld, Samuel J. "Experimental Propaganda Techniques and Voting Behavior." *Am. Polit. Sci. Rev.* 50 (March 1956): 154–65.

Eldersveld, Samuel. "The Independent Vote: Measurement, Characteristics, and Implications for Party Strategy." *Am. Polit. Sci. Rev.* 46 (September 1952): 732–53.

Evarts, Dru, Darryl A. Ross, Max E. Shively, and Guido H. Stempel, III. "Network Television Coverage of the 1972 Presidential Campaign." Paper presented at the annual convention of the Association for Education in Journalism, Fort Collins, Colo., August 1973.

Fagen, Richard R. *Politics and Communication: An Analytic Study*. Boston: Little, Brown, 1966.

Farley, James A. *Behind the Ballots*. New York: Harcourt Brace, 1938.

Fishbein, Martin and Fred S. Coombs. "Modern Attitude Theory and the Explanation of Voting Choice." Paper presented at American Political Science Association Convention, Chicago, September 1971.

Flanigan, William H. "Partisanship and Campaign Participation." Unpublished doctoral dissertation, Yale University, 1966.

Fleitas, Daniel William. "The Underdog Effect: An Experimental Study of Voting Behavior in a Minimal Information Election." Unpublished doctoral dissertation, Florida State University, 1970.

Freedman, J.L. and D.O. Sears. "Voter's Preferences Among Types of Information." *Am. Psychol.* 18 (August 1963): 375.

Freeman, Howard E. and Morris Showel. "Differential Political Influence of Voluntary Associations." *Pub. Opin. Q.* 15 (Winter 1951–52): 704–14.

Fuchs, Douglas A. "Does TV Election News Affect Voters?" *Columbia Journalism Rev.* 65 (Fall 1965): 39–41.

Fuchs, Douglas A. "Election-Day Newcasts and Their Effects on Western Voter Turnout." *Journalism Q.* 42 (Winter 1965): 22–28.

This article is an examination of voting turnout as a function of exposure to early broadcast predictions. Voting behavior may be changed (in a small degree) by hearing computer predictions of election outcomes.

Method: survey; questionnaire. *Statistics*: frequencies. *Pop. (N)*: 344 persons from 17 polling places in Berkeley, California.

Findings: (1) Interest in voting seemed to have been increased generally by exposure to pre-election polls. (2) Two-thirds of the sample had heard a broadcast computer prediction of the outcome in the presidential election, yet still voted.

Fuchs, Douglas A. "Election-Day Radio-Television and Western Voting." *Pub. Opin. Q.* 30 (Summer 1966): 226–36.

This study directly investigated the correlation of voting behavior as a consequence of the media broadcasting the election results of the 1964 Presidential election. The sample was obtained from Western voters, because in this area, Johnson was declared the winner over radio and television before the polls had closed. Results indicated that voting turnout and voter switching were not affected by the early media broadcasting of Johnson as the winner.

Method: survey; questionnaire. *Statistics*: frequencies, correlations. *Pop. (N)*: 3 Pacific coast metropolitan areas, 900 people from each.

Findings: (1) Among those who listened to or viewed returns and voted, their exposure increased as the day wore on. (2) In neither the pre-election plans to listen to returns nor the actual post-election reports of listening were there any important differences between Goldwater and Johnson voters. (3) Voting turnout in the West was negligibly affected by the early prognosis of a Johnson victory. (4) The turnout percentage was almost identical for respondents exposed before voting and those who heard the returns only after voting. (5) 2.7% of all respondents switched preference on the presidential election, but there was slightly more switching among those who had been exposed to the returns broadcast before voting.

Fuchs, Douglas A. and Jules Becker. "A Brief Report on the Time of Day When People Vote." *Pub. Opin. Q.* 32 (Fall 1968): 437–40.

Gardner, Allan D. "Political Ads: Do They Work?" *Wall Street Journal* 179 (1 February 1972): 10.

The effectiveness of political advertising in a presidential campaign is overrated. *Conclusions*: (1) The most effective ad is the "straight-into-the-camera" type through which the candidate exhibits some guts and credibility. (2) Political ads make a candidate's name and face become well-known; they can focus on the basic appeal that distinguishes a candidate from his opponent. (3) Political advertising has bred its own bureaucracy; today's campaign manager knows more about television and charisma than canvassing or precinct captains. (4) The limitations Congress has placed on primary spending has made access to political office more difficult. These limitations favor incumbents.

Gazell, James A. "One Man, One Vote: Its Long Germination." *West. Polit. Q.* 23 (September 1970): 445–62.

Gelman, Morris J. "Television and Politics: '62." *Television Magazine* 19 (October 1962): 64–67, 82–87.

Gelman discusses the manner in which candidates for senatorial and gubernatorial elections in 1962 used television in their political campaigns. All candidates believed that television was an essential ingredient of a successful campaign. *Conclusions*: (1) Television telethons, when artfully done, can make a candidate appear exceptionally quick, candid, and capable. (2) Political parties must be concerned with the "television attractiveness" of their candidate. (3) Five-minute taped spots are useful in helping the candidate express his views on particular issues. (4) Television consultants, in some cases, are the real bosses of campaigns. Without their advice, "most candidates would come out like clowns on television" (p. 85). (5) Half-hour broadcasts and addresses usually wind up selling voters who have been sold for generations. "The open-minded voter who might tune in is almost certain to be alienated by the ... partisan review and back-slapping eulogy of the candidate" (p. 86). (6) The advantages of a televised debate almost always lie with the unknown candidate.

Gilbert, Robert Emile. "The Influence of Television on American Politics." Doctoral dissertation, University of Massachusetts, 1967.

Gilbert investigates the influence of television on American politics, both campaigns for public office and nonelectoral aspects of political life. *Conclusions*: (1) Since the president is the focal point of so much television publicity, his bargaining power should be strengthened. (2) Television has made a shift in attention away from state political leaders toward officials of national government. (3) The great expense of television campaigning has strengthened the two-party system since minor parties cannot normally afford the medium on such an extensive level. (4) Television plays a significant role in campaigns for political office and can be of major importance to the victory of one of the candidates (example of Kennedy and 1960 debates given). (5) Americans' reliance on television for political information, their preference for the medium in both informational and entertainment aspects, and their belief in its credibility are discussed.

Gittell, Marilyn. "Urban School Politics: Professionalism Reform." *J. Soc. Iss.* 26 (Summer 1970): 69–84.

Glaser, William A. "Television and Voting Turnout." *Pub. Opin. Q.* 29 (Spring 1965): 71–86.

Glaser discusses the influence of television on voter turnout, and how this influence differs from the effects of other mass media. He also suggests ways in which television could be used to increase voter turnout. The author examined such things as which media were remembered as encouraging voting, whether television had improved turnout, and whether the effect of television was different for various socioeconomic factors.

Method: survey; questionnaire. *Statistics*: cross-tabulation, chi-square. *Pop. (N)*: 1645 adults included in nationwide surveys by Gallup polling organization.

Findings: (1) Television leaves a more lasting impression than either radio or print. (2) Newspaper reading has more influence in effecting turnout. (3) Reading, however, is a habit associated with a different mode of life. When television and print are both used, high turnout rates occur. (4) Users of media have much higher turnout rate than nonmedia users. This appears to be a qualitative difference, however, because there is not a linear increase related to hours engaged with the media. (5) Television could effect greater turnout rates if it (propaganda) was designed to suit the nonvoter, instead of having wide, general appeal.

Glenn, Norval D. "Class and Party Support in the United States: Recent and Emerging Trends." *Pub. Opin. Q.* 37 (Spring 1973): 1–20.

Glenn, Norval D. and Michael Grimes. "Aging, Voting, and Political Interest." *Am. Sociol. Rev.* 33 (August 1968): 563–75.

Goldberg, A.S. "Discerning a Causal Pattern Among Data on Voting Behavior." *Am. Polit. Sci. Rev.* 60 (December 1966): 913–22.

Gomez, Rudolph and Robert L. Eckelberry. "The 1970 Elections in Colorado." *West. Polit. Q.* 24 (June 1971): 274–81.

Goodman, Walter. "Candidates and the Camera." *New Republic* 132 (9 May 1955): 13–16.

Conclusions: In reviewing a 1952 survey of 450 Ohio, Indiana, and Kentucky housewives, it was concluded that the election decision lay more in the realm of personalities than in any differences in platform planks or candidate proposals.

Gordon, Leonard V. "The Image of Political Candidates: Values and Voter Preference." *J. Appl. Psychol.* 56 (October 1972): 382–87.

Gordon, N. George. *Persuasion: The Theory and Practice of Manipulative Communication.* New York: Hastings House, 1971.

Gosnell, Harold F. *Non-Voting: Causes and Methods of Control.* Chicago: University of Chicago Press, 1924.

Gosnell, Harold F. and Margaret J. Schmidt. "Relation of the Press to Voting in Chicago." *Journalism Q.* 13 (June 1936): 129–48.

Gould, Jack. "Television Techniques on the Political Stage." *New York Times Magazine*, 25 April 1954, pp. 12–13, 42, 44.

Greenberg, Bradley S. "The Political Candidate Versus the Television Performer." Paper presented to the Pacific Chapter of the American Association for Public Opinion Research, Los Angeles, January 1962.

This study indicates that those individuals who have consistent cognitions about the way that they will vote and their expectations of the outcome of the vote will expose themselves to more campaign information than those who have inconsistent cognitions.

Method: survey; questionnaire. *Statistics*: analysis of variance. *Pop. (N)*: 468 interviews 21 or older.

Findings: (1) Voters who thought their side would win exposed themselves to more sources of information than voters who thought their side would lose. (2) Individuals could more selectively choose meetings to attend or pamphlets to read than radio or television content. (3) The voter with consistent cognitions was a different person, socially and psychologically, from the voter with inconsistent cognitions.

Greenberg, Bradley S. "Voting Intentions, Election Expectations and Exposure to Campaign Information." *J. Comm.* 15 (September 1965): 149–60.

Greenberg, Bradley S. and Edwin B. Parker, eds. *The Kennedy Assassination and the American Public*. Stanford: Stanford University Press, 1965.

Hager, David. "Scott Vs. Spong: Analysis of Media Use and Effects in the 1972 Virginia Senate Campaign." Paper presented to annual meeting of the American Political Science Association, New Orleans, September 1973.

This examination into the uses of the media, especially television, in the 1972 Scott-Spong Senate election campaign in Virginia reveals evidence which seems to be sufficient to conclude that media use did make the difference in deciding who won.

Hahn, Harlan. "Leadership Perceptions and Voting Behavior in a One-Party Legislative Body." *J. Polit.* 32 (February 1970): 140–55.

Hahn, Harlan and Timothy Almy. "Ethnic Political and Racial Issues: Voting in Los Angeles." *West. Polit. Q.* 24 (December 1971):719–30.

Hainsworth, Brad E. "The 1970 Election in Montana." *West. Polit. Q.* 24 (June 1971): 301–7.

Hamilton, Howard D. "The Municipal Voter: Voting and Nonvoting in City Elections." *Am. Polit. Sci. Rev.* 65 (December 1971): 1135–40.

Harkey, P. "Televising the Legislature in Oklahoma," in H.L. Marx, ed., *Television and Radio in American Life*. New York: Wilson, 1953, pp. 49–52.

Harris, Louis. "Polls and Politics in the United States." *Pub. Opin. Q.* 27 (1963): 3–8.

Harris, Louis. "Public is No Longer Blase on Watergate." *The Cleveland Plain Dealer*, 26 June 1973.

Harris, Louis. "Some Observations on Election Behavior Research." *Pub. Opin. Q.* 20 (1956): 379–91.

Hartle, Donald G. and Richard M. Bird. "The Demand for Local Political Autonomy: An Individualistic Theory." *J. Confl. Resol.* 15 (December 1971): 443–65.

Hartmann, George W. "Field Experiment on the Comparative Effectiveness of Emotional and Rational Political Leaflets in Determining Election Results." *J. Abnorm. Psychol.* 31 (April 1936): 99–114.

Method: survey; questionnaire. *Statistics*: frequencies. *Pop. (N)*: 45 males and females in 45 voting wards in Allentown, Pa.

Findings: (1) Increase in Socialist vote in areas receiving pro-Socialist propaganda leaflets was two to three times. (2) Emotional leaflets produced greater impressive and retentive effect than rational leaflets did.

Hartnett, R.C. "Political Motives of Voters." *America* 92 (6 November 1954): 144.

Haystead, Jennifer. "Social Structure, Awareness Contests, and Processes of Choice." *Sociol. Rev.* 19 (February 1971): 79–94.

Hillinger, Claude. "Voting on Issues and on Platform." *Behav. Sci.* 16 (November 1971): 564–66.

Hirsch, Robert Oliver. "The Influence of Channel, Source, and Message Variables on Voting Behavior in the 1972 Illinois Primary Election." Unpublished doctoral dissertation, Southern Illinois University, 1972.

Hirsch investigates the influence of channel, source, and message variables on voting behavior in the 1972 Illinois primary election. He also considers the influence of candidate image and selected demographic characteristics in the same election. *Method*: survey; questionnaire. *Statistics*: factor analysis, multiple regression analysis, z-scores. *Pop. (N)*: 169 voters.

Findings: (1) Demographic characteristics are important variables when predicting voting behavior. Religious beliefs, sex, and age are some of the more important characteristics. (2) The communication variables (channel, source, and message) do not appear to significantly influence the electorate's voting behavior. (3) There is a low positive correlation between the channel, source, and message type in which the electorate places its greatest confidence and the channel, source, and messages type from which voters gain the most information.

Hovland, Carl I. "Effect of the Mass Media of Communication," in Gardner Lindzey, ed., *Handbook of Social Psychology*, vol. 2. Cambridge, Mass.: Addison-Wesley, 1954, pp. 1062–1103.

Hy, Ronn. "Mass Media in Election Campaigns (Extent to Which Voters Are Affected by Political Advertisement in the Mass Media)." *Pub. Admin. Surv.* 20 (January 1973): 1–6.

Isaacs, Jeremy. "Television and the Election." *Listener* 83 (18 June 1970): 822.
Isaacs discusses the use of BBC television during election time. During this time television lacks analysis and coverage of events. The author calls for a more active role on the part of television during election and a regular program dealing exclusively with politics between elections.

Jackson, John S., III, and Roy E. Miller. "Campaign Issues, Candidate Images, and Party Identification at Multiple Electoral Levels." Paper presented at Midwest Political Science Association Convention, Chicago, May 1973.

Jacobson, Gary Charles. "The Impact of Radio and Television on American Election Campaigns." Unpublished doctoral dissertation, Yale University, 1972.

Jennings, M. Kent and L. Harmon Zeigler, eds. *The Electoral Process*. Englewood Cliffs, N.J.: Prentice-Hall, 1966.

Johnson, Gerald W. "Political Correlatives of Voter Participation: A Deviant Case Analysis." *Am. Polit. Sci. Rev.* 65 (September 1971): 768–76.

Jones, Frank H. and Dan E. Jones. "The 1970 Election in Utah." *West. Polit. Q.* 24 (June 1971): 339–49.

Kaid, Lynda Lee. "A Selected, Indexed Bibliography on Political Campaign Communication." Unpublished master's thesis, Southern Illinois University, 1972.

Kaplowitz, Stan. "Using Aggregate Voting Data to Measure Presidential Coat-tail Effects." *Pub. Opin. Q.* 35 (Fall 1971): 415–19.

Katz, Elihu. "Platforms and Windows: Broadcasting's Role in Election Campaigns." *Journalism Q.* 48 (Summer 1971): 304–14.
This article reviews the latest empirical findings on studies related to the election campaign and the voter. The use of media for these campaigns would be considered facilitative if they would become an active initiator in presenting campaign coverage that was free from bias and political freedom. To function at this level, broadcasting must primarily consider the method of dividing broadcasting time and the overall division of labor in the production of political broadcasts.
Conclusions: (1) Of the mass media, only the press tried to sort things out for the voter. (2) Typically, 80% of the voters had made up their minds about their vote before the campaign began. (3) Shifters from one party to another were found to be relatively uninterested in the election and its outcome. (4) The combination of a low degree of loyalty and yet some exposure to election communications has become a more probable combination in the era of television. Television activates people to form opinions and talk about them. (5) Media are used for "reinforcement seeking." (6) Mass media campaigns, not just political campaigns, convert very few people.

(7) Voters expect the function of surveillance to be practiced by the media. (8) "The media themselves—not just the parties—must take an active share in presenting the candidates, introducing the issues, challenging the parties to take clearcut stands on the issues, and in general, 'representing' the intelligent voter in trying to make sense of the campaign" (p. 314).

Katz, Elihu and Jacob Feldman. "The Debates in the Light of Research: A Survey of Surveys," in Sidney Kraus, ed., *The Great Debates.* Bloomington: Indiana University Press, 1962, pp. 173–223.

Katz, Elihu and Paul Lazarsfeld. *Personal Influence.* New York: Free Press, 1955.

Kelley, Stanley, Jr. "Elections and the Mass Media." *Law Contemp. Probl.* 27 (Spring 1962): 307–26.

Examination of the role of mass media in the electoral process and outlines its consequences and potentialities.

Conclusions: (1) "The media transmit campaign propaganda to large numbers of persons" (p. 307). (2) "Media transmit propaganda selectively" (p. 307). (3) The media transmit propaganda in certain conventional forms, and "lead politicians to say things differently and to say different things" (p. 307). (4) "The media present campaign propaganda in the context of materials they themselves originate" (p. 307). (5) The media "encourage a more or less unquestioning faith in the significance of the electoral process, and of the citizen's role in it, among a great many people" (p. 309). (6) Mass media is not a direct and potent force in changing voting behavior. "How a person votes and whether he votes seems most closely related to his party affiliation, his perceptions of the interests of the groups with which he identifies himself, his opinions about several long-standing issues of public policy, his perceptions of the personal qualities of candidates, and his view of party performance in the management of governmental affairs" (pp. 309–10). (7) Campaign communication is more likely to reinforce than alter these views, opinions, etc. (8) Campaign discussion in the media does have a significant effect on voting by inducing "marginal changes in opinions about parties, issues, and group interests" and by exerting influence "on the voter's perceptions of the personal qualities of candidates" (p. 310). (9) Mass media help to overcome voter apathy about campaign talk by dramatizing elections. (10) Kelley argues "that interest in politics varies strongly with the entertainment value of politics and that the media arouse interest in elections by exploiting their value as entertainment" (p. 313). (11) "Both the (political) machine and the mass media can enable the politician to establish a relationship with voters and to give partisan direction to their opinions and actions" (p. 315). (12) "The mass media are useful to the politician as instruments of propaganda" (p. 316). (13) The mass media "force the politician to give his campaign a pace, an appearance of movement" (p. 317). (14) Debates "tend to increase the accuracy, specificity, and relevance to the voting decisions of statements in campaign discussions" and "tend to force candidates to take responsibility for arguments made on their behalf or to disavow such arguments" (p. 318).

Kelley, Stanley, Jr. *Political Campaigning: Problems in Creating an Informed Electorate.* Washington, D.C.: The Brookings Institute, 1960.

Kelley, Stanley, Jr. *Professional Public Relations and Political Power.* Baltimore, Md.: Johns Hopkins University Press, 1956.

Key, V.O., Jr. *Public Opinion and American Democracy.* New York: Knopf, 1961.

Key, V.O., Jr. *The Responsible Electorate.* Cambridge, Mass.: Harvard University Press, 1966.

Kirkpatrick, Samuel A. "Political Attitude Structure and Component Change." *Pub. Opin. Q.* 34 (Fall 1970): 403–7.

Kirsch, Arthur D. "Social Distance and Some Related Variables in Voting Behavior," in H.H. Remmers, ed., *Anti-Democratic Attitudes in American Schools*. Evanston, Ill.: Northwestern University Press, 1963, pp. 73–97.

Kitt, Alice S. and David B. Gleicher. "Determinants of Voting Behavior: A Progress Report on the Elmira Study." *Pub. Opin. Q.* 14 (Fall 1950): 393–412.

Klapper, Joseph T. "The Social Effects of Mass Communication," in Wilbur Schramm, ed., *The Science of Human Communication*. New York: Basic Books, 1963, pp. 65–76.

Korpi, Walter. "Some Problems in the Measurement of Class Voting." *Am. J. Sociol.* 78 (November 1972): 627–42.

Kramer, Gerald H. "The Effects of Precinct-Level Canvassing on Voter Behavior." *Pub. Opin. Q.* 34 (Winter 1970–71): 560–72.

Kramer, Gerald H. "Short Term Fluctuations in U.S. Voting Behavior, 1896–1964." *Am. Polit. Sci. Rev.* 65 (March 1971): 131–43.

Kraus, Sidney. "The Political Use of TV." *J. Broadcast.* 8 (Summer 1964): 219–28.

Kraus, Sidney. "Presidential Debates in 1964." *Q. J. Speech* 50 (February 1964): 19–23.

Kraus, Sidney, ed. *The Great Debates—Background, Perspective, Effects*. Bloomington: Indiana University Press, 1962.

Kraus, Sidney and Steven H. Chaffee, eds. *Communication Research* 1, 4 (October 1974).

Kraus, Sidney and Raymond G. Smith. "Issues and Images" in S. Kraus, ed., *The Great Debates*. Bloomington: Indiana University Press, 1962, pp. 289–312.

Krischak, Donald Eugene. "An Analysis of an Unsuccessful Rural Community College Millage Election to Determine How Selected Communication Techniques and Demography Interacted to Influence Voter Decision." Unpublished doctoral dissertation, Michigan State University, 1971.
    The purpose of Krischak's study was to determine how selected communication techniques and demography interacted to determine voter decision in an unsuccessful community college millage election.
    Method: survey; questionnaire. *Statistics*: frequencies. *Pop. (N)*: 410 voters.
    Findings: (1) More voters rely on the newspaper than upon any other source for millage information. (2) Almost one-half of the voters were not influenced by any of the communications techniques used during the campaign. (3) The radio does not appear to affect voter decision.
    In general, the findings of the study supported the idea that an "anti-tax" climate existed in the county before and during the millage campaign.

Kumar, Krishan. "The Political Consequences of Television." *Listener* 82 (3 July 1969): 1–3.

Lane, Robert. *Political Life*. New York: Free Press, 1959.

Lang, Kurt. "Book Review of Jay G. Blumler and Denis McQuail, *Television in Politics: Its Uses and Influences*." *Pub. Opin. Q.* 33 (Winter 1969–70): 645–48.

Lang, Kurt and Gladys Engel Lang. "Ballots and Broadcasts: The Impact of Expectations and Election Day Perceptions on Voting Behavior." Paper presented at 1965 Annual Conference of American Association for Public Opinion Research, May 1965.

Lang, Kurt and Gladys Engel Lang. "The Mass Media and Voting," in Bernard Berelson and Morris Janowitz, eds., *Reader in Public Opinion and Communication*, 2d ed. New York: Free Press, 1966.

Lang, Kurt and Gladys Engel Lang. "Mass Media and Voting," in Eugene Burdick and Arthur J. Brodbeck, eds., *American Voting Behavior*. Glencoe, Ill.: Free Press, 1959.

Lang, Kurt and Gladys Engel Lang. "Ordeal by Debate: Viewer Reactions." *Pub. Opin. Q.* 25 (Summer 1961): 277–88.

Data from an examination into viewers' reactions to the Nixon-Kennedy debates indicate that exposure to the televised debates resulted in some dramatic changes in candidate image, but that vote intentions changed much less.

Method: survey; questionnaires. *Statistics*: frequencies. *Pop. (N)*: 95 New York viewers.

Findings: (1) Among the subjects there was an immediate and dramatic improvement of the Kennedy image right after the first debate, but this improvement was not accompanied by shifts in voting intentions of anywhere near comparable proportions. (2) There were 22 intracampaign vote changes, consisting of 18 crystallizers and 4 switchers. Kennedy drew his strength (11 out of 18) from weak Democratic Party identifiers, 9 of whom had been too young to vote in the 1956 election and 2 of whom had defected to vote for Eisenhower in 1956. Nixon won 2 votes from Democrats for Stevenson in 1956 together with one vote from a Democrat who had voted for Eisenhower and another from a new voter calling himself Independent. (3) There was a significant difference between the expectations of Nixon partisans and Kennedy partisans. Two-thirds of the Nixon partisans felt confident of their candidate's superior debating skills; only 4 out of 33 thought Kennedy might do better. (4) 89% of those who watched or heard the televised debate (the first encounter) thought Kennedy had bested Nixon or at least fought him to a draw. The single most important result of the debate lay in its destruction of the image, so widely held, of Nixon as champion debater and television politican par excellence. (5) Among the sample there was no evidence that dissonance introduced by the first debate led to a general curtailment or to an increase of exposure. The number of debates watched was unrelated to initial candidate preference, judgment of who had won the first debate, amount of change in image, or education.

Lang, Kurt and Gladys Engel Lang. *Politics and Television*. Chicago: Quadrangle Books, 1968.

Lang, Kurt and Gladys Engel Lang. "Reactions of Viewers," in Sidney Kraus, ed., *The Great Debates*. Bloomington: Indiana University Press, 1962, pp. 313–30.

Lang, Kurt and Gladys Engel Lang. *Voting and Nonvoting: Implications of Broadcasting Returns Before Polls Are Closed*. Waltham, Mass.: Blaisdell, 1968.

Laskin, Richard and Richard Baird. "Factors in Voter Turnout and Party Preference in a Saskatchewan Town." *Can. J. Polit. Sci.* 3 (September 1970): 450–61.

Lawrence, Gary Caldwell. "Media Effects in Congressional Election." Unpublished doctoral dissertation, Stanford University, 1972.

Lazarsfeld, Paul F. "The Election is Over." *Pub. Opin. Q.* 8 (Fall 1944): 317–30.

Lazarsfeld, Paul F., Bernard Berelson, and Hazel Gaudet. *The People's Choice: How the Voter Makes Up His Mind in a Presidential Campaign*. New York: Duell, Sloan and Pearce, 1944 (2d ed., New York: Columbia University Press, 1948; 3d ed., 1968).

Lee, R.W., ed. *Politics and the Press*. Washington, D.C.: Acropolis Books, 1970.

Leventhal, Howard, Robert L. Jacobs, and Nijole Z. Kudirka. "Authoritarianism, Ideology, and Political Candidate Choice." *J. Abnorm. Soc. Psychol.* 69 (November 1964): 539–49.

Lewis, Chester, Godfrey Hodgson, and Bruce Page. *An American Melodrama: The Presidential Campaign of 1968*. New York: Viking, 1969.

Lipset, S.M., P.F. Lazarsfeld, A.H. Barton, and J. Linz. "The Psychology and Voting: An Analysis of Political Behavior," in G. Lindzey, ed., *Handbook of Social Psychology*, vol. 2. Cambridge, Mass.: Addison-Wesley, 1954, pp. 1124–75.

Lipset, S.M., M.A. Trow, and S.J. Coleman. *Union Democracy*. Glencoe, Ill.: Free Press, 1956.

Liston, R.A. *Politics from Precinct to Presidency*. New York: Delacorte Press, 1968.

Lyle, Jack and Richard A. Stone. "Election Coverage and Audience Reaction."

Unpublished manuscript. University of California at Los Angeles, August 1971.

Maass, Arthur. "Foreword," in V.O. Key, Jr., *The Responsible Electorate: Rationality in Presidential Voting, 1936–1960*. Cambridge, Mass.: Harvard University Press, 1966.

Maceda, E.M. "Television as a Political Advertising Medium." Unpublished master's thesis, University of Illinois, 1961.

MacNeil, Robert. "Marketing the Candidates—The Use of Television in the American Election." *Listener* 80 (14 November 1968): 631–32.
This article briefly describes the televised political advertisements used in the 1968 presidential campaign. Candidates evaded televised debates and relied on television, promoting a positive image of themselves at the expense of the opposing candidates. With more people depending on the medium for information, it is becoming evident that coverage of political events on television will have to improve.
Conclusions: (1) "Since most of Humphrey's television blitz was concentrated in the last ten days of the campaign and since he was coming up very fast in the end, it may be that his half-hour film (including the retarded granddaughter) and his short commercials did have an effect" (p. 632). (2) "Possibly the emotional montages on domestic violence and the Viet Nam horror broadcast for Nixon throughout the campaign helped to maintain his lead" (p. 632).

MacNeil, Robert. *The People Machine; The Influence of Television on American Politics*. New York: Harper & Row, 1968.

Manheim, Jarol B. "The Effects of Campaign Techniques on Voting Patterns in a Congressional Election." Unpublished doctoral dissertation, Northwestern University, 1971.

Margolis, Michael Stephen. "The Impact of Political Environment, Campaign Activity, and Party Organization on the Outcomes of Congressional Elections." Unpublished doctoral dissertation, University of Michigan, 1968.

Marr, Theodore J. "A New Method of Analysis for Panel Data on Political Candidate Image and Voter Communication Behavior." Paper presented at Speech Communication Association Convention, Chicago, December 1972.

Marshall, Mac. "The Impact of Television on Politics." Columbia: Freedom of Information Center, University of Missouri, 1968.

Martz, John D. "Democratic Political Campaigning in Latin America: A Typological Approach to Cross-Cultural Research." *J. Polit.* 33 (May 1971): 370–98.

Maurer, W.H. "Politics and the Press," in S.L. Stokes and L.W. Eley, eds., *The 1959 Summer Institute in Practical Partisan Politics*. Ann Arbor: University of Michigan, Institute of Public Administration, 1960.

May, Robert M. "Some Mathematical Remarks on the Paradox of Voting." *Behav. Sci.* 16 (March 1971): 143–51.

McBath, James H. and Walter R. Fisher. "Persuasion in Presidential Campaign Communication." *Q. J. Speech* 55 (February 1969): 17–25.
The authors analyze campaign communication as a special "species of persuasion" (p. 17).
Conclusions: (1) The political campaigner does not seek or expect to alter ideologies, but he attempts to use them. (2) Political persuasion operates on the basis of images and signs of consubstantiability rather than the presentation of facts or arguments. "The attempt is to show the candidate as possessing a view of the world which corresponds with that of potential voters" (p. 18). (3) The persuasive role of the vice-presidential nominee is "balancing the ticket" in geographical terms and modifying the presidential candidate's image. (4) Political parties should reform to accommodate the forces of social change and should be willing to establish communication with the dissident, the disillusioned, and the disadvantaged, or they will be

discarded for more effective means of communication between the American people and those who lead them.

McClenghan, Jack Sean. "Effect of Endorsements in Texas Local Elections." *Journalism Q.* 50 (Summer 1973): 363–66.

"The high degree of agreement between newspaper endorsements and the voting results of Texas municipal elections examined in this study confirms the generalization that the press is a major influence in the affairs of local government" (p. 366). *Method*: content analysis. *Statistics*: frequencies, means. *Pop. (N)*: 10 Texas newspapers.

Findings: (1) Nearly nine out of ten candidates endorsed by the Texas newspapers studied won their elections. The figure was slightly higher for council candidates than for mayoral candidates. (2) Endorsed candidates received more space than their opponents in the election campaigns. The endorsed candidates had a much wider margin, however, in advertising space (presumably not related to the endorsement). (3) The endorsed candidates fared better in the letters column, with 61% of the letters published supporting the endorsed candidate. (4) Picture coverage favored the opponents of the endorsed candidates by a 55–44 margin.

McClure, Robert D. and Thomas E. Patterson. "Television News and Voter Behavior in the 1972 Presidential Election." Paper presented for delivery at the 1973 annual meeting of the American Political Science Association, New Orleans, 4–8 September 1973.

This paper deals with television campaign effects. The authors examined the content of the nightly network television news shows broadcast during the 1972 presidential general election campaign and the voter response to this content. They found that inherent in the production, technology, and format of television news are several factors which severely limit its direct impact on voters; that most television news is subject to mediating effects; that the independent effects of television news are minimal, but that during the campaign, the electorate improved its knowledge of the candidate's issue positions and that the mass media as a whole played a substantial role in that information gain; and that effects on voters' beliefs due to television news exposure are much more likely to occur with regard to certain types of political stories and situations than others.

Method: survey; questionnaires (panel study) and content analysis. *Statistics*: percentages, means. *Pop. (N)*: wave 1 = 731, wave 2 = 650, wave 3 = 650, wave 4 = 692; random sample of adults in Syracuse, N.Y.

Findings: (1) Concerning Watergate, media impact was substantially mediated by voter cynicism and partisan loyalties. (2) On the Vietnam withdrawal issue: "Belief change about Nixon's position on immediate withdrawal was related to vote intention. Although exposure to network news was still unrelated to change, the data indicate that candidate preference, just as it did on the corruption items, mediated voter acceptance of news information on Vietnam" (p. 19). In the 1972 presidential campaign, television news had few direct and independent effects on voters. Two factors limit the scope of this conclusion: first, the authors' findings apply only to the impact of television news on voters' reactions to issues, and second, the findings apply only to the question of whether television news had effects independent of, and separate from, other channels of communication. Their concluding section discusses limiting factors, as well as the conditions they believe necessary for television news to produce unique and isolated effects on the American electorate.

McCombs, Maxwell. "Editorial Endorsements: A Study of Influence." *Journalism Q.* 44 (Autumn 1967): 545–48.

McCombs, Maxwell and David Weaver. "Voter's Need for Orientation and Use of Mass Communication." Paper presented at International Communication Association Convention, Montreal, April 1973.

McCurtain, Marilyn E. "An Investigation of the Voter's Decision Process and His Political Behavior." Unpublished doctoral dissertation, University of Washington, 1965.

McDonald, Lynn. "Social Class and Voting: A Study of the 1968 Canadian Federal Election in Ontario." *Br. J. Sociol.* 22 (December 1971): 410–22.

McGinniss, Joe. *The Selling of the President, 1968.* New York: Trident Press, 1969.

Meadow, Robert G. "Cross-Media Comparisons of Coverage of the 1972 Presidential Campaign." *Journalism Q.* 50 (Autumn 1973): 482–88.

In this study, newspaper and media coverages of the 1972 presidential campaign were compared, revealing similar time and space devoted to Nixon and McGovern. *Method*: historical survey, content analysis. *Statistics*: percentages. *Pop. (N)*: network and news coverage period from 2 October to 3 November 1972.

Findings: (1) "The most striking pattern is the uniformity of coverage across several media sources" (p. 485). (2) McGovern had slightly more media coverage than Nixon in terms of the campaign, but had less media coverage in general because of Nixon's use of media for administrative purposes. (3) Agnew's criticisms of the media gave him markedly greater coverage by the media than Shriver. (4) "While aggressive campaigns may be exciting and capture public attention, it remains a possibility that a curvilinear relationship exists between aggression and public attention such that beyond some saturation point aggressive campaigning may appear as inflammatory and reckless, ultimately harming the aggressive campaigner" (p. 488). (5) "How the audience compares the credibility of words uttered by such "opinion leaders" as John Chancellor, Walter Cronkite, Harry Reasoner or Howard K. Smith with the credibility of an anonymous press service reporter has yet to be documented" (p. 488).

Mehling, Reuben, Sidney Kraus, and Richard D. Yoakman. "Pre-Debate Campaign Interest and Media Use," in S. Kraus, ed., *The Great Debates*. Bloomington: Indiana University Press, 1962, pp. 224–31.

Meller, Norman. "The 1970 Election in Hawaii." *West. Polit. Q.* 24 (June 1971): 282–91.

Mendelsohn, Harold. "Election-Day Broadcasts and Terminal Voting Decisions." *Pub. Opin. Q.* 30 (Summer 1966): 212–25.

There was no significant evidence that media presentation of poll results affected the voting behavior of the viewers. The study does indicate that media create an increase in the amount of discussion about voting among people. *Method*: survey; questionnaire. *Statistics*: correlation. *Pop. (N)*: 2,270 voters.

Findings: (1) The vast majority of the voters studied had made their decisions sometime before Election Day. (2) Political partisanship was the most important influence in determining the great majority of votes that were cast for either candidate. (3) There was generally low salience of the broadcasts in the terminal decision-making process. (4) Last-minute influences on last-day deciders can be seen as serving a crystallizing function of helping the voter to come to some decision immediately before he has to vote. (5) The majority of last-day deciders must have been exposed to "crystallizing" influences other than election television or radio broadcasts on Election Day itself. (6) One-fifth of the sample reported that as a consequence of listening to or viewing Election Day broadcasts, they personally urged others to vote. Conversely, only 3 of the total sample voters admitted that they tried to convince others not to vote as a result of hearing Election Day broadcasts.

Mendelsohn, Harold and Irving Crespi. *Polls, Television and the New Politics*. San Francisco: Chandler, 1970.

Mendelsohn, Harold and Melvyn M. Muchnik. "Public Television and Political Broadcasting: A Matter of Responsibility." *Educ. Broadcast. Rev.* 4 (December 1970): 3–9.

An analysis of the television broadcasting of the 1968 election campaigns reveals that, according to the authors, the coverage was substandard.

Method: survey; questionnaire. *Statistics*: frequencies. *Pop. (N)*: 133 television stations (public television).

Findings: (1) A total of 1,938 hours of campaign-related programming (mean of "14.2 hours totally per PTV outlet") was telecast in 1968. (2) No more than 1.8% of total PTV broadcasters on-air time was devoted to political broadcasts during the period following the Republican Convention through Election Day 1968. (3) 8.7 of the mean 14.2 hours of political broadcasts which respondents said they aired in 1968 were reported to have originated from programming sources other than the stations themselves (p. 5). (4) In all, 72 outlets (54% stations responding) reported having originated any political programming on their own. This is in contrast to the 111 stations (84% of total) which indicated they had carried political programming that had originated from sources other than themselves (p. 6). (5) Political programming presented by PTV during the 1968 election campaigns focused mainly on candidates for state and congressional office as well as on state issues. (6) Totally, PTV stations in the survey reported having used 2.1 hours for the presentation of candidates for state/congressional offices and 1.6 hours for discussions of state candidates and issues. 0.7 hour was devoted to presentations of local candidates and 0.7 hour to discussions of local issues and candidates (p. 7). (7) 19% of the station executives assessed their own stations' treatment of 1968 election campaigns as poor; 50% placed their efforts as fair; 13% considered their performance excellent; 18% refused to evaluate their performance. (8) The authors believe "it is perfectly feasible for every PTV station in the country to devote no less than two weeks of its fall night time and week-end schedules in full to political broadcasts during national presidential campaigns and one full week during local, state and congressional campaigns" (p. 9).

Merriam, Charles E. and Harold F. Gosnell. *Non-Voting.* Chicago: University of Chicago Press, 1924.

Meyer, Alan S. "The Independent Voter," in William N. McPhee and William Glaser, eds., *Public Opinion and Congressional Elections.* New York: Free Press, 1962, pp. 65–77.

Mickelson, Sig. *The Electric Mirror: Politics in an Age of Television.* New York: Dodd, Mead, 1972.

Mickelson, Sig. "TV and the Candidate." *Saturday Rev.* 43 (16 April 1960): 13–15, 51.

Television has made for a better democracy and a better government by allowing citizens to become informed, and it has placed additional responsibilities on the politicians.

Conclusions: (1) Television has brought about a broadening of public participation in the democratic process. (2) Television has increased the degree of independent thinking and decreased the influence of the party. (3) Television has made the public's contact with political life a continuing process; this contact is not limited to political candidates, but extends through all the issues about which the electorate must be informed. (4) Television has brought political office within reach of a larger segment of qualified persons. (5) Television has tended to keep election campaigns honest since a candidate cannot risk being inconsistent among the television's large audience. (6) Television has created a more knowledgeable and sophisticated voter.

Middleton, Russell. "National Television Debates and Presidential Voting Decisions." *Pub. Opin. Q.* 26 (Fall 1962): 426–29.

This article considers the impact of Kennedy-Nixon debates on voters in Tallahassee, Florida.

Method: survey; questionnaire. *Statistics*: frequencies. *Pop. (N)*: 127 Negroes, 143 whites.
Findings: (1) "Although the voting decisions of a majority of the registered voters in Tallahassee were not significantly affected by the television debates, almost one-third were influenced to some degree" (p. 429). (2) "The debates played an 'extremely important' role in the decisions of one out of every eight registered voters" (p. 429). (3) "Respondents who were committed to a particular candidate prior to the debates almost always felt that their candidate had made a better impression in the debates or that he had at least held his own. Those who were both uncommitted and un-influenced tended more often to see the debates as a 'draw'" (p. 428).

Miller, W.E. "Analysis of the Effects of Election Night Predictions on Voting Behavior." University of Michigan, Survey Research Center, unpublished report, Political Behavior Program, 1965.

Mitchell, William C. "The American Policy and the Redistribution of Income." *Am. Behav. Sci.* 13 (November-December 1969-70): 201-14.

Morgan, Roy. "Last-Minute Changes in Voting Intention." *Pub. Opin. Q.* 12 (Fall 1948): 470-80.

Mueller, John E. "Choosing Among 103 Candidates." *Pub. Opin. Q.* 34 (Fall 1970): 395-402.

Mueller, John E. "Presidential Popularity from Truman to Johnson." *Am. Polit. Sci. Rev.* 64 (March 1970): 18-34.

Napolitan, Joseph. *The Election Game and How to Win It.* Garden City, N.Y.: Doubleday, 1972.

Natchez, Peter B. "Images of Voting." *Pub. Policy* (Summer 1970): 553-88.

Natchez, Peter B. and Irvin C. Bupp. "Candidates, Issues and Voters." *Pub. Policy* 17 (1968): 409-37.

Neustadt, Richard E. *Presidential Power, the Politics of Leadership.* New York: Wiley, 1961.

Nimmo, Dan. *The Political Persuaders: The Techniques of Modern Election Campaigns.* Englewood Cliffs, N. J.: Prentice-Hall, 1970.

Nwankwo, Robert L. "The Mass Media and Political Culture in Africa." Paper presented to the annual convention of the Association for Education in Journalism, Fort Collins, Colo. August 1973.

O'Donnell, Kenneth P. "TV in the Political Campaign." *Television Q.* 5 (Winter 1966): 20-23.

Orbell, John M., Robyn M. Dawes, and Nancy J. Collins. "Grass Roots Enthusiasm and the Primary Vote." *West. Polit. Q.* 25 (June 1972): 249-59.

Ordeshook, Peter C. "Extensions to a Model of the Electoral Process and Implications for the Theory of Responsible Parties." *Midwest J. Polit. Sci.* 14 (February 1970): 43-70.

Orum, Anthony M. and Edward W. McCranie. "Class, Tradition, and Partisan Alignments in a Southern Urban Electorate." *J. Polit.* 32 (February 1970): 156-76.

Oxford Research Associates, Inc. *Influence of Television on the Election of 1952.* Oxford, O.: Miami University Press, 1954.

Page, Benjamin I. and Richard A. Brody. "Policy Voting and the Electoral Process: The Vietnam War Issue." *Am. Polit. Sci. Rev.* 66 (September 1972): 979-95.

Paletz, David L. "Delegates' Views of TV Coverage of the 1968 Democratic Convention." *J. Broadcast.* 16 (Fall 1972): 441-52.
This study found a possible negative impact of television in circumstances similar to the 1968 Democratic convention as indicated by the vehemence with which the delegates replied to the question of television's influence on their decisions.

Method: survey; questionnaire. *Statistics*: frequencies. *Pop. (N)*: North Carolina Democratic delegates.

Findings: (1) $\frac{3}{10}$ of the delegates denied watching any television coverage at all; $\frac{1}{10}$ admitted to viewing for longer than one hour daily. (2) The highest proportion of respondents (only $\frac{2}{5}$) said they watched television to obtain factual information about events which had transpired at the convention. A number of delegates said they watched television to learn what was occurring outside the convention hall in the streets. (3) All the delegates were very critical of television coverage of the convention; nearly all respondents disagreed with the statement that television coverage mainly showed formal convention events such as speeches and platform debates. (4) Most of the liberal delegates disagreed with the statement that television coverage emphasized controversy within the convention. The conservative delegates were distressed that television coverage publicized discord within the party in the convention hall. (5) Only three delegates thought that they had been influenced at all by television coverage. Most delegates offered vehement negative comments along with their negative responses.

Patterson, Thomas E. and Robert D. McClure. "Political Advertising: Voter Reaction." Department of Political Science, Syracuse University. Paper presented at annual meeting of AAPOR, Asheville, N.C., May 1973.

This study considered effects of political advertising on voters' attitudinal change. It looked at attitudes and beliefs separately to fully understand the impact of political commercials.

Method: survey; questionnaire. *Statistics*: correlations, percentages. *Pop. (N)*: wave 1 $N = 731$, wave 2 $N = 650$, wave 3 $N = 650$, wave 4 $N = 646$.

Findings: High-television-exposure subjects changed more than low-exposure subjects. Subjects with moderate and low political interest changed more than high-interest subjects. Moderate subjects changed more than those with low political interest. Party commitment played a role in the change, but it depended upon what attitude or belief the commercial was trying to change. Authors found four critical factors that vary the impact of these commercials: (1) the amount of exposure to television advertising; (2) the accuracy of voters' beliefs before exposure; (3) the extent to which the voters ignore alternative sources or selectively ignore certain messages from alternative sources; (4) the extent to which voters are interested in political information but are willing to attend to sources requiring effort. Two more factors are hypothesized: the degree to which the voter possesses the necessary skills to process and conceptualize new information; and the degree to which information contained in commercials also is available through other communication channels.

Payne, Alvin N. "A Study of the Persuasive Efforts of Lyndon Baines Johnson in the Southern States in the Presidential Campaign of 1960." Master's thesis, Abilene Christian College, 1968.

Payne, Thomas, ed. "The 1966 Election in the West." *West. Polit. Q.* 20 (June 1967): 517–19.

Pearson, Kathy. "Campaign '72: Politics and the Media." *Washington University Magazine* 43 (Winter 1973): 34–35.

Pepper, Robert. "An Analysis of Presidential Primary Election Night Coverage." *Educ. Broadcast. Rev.* 7 (June 1973): 159–66.

Perentesis, John L. "Effectiveness of a Motion Picture Trailer as Election Propaganda." *Pub. Opin. Q.* 12 (Fall 1948): 465–69.

Perry, Paul. "A Comparison of Voting Preferences of Likely Voters and Likely Non-voters." *Pub. Opin. Q.* 37 (Spring 1973): 99–109.

Philips, Kevin. *The Emerging Republican Majority*. New Rochelle, N.Y.: Arlington House, 1969.

Polsby, Nelson W. and Aaron B. Wildavsky. *Presidential Elections*. New York: Scribner's, 1968.

Pomper, Gerald M. "Control and Influence in American Elections (Even 1968)." *Am. Behav. Sci.* 13 (November-December 1969-70): 215-30.

Pomper, Gerald M. *Elections in America: Control and Influence in Democratic Politics*. New York: Dodd, Mead, 1968.

Pomper, Gerald M. "Ethnic and Group Voting in Nonpartisan Municipal Elections." *Pub. Opin. Q.* 30 (Spring 1966): 79-98.

Pool, Ithiel de Sola. "The Effect of Communication on Voting Behavior," in Wilbur Schramm, ed., *The Science of Human Communication*. New York: Basic Books, 1963, pp. 128-38.

Pool, Ithiel de Sola. "The Mass Media and Politics in the Modernization Process," in Lucian Pye, ed., *Communications and Political Development*. Princeton, N. J.: Princeton University Press, 1963, pp. 234-53.

Pool, Ithiel de Sola. "TV: A New Dimension in Politics," in E. Burdick and A.J. Brodbeck, eds., *American Voting Behavior*, Glencoe, Ill.: Free Press, 1959, pp. 236-61.

Pool, Ithiel de Sola, Robert P. Abelson, and Samuel L. Popkin. *Candidates, Issues, and Strategies*. Cambridge: Massachusetts Institute of Technology Press, 1965.

Prewitt, Kenneth. "From the Many Are Chosen the Few." *Am. Behav. Sci.* 13 (November-December 1969-70): 169-88.

Price, Granville. "A Method for Analyzing Newspaper Campaign Coverage." *Journalism Q.* 31 (Fall 1954): 447-58.

Priest, Robert F. and Joel Abrahams. "Candidate Preference and Hostile Humor in the 1968 Elections." *Psychol. Rep.* 26 (June 1970): 779-83.

Prisuta, Robert H. "Mass Media Exposure and Political Behavior." *Educ. Broadcast. Rev.* 7 (June 1973): 167-73.

This study of the 1968 presidential campaign examines the relationships of mass media exposure to political behavior.

Method: survey; questionnaire. *Statistics*: correlation coefficient and chi-square. *Pop. (N)*: 1400 Survey Research Center interviews.

Findings: (1) Newspapers displayed the strongest relationship with political variables, followed by print and then broadcasting. (2) The number of people exposed to various media varies greatly. (3) Newspapers were the only medium to correlate significantly with voter turnout. The other media showed little relationship. (4) When media exposure and time of voting decision were examined, further evidence was found that media-political interaction is an ongoing process, rather than one which takes place only during the campaign. (5) The more highly exposed the voter, the more likely he or she was to have decided before the conventions, thus before the campaign. (6) In the relationship between media exposure and political information, as exposure rose, so did the level of political information. (7) High media use is most strongly correlated with self-perceived information level, less so with evaluated level, and still less with indirect assessment. (8) The independent variable of exposure affects the dependent variable of turnout differently with each medium utilized, thus making the medium under consideration a primary factor. (9) The print media were a mobilizing factor for the Republicans in the 1968 election, whereas the broadcast media were a mobilizing factor for the Democrats.

Pulse, Inc. "How Viewers Vote: A Special Pulse Study Checks Before and After Effects of TV on Attitudes Toward Candidates." *Television Age* 3 (1956): 56-57+.

Ray, Joseph M., ed. *The President: Rex, Princeps, Imperator?* Proceedings: 1968 Presidential Election Symposia, University of Texas, El Paso, April and September 1968. El Paso: Texas Western Press, 1969.

Reinsch, J. Leonard. "Broadcasting the Political Conventions." *J. Broadcast.* 12 (1968): 213–24.

Repass, Donald E. and Steven H. Chaffee. "Administrative vs. Campaign Coverage of Two Presidents in Eight Partisan Dailies." *Journalism Q.* 45 (Autumn 1968): 528–31.

Rice, Ross R. and Dickinson L. McGaw. "The 1970 Elections in Arizona." *West. Polit. Q.* 24 (June 1971): 243–51.

Richard, John B. "The 1970 Election in Wyoming." *West. Polit. Q.* 24 (June 1971): 362–68.

Rider, John Russell. "The Charleston Study: The Television Audience of the Nixon-Kennedy Debates." Unpublished doctoral dissertation, Michigan State University, 1963.

This study provides a descriptive analysis of the impact of the Great Debates. This impact is evaluated in terms of four criteria: educational level of respondent, family size, political preference, and media activity.

Method: survey; questionnaire. *Statistics*: frequencies. *Pop. (N)*: 100 adults in Charleston, Ill.

Findings: The Charleston Study supports a theory that has four elements: (1) change of opinion in political broadcasting is directly related to the amount of use the viewers make of the mass media; (2) television and print media used together are more effective in changing opinions than use of television programs by themselves; (3) the combined effect of television and print media is greater where controversy is concerned; (4) print media serve as an interpretive agent for the messages which a viewer receives from television.

Essentially, the *Charleston Study* found no solid basis for a belief that a significant number of people changed their minds about voting because of the debates. The issues were not clearly discerned by most viewers. Rather, the Great Debates led to a more positive conception of the men themselves.

Roberts, Churchill. "Voting Intentions and Attitude Change in a Congressional Election." *Speech Monogr.* 40 (March 1973): 49–55.

Robinson, John P. "Mass Media and Interpersonal Influence During the 1968 Election." Paper presented to the American Sociological Association, August 1972.

"The voting behavior of individuals exposed to various media and interpersonal political communication was ... compared with the voting behavior of individuals not so exposed, holding several other factors constant as an indicator of the influence of each of these message sources."

Method: survey; questionnaire. *Statistics*: frequencies, multiple classification analysis. *Pop. (N)*: national sample, Michigan Survey Research Center data, 1968.

Findings: Contrary to the two-step flow model of political communication, the data did not support a simple division of the electorate into opinion givers and receivers with 68% of opinion givers reporting that they were in turn receivers of influence attempts compared to only 26% of nongivers. Opinion-givers seldom voted for the candidate they did not verbally support.

Robinson, John P. "Perceived Media Bias and the 1968 Vote: Can the Media Affect Behavior After All?" *Journalism Q.* 49 (Summer 1972): 239–46.

Examines the effect of media on the outcomes of political campaigns. Subjects were asked how they perceived political allegiance in media.

Method: survey; questionnaire. *Statistics*: frequencies, percentages. *Pop. (N)*: 1,346 Americans 21 years and over.

Findings: "The public ranked television as its most important and relatively unbiased source of campaign news in 1968" (p. 245). With other variables controlled, it was estimated that a newspaper's perceived support of one candidate rather than another was associated with about a 6% edge in vote for the endorsed candidate over his opponent.

Robinson, Michael J. "Television and the Wallace Vote in 1968: Are There Implications for 1976?" Unpublished paper, n.d.
An explanation of the "Wallace movement" in 1968, with some predictions about the 1976 campaign. Robinson contends that those who followed politics principally through television in 1968 showed a greater affinity for Wallace than those who did not.
Method: survey; questionnaire. *Statistics*: frequencies, correlations, cross-tabulation. *Pop. (N)*: national samples 1960–68, Michigan Survey Research Center data.
Findings: Statistical relationship shows positive correlation between reliance on television and Wallace support. Positive correlation is maintained even with controls for age, education, SES. There is some indication that television aided Nixon. Television-dependent voters were apparently rendered conservative (Wallace) or hostile to incumbent (Nixon vote). Television news in 1968 created a very significant climate; its issue presentation fostered the Wallace campaign in a very special way.

Roper, Elmer. "Election Study II: Concerning Issues and Candidates." October 1960, unpublished.

Rose, Richard. *Influencing Voters: A Study of Campaign Rationality*. London: Faber and Faber, 1967.

Rose, Richard and Harve Mossawir. "Voting and Elections: A Functional Analysis." *Polit. Stud.* 15 (June 1967): 173–201.

Rossi, Peter H. "Four Landmarks in Voting Research" in E. Burdick and A.J. Brodbeck, eds., *American Voting Behavior*. Glencoe, Ill.: Free Press, 1959, pp. 5–54.

Rossi, Peter H. "Trends in Voting Behavior Research: 1933–1963," in E.C. Dreyer and W.A. Rosenbaum, eds., *Political Opinion and Electoral Behavior*. Belmont, Calif.: Wadsworth, 1966, pp. 67–78.

Rothschild, Michael L. "The Effects of Political Advertising Upon the Voting Behavior of a Low Involvement Electorate." Unpublished paper, Stanford University.

Rothschild, Michael. "The Effects of Political Advertising Upon the Voting Behavior of a Low Involvement Electorate Marketing Area." Unpublished article, n.d.

Rothschild, Michael L. and Michael L. Ray. "Involvement and Political Advertising Effectiveness: A Laboratory Repetition Experiment." Paper presented to the AAPOR Conference, Asheville, N.C., May 1973.
This experiment is concerned with involvement in elections and the effectiveness of political advertising.
Method: experiment. *Statistics*: means, frequencies. *Pop. (N)*: 160 adults.
Findings: Increasing advertising exposure in most involving presidential race produced steady increases in advertising recall, moderate improvements in attitude, and no effect on voting intention. Least involving state assembly race produced the most dramatic repetition effects for advertising recall and voting intention and no effect on attitude. Political efficacy and volunteering scales separated individuals into "high and low" groups. Highs seemed "turned-off" by heavy advertising in the presidential race, e.g., the more advertising, the less voting intention. Highs were affected more than lows by the advertising for State Assembly. The results can be attributed to a sophisticated learning attitude-intention process under high involvement and a simple perceptual shift-intention process under low involvement.

Roucek, Joseph S. *Influence of Television on American Politics*. Bridgeport. Conn.: University of Bridgeport, 1963.

Rubin, Bernard. *Political Television*. Belmont, Calif.: Wadsworth, 1967.

Rusk, Jerrold G. "The Effect of the Australian Ballot Report on Split-Ticket Voting, 1876–1908." *Am. Polit. Sci. Rev.* 64 (December 1970): 1220–38.

Rusk, Jerrold G. and Herbert F. Weisberg. "Perceptions of Presidential Candidates: Implications for Electoral Change." *Midwest J. Polit. Sci.* 16 (August 1972): 388–410.

Russell, Charles G. "A Multi-variate Descriptive Field Study of Media and Non-Media Influences on Voting Behavior in the 1970 Texas Gubernatorial Election." Unpublished doctoral dissertation, Southern Illinois University, 1971.

Russell's study sought to discover the relationships between voting behavior and many of the variables said by the literature of political science and communications to influence voting behavior. He collected seventy-two items of information from each subject during three interviews, two before and one after the election. *Method*: survey; questionnaire. *Statistics*: regression analysis. *Pop. (N)*: 33 voters in Travis County, Texas.

Findings: (1) The data suggest that the credibility which a voter attaches to a source is a better prediction of his voting behavior than the amount of information gained from the source. (2) Demographic data such as sex, political party affiliation, and educational level are highly predictive of voting behavior.

Salant, Richard S. "The Changing Use of TV in Campaign Politics." Paper presented at annual meeting of the American Political Science Association, St. Louis, 1961.

Salant, Richard S. "The 1960 Campaigns and Television." Unpublished doctoral dissertation, University of Missouri, 1961.

Salant, Richard S. "The Television Debates: A Revolution That Deserves a Future." *Pub. Opin. Q.* 26 (Fall 1962): 335–50.

A case is made for the continuance of debating in presidential campaigns. The author discusses the effects of the 1960 Kennedy-Nixon debates.

Conclusions: (1) "Almost 90% of American families have one or more television sets; they use them, on the average, more than five hours a day" (p. 337). (2) "A total of about 115 million people attended, through radio and television, at least some part of the four 1960 debates" (p. 338). (3) A 1956 Michigan study by Samuel Eldersveld showed 38% of the people stated they received most of their political information from television, 38% from newspaper, 9% from radio (p. 338). (4) Debates may "have a greater impact and produce more conversions than single, set appearances controlled by the candidate" (p. 341).

Scheff, Edward A. "The Application of the Semantic Differential to the Study of Voter Behavior in the 1964 Political Campaigns." Unpublished doctoral dissertation, University of Kansas, 1965.

Schramm, Wilbur and Richard F. Carter. "Effectiveness of a Political Telethon." *Pub. Opin. Q.* 23 (Spring 1959): 121–26.

This study of the effectiveness of the political telethon of Senator Knowland in October 1958 supports the generalization that their predispositions can reduce the dissonance resulting from a challenge to those predispositions. *Method*: survey; questionnaire. *Statistics*: frequencies. *Pop. (N)*: 563 persons.

Findings: (1) Only 65 of 563 persons interviewed watched some part of the telethon. Republicans were twice as likely to see the program as Democrats were. (2) 44 of the 65 viewers did not tell anyone of the telethon; 17 told friends the program was on the air; 6 told other members of their family. (3) Republicans found the program more worthwhile, higher in quality, and more impressive generally than did Democrats. (4) The telethon did not bring about great changes in viewers' intention to vote; 2 of the 65 viewers said it helped them to make up their minds—one to vote for, one to vote against Knowland. (5) The main result of the telethon seemed to have been to confirm the impressions of Knowland and the voting intentions which the viewers brought to the program.

Schreiber, E.M. "Vietnam Policy Preferences and Withheld 1968 Presidential Votes." *Pub. Opin. Q.* 37 (Spring 1973): 91–98.

Schwartz, Alan J. "An Analysis of Selected Television Political Debates Produced in New York by WCBS-TV and Transmitted Locally During the Elections of 1962 and 1966." Unpublished doctoral dissertation, New York University, 1970.

Seagull, Louis M. "The Youth Vote and Change in American Politics." *Ann. Am. Acad. Polit. Soc. Sci.* 397 (September 1971): 88–96.

Segal, David R. "Status Inconsistency and Party Choice in Canada: An Attempt to Replicate." *Can. J. Polit. Sci.* 3 (September 1970): 462–70.

Seymour-Ure, Colin. *The Political Impact of Mass Media.* London: Constable; Beverly Hills, Calif.: Sage, 1974.

Shaffer, William R. "Partisan Loyalty and the Perception of Party, Candidates, and Issues." *West. Polit. Q.* 25 (September 1972): 424–33.

Sherrod, Drury R. "Selective Perception of Political Candidates." *Pub. Opin. Q.* 35 (Winter 1971–72): 554–62.

Shinn, Allen M., Jr. "A Note on Voter Registration and Turnout in Texas, 1960–1970." *J. Polit.* 33 (November 1971): 1120–29.

Siebert, Joseph C. *The Influence of Television on the Election of 1952.* Oxford, O.: Oxford Research Associates, 1954.

Sigel, Roberta S. "Effect of Partisanship on the Perception of Political Candidates." *Pub. Opin. Q.* 28 (Fall 1964): 483–96.

Simon, Herbert A. and Frederick Stern. "The Effect of Television Upon Voting Behavior in Iowa in the 1952 Presidential Election." *Am. Polit. Sci. Rev.* 49 (June 1955): 470–77.

Investigation of the effect of television on voting participation and party division of the vote in Iowa in 1952. Comparison of counties of high television density with counties of low television density.

Conclusion: "The data do not reveal any reliable difference either in the voting turnout or in the percentage of the vote cast for the Republican candidate between high television density and other areas" (p. 471).

Sizemore, Afton A. "Television and Presidential Politics, 1952–1970." Unpublished master's thesis, University of Kansas, 1970.

Smith, C.W., Jr., "Measurement of Voter Attitudes." *Ann. Am. Acad. Polit. Soc. Sci.* 283 (September 1952): 148–55.

Smith, David E. "Recent Trends in Canadian Politics." *West. Polit. Q.* 23 (June 1970): 348–63.

Smith, Harrison. "The Campaign and Television." *Saturday Rev.* 39 (17 November 1956): 26.

This editorial considers the effects of television on political campaigns.

Conclusions: (1) Television has eliminated the necessity of group gatherings and discussions; all information can be communicated to the individual via television. (2) Paid political broadcasts should be no substitute for independent reporting of the political scene (which Jack Gould believed was the case). (3) Radio does a better job in dealing with the truth since its broadcasters permit argument and debate.

Sternthal, Brian. "Persuasion and the Mass Communication Process." Unpublished doctoral dissertation, Ohio State University, 1972.

Stillings, Edwin J. "Turnout and Electoral Trends, 1870–1950." Unpublished doctoral dissertation, Chicago, 1953.

Stokes, D. and D. Butler. *Political Change in Britain.* New York: St. Martin's Press, 1969.

Stratman, William Craig. "A Concept of Voter Rationality." Unpublished doctoral dissertation, University of Rochester, 1972.

Suchman, Edward A. "Television," in Joseph S. Roucek, ed., *Social Control*. Princeton, N.J.: Van Nostrand, 1956, pp. 504–21.

Surlin, Stuart H. and Joseph R. Dominick. "Television's Function as a 'Third Parent' for Black and White Teen-agers." *J. Broadcast*. 15 (Winter 1970–71): 55–64.

Swanson, David L. "The New Politics Meets the Old Rhetoric: New Directions in Campaign Communication Research." *Q. J. Speech* 58 (February 1972): 30–40. The study of campaign communication must take new and more demanding steps to respond to the challenge of the new politics.
Conclusions: (1) "The most productive investigation of the issues and methods of the new politics must be rooted in a reconceptualization of campaign communication and of the role of the communication researcher" (p. 31). (2) Campaigns which are cited as examples of new politics are those whose strategy is grounded in scientific theory and research, and which seem to make extensive use of the mass media of communication and of television particularly. (3) David Mortensen suggests "that the format of political television messages tends to influence the content of discussion" (p. 33). (4) "Productive study of the communications of the new politics seems to require abandoning the political speech making orientation in favor of a 'full-blown' view of rhetoric in the campaign context" (p. 37).

Swanson, David L. "Persuasion and the New Politics: Foundations for a Strategy of Communication in the Modern Presidential Campaign." Unpublished doctoral dissertation, University of Kansas, 1971.

Swanson, David L. "Political Information, Influence, and Judgement in the 1972 Presidential Campaign." *Q. J. Speech* 59 (April 1973): 130–42.
A pilot survey of voters' evaluations of the 1972 presidential campaign and of sources of political information and influence.
Method: survey; questionnaire. *Statistics*: frequencies. *Pop. (N)*: 65 Illinois voting-age adults.
Findings: (1) A higher percentage of 1972 voters than usual decided for whom to vote before the conventions, a higher percentage than usual decided during the convention period, and fewer voters than expected decided during the campaign itself. This indicates that the 1972 conventions had a greater impact on crystallizing the vote decision than is normally the case. (2) Voters are generally aware of major campaign events and activities. (3) Campaign features which were mentioned as prominent features in the campaign were not mentioned as important reasons why 17.8% Nixon voters and 19.2% McGovern voters changed their minds about who to support. This leads to a speculation that events during the campaign help voters form voting decisions. (4) Television ranks first and newspapers second as sources of campaign information. (5) Retention loss for television commercials was 50–80% lower than that for half-hour television programs or radio programs. (6) The data do not clearly validate the operation of selective exposure and retention. (7) Non-partisan mass communication is an important and credible source of political information for most people. (8) When asked to list party preference of their three closest friends, 60.7% of Nixon voters and 61.7% McGovern voters had party preference the same as their friends (p. 141). (9) The preference of 78.5% of Nixon voters' three closest friends favored voting for Nixon; 80.7% of McGovern voters found social support among their three closest friends for their vote decision. This suggests that interpersonal communication among friends is an important influence on final voting decisions.

Swanson, Wayne R., Jay S. Goodman, and Elmer E. Cornwell. "Voting Behavior in a Non-Partisan Legislative Setting." *West. Polit. Q.* 25 (March 1972): 39–59.

Taylor, Michael. "The Problems of Salience in the Theory of Collective Decision Making." *Behav. Sci.* 15 (September 1970): 415–30.

Thomson, Charles A.H. *Television and Presidential Politics.* Washington, D.C. : The Brookings Institution, 1956.

Topping, Malachi C. and Lawrence W. Lichty. "Political Programs on National Television Networks: 1968." *J. Broadcast.* 15 (Spring 1971):161–79.

Truman, David B. *The Governmental Process.* New York: Knopf, 1953.

Tuchman, Sam and Thomas E. Coffin. "The Influence of Election Night Broadcasts on Television in a Close Election." *Pub. Opin. Q.* 35 (Fall 1971): 315–26.

This study of the 1968 presidential election attempts to discover if broadcasts prior to voting lead people to change their voting plans.

Method: survey; questionnaire (pretest-posttest). *Statistics*: frequencies. *Pop. (N)*: 1455 voters in Pacific Time Zone, 517 voters in Eastern Time Zone.

Findings: (1) There was no significant difference in the incidence of change in voting turnout plans between exposed and unexposed groups. (2) There was no significant difference in the level of candidate-switching between exposed and unexposed groups. (3) Election night broadcasts did not significantly influence those voters who changed turnout plans and switched candidates. (4) Eastern voters were more likely than Western voters to make last-minute changes in their voting turnout plans. (5) There was no indication that voters who were undecided about whether to vote employed election night broadcasts to reach decisions.

"TV and the Ballot Box." *Television Age*, 27 June 1960, pp. 30–31.

"TV as a Political Weapon." *Sponsor* 19 (18 January 1965): 33.

Ulmer, S. Sidney, ed. *Proceedings: Political Decision-Making Conference* (University of Kentucky, Lexington, 1968). New York: Van Nostrand Reinhold, 1970.

University of Michigan. *Television and the Political Candidate.* New York: Cunningham and Walsh, 1959.

Veblen, Eric Paul. "Newspaper Impact in Election Campaigns: The Case of Two New England States." Doctoral dissertation, Yale University, 1969.

The main focus of this study is the nature and degree of newspaper impact on a candidate's strategies and campaign activities.

Conclusions: (1) An analysis of the New Hampshire *Union Leader*'s impact on candidates concludes that two main influence bases of the newspaper are the candidates' beliefs that it exerts a strong impact on electorate and the candidates' desire to avoid personal attacks in editorials. (2) Perception of a Vermont newspaper's influence on voters is based on its large circulation and its vigorous political advocacy. (3) The "study demonstrates the great potential power which accompanies the control of a dominant communications medium in a political entity."

Vinyard, Dale and Roberta S. Sigel. "Newspapers and Urban Voters." *Journalism Q.* 48 (Autumn 1971): 486–93.

This study on the way people use mass media indicates that none of the three media alone seems to constitute the only source of news for the average and even the not-so-average consumer.

Method: survey; questionnaire. *Statistics*: frequencies. *Pop. (N)*: 250 Detroit registered voters.

Findings: (1) Reliance on a diversity of media increases as education increases. (2) 98% of the respondents reported that they read one or both of the daily newspapers (p. 487). (3) 87% of the respondents reported that they regularly watched television news broadcasts and public affairs programs (p. 488). (4) 66% of the respondents reported that they listened to radio news broadcasts. (5) News magazine readers were heavily concentrated among the more highly educated. (6) During a newspaper strike, the upper status group sought substitutes for the local newspaper and placed major reliance on the electronic media, especially television. (7) Newspapers ranked as the most important source as a means to keep informed. The reason given for this preference is their relatively complete news coverage. (8) 60% of the respondents reported great dependence on the papers in local candidate selections while experiencing much less need for newspapers in national or state races (p. 491). (9) Dependence on the newspapers extends even to dependence on the paper's electoral advice. (10) 47% of the respondents said all three media (television, newspaper, radio) were equally truthful; 21% believed television most truthful, and 21% named the newspaper as the most truthful.

Weinberg, Leonard and Joseph Crowley. "Primary Success as a Measure of Presidential Election Victory." *Midwest J. Polit. Sci.* 14 (August 1970): 506–13.

Weisberg, Herbert F. and Richard G. Niemi. "A Pairwise Probability Approach to the Likelihood of the Paradox of Voting." *Behav. Sci.* 18 (March 1973): 109–17.

Weisberg, Herbert F. and Jerrold C. Rusk. "Dimensions of Candidate Evaluation." *Am. Polit. Sci. Rev.* 64 (December 1970): 1167–85.

Weisberg, Robert. "Adolescents' Perceptions of Political Authorities: Another Look at Political Virtue and Power." *Midwest J. Polit. Sci.* 16 (February 1973): 147–67.

Weitzel, Al. "Candidate and Electorate Perceptions of the Nature and Function of Media Messages: A Case Study Approach." Paper presented at the International Communication Association Convention, Montreal, April 1973.

Whale, John. *Half-Shut Eye: Television and Politics in Britain and America.* New York: St. Martin's Press, 1969.

"What Air Media Did to Swing the Vote." *Sponsor* 6 (3 November 1952): 25.

White, Theodore H. *The Making of a President, 1960* (also *1964, 1968, 1972*). New York: Atheneum, 1961, 1965, 1969, 1973.

Wicker, Tom, Kenneth P. O'Donnell, and Rowland Evans. "Television in the Political Campaign." *Television Q.* 5 (Winter 1966): 13–26.

Three political pundits agree that television makes it possible for a better informed electorate, but they also agree that television's effectiveness has limitations.

Conclusions: Tom Wicker: (1) Television raises the dangers that are inherent in political fund-raising. (2) Television puts greater emphasis on, and rewards in higher proportions, the production and merchandising of talent. (3) Television allows increase in the public's interest in, and knowledgeability about, candidates and races. (4) The shape of events of a campaign tends to soften the issues in a campaign; it puts emphasis on blurring over the hard questions of choice between two courses. (5) Although television may change political tactics and strategy, it will not fundamentally change American politics.

Kenneth O'Donnell: (1) While it is true that television thrusts people into prominence, in order to remain there they must have qualities of greatness; television can only transmit what is there. (2) The role of television in politics may be unfair, since an incumbent has greater access to the media than does the other candidate. (3) Television can control a candidate's statements. For example, if television reporter asks a candidate a question he does not want to answer, he is either pressured into answering or made to appear that he is "ducking" the question.

Rowland Evans: (1) Despite the importance of the "living room" campaign, television will never substitute for the traditional campaign. (2) Television exposes voters— who would normally never be exposed—to the candidate of the other party. (3) While television gives every voter a chance to measure his candidate, every candidate is not given an equal chance to be measured. (4) Television can be used by candidates to create images of themselves. For example, a candidate might expose himself to hostile questions in order to create sympathy in the audience and an image of himself as a "good-guy" being "picked on" by television.

Willis, Edgar E. "Radio and Presidential Campaigning." *Central States Speech J.* 20 (Fall 1969): 187–93.

"The advent of radio broadcasting brought some significant changes into presidential campaigns but it failed to produce other changes that one might have expected to arise from the use of this new communications medium. This paper describes the changes that took place and examines the reasons for certain expected changes failing to materialize" (p. 187). Examination of radio's effect on candidates, convention, campaigning, and the voter.

Conclusions: Radio had the capacity to confer almost instant fame on those presidential aspirants who were successful in meeting its demands. If they continued to use it well, it materially advanced their cause. It did reveal ineptitude in otherwise competent men. The use of radio diminished the influence of newspapers. It made personal appearances less necessary. People had a chance to participate directly in political events. Radio's persuasive power is most fully utilized through political commercials. The 1948 campaign was the last one in which radio played a dominant role.

Wolf, T. Philip. "The 1970 Election in New Mexico." *West. Polit. Q.* 24 (June 1971): 316–22.

Wolfinger, R.E. "The Influence of Precinct Work on Voting Behavior." *Pub. Opin. Q.* 27 (Fall 1963): 387–98.

Worsnop, R.I. "Television and Politics." *Ed. Res. Rep.* no. 19, 1 (1968): 363–84.

Traces the use of television by politicians. Points to the rising costs both for television and for the politicians. Examines the use of radio in the campaigns of F.D. Roosevelt. Suggests that an effective use of television by a politician might help him gain political prominence.

Wright, James E. "The Ethnocultural Model of Voting." *Am. Behav. Sci.* 16 (May-June 1973): 653–75.

Zechmeister, Kathleen and Daniel Druckman. "Determinants of Resolving A Conflict of Interest: A Simulation of Political Decision-Making." *J. Confl. Resol.* 17 (March 1973): 63–88.

Zeidenstein, Harvey. "Presidential Primaries—Reflections of 'The People's Choice'?" *J. Polit.* 32 (November 1970): 856–74.

Zeigler, L. Harmon and Barbara Leigh Smith. "The 1970 Elections in Oregon." *West. Polit. Q.* 24 (June 1971): 325–38.

Zemsky, Robert. "American Legislative Behavior." *Am. Behav. Sci.* 16 (May-June 1973): 675–95.

Zimmerman, Fred L. "Contrary to Theory, More Than Just a Pretty Ad is Needed to Win in Politics, The Candidates Find." *Wall Street Journal* 179 (10 May 1972): 34.

Today's sophisticated media audience can see through phony campaign ads; to be successful, ads must be truthful, realistic, and consistent.

Conclusions: (1) Television political material is bound to fail unless it is limited to a few clear-cut themes that jibe with other information voters are getting about the candidate. (2) One problem facing media men is that so much has been written about television's capacity for image-making that voters are becoming increasingly skeptical of political ads of all sorts. (3) The most successful campaign ads of 1972 appear to have been those which were excerpts of the candidates in ordinary conversation with different groups of people.

4

Mass Communication and Political Information

In the previous two chapters we focused on political socialization, a social psychological process, and election campaigns, a social organizational process. In the remaining chapters, we will consider how various models of communication processes relate to political phenomena. Although one of our prime objectives remains a comprehensive review of the literature in political communication, we will give greater attention to those studies which are based on certain conceptualizations. Our purpose is to present these conceptualizations in a critical perspective which can guide future research in political communication.

Information and Political Institutions

The creation, organization, and dissemination of information is a central process in any modern society. This process uses various forms of communication. It is a political process to the extent that it influences or is influenced by political institutions. In most industrialized societies the control of information has become an increasing concern of government. In the nations of Eastern Europe, the Soviet Union, and China, the control of information has become an accepted function of government. Only in this way, it is argued, can information be made to serve the whole society rather than elite groups. In the nations of Western Europe and North America and in Japan information processes are probably as structured as those of Communist societies, but control is decentralized. There are many historical reasons for the specific form which this decentralization has taken in each nation. Most structures have been strongly influenced by theories of democratic government which were advanced during the eighteenth century. In general, these theories held that free access to information and the freedom to create and to disseminate information were important rights of the individual. These rights were considered to be part of the basis of a democratic social order.

In the course of history, social structures which affect the control of information have been viewed as politically important, so much so that particular forms of government have become associated with specific structures. Thus, a free press and independent, tuition-free public schools have become characteristic structures of Western nations, while Eastern nations are characterized by government-controlled newspapers and more direct government control of public schools. Though such structures clearly influence and are influenced by political phenomena, only a rudimentary effort has been made to understand scientifically their political implications or the processes of information creation, organization, and dissemination behind them. Centuries of speculation concerning these processes exist, but very little empirical knowledge exists which is not simply descriptive.

Recently, communication theorists and researchers have begun to develop and evaluate models for mass communication systems. In most industrialized societies these mass communication systems are an increasingly dominant part of information-related processes. In Chapter 2 we argued that the significance of these systems for political socialization of children is increasing. In this chapter we will attempt to demonstrate that creation, organization, and transmission of information by mass communication systems is also of increasing importance to the political beliefs, attitudes, and behavior of adults. We will also be concerned with the development of conceptualizations of mass communication systems which facilitate our understanding of information-related processes, so that the political implications of changes in mass communication system structures can be anticipated. We will argue that a "transactional model" of political communication offers the best hope of understanding political communication in a way which is consistent with democratic ideals and goals.

Information and Democracy

Political scientists and politicians have a long-standing concern for the social structures by which political information is used by the public and controlled. Traditionally, these structures have been conceived of as the basis for a liberal, democratic society. Eighteenth-century political theorists argued that democracy is based on an educated and informed public which acts responsibly on what it knows. They suggested social structures which would enhance education and the free flow of information.[1] Building on these ideas, American planners wrote the First Amendment to the Constitution, which guarantees free speech and freedom of the press. This amendment was intended to establish the basic conditions for a democratic state. Its authors foresaw an open "marketplace of ideas" in which every citizen could participate and become informed. One assumption underlying this concept was that in the "marketplace" good ideas would be more likely to prevail and win acceptance.[2]

The two theses of this chapter are that the social structures which create, organize, and transmit information have been transformed; and these structural changes have had and will continue to have significant consequences for the functioning of our democracy. These theses are not novel. They have been advanced and discussed by many communication theorists, particularly those who have considered the structure and functioning of national communication systems. Our purposes here are fourfold: first, to consider these theses with reference to political information; second, to discuss the possible social consequences of structural changes in the light of recent communication research; third, to indicate those areas where additional information is necessary to improve our understanding of the relationships among particular structures of communication systems and the political consequences of those structures; and finally, to consider the role of communication research in relation to policy making which affects the design and operation of future communication systems.

Theories of National Communication Systems

Traditionally, communication theorists have classified national communication systems into four categories based on a typology advanced by Siebert, Peterson, and Schramm.[3] The four categories are Soviet-Communist or totalitarian, libertarian, social responsibility, and authoritarian. Not surprisingly these categories parallel four popular normative theories of government. Clearly, an essential link was perceived between the governmental structure of a society and its communication system. However, the nature of this link was not completely understood. Early theorists made assumptions about the transmission of political information in the different types of communication systems. Below, these presumed links will be reviewed and then evaluated critically.

According to the theories, in totalitarian or authoritarian systems, the flow of information moves strictly from the "top down." In such a system all information is more or less political because its transmission and use have direct or indirect consequences for the political system. Thus even entertainment content is closely controlled because of its potential consequences for the political system. A smoothly functioning, well-planned communication system, efficiently transmitting information chosen or screened by government officials, is essential to the maintenance of a totalitarian government and to the implementation of its policies. The other types of communication systems vary in the degree to which information is controlled by the political system. Under authoritarian regimes, communication systems are closely monitored by government for the purpose of encouraging information viewed as supporting government policies and discouraging antigovernment information. Wright (1959) classifies the communication systems of most developing countries as authoritarian because of the direct control exercised by governments over media content.

Social responsibility communication systems are characterized by a high degree of "self-censorship." In such systems media professionals, not government officials, make decisions about what information should be transmitted. The prime criterion in their decision-making is that the information transmitted be of benefit to the society as a whole, not just to the government. Libertarian communication systems simply transmit any information which is desired by someone who gains access to a medium. No restrictions are placed on access to or transmission of information on the assumption that the "best information" (that is, the most useful, most truthful, most accurate) would eventually reach the widest audience. Free access to the communication system is viewed as a right of the individual which should not be infringed upon by the state. The libertarian system closely resembles the "marketplace of ideas" notion mentioned above. Presumably, such a system could extend the "marketplace" to a national audience.

This view of communication systems has proved inadequate for several reasons. First, this typology assumes that it is possible to anticipate the social consequences of the transmission of any form of information. Unless totalitarian or authoritarian governments can anticipate all such consequences, it is not possible for them to plan and to administer communication systems effectively. Recent studies of the operation of the Soviet communication system by Markham[4] indicate that it is hardly as efficient in mobilizing citizen support as was implied by early theorists. In fact, a certain amount of contradictory, useless, or even politically volatile information is transmitted, especially during periods in which communication policies are revised. Similarly, social responsibility systems have faltered because of an inability to anticipate the social consequences of information transmission. Changes have been made in these systems (for example, the Independent Television Authority was established in Britain) to take into account the consequences of certain policies for information transmission.[5]

Second, the technologies of the emerging mass communication media are enormously expensive and require increasingly well-educated and well-organized personnel to operate them. In most countries, centralized media bureaucracies have emerged which severely limit access to the media by nonprofessionals. An individual cannot easily buy a public forum for his ideas. In countries with traditionally libertarian or social responsibility systems, these bureaucracies are defended as the only means of efficiently providing top quality, useful media content. Access by nonprofessionals is viewed as threatening to the efficient operation of the media bureaucracies.[6] In countries with totalitarian or authoritarian systems of communication, large-scale, centralized media bureaucracies have been encouraged by an additional factor. Centralization of facilities and "professionalization" of personnel can increase the ability of government to monitor and control the media system.

Third, pure libertarian systems of communication are nonexistent today. Even the United States system, which historically has had the least direct government control, is regulated. The Radio Act of 1934, which instituted the Federal Communications Commission, established the government's right to ensure that the broadcast media are operated in the public interest. Codes of ethics adopted by American journalists recognize the "social responsibility of the press." Thus the "marketplace of ideas" has become subject to two types of constraint.[7]

Recently, economic theorists have noted a convergence of communist, socialist, and capitalist economic systems. Not surprisingly, this convergence can be found to extend to communication systems, particularly if only the technological features of these systems are compared. We are faced with the problem of understanding media systems which appear to be developing in accord with the evolution of the technologies that underlie them. This is a problem faced by those who seek to understand communication systems, no matter what the historical or ideological origins of those systems. We are repelled by and yet resigned to the thought of our technology "running wild," propelling us into an uncertain future such as that envisioned by Orwell for 1984.[8]

There is a clear need for a comprehensive conceptualization of communication systems which goes beyond the descriptive, normative, and ideologically based typologies of early theorists. This conceptualization should guide the development of existing media systems so that they enable us to achieve social goals. This has been one of the primary aims in the development and implementation of economic theory. It is not an impossible goal for communication theory.

Recent communication research suggests that most previous assumptions about information control should be questioned and discarded. These new findings make it clear that the processes by which political information is created, transmitted, and used are complex. They are interactive processes in which the creation of public involvement is necessary for effective dissemination of information. Let us turn to these findings, the communication models which they suggest, the gaps which they leave in our understanding, and the research necessary to fill those gaps.

Models of Information Communication

A review of the literature in the communication of political information reveals four models which have explicitly or implicitly guided communication research in this area. These models differ substantially from one another in the way that relationships between mass media and the public are conceptualized. Yet each of these models is historically related to all of the others. Each subsequent model serves to elaborate on rather than completely supplant the models which preceded it.

The earliest of these models is the so-called hypodermic needle model (Rogers 1971, p. 203). It assumes that information is directly transmitted by the mass media to the public. The media are conceived of as a needle which "injects" information directly into the mind. This model was developed during World War I and was used to explain the success of propaganda in manipulating national audiences.[9] It was demonstrated to be inadequate by psychological experiments and sociological surveys.[10] This model failed to account for the way in which individuals were found to expose themselves to media information, or to perceive and retain information following exposure. Moreover, it did not take into account the social situation in which media information is received, and thus did not isolate those social variables that were later found to reinforce or impede the transmission of information.

These research findings led to the formulation of the social influence model or "two-step" flow model.[11] This model emphasized the influence of the social environment upon the transmission of information. An individual's exposure to, perception of, and retention of information were viewed as controlled by the groups to which he belonged. Opinion leaders were thought to mediate access to certain types of information for followers. Subsequent research revealed several inadequacies in this conceptualization. Certain types of information were found to be directly transmitted to mass audiences; other types of information were transmitted through several steps before being retained. A variety of opinion leaders was found to exist whose roles in information transmission, interpretation, and retention varied greatly; some of these "leaders" were discovered to be heavily influenced by followers. Moreover, mass media were found to differ in their capacities to transmit information, and the social situations of individuals were found to vary greatly. Finally, this model diverted attention from the eventual use of information transmission to guide behavior.

The social influence model was superseded by the diffusion model.[12] This model takes into account the multistep flow of various types of information as it passes from various mass media, through persons who play crucial roles in facilitating transmission, interpretation, and acceptance of information, to individuals in a variety of social situations who are eventually motivated to act in terms of information.

The chief drawback of the diffusion model is its emphasis on the downward flow of information. It permits the design of information campaigns which are most effective when the responses of the audience to the information can be predicted and controlled. It is useful also where one is interested in motivating certain types of action with a minimal concern for how those actions are understood by the persons who perform them.

Later in this chapter we shall propose that a new model is necessary to understand political information communication. This model elaborates upon the diffusion model, but modifies it to consider the flow of communication from individuals back to the sources of political communication. This model highlights consideration of the social and psychological conditions which structure this two-way flow. It elaborates Bauer's (1964) argument for a "transactional" model of communication.

We shall now discuss each of the models, together with the research which is related to it. Our purpose is to show how conceptualizations have changed in response to research findings and to provide a basis for new conceptualizations which can guide future research.

The Hypodermic Model[13]

Early mass communication researchers sought to understand the effects of propaganda during and following World War I. This research continued throughout the 1920s and 1930s and reached a high point in the Office of War Information studies conducted during World War II. In general, this research used the experimental methods of psychology or the developing technique of content analysis to draw inferences about the effects of propaganda. Thus researchers attempted to ascertain the presence of Nazi propaganda from a careful analysis of the pro-German magazine, *The Galilean*.[14] Likewise, Hovland et al. (1949) conducted a series of informal experiments to determine the influence of Allied propaganda in changing attitudes.

Early researchers worked from a view of man which assumed that mass media messages had direct impact upon the mind which inevitably produced predictable behaviors. These effects were thought to occur no matter what differentiating social or psychological attributes characterize an individual. Every person was an equivalent member of a mass audience who responded in similar ways to similar media stimuli. Mass media audiences were thought to be comparable to "mobs" which could be moved to common action by persuasive speakers. The flow of this communication was directly from the media to the individual. Its impact on the mind was immediate and not subject to the conscious control of the individual. Messages were literally conceived of as being "injected" into the mind where they were "stored" in the form of changes in feelings and attitudes. Eventually such feelings or attitudes produced the behavior desired by the message source.[15] This theory appeared plausible to researchers who frequently observed the apparently irrational yet well-coordinated actions of large groups, particularly during the war and again during the Depression era. Berelson (1948) suggests that Roosevelt's use of radio was regarded by these researchers as capable of directly influencing masses of the American public. The rise of Nazi Germany appeared to be proof of the theory, particularly to outside observers unaware of the underlying social and psychological dynamics of the National Socialist movement.[16]

The Social Influence Model

In the 1940s new methods of data collection and analysis began to produce evidence which contradicted the hypodermic model. Using survey research and simple correlational analysis techniques, Lazarsfeld, Berelson, and Gaudet (1944) found that several factors appeared to moderate political information or even prevent it from having an impact. These researchers found that in the 1940 presidential election campaign propaganda had a minimal impact. Their study, conducted in Erie County, Ohio, showed that very few people changed their vote in response to the campaign and that, of those who did change, very few attributed their change to media information. The researchers were able to offer two explanations for their findings. First, if a media message is in conflict with group norms, it will be rejected. Since groups have opinion leaders who transmit mass media information to individuals who do not attend to the media, these leaders influence whatever opinion change takes place in followers; media messages do not have direct impact. Second, individuals selectively expose themselves to campaign messages. They will choose to listen to or read those messages which are most consistent with their existing beliefs, attitudes, or values. These two explanations are compatible with one another. They can be seen respectively as sociological and psychological explanations of the same phenomenon.[17] These two explanations have guided research grounded in different disciplines using a variety of data-collecting techniques. Even though this research often produced inconsistent findings, these inconsistencies often were explained by methodological failures rather than inadequacies in the theory. The power of this paradigm for research is evidenced by its continued influence upon mass communication studies.

Perhaps part of the power of this paradigm stems from its reaffirmation of a uniquely American view of politics and the social order. It is consistent with how we have traditionally viewed our political process and it restores our faith that the future will be consistent with the past. Elihu Katz (1957) states, "The authors themselves (Lazarsfeld, Berelson, Gaudet) were intrigued by its [two-step flow hypothesis] implications for a democratic society. It was a healthy sign, they felt, that people were still most successfully persuaded by give-and-take with other people and that the influence of the mass media was less automatic and less potent than had been assumed." The mass media have not transformed society according to this paradigm nor do they threaten to do so. They are our servants, not our masters. Our fellow Americans are not an unruly, irrational mob. They are "homefolk"—loyal, committed members of their families, their professional groups, their labor unions, and most of all their political parties. Their beliefs, attitudes, and values are not at the mercy of a demagogue who can seize or buy control of a few newspapers or radio stations. They can be trusted with the destiny of this nation because their minds and their actions are grounded in inherently stable social institutions. The "stars" of the mass media can come and go with little or no influence upon American politics.

Of course, not everything in this vision of political communication was flattering. It implied that most individuals did not vote on the issues. Commitments to groups outweighed commitments to rational decision making. Still there was evidence that with a balanced, two-party system these "loyalists" would cancel each other out and elections would ultimately be decided by a rational minority. Also, opinion leaders were conceived of as rational individuals who would properly direct their followers to vote for the right candidate. Such was the inherent "wisdom" of our democratic system.

Much subsequent research confirmed this view, although not all researchers were as optimistic about the ultimate consequences of a political communication process grounded in social influence and selective exposure. Hyman and Sheatsley (1947) demonstrated that for a variety of political issues, both domestic and foreign, only a minority was even partially informed. This minority was not guided by reason but attended to those messages which fit its previously formed beliefs and attitudes. Where information threatened previously held attitudes, the researchers argued it would be ignored or misinterpreted. However, they could provide no direct test of this hypothesis. Furthermore, a hard core of consistently "chronic know-nothings"[18] seemed to exist who lacked information about issues that the researcher defined as being of the greatest national importance. This research cast doubt upon the existence of reasoned, informed opinion leaders and increased pessimism about the free flow of vital political information to mass audiences.

A rapid succession of impressively mounted studies during the mid-fifties carried the social influence model to the apex of its acceptance. Berelson, Lazarsfeld, and McPhee (1954) focused concern on identifying opinion leaders and the way in which they exerted their influence on other group members. They found that followers look to leaders who closely resemble themselves, particularly in terms of their attitudes. Thus the influence of leaders appeared to be limited to a relatively homogeneous group of followers. Wright (1955) stressed the "personalizing" dimension of opinion leader influence. Such leaders succeeded where mass media failed because they were able to make abstract political information relevant to the lives of followers. They made political communication a "human" process.

The Two-Step Flow Model

In 1955, Katz and Lazarsfeld reported the results of a large-scale study of personal influence in Decatur, Illinois. This research confirmed the basic social influence model and produced a tighter, more closely reasoned conceptualization known as the two-step flow hypothesis. According to this conceptualization, opinion leaders are necessary for effective information transmission from the mass media to the general public. The media must first reach opinion leaders who will subsequently relay information to their followers. While their data confirmed this hypothesis in an indirect manner, they failed to provide conclusive evidence. Subsequent efforts to provide such evidence have produced conflicting results.

It was clear from their data that women in Decatur were willing to admit significant influence by other women on several topics. These women were less willing to attribute important influence to the mass media. Opinion leaders differed from topic area to topic area and leaders for each topic shared social and psychological characteristics which differentiated them from leaders in other areas. This suggested that political information was mediated by a pluralistic group structure in which no single opinion leader exercised widespread control over the beliefs of others. The study also indicated that the transmission of information and influence was usually horizontal, within rather than between social strata, although there was some evidence for the vertical transmission of public affairs information.

The finding that emerged from this study which most discouraged subsequent efforts to look for media influences was that opinion leaders[19] were no more likely than followers to attribute influence upon their beliefs or opinions to the mass media. If leaders are not influenced by the media, and followers cannot be influenced directly by the media, then the role of the mass media in political communication appears to be minimal indeed. Even a two-step flow of communication is apparently of minor importance. Researchers looked to interpersonal communication networks when attempting to locate *significant* sources of political information transmission and influence. Media exposure was presumed to be short-circuited by such interpersonal networks. Relationships between exposure and certain observed effects could be regarded as possibly spurious. Such relationships could be expected to be sharply attenuated when interpersonal communication variables were controlled. In studies of opinion leaders, media variables were often treated as dependent variables. Research done by Robert Merton (1949) in Rovere, New Jersey, took for granted the importance of interpersonal influence and proceeded to try to find the people who play key roles in its transmission. He assumed that opinion leaders used media to keep informed, and that media influence was dependent on how opinion leaders used them.

The Selective Exposure Model

While the two-step flow hypothesis was receiving support from sociologists during the 1950s, selective exposure was being evaluated by psychologists. In Chapter 3 we summarized our criticisms of this research. We argued that it is unwise to attribute causal influence to unobservable psychological states before exploring the influence of more directly observable variables such as patterns of mass media use.

Sears and Freedman (1967) reviewed the literature on selective exposure with specific reference to information. They point out that while studies of the composition of media audiences suggest that selective exposure operates, direct experimental tests for the existence of "psychological preference for supportive information" failed to demonstrate conclusively that such a predisposition guides most information seeking.[20] Researchers were forced to qualify their findings to suggest that selective exposure occurs only under certain conditions: when information is perceived as necessary to support an important decision (Mills, Aronson, and Robinson, 1959), or when information is perceived to reduce cognitive dissonance. However, research using both these conditions has failed to produce consistent findings; Sears and Freedman (1967) conclude that researchers might generate more useful findings if they studied *voluntary* exposure to information rather than exposure compelled by unconscious predispositions. They suggest four factors that can be expected to influence voluntary exposure: education, social class, utility of the information, and past history of exposure to the media.

Later Studies of the Social Influence Model

Subsequent studies of the social influence model, while critical of the two-step flow notion, did not question the basic tenets of the overall model. Troldahl (1966), for example, demonstrated that the mass media sometimes cause followers to seek out leaders. This happens especially when the media communicate information which is inconsistent with an individual's predispositions. Thus the media might be important because they encourage communication which ultimately results in influence. However, if opinion leaders usually share followers' predispositions, they can be expected to reject inconsistent media messages and thus attenuate media influence. Again, social influence was viewed as predominant over media influence.

Lazarsfeld and Menzel (1963) described a "multistep flow" of influence in which several opinion leaders relay information to one another before it is finally passed on to followers. In this conceptualization of the model, media have even less influence. Information must pass through several leaders, any one of whom can act as a "gatekeeper."[21] Thus the logical extension of the social influence model appears incompatible with the view of the media as being even indirectly influential. However, Lazarsfeld and Menzel do suggest that "when it comes to the mere conveying of information rather than the exerting of influence . . . the direct impact of the mass media should be correspondingly greater" (p. 111).

Studies reported in 1970 by Douglas et al. and Bostian suggest a further refinement of the multistep flow model. Douglas et al. report evidence which suggests that personal communication served simply to reinforce and extend a media campaign designed to communicate information about mental health. They conclude, "In this study we have, of course, found strong support for the hypothesis that the media campaign is 'relayed' via interpersonal sources. But instead of counteracting the media campaign as the 'two-step' school holds, the effect was to supplement and extend the campaign. The primary causal agency was the media campaign; interpersonal processes provided a secondary communication campaign" (p. 492).

Bostian (1970) concludes his review of two-step flow studies by arguing that most of them do not establish the existence of a two-step flow for media in general. Rather, he finds that such a flow of influence has been established only for certain media transmitting specific messages to audiences in particular social situations. He criticizes the hypothesis as too simplistic. Bostian cites several reasons why the two-step flow notion is of very limited usefulness in understanding communication in developing nations. Mass communication is often not available. When present, the mass media are typically not looked to for information. When media are seen as relevant for information, they are more influential. Followers often initiate the flow of information. In studying developing nations, information *seeking* should be stressed over information *avoidance.*[22]

Other studies of the social influence model which relate directly to political information are even more critical of its usefulness. Harik (1971) questions the existence of a two-step flow in his study of an Egyptian village. He found that mass media use was highly correlated with political awareness. The only individuals who turned to others for information were those who lacked personal access to the mass media. In this study, interpersonal communication was found to be a "mere conveyor of information," while the mass media created "awareness." Trenaman and McQuail (1961) failed to find evidence of a two-step flow during a political campaign. They reasoned that if such a flow exists, those persons who report more discussion of the campaign (opinion leaders) should report greater attitude change which could be attributed to the mass media.[23] Instead, the campaign was not found to influence the attitudes of either those who discussed more or those who discussed less. However, television apparently increased the political knowledge of everyone since exposure to campaign programming correlated with political knowledge. Blumler and McQuail (1968) found that during a political campaign in Britain, individuals were quite unselective in their viewing of public affairs programs. Only Conservatives with a strong motive to follow the campaign appeared to use the media to reinforce ideas. While these researchers did not observe a big shift in candidate preferences during the campaign, they suggest that such a shift may have occurred prior to the campaign and may, in part, have been influenced by the mass media. Lang (1969–70), in his review of this study, argues that research should be done before campaigns to detect such shifts.

The social influence model can be viewed as a reflection of the mid-twentieth-century society in which it was formulated and evaluated. It depicts a social order in which political influence is divided among many heterogeneous groups. Information flowing from the central government is evaluated by group opinion leaders who interpret it for their members. Their interpretation determines whether information will be received and used. Obviously, this two-step flow places a severe limitation on the power of a central government, whether state or federal. While such a flow of information restricts the ability of government to make rapid social changes, it appears to provide the basis for a stable, gradually evolving society. This model and the data which supported it provided important reconfirmation that the examples of Nazi Germany and Bolshevik Russia would not be repeated in America. Though Kate Smith or Orson Welles might instigate disturbing instances of mass action through the use of the mass media,[24] there were other data which suggested that a leader like Hitler could not influence the average American directly on a continuing basis.

Challenges to the Social Influence Model Assumptions

The sixties challenged many of the assumptions about the American social order which grounded the social influence model. Central governments continued to expand, particularly at the federal level. Simultaneously, the mass media system grew exponentially with the widespread adoption of television. Television viewing replaced interpersonal conversations and meetings as a leisure time activity for some individuals. For everyone, access to mass media greatly improved as the income of Americans steadily increased. The quiescent fifties gave way to a decade of disquieting social movements. Beginning with the civil rights movement, large-scale social movements appeared which linked numerous local groups into relatively cohesive national organizations. The strategies for recruiting, organizing, and maintaining such movements were grounded in the effective use of various forms of mass communication.[25] Such communication provided important links among local groups and made it possible for national leaders to effectively wield the power of their movements. Many social commentators have pointed out that the national news media appeared to provide an important catalyst for such movements by making them appear credible. They did so by conferring status on their leaders and suggesting that they possessed influence far beyond their initial strength. Singer (1973) offers an extended discussion of such an effect upon the civil rights movement.

The growth of such movements suggests a decline in the influence of pluralistic, locally based groups and their traditional leaders. It further suggests the possibilities of using political communication as an effective means of bringing about rapid social change on a national scale. While the influence of many of the movements of the sixties has waned, the basis for their power may not have disappeared. In a later chapter, we shall consider at length the topics of political participation and alienation and the relationship between these variables and political communication. We will attempt to demonstrate more clearly the potential for massive political influence which still exists. In part, the basis for this influence lies in the media of mass communication. A new model of political communication is called for which considers this potential.

Figure 3 depicts the relationship of the social influence studies to the development of television as a medium for political information. The years in which the strongest evidence was found for social influence were the years

Figure 3

CONTIGUOUS EXAMINATION OF THE APPEARANCE OF SELECTED
BENCHMARK POLITICAL INFORMATION AND MEDIA STUDIES WITH THE
DEVELOPMENT OF TELEVISION'S ROLE IN THE POLITICAL PROCESS

Information and Mass Communication Studies	Year	Introduction of Significant Political Information Programming on Television[1]	Television Stations[2] Public	Television Stations[2] Commercial
				Year
Propaganda Techniques in The World War	1927		0	1949 69
			1	1952 108
Radio and the Printed Page	1940	No Television	1	1953 198
			6	1954 402
			11	1955 458
The People's Choice	1944		47	1960 579
			59	1962 571
Mass Persuasion	1946		79	1964 582
	1947	TV Enters Elections	92	1965 589
Some Reasons Why Information Campaigns Fail	1948	Today/See It Now	127	1967 626
	1949		199	1971 695
United Nations Information Campaign	1951	First commercials in political campaigns		
	1952	Political conventions televised		
	1953			
Experiments on Mass Communication	1954			
	1955	Meet the Press		
Personal Influence		Army-McCarthy Hearings		
News Diffusion Studies Include Television[3]	1960	Presidential press conferences		
Diffusion of Innovations The Great Debates	1962	Televised presidential debates		
The Kennedy Assassination and the American Public	1965	Televised coverage of John Kennedy assassination		
	1967			
Politics and Television	1968	National Drivers Test[4]		
Some Reasons Why Information Campaigns Succeed	1973 1974	Public Broadcasting Corporation established		
Watergate and Mass Communication (in press)		Watergate Senate Hearings		
		Impeachment Hearings		

[1] Source for most programs: Erik Barnouw, *The Image Empire* (New York: Oxford University Press, 1970).

[2] Source: Federal Communication Commission, *Annual Report, Fiscal Year* 1971. (Washington, D.C.: U.S. Government Printing Office, 1971).

[3] For example: Deutschmann and Danielson (1960).

[4] Drivers test demonstrated an apparent ability of information broadcasts to directly produce desired actions.

when television was developing as a medium for political information. New uses were being pioneered for television as a vehicle for political campaigns or public affairs. Political conventions were first televised at length in 1952. Public affairs programs like *See It Now* began production in the early fifties. Educational television developed more slowly than commercial television. Only a few stations were operating by the mid-fifties and these were broadcasting content which appealed to a select audience. More recent diffusion studies have demonstrated that television can transmit information effectively to a heterogeneous mass audience. The development of television as a medium for political information may have reduced the relative importance of social influence in transmitting political information.

The Diffusion Model

During the past two decades mass media researchers have developed the diffusion model of communication concurrently with the social influence model. Although the two have long shared many theoretical assumptions and are grounded in similar methodologies, the diffusion model has one central tenet which is in conflict with the social influence model: under certain conditions of access to mass media, for particular social relationships, for certain types of information, media transmission of information will have a direct impact upon individuals and can produce changes in their knowledge, attitudes, or actions. Despite this basic difference, it has been possible for researchers to incorporate most of the findings of social influence research into their conceptual framework. Also, social influence researchers frequently cite diffusion studies as support for their views.

The diffusion model was not the creation of media researchers. Katz, Levin, and Hamilton (1963) and Rogers and Shoemaker (1971) have explained how the model was used by social scientists in several disciplines—notably anthropology, rural sociology, and education—several years before it was adopted by communication researchers. Before that the model was used by physical scientists, particularly physicists.[26] The model still bears some traces of its origins. Strictly interpreted, it describes a mechanistic process. It suggests that messages flow from sources and are eventually absorbed and used by individuals just as rainwater influences the growth of plants. This linear, deterministic process can always be expected to have certain consequences if input variables (rain, messages) are properly controlled. Not many researchers use the model in this way. Most would consider the close comparison of human communication systems to biological systems as useless or even potentially dangerous.

The diffusion model which has been developed is essentially descriptive in nature. It can sensitize communication professionals to potential barriers to communication, or to the process, or to *useful* strategies to encourage desired consequences, but it cannot accurately predict when these strategies will prove successful. It cannot predict when barriers will appear or even how seriously to take various barriers when they do appear. The model certainly cannot begin to predict the output which will result from a given level of input and can only crudely describe the stages through which the input is processed.

These remarks do not imply that the diffusion model has not proved useful to communication research. It has enabled researchers to progress from a stage at which only input and output were observed and correlated to the present stage at which several significant intervening variables in the process have been specified. Let us review the development of this model in communication research.

Early Diffusion Studies

Early studies using the diffusion model were concerned with understanding the transmission of news. They found that when significant news events occurred, most people quickly became aware of them. Apparently, when such information was involved, very few "know-nothings" were likely to be found. Also, interpersonal communication, when it occurred in relation to such information, was likely to play a subordinate role in its transmission. Deutschmann and Danielson (1960) argued that interpersonal communication occurs *after* the mass media transmit information about news events and that it is a *response* to mass media reports. Interpersonal communication with opinion leaders reinforces and supplements information initially received from the mass media.

This view of interpersonal communication contrasts sharply with the view contained in the social influence model. It is a view which has been fairly consistently supported by researchers who use the diffusion model. In part, this consistent support may be due to the research designs they use. Just as social influence research has often attributed a priori influence to interpersonal communication variables, diffusion research designs have frequently begun with the assumption that "independent messages flow down from mass media to mass audiences." The studies were designed to measure the extent to which messages diffused. Typically, the messages studied were simple to understand and repeated frequently by the mass media. Often, the messages concerned news events.[27] The messages were considered to have had an impact if substantial numbers of people learned something from them.

Early diffusion studies usually omitted important variables which might have permitted the development of more complete explanations of the diffusion process. Thus, the way in which individuals used the mass media when they received the message was not considered. It was assumed that most people want to learn about news events and that the mass media are simply serving this basic interest in news. Only rare attempts were made to determine how accurately people learned about events, how long they remembered news about events, or whether news about events affected important beliefs, attitudes, or behavior. The findings of early studies are not invalid but their narrow design limits their usefulness.

Several studies support the view that the mass media are the predominant source of information about political news events. Larsen and Hill (1954) found that the media informed most people about the death of Senator Taft. Interpersonal discussion *followed* effective transmission of news about the event. Danielson (1956) identified radio and newspapers as the most effective sources of information about Eisenhower's decision to seek the Presidency a second time. The Deutschmann and Danielson (1960) study described above found radio and television to be the most effective media in informing people about the Explorer satellite, Alaskan statehood, and an illness of President Eisenhower. In several other studies the broadcast media were found to be the primary sources of information about the following events: a local racial incident (Warren, 1972), the dropping of Eagleton as vice-presidential candidate (Sheinkopf and O'Keefe, 1973), and the assassination of President Kennedy (Mendelsohn, 1964; Greenberg and Parker, 1965). Only in the case of the last event has the predominance of the mass media been questioned. Spitzer (1964–65) cited studies which suggest that inter-personal communication was as important as mass communication. He argues that the media may be important sources of information about poli-tical news events except in the case of extremely important events such as the assassination. However, even for such events, the contribution of the media is significant because it is unlikely that interpersonal communication does more than relay information initially received from the mass media.

These findings are of limited usefulness because, while they demonstrated that the mass media are capable of transmitting information about significant events, they do not permit us to ascertain the impact of this information beyond increasing the level of public knowledge. Danielson (1956) attempted to assess the impact of Eisenhower's announcement to seek reelection upon attitudes and found the effect very limited. Respondents were *not* more likely to say they would vote for Eisenhower but did see an improvement in Republican chances for winning the election. Republicans showed increased optimism about peace and prosperity but Democrats did not. Warren (1972) found that diffusion of information about a racial incident in Detroit seemed to polarize the attitudes of blacks and whites. Persons who got news from television showed the greatest polarization in their views of the incident. These views were demonstrated to persist for several weeks. On the other hand, persons who heard about the incident from neighbors showed less polarized attitudes. However, it may be misleading to infer that television viewing caused people to develop extreme views. Persons with initially polar-ized attitudes may have been more likely to use television as a source of information.

Rogers' Use of the Diffusion Model

For more than a decade, Everett Rogers has continued to be the most system-atic and comprehensive researcher using the diffusion model, His book *Diffusion of Innovations* (1961) is one of the first efforts to elaborate this model for use in communication research (elaborated further by Rogers and Shoemaker, 1971). Though many of the propositions summarized by Rogers are derived from previous research by others, his synthesis has proved instructive. The primary advantage of Rogers' approach lies in the explication of a multistage process underlying innovation transmission. The transmission of information is only a part of this process, albeit an essential part. Rogers' approach links the transmission of information to a variety of social and psychological effects. Information from the mass media is viewed as capable of initiating acceptance of innovations when the right social conditions are present. This conceptualization has served to guide and synthesize research concerned with only one or two stages of the overall process. Thus each stage could be studied separately and the social or mass communication variables which affected each stage could be specified. Such isolated studies then could be synthesized into a larger framework. Findings on information transmission could be integrated with findings on why people are persuaded to adopt a new invention.

Rogers and Shoemaker (1971) identify four stages of innovation diffusion: information or knowledge stage; persuasion stage; decision or adoption stage; and confirmation or reevaluation stage. In general, the mass media are viewed as predominant only in the information stage. The media can create an interest in an innovation and create an understanding of it which facilitates the completion of the subsequent stages. Under certain conditions the mass media can dominate these later stages as well. For example, when an innovation is simple to understand, easy to adopt, and communicated about by a respected mass media source, individuals are likely to adopt it without much additional communication. Modern advertising appears to be heavily dependent on this principle for its success. For this reason, advertising could be expected to fail in a developing country where most products would be unfamiliar, hard to understand, and difficult to adopt.

Rogers and Shoemaker believe, with the social influence researchers, that interpersonal communication is predominant under most conditions during the last three stages for most people. An individual can be expected to look to others for confirmation and interpretation of the information he gets from the mass media. In the case of the transmission of most significant, complex innovations, only a few extraordinary individuals can be expected to be persuaded by the mass media information alone. These individuals, whom Rogers initially labeled "innovators," are typically relatively affluent, risk-taking persons. They are willing and can afford to speculate on the adoption of something merely because the mass media present information about it. When these individuals prove that an innovation can be used successfully, community leaders will adopt it. The majority of persons will eventually be influenced by these leaders to adopt. However, the ability of the media to convince even a few innovators to adopt an innovation may be critical for the overall process.

Rogers' model is primarily concerned with the diffusion of material inventions. He argues for its applicability to the transmission of new ideas or ideologies in advanced industrial nations, but its usefulness has been empirically demonstrated best for the transmission of inventions or specific techniques in developing nations. There are some reasons to question the applicability of this model to the transmission of political information in the United States. Unlike a new agricultural practice, the significance of such information can rarely be demonstrated empirically. Thus innovators cannot influence community leaders merely by showing them that an innovation will have immediate practical benefits. Furthermore, the literature in political science or political communication can demonstrate no consistent correlation between level of knowledge and certain types of political actions. Actions may precede knowledge, as when a person votes for a candidate and then becomes informed about him when he takes office. Innovators in politics may exercise much greater relative influence than innovators in agriculture without the necessity of persuading masses of people to follow their example; a political innovator may change a government bureaucracy to conform to his knowledge and ideas, while very few members of the public who support him have any knowledge of or concern about his reasons for acting as he does. This difference partially accounts for why political scientists have historically focused their concern about political communication on communication that goes on within and between certain elite groups. They believed it was more important when a particular political leader was converted to an ideology than when relatively large numbers of uninfluential people were converted.

Diffusion and Selectivity

The notions of selective exposure, perception, and retention are an essential part of the social influence model. Diffusion researchers have generally not found these concepts useful. In part, this lack of use stems from the effects which were usually observed by researchers studying the diffusion of information about news events. In contrast to the complex opinion or behavior change effects which Lazarsfeld et al. (1944) sought to associate with exposure to the mass media, diffusion researchers have often been content to associate knowledge of an event with exposure to a news report about the event, although recently, more demanding research designs, such as that advocated by Rogers, have used more conceptually interesting dependent variables. In general, early diffusion researchers were simply concerned with demonstrating that certain messages would be accepted by large proportions of the public. The messages tested rarely were threatening to social groups. They were publicized well and were simple to understand so that even systematically uninformed people were likely to know something about them. Thus levels of exposure were often so high that researchers were unconcerned about explaining why a relatively small minority failed to become informed.

Another factor which discouraged diffusion researchers from considering selectivity was the fact that they usually found that interpersonal communication played a minor role in the transmission of information about news events. Since opinion leaders who acted as "gatekeepers" were not found, their selective predispositions could not affect what the majority of the public found out about an event.

Diffusion researchers have developed a concern about conditions which may mediate the flow of information about events. It is important to note how these conditions differ from those posited earlier by social influence researchers. Often these conditions can be viewed as patterns of media perception or media use. These patterns are clearly the result of learning which occurs in some social context. While these patterns can result in de facto selectivity, they do not wholly determine reception. Messages which disrupt normal patterns of media perception and use will be received and responded to.

Earlier, we argued that emphasis on patterns in the perception and use of the mass media offers an important alternative to emphasis on selective exposure in the conceptualization of information transmission and its effects. Such patterns can be observed more directly and can be linked to specific situations in which they are learned. In addition, the effects of variables like education can conceivably be traced to the impact which they have on patterns of media perception and use. For example, educational institutions may exert continuing influence throughout an individual's life because of the way they teach students to perceive and use mass media for information. McCombs and Mullins (1973) suggested that college students learn habits of scanning the mass media for information. Scanning of the media raises the students' interest in politics, which leads them to seek out specific political information. It may be erroneous to assume that education's greatest influence lies in the *quantity* of knowledge, rather than in the *approach* to knowledge, which it instills. Nevertheless, educators generally neglect teaching how to use media to acquire knowledge. It may also be a mistake to conceive of interest as an independent variable. Interest in a subject may rise when media use habits enable an individual to acquire a critical amount of knowledge about an area.

According to the concept of patterns of media perception and use, individuals exercise a certain degree of voluntary control over their behavior. The selectivity model presumes that individuals are unconsciously predisposed to avoid or distort or forget certain types of information. On the other hand, if individuals learn patterns of media use, though these patterns may routinely structure an individual's behavior, the individual can consciously choose to break them. Thus a man can choose to forgo Sunday afternoon football to watch a program his children prefer. This does not mean that the range of voluntary control over patterns of media perception and use is great. Dominant patterns may be rarely changed. Most people use media in highly specific, routinized ways. Only extraordinary circumstances upset such uses of the media and produce unusual effects. The explication of media use patterns which follows provides an addition to the diffusion model and the basis for understanding the transactional model of mass communication which is developed in Chapter 5.

Media Perception and Use Patterns

Patterns of media perception and use can be divided into several categories. These categories, which differentiate the functions of various sets of patterns for the overall process of information diffusion, include the following: (1) *attention*—patterns which accelerate the flow of information by increasing the likelihood that individuals will attend to information; (2) *trust*—patterns which increase the acceptance of the truthfulness and usefulness of information by increasing people's trust in various mass media of communication; (3) *accuracy*—patterns which increase the flow of accurate, undistorted information by increasing people's ability to interpret information correctly; and (4) *interpersonal communication*—patterns which reinforce the flow of information by encouraging interpersonal communication about the information.

Although other categories could be mentioned, these four illustrate the thrust of this argument. We shall discuss each of them along with research which illustrates how it can be studied. Taken together, these categories constitute an explanation of how, in certain situations, the mass media can serve as powerful channels of information which ultimately have an important impact on the political process. For example, a combination of patterns which compel attention to a message, make it appear credible, ensure its accurate transmission, and reinforce it through interpersonal communication would provide the media with an audience which receives the message and acts in terms of it. Likewise, of course, when these patterns are absent, or further, when the patterns present are functionally opposed to these, then the media can be expected to exert little or no influence. As we shall see, there is every reason to believe that our society is encouraging many patterns which are increasing the influence of the media, at least for certain segments of our population. However, certain institutionalized activities, like political campaigns, may temporarily reduce the influence of certain media messages. As we indicated in Chapter 3, people may perceive many campaign messages as partisan propaganda.

Attention Patterns

Media researchers have long been concerned with specifying social and psychological variables which explain the public's attention to the mass media. Social influence researchers explained attention by the selective exposure model. Some individuals were conceived of as predisposed by psychological states to seek certain content and avoid other content. Unfortunately, the notion of selective exposure was frequently taken for granted by researchers and rarely systematically evaluated in field settings. Researchers identified a substantial minority of the population as "chronic know-nothings." Hyman and Sheatsley (1947) found persons in this category to be much less interested in public affairs topics. Presumably, such persons remained uninformed because they did not seek out or actively avoided information about public affairs. Only when they talked to other people were they likely to become informed. As we saw above, however, the flow of interpersonal influence is not unstructured. Opinion leaders tend to be like followers. Followers are most likely to be influenced by persons like themselves. Thus it would follow that "know-nothings" are most influenced by other "know-nothings." Research on the two-step flow should not lead to confidence that personal communication will always fill in gaps left by mass communication.

Media perception and use patterns which affect the flow of information can be categorized into two types. One type consists of those patterns in which an individual voluntarily uses a medium to seek out specific information. The second type involves those patterns which encourage generally high levels of media use so that information is learned incidentally. Patterns of the first type can be referred to as information-seeking patterns. Patterns of the second type can be labeled incidental learning patterns. Persons exhibiting the first type of pattern are said to be *using* the media, whereas persons exhibiting the second type are said to be gratifying needs. Both types result in exposure to the media but the consequences of this exposure may differ greatly.

INFORMATION-SEEKING PATTERNS. Some researchers have argued that individuals seek out information which has the greatest personal relevance for them. Information may be relevant for a variety of reasons. Adams, Mullen, and Wilson (1969) argued that news about a papal encyclical should be most relevant to Catholics. While Catholics were only slightly more likely to have heard of the encyclical (60 percent Catholics versus 55 percent non-Catholics), 24 percent of the Catholics tried to verify the event by checking another communication medium while only 11 percent of the non-Catholics did so. Thus, while exposure levels were similar, the news of this event led to greater action by those for whom it was relevant.

Hanneman and Greenberg (1973) point out that studies of information seeking motivated by personal relevance have produced contradictory results. They report that O'Keefe and Timothy[28] did not find heart specialists any more likely than other doctors to seek out news about the first heart transplant. Their own study attempted to define personal relevance in a more useful way. They differentiated two important dimensions of this variable for diffusion of a papal encyclical: religiosity and salience. They found that religiosity was related to hearing of the encyclical and being able to accurately recall information about it. Salience was defined as the amount of interest a person had in the encyclical and its perceived importance. Salience was found to be related to telling others about the encyclical.

Sheinkopf and O'Keefe (1973) report that relevance was a factor in the diffusion of news about McGovern's decision to drop Eagleton as a vice-presidential candidate. Though almost everyone in their sample had heard of the event (92 percent), those who were registered party members were more likely to have talked about it.

The results of studies using personal relevance as a variable have not been impressive in explaining exposure to information. McLeod (1965) found that party affiliation or political attitude did not predict information seeking from Madison newspapers nor did these variables predict what individuals learned from the papers. Party members who attended to one of two politically conflicting newspapers were as likely to learn information which ran counter to their political position as were non-party members. Chaffee and McLeod (1973) have argued that variables like personal relevance may not be useful in predicting whether a person will seek political information. They report that on the basis of their research "there seems to be no consistent information seeking pattern due to relevance based on intention to vote" (p. 240). Instead, they found that those persons who had discussed the campaign more or who anticipated discussing the campaign in the future were the most likely to request campaign literature. These persons were presumed to seek information because of the communication utility which it served for them. Thus communication utility may result in the development of information-seeking patterns. Atkin (1972) has reported several findings which confirm the usefulness of this variable. Discussion of a political campaign was found to be significantly correlated with exposure to newspaper coverage, magazine campaign coverage, television political convention coverage, and television news and public affairs programming. Atkin points out, however, that individuals do not seem to plan to use the media for this purpose. "Instead, users may routinely seek information for short-term storage without a target conversation clearly in mind" (p. 198). Atkin suggests that it may be useful to differentiate types of communication utility.

Starck (1973) has suggested that people have systems of values which determine which media they choose for information. His findings indicate that the mass media are more likely to be used than interpersonal communication when an individual is seeking information relevant to the values "imaginative" and "world of beauty." His research indicates a need to specify media use patterns which are related to personal values.

The McCombs and Mullins (1973) study cited above suggests that it would be useful to isolate habitual media scanning patterns which are produced by education. These very general patterns of media use may provide the basis for other, more specific patterns such as the seeking of political content. McCombs and Mullins found some evidence of this. Further study of media perception and use patterns seems likely to reveal that certain patterns cause or reinforce other patterns. Thus, a habit of reading newsmagazines which is encouraged by parents may be reinforced by the personal relevance of political information and the communication utility of that information. It would not be wise for media researchers to exclude certain patterns from consideration because they appear to serve similar functions. Another study by McCombs (1968) consisted of a secondary analysis of Survey Research Center data. He found that media use for political information had increased sharply among blacks during the period from 1952 to 1964. Most of this increase was accounted for by increased use of television for political information. This political use of television may have been an offshoot of an initial increase in their access to and use of television for entertainment.

A more recent paper by Kline (1973) has suggested an approach to studying information campaigns which combines personal relevance and communication utility. Persons were asked to list societal problem areas that they considered important and were asked about their discussion of these problem areas with others. Preliminary analysis of a data set showed evidence of greater information seeking when topic areas were of personal relevance and persons were likely to talk to others. Lazarsfeld, Berelson, and Gaudet (1944) pointed out that individuals appear to use several media for the same information. People who use one medium during a political campaign for information are more likely to use other media. This finding may reflect the overlap of various media use patterns. Use of media for one purpose makes it more likely that another medium will be used for the same or different purposes. Thus information seeking could "snowball" so that individuals become highly informed. In the opposite case, the absence of certain general media use patterns might explain "chronic know-nothings."

Several studies have indicated that information campaigns fail because they do not attract the attention of audiences. Wright (1955) argues that the Star-Hughes campaign to promote the United Nations failed because only those persons who had an initial interest in or opinion about the United Nations paid attention to it. It is important to know those social factors which create interest in or opinions about a topic. A media campaign designed to influence these factors might attract more attention. When campaigns are able to gain the attention of audiences they can succeed. Douglas et al. (1970) showed that a campaign can increase information and that this increase in information can produce a change in attitudes which is consistent with the information, not with other attitudes held by the person. A review of successful campaigns by Mendelsohn (1973) suggests the necessity of delineating target audiences that are likely to be receptive to particular messages. While the mass audience may be unreceptive to a single message, a well designed campaign using a variety of messages in several media should be successful. For example, Mendelsohn points out that the CBS program, "National Driver's Test," was apparently able to encourage a threefold increase in enrollment in driver improvement programs. The program broadcast a variety of messages each of which may have been able to overcome the indifference of a segment of the audience. Mendelsohn is not optimistic about the power of the media to influence social change, but he argues that the potential for encouraging such change may exist if social scientists can devise effective strategies for reaching particular audiences.

INCIDENTAL LEARNING PATTERNS.   Researchers have noted that the transmission of political information often has the greatest impact upon beliefs, attitudes, or behavior when the individual is relatively uninformed. However, persons who are uninformed are also the least likely to attend to informational messages. If what we have argued in the preceding section is true, persons remain uninformed if they have developed few information-seeking media use patterns. These persons will not be reached by an information message unless it interrupts their normal use of the mass media or is somehow a part of the messages which they normally receive. Let us consider patterns of media use which are intended to gratify other needs but which may result in the reception of information under certain conditions.

Kelley (1962) argues that many people view political campaigns as a game. They watch the game because of the excitement or drama with which it is played. Thus, the Great Debates between Kennedy and Nixon were sought out by many viewers because of the inherent entertainment which they offered and not because these viewers desired to become informed about the candidates. Blumler (1969) found that producers of a series of election campaign analysis programs in Britain made a deliberate attempt to attract and hold an audience for their program by increasing its entertainment value. A program format was selected which highlighted the dramatic, exciting, tragic, comic, or ironic possibilities of campaign situations. Producers perceived this format as a means of relieving the boredom of the campaign.

Similar attempts by public affairs program producers to attract persons who are not seeking information are apparently successful. Lang (1969) points out that Blumler and McQuail (1968) found that audiences for British public affairs programs during the campaign of 1964 included persons who expressed low interest in politics and low participation in political activities.

Wamsley and Pride (1972) have argued that news or public affairs programs, which attract some people primarily because of their entertainment value,[29] should influence these persons in several ways. They contend that broadcasts which highlight dramatic events have an emotional impact which makes the information they contain more significant. Coverage of specific dramatic events may stand out and serve as potent symbols which focus people's attention during a campaign. They argue that this focusing may result in gradual, long-term shifts in public attitudes, especially among those who use the media for gratification.

Patterson and McClure (1973) concluded that television commercials most affected the beliefs of those persons who had some interest in the information presented but were unwilling to attend to alternate sources requiring greater effort. This finding suggests that information-seeking and incidental learning patterns of media use may reinforce one another. Where the former are weak, uses of the media for gratification may result in learning information. Thus commercials which are both entertaining and informative may reach a particular audience and change its beliefs. Patterson and McClure found no evidence that such short-term changes in beliefs had any effect on an individual's political attitudes. However, they contend that if enough belief changes occur over a sufficient period of time, attitudes may be influenced. They reject the hypothesis that campaign commercials can produce immediate changes in political attitudes.

McClure and Patterson (1973) found evidence that television news can have an impact on beliefs. They found that persons with low political interest were likely to change their beliefs about McGovern in a direction consistent with information being presented on television network evening news broadcasts. Apparently, such persons had little reason to doubt the veracity of network news and were not motivated by sufficient interest or alternate media use patterns to check this information against other sources. Persons attracted to news broadcasts because of their entertainment value may learn information from them which would not be validated by other sources. Blumler and McQuail (1968) found evidence of this in Britain. They concluded that television campaign broadcasts had the greatest influence on marginally involved voters. They attributed this influence to the nonpurposive viewing of these voters and their lack of resistance to counterpropaganda.[30] Future research should ascertain the size of this category of viewers[31] and attempt to gauge the extent to which their beliefs and their attitudes on political matters can be shaped almost exclusively by television.

Credibility

Besides attention, a second important factor in the transmission of information may be people's willingness to regard a particular medium or a particular source as trustworthy. Experimental research has suggested that source credibility is an important variable in the transmission of information and ideas from a speaker to his audience.[32] While this variable has been shown to influence the transmission of information by mass media in experimental settings, we lack conclusive data on its influence in everyday life situations. We do, however, have much information about people's willingness to express a trust in various mass media as sources of news or information. Roper surveys continue to show that television is increasing its trustworthiness relative to newspapers. Forty-eight percent of the respondents in a 1972 national survey said they would trust a news story reported by television most over conflicting stories in newspapers or on radio or in magazines.[33] This credibility extends beyond a trust in the accuracy of news content. Many people even regard the situations depicted in television entertainment content as real.

This credibility may be an important source of media influence. When media are credible people may tend to rely heavily on them for certain types of information. This appears to be especially true of specialized media, such as special interest magazines. One of the few findings of media influence in *The People's Choice* study (1944) was the apparent influence of a specialized magazine, *Farm Journal*, on voting intention. Several studies report people's perception of reliance on newspapers for local news information: Alexander (1969), The American Institute (1969), Rarick (1970), McClenghan (1973) and O'Keefe and Spetnagel (1973). These studies, however, do not explore the social situations which produce and sustain this relationship of trust. Such knowledge would provide greater understanding of how certain media are able to transmit particular kinds of information which cannot be transmitted by other media.

In the discussion in Chapter 6 we shall deal at length with the power of the media to influence public conceptions of reality. Much of this power may derive from the public's inability to perceive a difference between the way in which the mass media represent situations and the way those situations are in reality. In a sense, the public can be said to lack a "critical distance" from media content. Thus, the world as presented each evening by Walter Cronkite may be all too readily accepted by many individuals.

Just as attention to various media and their messages may be linked to social variables, it should be possible to link such variables to media credibility and dependence on particular media for knowledge of "reality." Almost no research exists in this area, particularly research which uses political variables. Some suggestive studies have been conducted. Singer (1973) cited evidence that American blacks were encouraged to organize and act for social change because they trusted the television portrayal of the growing success and power of the civil rights movement. Thus blacks, because of their dependence on television and their willingness to trust its messages, were apparently reached by a wide variety of political information and opinions.[34] In this way, television may be shaping the very reality that it purports to depict. In the case of television coverage of racial incidents such as those described by Warren (1972), trust in television messages may help polarize views of crucial events.

As we pointed out in Chapter 3, election campaigns may influence the degree to which individuals trust messages from the mass media. McClure and Patterson (1973) argued that McGovern was not able to effectively communicate his arguments about corruption in the Nixon administration because the public expects to be confronted by partisan views during a campaign and rejects most as partisan propaganda. Blumler and McQuail (1968) have argued that this is one of the reasons why political attitudes change so little during a campaign. They argue that it is likely that attitudes change more frequently before campaigns start. A campaign may actually "freeze" the attitudes of most persons while at the same time rapidly increasing their store of political information. Only after the campaign will this information begin to have its effect on attitudes. They believe that this partially accounts for why major shifts in party affiliation seem to occur when no campaign is taking place. In the 1964 election they studied, a large shift to the Labor Party had occurred prior to the campaign, but the shift did not continue during the campaign.

Nevertheless, media may serve as credible and influential sources of certain kinds of information during campaigns. McClenghan (1973) found that in local elections in Texas, 90 percent of the candidates endorsed by newspaper editorials won the election.[35] This relationship was found despite the fact that content analysis could discover no overt, systematic bias in the news coverage given opposing candidates. There was if anything a tendency for nonendorsed candidates to be pictured more often. McClenghan argues that in local elections few alternate, credible sources of political information exist. Individuals apparently assume that newspaper editors are informed enough to make decisions that are worth following. Further research is necessary to determine whether media are more influential in local races. Most attention has been given to national election contests.

Accuracy Patterns

Accurate or undistorted perception of information can be linked to several media use patterns. These patterns in turn are shaped by social situations. Mass communication research has revealed that people's willingness and ability to interpret mass media information accurately both vary greatly. However, the ability to interpret information accurately is not as well correlated with existing attitudes and values (as implied by the selective exposure model) as it is with such variables as age, education, and socio-economic status. Tichenor, Donohue, and Olien (1970) and Tichenor, Roden-kirchen, Olien, and Donohue (1974) have reviewed a number of studies concerned with accuracy of information transmission and have conducted several original surveys. Their work indicates that several media use patterns are being encouraged by our society which lead to differential transmission of information. They have argued (1970) that one of the results of this is an increasing knowledge gap between persons in different social strata; persons with better educations and higher status are more likely to be able to read science news and then give accurate reports of what they have read. Apparently these persons have been taught how to read and understand information contained in print media. These acquired patterns of media use give them effective access to information which is denied to persons who have not learned to use media in this way. This knowledge gap can be viewed as the logical outcome of the way in which our society has structured access to various media. Access to print media is restricted by the failure of school systems to teach more than basic literacy. On the other hand, a medium like television is available to everyone, but because it transmits a minimal amount of information it is likely to be used primarily for entertainment. In fact, as we have argued above, attention to television for gratification purposes by blacks and by persons in particular social strata may be encouraged. Tichenor et al. (1974) report evidence that when conflict situations arise in communities and encourage attention to media for conflict-related information, this information can close the knowledge gap. Apparently situational factors can produce specific media use patterns which overcome the effects of other general patterns of media use.

Research conducted in other nations suggests that media can bridge the knowledge gap when media content contains much information and this information is repeated frequently. Bishop (1973) posited that television could be an effective medium for transmitting political information successfully over such barriers as low education. McLeod et al. (1968–69) found modest correlations between media exposure and political knowledge which are consistent with Bishop's views. Harik (1971) found even more impressive correlations between knowledge and media use among poorly educated

Egyptian villagers. Reviewing American studies, Robinson (1972) indicates that high exposure to an issue through the mass media can produce accurate knowledge of the issue despite differences in education.

This research highlights the necessity of specifying those variables which explain why persons develop patterns of media use which enable them to obtain accurate information from the media. This research should not simply probe why some people are better able to understand messages from certain media. We ought to know why some individuals are able to approach such information more critically and to arrive at judgments about it which are based on the evaluation of information from other sources. No one message, no one source, no one mass medium should be expected to communicate the only necessary information about any topic.

Yet, as noted previously, many people attend exclusively to television for news and political information. There is some reason to doubt that television can transmit political information accurately. Wamsley and Pride (1972) point out that television news broadcasts are typically chaotic. They follow no set order, interject reporters into events, focus on dramatic, visually exciting events, and condense much information into a very short period of time. Their suspicions about the effectiveness of such news broadcasts are confirmed by McClure and Patterson (1973), who found that immediately after a network news broadcast most respondents could not recall what they had seen. McClure and Patterson conclude that the brevity of most campaign stories (the average length was 100 seconds) creates a "montage effect" that reduces the impact of information even though substantial proportions of news time are devoted to election coverage.

Westley and Barrow (1959) found evidence that individuals can learn to receive information accurately from the mass media. They studied more than 200 grade school students and found that some had learned news seeking attitudes which enabled them to accurately perceive the relevance of information for them and to apply it in structuring their views of the environment. These students were no more likely to exhibit short-term learning from media presentations but were more likely to recall information after time elapsed.

A series of studies conducted by the Wisconsin Mass Communication Research Center (see Chapter 2 Abstracts and Bibliography for a consideration of some of the most important research produced by this group) indicated that certain family situations encourage accurate use of the mass media, particularly the use of television for public affairs information (Chaffee, McLeod, and Wackman, 1966). Children in families that encourage free and argumentative discussion of social and political topics are more likely to use television for public affairs information. Children in families which discourage such discussion and seek close control of children's behavior tend to use television more for entertainment. This research suggests that the family plays an important role in developing certain media use habits which later enable individuals to seek out information and process it accurately. A 1970 study (Chaffee, Ward, and Tipton) established that those adolescents who used television and newspapers for information in May knew more about a political campaign in November.

Kraus, Meyer, and Shelby (1974) have isolated yet another factor which may affect the accurate perception of information from the mass media. Because their study took place during a political campaign, its findings may be limited to campaign situations. Nevertheless, the results are intriguing. They report that exposure to the media was *negatively* correlated with knowledge of political candidates. They argue that "selective retention" or the "clutter effect" may account for this result. A political campaign may so overload some individuals with information that they selectively forget some of it. Thus there may be real limits to the quantity of information which the media can communicate accurately during a campaign.

Research is necessary to determine what media use patterns permit or encourage accurate perception of information. What social situations encourage such patterns of use? Can families or schools teach media use patterns that facilitate access to certain types of information and insure accurate processing of it? What are the societal consequences of inaccurate transmission of political information, especially during political campaigns?

Reinforcement by Interpersonal Communication

The influence of certain mass media messages may be greatly increased by discussion of these messages after exposure to them, especially when discussion is routinized and when it occurs in response to certain types of messages. Individuals who can expect to interact with others after exposure to the media may tend to increase their attention to the media (communication utility). Routine discussion of media content can be viewed as an essential part of certain patterns of mass media use. Such patterns may vary in the degree to which they are formalized by society.

Rogers and Shoemaker (1971) have described how radio forums in developing nations such as India greatly increase the effectiveness of mass communication. These forums routinize discussions of informative media content. Village residents gather to listen to an informative program on agriculture. After the program, discussions are led by person(s) knowledgeable in agriculture. Rogers and Shoemaker argue that in this situation the radio informs while discussion makes the information relevant to the farmers and persuades them to put the information into practice. Such discussion should also greatly improve the accuracy with which information is transmitted. Individuals who misunderstand the media can be corrected and information which has been missed by some can be resupplied by others.

Atkin (1972) has argued that when interaction and discussion can be expected to follow political campaign coverage, individuals are more likely to expose themselves to media coverage. He uses the concept of communication utility to refer to this expectation. He observed significant correlations between media exposure and interpersonal conversations. In addition, he cites a study of high school students which indicated that when students were told they might discuss a topic area, they were subsequently more likely to recall relevant content from mass media presentations. Sheinkopf, Atkin, and Bowen (1973) provide additional support for the view with their finding that 65 percent of political party workers interviewed reported that viewing television political advertisements was useful to them "for subsequent persuasion activities." Chaffee and McLeod (1973) found evidence that people read partisan political pamphlets to be able to discuss their side intelligently.

Tichenor et al. (1970) suggest that one of the reasons why a knowledge gap is growing in our society is that those who are uninformed lack social contacts which might encourage them to seek media-provided information and to process it accurately. Warren (1972) reports findings that indicate that only those persons who relied on interpersonal communication to find out about a racial incident were likely to become consistently less polarized in their views of the incident. Those who relied on mass media tended to become more polarized over a six-week period. Discussion of this subject may have served to make the views of some persons less extreme.

Toward a Transactional Model

In the last section we argued that diffusion of information by the mass media is dependent upon the development of four patterns of mass media perception and use. These patterns assure that the media will be *attended to*, be perceived as *credible* and relied upon for information, be *interpreted accurately*, and be *reinforced by interpersonal communication*. Where such patterns exist the media can act as powerful transmitters of information. It is clear that this power of the media is grounded in social situations which give rise to these patterns of media perception and use. However, once formed, these patterns can give media the power to reshape the situations which initially gave them influence. This is why, in certain situations, the media can instigate change in a basically quiescent social order. Once patterns of media perception and use are formed, the social situation which produced them may lose its influence over the individual. For example, if parents teach their children to regard television as a babysitter and encourage them to spend much of their leisure time in front of the television, the patterns of media perception and use which the child learns are likely to increase the probability that he will be more influenced by television than his parents.

This argument suggests that every national system of mass communication is linked with a particular social order in a relationship which is potentially symbiotic but also potentially destructive. The social order produces patterned use of the media system and in this way grants the media a certain sphere of influence within the nation. The media system in turn gives the nation certain new capacities for social change, cultural enrichment, and amplification of knowledge.

Under certain conditions a social order may foster uses of the mass media which are detrimental. Just as parents can unsuspectingly surrender influence over their children, mass media may be granted an inordinate amount of influence. Thus in some societies masses of individuals may come to place too much reliance on certain media for certain purposes and fail to evaluate the accuracy of the messages which they receive. In such a social order, it is possible that a few individuals could control the actions of most other members of society.

This analysis of information flow points toward a new approach to the evaluation of national mass media systems. This approach would focus on media use patterns and the social situations which teach these patterns. These social situations and use patterns are, of course, related to the political system of a nation, its technological development, and the development of the mass media. However, this relationship is not a simple one.[36] We can expect to find as many similarities as differences in comparing situations and use patterns in totalitarian and democratic nations. Such comparative studies could provide much insight into the nature of media systems and their relative power for a particular nation. It is clear that media systems cannot be regarded as simple amplifying transmitters. One does not increase the information flow in a society simply by building more television sets or by publishing more newspapers.

The view we have presented here goes beyond a diffusion model of information flow. It can be more appropriately regarded as a *transactional model of communication flow*. In this model the flow of influence does not simply come down from sources of mass communication. The messages from these sources are only part of the process. Influence also is grounded in social situations. These situations teach individuals the value of carrying on certain transactions with the mass media and in some cases reward individuals for carrying on these transactions. Media influence can be created or destroyed from the "top" or from the "bottom." In addition, because this influence is ultimately situated in patterns of media perception and use, the potential remains for individuals to resist some forms of influence.

Bauer (1964) argues that a transactional model of the communication process provides the most useful approach to understanding mass media influence. He points out that while media effects are not always direct, media do have such effects when people choose to use them in certain ways. Bauer cites a communication study done in the Soviet Union by Inkeles in which respondents failed to mention political meetings as a source of information about what was happening despite the fact that such meetings were common. Later they realized that respondents were telling them where they heard information that they wanted to know, not where they learned what the government wanted them to know. Persons most involved in the government made extensive use of word-of-mouth sources as a means of understanding official media. Thus patterns of media use developed which best served the needs of the individual and which, in this case, moderated the influence of the mass media.

The transactional model suggested by Bauer has not been systematically developed. Two new trends in communication research may support a renewed effort to develop such a model. These trends are the *uses and gratifications* approach and the *agenda setting* approach. Together these approaches may eventually provide a body of research findings which enable us to begin to specify (1) the range of uses which people have for the mass media, (2) the way in which people assimilate and apply media content which they do use, (3) the ways to organize and present media content so that it will be used, (4) the types of transactions in which media content is offered and accepted, and (5) the social consequences of existing patterns of media use.

In subsequent chapters we will elaborate the transactional model and demonstrate how it can be evaluated and revised building on the results of studies employing the uses and gratifications and agenda setting approaches. The transactional model recognizes the necessity for broad social participation in the development of any national media system. For a system to have maximal effectiveness it should be responsive to the needs and desires of the public. In considering political participation and alienation we have attempted to demonstrate that a political communication system will not be effective unless it responds sensitively to the perceptions which people have of the mass media and the *patterned* way in which they use the media.

In subsequent chapters we will also argue that a mass communication system can provide a means of shaping political policies through transactions with the public. Such transactions should encourage increased political participation. The basic alternative to this approach is the use of the mass media system to "sell" political policies with one-sided, one-way promotional communication. Although this strategy seems to have gained acceptance with many politicians, it may be conducive to widespread political alienation. The transactional model suggests an alternate approach to political communication which is more consistent with the democratic ideals that underlie the media system implicit in the First Amendment to the Constitution.

Notes

1. John Dewey presents a systematic argument for a particular structuring of public education to serve democratic goals in *Democracy and Education* (New York: Free Press, 1966; a reprint of a 1916 publication).
2. Gerbner has made a similar argument. See George Gerbner, "Toward a General Model of Communication," *Audio-Visual Communication Review* 4 (1956): 171–99.
3. F.S. Siebert, T.B. Peterson, and W. Schramm, *Four Theories of the Press* (Urbana: University of Illinois Press, 1956).
4. James W. Markham, *Voices of the Red Giants* (Ames: University of Iowa Press, 1967).
5. For a discussion of how Europeans have attempted to shape their mass media systems to serve social objectives see Chapter 5, "Programs: Information" in Berton Paulu, *Radio and Television Broadcasting in the European Continent* (Minneapolis: University of Minnesota Press, 1967).
6. Jerome Barron provides an extensive review of this subject in *Freedom of the Press for Whom?* (Bloomington: Indiana University Press, 1973).
7. Perhaps the most systematic attempt to set policy for American television broadcasting is the Report of the Carnegie Commission on Educational Television. See *Public Television, A Program for Action* (New York: Bantam Books, 1967).
8. George Orwell, *1984* (New York: Harcourt, Brace, 1949). For other recent analyses of the media see Ben Bagdikian, *The Information Machine* (New York: Harper & Row, 1971), p. 303, and Robert MacNeil, *The People Machine* (New York: Harper & Row, 1968), p. 325.
9. For a discussion by a social scientist of the apparent effects of war propaganda see Harold D. Lasswell, *Propaganda Techniques in the World War* (New York: Knopf, 1927). Though Lasswell notes some important limitations of propaganda, he concludes that it is "one of the most powerful instrumentalities in the modern world" (p. 220). He argues that emotional appeals can trigger massive effects.
10. Elihu Katz and Paul Lazarsfeld have reviewed some of this research in *Personal Influence* (New York: Free Press, 1955), pp. 15–30.
11. This model was first discussed as an empirical generalization emerging from the 1940 election campaign study reported in P.F. Lazarsfeld, B. Berelson, and H. Gaudet, *The People's Choice* (New York: Columbia University Press, 1948).
12. See Katz, Levin, and Hamilton (1963) for a discussion of the origin of this model.
13. DeFleur has argued that the term "hypodermic needle" model does not adequately communicate the implicit psychological assumptions which underlie this model. He has introduced the term "mechanistic stimulus-response model" which is a more adequate, though less well known, label for this model. See M. DeFleur, *Theories of Mass Communication* (New York: David McKay, 1970), pp. 112–18.
14. Lasswell, Leites, and Associates describe how content analysis was used to establish

that antidemocratic propaganda was being disseminated by a pro-German magazine, *The Galilean*. See *Language and Politics* (Cambridge: M.I.T. Press, 1965), pp. 173–232.

15. See DeFleur (1970, pp. 112–18) for a similar discussion of this model.

16. Colin Cherry has discussed the apparent effectiveness of Goebbel's propaganda and points out that it was only after World War II that the limitations of his work were discovered. See *World Communication: Threat or Promise* (New York: Wiley-Interscience, 1971), pp. 115–16.

17. We have chosen to treat the notions of social influence and selective exposure as parts of the same paradigm. Many researchers do not do so. Not suprisingly, most experimental studies have evaluated selective exposure as a purely psychological phenomenon. However, the concept of selective exposure is useful for prediction and explanation only if large numbers of people are guided by similar predispositions. It is our view that such predispositions would be most likely to arise in group situations. Thus the two concepts can be said to be inextricably interwined.

18. Hyman and Sheatsley introduced this term into the communication literature. "Know-nothings" could not be reached, let alone influenced by the mass media. The authors comment, "Instead there is something about the uninformed that makes them harder to reach, no matter what the level or nature of the information" (p. 413).

19. Only fashion leaders were found to attribute greater influence to the media. Results were inconclusive for other leaders (p. 318).

20. Information-seeking behavior has been studied at least indirectly since quantitative studies of mass media audiences were initiated. For example, the research reported by Paul Lazarsfeld in *Radio and the Printed Page* (New York: Duell, Sloan and Pearce, 1940) compares use of radio and newspapers for news. Recently researchers have studied information seeking more directly. These researchers are concerned about the voluntary, systematic, and habitual use of particular media for information which serves certain purposes. Thus some individuals can be isolated who consistently choose to read newspaper reports of election campaigns because they believe that these reports will aid them in their voting choices. This research is concerned about specifying *patterns* of use of the mass media for information, not simply counting how many people read the newspaper. We refer to several such studies later in this chapter.

21. The concept of the "gatekeeper" has been used frequently by researchers who study mass media bureaucracies. One of its earliest uses was in a study by David M. White, who analyzed some of the criteria which guide wire-service news editors in deciding what to print. Because these men allow only a small amount of the news which comes in over the wire to be printed, they can be said to act as "gatekeepers." Subsequent studies have used the term to refer to individuals or groups who exercise control of the information which other persons receive. See D.M. White, "The 'Gate Keeper': A Case Study in the Selection of News," *Journalism Quarterly* 27 (Fall 1950): 383–90.

22. Bostian's call for more research on information seeking is reasonable given the present state of communication research. Previous studies have speculated on and probed many of the reasons why information is avoided but have not systematically studied information-seeking patterns. It is important to learn how such patterns are formed and what can be done to encourage them. This does not mean that information avoidance should not be studied but that such research needs to be balanced by information-seeking studies.

23. This coincides with the reasoning of Katz and Lazarsfeld (1955) discussed previous-

ly. Opinion leaders should report greater exposure to and influence by the mass media. This influence is then transmitted to followers. Katz and Lazarsfeld only found this to be true for fashion leaders. It is important to note that this rationale hypothesizes a "two-step flow" of *influence.* Such a flow may not exist even though a "two-step flow" of *information* is present. Researchers have frequently confused these two types of "flows," perhaps because transmission of information has often been considered synonymous with influence.

24. See R.K. Merton, *Mass Persuasion; The Social Psychology of a War Bond Drive* (New York: Harper & Brothers, 1946) for a case study of the impact of Kate Smith's war bond appeal. H. Cantril, H. Gaudet, and H. Hertzog considered the impact of Welles' invasion from Mars radio hoax in *The Invasion From Mars* (Princeton, N. J.: Princeton University Press, 1940).

25. See Sidney Kraus, "The Role of the Mass Media in Social Movements," paper presented at the Annual Meeting of the Speech Communication Association, Chicago, December 1972.

26. For a review of research in physics using diffusion models, see Wilheim Jost, *Diffusion in Solids, Liquids, Gases* (New York: Academic Press, 1952).

27. See, for example, Deutschmann and Danielson (1960), Larsen and Hill (1954), and Sheinkopf and O'Keefe (1973).

28. G. O'Keefe and M. Timothy, "The First Heart Transplant: A Study of Diffusion Among Doctors," *Journalism Quarterly* 46 (Spring 1969): 237–42.

29. In recent years local television news formats have been altered to include elements of entertainment. Music, jokes, brightly colored settings, and film and tape renditions of "news" with comic overtones have found their way into the newscasts.

30. One of the pretelevision findings was that the voting behavior of those least informed was most susceptible to influence (Lazarsfeld, Berelson, and Gaudet, 1944). However, such persons were not likely to be exposed to campaign information. Television would appear to have increased the likelihood that such persons will be exposed to political information.

31. Some estimate of the size of this group can be made by considering that a Roper survey in 1972 showed that 33 percent of the public relies on television exclusively for news and refers to no other media. Sixty-five percent say that they are most likely to become acquainted with candidates for national office by watching television. Fifty-four percent say that television gives them the clearest understanding of candidates and issues in national elections. Roper Organization, Inc., "What the People Think of Television and Other Mass Media" (New York: Television Information Office, 1973).

32. See C. Hovland, I. Janis, and H. Kelly, *Communication and Persuasion* (New Haven: Yale University Press, 1953); C. Hovland and W. Weiss, "The Influence of Source Credibility on Communication Effectiveness," *Public Opinion Quarterly* 15 (1951): 635–50; and W. Weiss, "A 'Sleeper Effect' in Opinion Change," *Journal of Abnormal Social Psychology* 48 (1953): 173–86. See also B.S. Greenberg and G.R. Miller, *The Effects of Low Credible Sources on Message Acceptance: Four Experimental Studies in Persuasion* (East Lansing: Michigan State University, 1966); K.E. Anderson and T. Clevenger, Jr., "A Summary of Experimental Research in Ethos," *Speech Monographs* 30 (June 1963): 59–78; and S.W. Littlejohn, "A Bibliography of Studies Related to Variables of Source Credibility," in N.E. Shearer, ed., *Bibliographic Annual in Speech Communication* (New York: Speech Communication Association, 1971), pp. 1–40.

33. Roper, 1973, p. 3.

34. We have previously documented the viewing behavior of blacks (see Chapter 2 and Greenberg et al., *Use of the Mass Media by the Urban Poor* [New York: Praeger,

1970]), and we have referred to the political socialization of this minority group. It is interesting to note the difference in trust which blacks feel for the mass media on one hand and the government on the other. Blacks trust television and do not trust the government and the political system generally. Arthur Miller et al., "Social Conflict and Political Estrangement, 1958–1972" (paper produced by the Center for Political Studies of the Institute for Social Research at the University of Michigan, 1974) found that between 1968 and 1972 blacks' trust in government deteriorated four times as rapidly as that of whites. Singer's data should be considered along with the data presented by Kent Jennings and Richard G. Niemi ("Media Exposure and Political Discourse," unpublished paper, 1973) reported in Chapter 2. They found that as blacks took more civics courses in high school, their dependence on television for political items decreased.

35. Other studies of the effectiveness of editorial endorsements will be discussed in Chapter 5.

36. Several studies point to these variables as paramount in successful nation-building. We are particularly impressed by Daniel Lerner, *The Passing of Traditional Society, Modernizing the Middle East* (New York: Free Press, 1958) and Leonard W. Doob, *Communication in Africa, A Search for Boundaries* (New Haven: Yale University Press, 1961). Lerner has demonstrated that "rising media participation tends to raise participation in all sectors of the social system" (p. 62) and Doob observes:

> It is always important to note, when possible, who has understood or responded favorably to a communication and who has not. In a miscellaneous group of adult males, whom the chief of a small village in Northern Nigeria once hastily assembled as this writer and his friends suddenly appeared, only one old man could be found who had any knowledge about world affairs, including some recent developments in the field of atomic warfare. To all the rest it seems the mass media had failed to communicate such information, but with him they had been successful, undoubtedly because he alone in the village had a radio. (pp. 330–31)

Abstracts and Bibliography

Adams, John B., James J. Mullen, and Harold M. Wilson. "Diffusion of a 'Minor' Foreign Affairs News Event." *Journalism Q*. 46 (Autumn 1969): 545–51.
A field study was conducted following Pope Paul VI's national statement about his views on birth control, tracing how the news of the event was disseminated to the American public. The study confirmed previous hypotheses of diffusion of events isolating sex, education, and age as important variables.
Method: survey; questionnaire. *Statistics*: chi-square. *Pop. (N)*: 2646 respondents in 13 American cities.
Findings: (1) The hypothesis that more learners of the event would be male, possess a higher education, and be young rather than old was confirmed. (2) The interviews began about 6 hours after the first word reached America. 55% of the respondents had heard of the event by the time they were called. (3) Catholics, who were predicted to be more concerned about the event, were more likely to have heard the event, have attempted to verify it, and to have others tell them about it, than were people of other religious denominations. (4) 39.6% of the respondents first learned of the statement through newspapers, 30.3% through radio, and 26.8% through television.

Alexander, Herbert E. "Communications and Politics. The Media and the Message." *Law Contemp. Probl.* 34 (Spring 1969): 255–77.

Alper, S.W. and T.R. Leidy. "The Impact of Information Transmission Through Television." *Pub. Opin. Q.* 33 (Winter 1969–70): 556–62.

This study measured students' knowledge of constitutional rights and obligations. The students were polled before and after viewing the CBS National Citizenship Test. The study also included those who had not viewed the program.

Method: survey; questionnaire. *Statistics*: single-factor analysis. *Pop. (N)*: 4515 high school students.

Findings: There was a significant difference between viewer and nonviewer groups in both knowledge covering information presented in the program and also opinions covering that information. There was also a follow-up study 6 months after the presentation, utilizing questionnaires from 9000 students. Trends indicated that the impact of the National Citizenship Test on knowledge and attitudes had dissipated but had not disappeared.

The American Institute for Political Communication. *Evolution of Public Attitudes Toward the Mass Media During An Election Year*. Washington, D.C.: American Institute for Political Communication, November 1969.

Anderson, Bo. "Opinion Influentials and Political Opinion Formation in Four Swedish Communities." *Int. Soc. Sci. J.* 14, 2 (1962): 320–36.

Arons, L. and M.A. May. *Television and Human Behavior*. New York: Appleton-Century-Crofts, 1963.

Atkin, Charles K. "Anticipated Communication and Mass Media Information-Seeking." *Pub. Opin. Q.* 36 (Summer 1972): 188–99.

An analysis relating news media use to interpersonal discussion of news events indicates a positive relationship between the amount of interpersonal discussion and exposure to relevant mass media materials.

Method: survey; questionnaire. *Statistics*: frequencies. *Pop. (N)*: 167 Wisconsin adults, 69 Wisconsin high school seniors.

Findings: (1) Information seeking comprises two modes of message exposure: information search and information receptivity. (2) "An individual seeks information for communicatory utility when he perceives a likelihood of face-to-face communication on a topic" (p. 191). (3) "The number of groups in which news is discussed often correlates significantly with the number of newspapers read daily and is positively related to the amount of time spent reading newspapers and magazines" (p. 191). (4) "The basic pattern of mass media use of the high school seniors in this study is one of strong receptivity to useful content but very little active information search" (p. 197). The basic thrust of the findings is that if the person attending to the media anticipates social uses for what he learns, this "communicatory utility" of the media exposure will lead to increased interpersonal communication.

Bailey, Robert Lee. "Network Television Prime-Time Special Political Programs." *J. Broadcast.* 12 (Summer 1968): 287–88.

The article is a brief summary of a doctoral dissertation indicating that a large number of special programs from the years 1948–66 could be characterized as "political." There are four types of political program: speeches by candidates or supporters; debates; programs produced by networks about candidates; and convention and election returns.

Findings: From 1948 to 1966 (excluding 1948 convention coverage) stations presented 398 political programs preempting 551 hours and 33 minutes of regular prime-time programs.

Barnow, Erik. *A Tower in Babel*. New York: Oxford Press, 1966.

Bauer, Raymond A. "The Obstinate Audience: The Influence Process from the Point of View of Social Communication." *Am. Psychol.* 19 (1964): 319–28.

Berelson, Bernard. "Communications and Public Opinion," in Wilbur Schramm, ed., *Communications in Modern Society.* Urbana: University of Illinois Press, 1948, pp. 167–85. See abstract in Chapter 3.

Berelson, Bernard, Paul F. Lazarsfeld, and William McPhee. *Voting: A Study of Opinion Formation in a Presidential Campaign.* Chicago: University of Chicago Press, 1954.

Bishop, Michael E. "Media Use and Democratic Political Orientation in Lima, Peru." *Journalism Q.* 50 (Spring 1973): 60–67, 101.

The author investigates the relationship between media use, political knowledge, and political orientation in Lima, Peru. There has been little empirical study in this area. The results indicated the following flow of relationships: political information seeking predictors → mass media use → political knowledge → democratic political orientation. For these people, it is possible that media use compensated for education in acquiring political knowledge.

Method: survey; questionnaire. *Statistics*: cross-tabulations, Simon-Blalock causal analysis. *Pop. (N)*: 632 male subjects, 18 and above. Multistage, stratified sampling. *Findings*: (1) Highest political interest and media use were among younger members of the sample. Political knowledge was highest for middle-age respondents, and democratic orientation was most commonly found among older respondents (p. 64). (2) Probably paths of causal relationships fit closest in the path from mass media through political knowledge to democratic orientation. (3) The results indicate that the adult male in Lima may be able to compensate for lack of education with high media use in order to shore up political knowledge (p. 67). (4) In addition to their direct contributions to increasing political knowledge, the media may be important in a causal process leading to democratic orientation (p. 67). (5) The results reported here suggest that a pattern of political information seeking in a relatively free media system may be associated with the acquisition of a democratic orientation.

Blackman, Edwin T. "Patterns of Information-Seeking in Presidential Campaigns." Unpublished master's thesis, University of North Carolina, 1968.

Blumberg, Nathan B. *One-Party Press?* Lincoln: University of Nebraska Press, 1954.

Blumer, H. "Suggestions for the Study of Mass Media Effects," in E. Burdick and A.J. Brodbeck, eds., *American Voting Behavior.* Glencoe, Ill.: Free Press, 1959, pp. 197–208.

Blumler, Jay G. "Producers' Attitudes Towards Television Coverage of an Election Campaign: A Case Study." *Sociol. Rev. Monogr.* 13 (January 1969): 85–115.

The author studies producers' attitudes toward television coverage of an election campaign in England. He groups these attitudes under four headings: "the structure of rules and policies that is supposed to govern their activities; their sources; the needs of their audience; and the events they are supposed to cover" (p. 86). *Method*: interview; observation. *Pop. (N)*: BBC political program producers. *Findings*: The producers' strategy for strengthening the contribution of television to the 1966 campaign embraced at least four objectives. (1) "They aimed to encourage party spokesmen to confront each other in face-to-face discussions" (p. 88). (2) "The producers were keen to help to promote a top-level party leader debate between the Prime Minister and his Conservative and Liberal counterparts" (p. 88). (3) "The producers were determined to circumvent any attempts by one or another political party to veto the airing of an election issue by refusing to supply a speaker to discuss it on television" (p. 89). (4) The producers wished to ensure that television did not pay more attention to the Liberal Party than it deserved. The general influences on producers were the following: the internal role definition of their position to which television journalists subscribe; the character of the existing body of rules and policies; and the place of producers in the authority structure of the BBC. Two styles of producer-audience relationship were revealed: a sacerdotal approach versus a pragmatic approach to election coverage. The sacerdotal type of producer tended to think of himself as providing a "service" and of an election as an intrinsically important event which entitled it to substantial coverage as a right, while the pragmatic type denied the intrinsic right of election material to program prominence and repeatedly asserted that it must "fight its way in" on its merits. They wished to avoid creating any impression that they felt obliged to cover the campaign.

Blumler, Jay G. and Denis McQuail. "Television and Politics." *New Society* 12 (5 December 1968): 834–35.
An inquiry into use and influence of television in the British general election of 1964, this article stems from a book written by the authors, *Television in Politics*.
Conclusions: (1) Though the less politically committed viewer is often less informed than the politically committed viewer, his capacity to learn about politics during an election campaign is not markedly inferior to that of a more interested viewer. (2) There is "an inverse relationship between social status and an interest in political personalities" (p. 834). (3) 36% of the less educated respondents claimed to notice the promises of campaigning politicians first, compared with only 13% of those who had stayed at school to age 16 or later. (4) "The proportion of respondents who said that the promises of campaigning politicians were 'usually unreliable' rose from 28% of those who were most politically interested to 54% among the least interested" (p. 834). (5) Political communication needs of the mass audience include easy access to political material, material which is understandable and geared to the capacity of the ordinary viewer, and communication in which ordinary people could place trust and confidence. (6) 48% of the sample, when asked how they preferred politicians to appear on television, opted for debate between candidates, 39% chose interviews with well-known television reporters, 10% preferred straight talk (p. 835).

Bogart, Leo. "Changing News Interests and the News Media." *Pub. Opin. Q.* 32 (Winter 1968–69): 560–74.

Bonato, Roland Richard. "The Effect of Source Credibility and Amount of Information on Opinion Change." Doctoral dissertation, University of Connecticut, 1961.

Bostian, Lloyd R. "The Two-Step Flow Theory: Cross Cultural Implications." *Journalism Q.* 47 (Summer 1970): 109–17. Assessing research on the 1940 Lazarsfeld et al. hypothesis, the author finds little support for explaining the communication process, except in personal influence. He advances propositions for testing the hypothesis in developing countries. "The two-step flow hypothesis appears to explain very few communication situations and is likely too simplified a concept for great utility in explaining the process of communication" (p. 116).
Conclusions: (1) There is a need for research which separates the relay function from the influence function. (2) There is a need to reevaluate ideas about the flow of information, especially the concept of an opinion leader as a voluntary transmitter of information. (3) The type of information being transmitted must be specified, and its usefulness to the receiver must be considered.

Bradley, Rulon Le Mar. "The Use of the Mass Media in the 1960 Election " Doctoral dissertation, University of Utah, 1962.

Brinton, J.E., C.R. Bush, and T.M. Newell. *The Newspaper and Its Public*. Stanford University Institute for Communication Research, 1959.

Brody, Richard A. and Benjamin I. Page. "The Impact of Events on Presidential Popularity: The Johnson and Nixon Administrations." Paper presented at annual meeting of the American Political Science Association, Washington, D.C., 5–9 September 1972.

The impact of news events on the president's popularity was indicated in this study. The authors proposed a "news discrepancy theory" which "postulates that the presidential popularity remains at a constant level as long as the news events are congruent with it; any discrepancies in the quality of the news event and the previous level of popularity will cause a shift in the direction of the discrepancy" (p. 11). Using a time-series study the popularity of the Johnson and Nixon administrations was compared with the events in Viet Nam and foreign and domestics news.

Method: survey, interview. *Statistics*: correlations, frequencies, multiple regression analysis. *Pop. (N)*: national sample, Gallup poll data.

Findings: (1) "Foreign and Viet Nam news had far more effect than domestic news on the popularity of both Presidents" (p. 16). (2) "Viet Nam news affected Johnson powerfully about twice as much as it affected Nixon" (p. 16). (3) "These were the years of heavy impact from foreign news" (p. 16). (4) "Some news may not have to be 'front page' to affect judgments of presidential performance" (p. 16). (5) "According to the news discrepancy theory, presidential popularity has great inertia; without a change in the balance of news, the level of popularity remains the same from one period to the next" (p. 17). (6) "Worse news did tend to lower Nixon's popularity, and better news did raise it, but news discrepancy correlated only .28 with opinion change, and could account for only 8% of the variance in it" (p. 18). (7) "For the Johnson administration ... news events have effects which are partly permanent and partly temporary" (p. 19). (8) In the Johnson administration, the theory can account for fully 84% of the variance in the level of presidential popularity. For the Nixon administration the findings are weaker but still substantial, being 55% of the variance.

Campbell, Angus. "Has Television Reshaped Politics?" *Columbia Journalism Rev.* 1 (Fall 1962): 10–13.

Chaffee, Steven H. "The Interpersonal Context of Mass Communications," in P.J. Tichenor and F. Gerald Kline, eds., *Current Perspectives in Mass Communication Research*. Beverly Hills, Calif.: Sage, 1973, pp. 95–120.

Chaffee, Steven H. and Jack M. McLeod. "Individual Vs. Social Predictors of Information-Seeking." *Journalism Q.* 50 (Summer 1973): 237–45.

Across measures of information-seeking, comparisons of the predictive power of social variables with individual variables show that differences were greater for the social predictors in 28 of 32 comparisons; this suggests that social variables are greater in predictive power than are individual variables.

Method: survey, questionnaire, *Statistics*: percentages. *Pop. (N)*: 221 Wisconsin residents (middle-aged).

Findings: (1) Those respondents who were determined to vote showed somewhat more interest in information supporting the candidate they intended to vote for, but were less likely to request the opposition and neutral information. There was no consistent information-seeking pattern due to relevance based on intention to vote. (2) The League of Women Voters' Pamphlet (neutral information) was much more popular than partisan pamphlets. Only one respondent in four asked for more than one pamphlet. Of the partisan pamphlets, there is a tendency to prefer that of one's own candidate. (3) There was a tendency to request the neutral pamphlet information and ignore the partisan pamphlet information among those who had already had the partisan communication from party workers. (4) While local party activity may have considerable influence on voting behavior, it appears to have little impact on information-seeking patterns. (5) Those respondents who said they were more interested in politics than their friends requested more opposition, impartial, and total pamphlets and fewer of their own candidates pamphlets. Those who felt their political interest level was the same as that of their friends were more likely to request a pamphlet

edge of the content covered by the broadcast. (2) The respondents in the experimental group changed their opinions to a significant degree in the direction of the predictions (of the commentator). The results indicated that exposure to a commentator's remark do change opinions and attitudes. (3) There is evidence indicating that the experimental group evaluated the news commentator somewhat more favorably than did the control group.

Funkhouser, G. Ray and Maxwell E. McCombs. "The Rise and Fall of News Diffusion," in Lee Thayer, ed., *Communication Theory and Research*. Springfield, Ill.: Charles C. Thomas, 1967, pp. 289–309.

Gieber, Walter and Walter Johnson. "The City Hall 'Beat': A Study of Reporter and Source Roles." *Journalism Q*. 38 (Summer 1961): 289–97.

Gilkinson, Howard, Stanley F. Paulson, and Donald E. Sikkink. "Conditions Affecting the Communication of Controversial Statements in Connected Discourse: Forms of Presentation and the Political Frame of Reference of the Listener." *Speech Monogr*. 20 (November 1953): 253–60.

The study's findings were similar to those of past studies of listener perceptions, in that the respondents' own bias and frame of reference affected the ways they perceived information.

Method: experiment; questionnaire. *Statistics*: chi-square. *Pop. (N)*: 476+.

Findings: (1) The subjects showed greater facility in the recognition of statements which conform to their bias than statements running counter to their bias. (2) "Both the Democratic and Republican subjects recognized more pro-Republican than pro-Democrat statements, but the trend was significantly stronger among the Republicans" (p. 259). (3) "The trend toward 'biased' listening was equally strong among men and women." (p. 259). (4) "The trend toward 'biased' listening was not affected by the forms of presentation employed" (p. 259).

Glock, Charles Y. "The Comparative Study of Communication and Opinion Formation." *Pub. Opin. Q*. 16 (Winter 1952–53): 512–23.

The author outlines some of the problems connected with understanding the influence of the mass media and informal channels of communication in the formation of opinion on a comparative world-wide basis. How accessible are the media to different segments of the population? What is the relationship between accessibility and actual exposure? What are the restrictions on accessibility and what are the resistances to exposure?

Conclusions: (1) Although one medium may be responsible to only one group, it may not be effective for a variety of reasons. For example, the minority group in Turkey (non-Moslems) are most exposed to radios, but the Moslems control the country. Therefore, the radio medium will have little effect on Turkey's political system. (2) Images of the media and general attitudes toward the media vary across cultures.

Greenberg, Bradley S. "Media Use and Believability: Some Multiple Correlates." *Journalism Q*. 43 (Winter 1966): 665–70, 732.

This study of media use reveals that television is as widely used as a principal news source as is the newspaper. Also, television is the more credible source. This study attempts to pinpoint factors that cause an individual to prefer one medium over another.

Method: survey; questionnaire. *Statistics*: frequencies. *Pop. (N)*: 500 adults.

Findings: (1) "The sex of the respondents by itself was significantly related to media credibility; 78% of the women and only 61% of the men would believe a television news report more than one in their newspaper" (p. 667). (2) "The less educated were more likely than the better educated to believe the television version of the news story than the newspaper version." (3) "Among respondents under 30, 72% chose television as the medium they would believe. 78% of those in their thirties made the same choice, 74% of those in their forties and 63% of those fifty and over. . . . Among the men, the younger were more likely than the older to choose television: 67% of those under thirty and 51% of those over forty. . . . Among women, however, the relationship was not linear" (p. 668). (4) "More women (56%) than men (40%) chose television over newspapers as the medium they depended on most for the news around them" (p. 668). (5) "Of the respondents with no college, 60% said they used television more, whereas only 33% of those with a college degree chose television" (pp. 668–69).

Greenberg, Bradley and Edwin Parker, eds. *The Kennedy Assassination and the American Public*. Stanford: Stanford University Press, 1965.

Hanneman, Gerhard J. and Bradley S. Greenberg. "Relevance and Diffusion of News of Major and Minor Events." *Journalism Q.* 50 (Autumn 1973): 433–37.

This study of the news diffusion of a major and minor papal encyclical indicates that news dissemination may be as much a function of the relevance and salience of news as of news value.

Method: survey; questionnaire. *Statistics*: frequencies. *Pop. (N)*: 228 persons; 147 persons.

Findings: (1) The more religious the respondent, the more likely he was to have heard the Pope's messages. (2) The more salient the message, the more likely the respondent told someone else, and the strength of this relationship across events attests to the utility of the predictions. (3) Neither religiosity nor salience predicted the accuracy of respondents' recall of the Pope's message for the second event, yet both were predictive for the first event. This may be attributed to the content of the messages.

Harik, Iliya F. "Opinion Leaders and the Mass Media in Rural Egypt: A Reconsideration of the Two-Step Flow of Communication Hypothesis." *Am. Polit. Sci. Rev.* 65 (September 1971): 731–40.

This study was conducted to determine how mass media messages reach the population of the village, to identify mediators of information, and to assess the relationship between mass media exposure and political awareness.

Method: survey; questionnaire; chi-square. *Pop. (N)*: 135 (men, ages 18–60).

Findings: 48% got information directly from mass media, 37% orally from mediators. (1) The study does not strongly support or disconfirm the two-step flow hypothesis. (2) The author confirms a positive but not commanding relationship between mass media and political knowledge.

Hill, Ruane B. "Political Uses of Broadcasting in the U.S. in the Context of Public Opinion and the Political Process, 1920–1960." Unpublished doctoral dissertation, Northwestern University, 1964.

Hovland, C.I., A.A. Lumsdaine, and F.D. Sheffield, *Experiments on Mass Communication*. Princeton: Princeton University Press, 1949.

Hyman, Herbert H. and Paul B. Sheatsley. "Some Reasons Why Information Campaigns Fail." *Pub. Opin. Q.* 11 (Fall 1947): 412–23.

The authors suggest that even if all physical barriers to communication were known and removed, many psychological barriers to the free flow of ideas would remain.

Method: survey; questionnaire. *Statistics*: frequencies. *Pop. (N)*: national NORC samples.

Findings: (1) There exists a group of uninformed persons who are hard to reach no matter what the level or nature of the information. (2) People tend to expose themselves to information which is congenial with their prior attitudes and avoid exposure to information which is not congenial. (3) A person's perception and memory of materials shown to him are often distorted by his wishes, motives, and attitudes.

(4) Once individuals are exposed to information they change their views differently, each in the light of his own prior attitude.

Jacobson, Harvey K. "The Credibility of Three Mass Media as Information Sources." Unpublished doctoral dissertation, University of Wisconsin, 1967.

Jacobson contends that studies of the credibility of mass media sources have been deficient in theoretical framework and objective measurement. His study is an attempt to advance a conceptualization of source credibility in the mass media, to isolate components, and to investigate the ability of four receiver variables to predict the connotative judgments of three mass media as sources of news. He uses four independent variables: preference, believability, use, and belief system. His independent variable, judgment of the source, was measured by means of an index whose twenty word-pairs were designed to measure credibility and noncredibility judgments. *Method*: survey; questionnaire. *Statistics*: frequencies. *Pop. (N)*: 627 adult Wisconsin residents.

Findings: A comparison of the three media as sources of news revealed that television was the most preferred source, newspapers the most used, and television the most believable. The results suggest that credibility is a multidimensional concept operative principally in the perception of newspapers, to a lesser extent for television, and little for radio. The results also indicate that the traditionally used unidimensional Roper question on believability should be employed with caution.

Katz, Elihu. "The Two-Step Flow of Communication: An Up-to-Date Report on a Hypothesis." *Pub. Opin. Q.* 21 (Spring 1957): 61–78.

Although this particular hypothesis has undergone a test by several studies, each study has attempted a different solution to the problem of taking into account interpersonal relations.

Conclusions: (1) Opinion leaders and the people whom they influence are very much alike and typically belong to the same primary groups. (2) Influentials and influencees may change roles when the sphere of influence changes. (3) Interpersonal relations are channels of information, sources of social pressure, and sources of social support, and each relates interpersonal relation to decision making in some different way.

Katz, Elihu and Paul F. Lazarsfeld. *Personal Influence: The Part Played by People in the Flow of Mass Communication*. Glencoe, Ill.: Free Press, 1955.

Katz, Elihu, Martin L. Levin, and Herbert Hamilton. "Traditions of Research on the Diffusion of Innovation." *Am. Sociol. Rev.* 28 (April 1963): 237–52.

Kelley, Stanley, Jr. "Campaign Debates: Some Facts and Issues." *Pub. Opin. Q.* 26 (Fall 1962): 351–66.

This article discusses the use of media by politicians during the early 1960s (after the Nixon-Kennedy debates). At issue in the article are the following: What are the alternatives to debates? How well do these alternatives work in stimulating political thinking in the electorate? Is rescinding Section 315 the only way to get debates on television? Some suggestions for style and format changes in debates are given, as are some tactics for using television for political campaigning.

Conclusions: (1) Politicians, through polls, surveys, and letters, have concluded that media use for campaigning is constructive and effective. (2) "The producers of party television programs have been engaged in an effort to make them visually interesting and to introduce audience participation, conflict, and other entertainment features into them" (p. 354). (4) "Audience survey data convinced politicians that voters are far more interested in hearing what candidates have to say for themselves than in hearing what other party leaders have to say for and about candidates" (p. 355). (5) Politicians say that the undecided voters are the voters least likely to watch political television shows. (6) "Political television in its usual forms cannot effectively compete for audiences with commercial entertainment" (p. 356). (7) Television news departments have discovered that a sizable section of the mass media audience is interested in the game aspects of elections. (8) The proponents of future debates are recommending the suspension of Section 315, the only question being whether the suspension be permanent or temporary.

Kline, F. Gerald. "Sources and Impact of Political Information in the 1972 Elections." Paper presented at annual conference of American Association for Public Opinion Research, Asheville, N.C., May 1973.

Past studies, summarized by Kline, point to a reinforcement function only in a consideration of the effect of mass media in a political campaign. That is, it had been generally assumed that conversion from Democrat to Republican does not usually happen for a person in the course of a political campaign through mass media effects. However, Kline's assumption was rather that "the *minimal* consequences in the context of political campaigns may be maximal when compared to other short-term forces at work" (p. 3). Kline begins by first offering data which give evidence that the media do set the agenda in a political campaign. He next measures such variables as candidate preference and partisan stability against the agenda-setting function of the media and ascertains the consequences. He found a strong relationship between agenda-setting and certain variables, among them candidate preference and partisan stability. Data collected from network news by Kline; other data are from Market Opinion Research of Detroit, National Media Analysts, Washington, D.C., Sindlinger and Co., Swarthmore, Pa., and Vanderbilt Television News Archive, Nashville, Tenn.

Kraus, Sidney, Timothy Meyer, and Maurice Shelby, Jr., "Sixteen Months After Chappaquidick: Effects of the Kennedy Broadcast." *Journalism Q.* 51 (Autumn 1974): 431–40.

This study charts media use by the public when coupled with a "salient media event," such as occurred when Senator Edward Kennedy made a television appeal to his constituency after the Chappaquidick incident.

Method: survey; questionnaire. *Statistics*: frequencies; cross-tabulation. *Pop. (N)*: 230.

Findings: Those who viewed Kennedy's 10-minute speech 16 months earlier were revealed likely to have voted in 1970, to have had a high interest in the campaign, to be female, to be heavy media consumers, to have recall of Kennedy's speech, and to have avoided Nixon's election eve television address. In general, the speech seemed to move the "fallen-away" Kennedy voter back to the fold. The astounding finding is this: heavy media consumers exhibited a *lower* recall of candidates. In this instance, counter to much else in this area of research, *media exposure was related to decreased learning.*

Lang, Gladys Engel and Kurt Lang. "The Inferential Structure of Political Communications: A Study in Unwitting Bias." *Pub. Opin. Q.* 19 (Summer 1955): 168–83.

This comparison study of three television networks' coverage of the same public event refutes the "alleged neutrality of video," for although no difference in proffered contextual information was in evidence, the preconceptions on which each network developed its own particular coverage showed through.

Method: content analysis; observation.

Findings: (1) The crucial variables in the structure of each particular coverage were: "(a) interpretation, or lack of interpretation, of a particular incident or picture unit affects the focus of attention; (b) the timing of specific information contributes to the frame of reference into which incidents and picture units are fitted; (c) this frame of reference upon crystallizing tends to overshadow subsequent information to the point at which even specific news information is ignored; (d) the television network's tone or attitude toward the convention, both explicit and implied, affects cognition and interpretation even when critical faculties are exercised" (p. 171). (2) "In his selection of dominant materials (picture and proceedings vs. development and interpretation), in his timing and linkage of these, the telecaster leaves his peculiar imprint on the event by creating an atmosphere and a set of expectations which constitute a context for interpretation of visual materials and of the 'facts' of the event itself" (pp. 181–82). (3) "Networks thus addressed themselves to three different interests inferred among the audience. In spite of their commitment to unbiased and accurate reporting, the networks failed to evaluate the possible effect due to the manner of reporting" (p. 182).

Lang, Kurt. "Book review of Jay G. Blumler and Denis McQuail, *Television in Politics: Its Uses and Influence*." *Pub. Opin. Q.* 33 (Winter 1969–70): 645–48.

Lang, Kurt and Gladys Engel Lang. "Ordeal by Debate: Viewer Reactions." *Pub. Opin. Q.* 25 (Summer 1961): 277–88.

Larsen, Otto N. and Richard J. Hill. "Mass Media and Interpersonal Communication in the Diffusion of a News Event." *Am. Sociol. Rev.* 19 (August 1954): 426–33. The study gives us insights into how information is diffused both through mass media and interpersonal sources in two different community settings: a university faculty community and an interracial laboring class. More people learned the news from a mass media source than through interpersonal communication. Larsen and Hill study the diffusion process through the observance of the public response to the deaths of President Roosevelt and Senator Taft. Differences in the acquisition of knowledge and information evolve between males and females and communities. *Method*: survey; questionnaire. *Statistics*: frequencies. *Pop. (N)*: 2 communities, university faculty community and laboring class, interracial community (256 total). *Findings*: The faculty community learned the news earlier than the laboring class community. Females learned the news earlier than males. Once the news became known similar patterns of interpersonal communications followed. Radio was the single most important initial source of news in both communities.

Lazarsfeld, Paul F., Bernard Berelson, and Hazel Gaudet. *The People's Choice*. New York: Columbia University Press, 1944.

Lazarsfeld, Paul F., Bernard Berelson, and Hazel Gaudet. "Radio and the Printed Page as Factors in Political Opinion and Voting," in Wilbur Schramm, ed., *Mass Communications*. Urbana: University of Illinois Press, 1960, pp. 513–26. This article discusses the results of the Erie County study of the presidential election of 1940. The authors were able to discern what media sources were used most and by whom. The general findings indicate that radio was a more credible source of information than newspapers, and that the individuals most likely to keep well informed on the campaign were those who already knew how they would vote, the better educated, better off, older, urban men. *Conclusions*: (1) The people who were exposed to a lot of campaign propaganda through one medium of communication were also exposed a lot through other media; those who were exposed to a little in one were also exposed to a little in the others (p. 515). (2) The primary distinction between people who saw and heard much campaign propaganda and those who saw and heard only a little was interest in the election (p. 516). (3) The interested were highly exposed and so were the undecided. (4) Asked which medium helped them make their decision, the voters mention radio and newspaper about equally. When they are asked for the "most important" source, however, radio gets a clear lead (p. 519). (5) To the extent that the formal media exerted an influence at all on vote intentions or actual vote, radio proved more effective than the newspaper. (6) Democrats utilized the radio, and the Republicans utilized the newspapers. (7) The average opinion leader has about twice as high a score as the ordinary citizen with reference to newspapers and radio.

Lazarsfeld, Paul F. and Herbert Menzel. "Mass Media and Personal Influence," in Wilbur Schramm, ed., *The Science of Human Communication.* New York: Basic Books, 1963, pp. 94–115.

A review of major studies (1940 to early 1960s) dealing with mass media and personal influence reveals that "personal relations and mass media interact in many ways, sometimes reinforcing, sometimes modifying each other" (p. 113).

Conclusions: (1) Lazarsfeld et al., 1948: Communications flow in two steps, from radio and print to opinion leaders and from these to the less active section of the population. (2) Merton, 1949: Opinion leadership is not a general characteristic of a person, but is always limited to particular issues. (3) Katz and Lazarsfeld, 1955: Personal influence played a more frequent and more effective role than any of the mass media. The influential people proved to be fairly evenly distributed through all educational and income classes and generally not very different from those they had influenced. (4) Berelson et al., 1954: There is a multistep flow of communication— from the mass media through several relays of opinion leaders who communicate with one another, to the ultimate followers. People tend to have discussions primarily with others who agree with them; political discussions are most frequent among those who are most interested in politics. (5) Beal et al., 1957: Different channels of communication play qualitatively different roles in leading persons to a decision. (6) Leaders do not deviate very far from the norms of the groups they lead; if anything, they live up to them with consistency. (7) When it comes to the mere conveying of information, the impact of the mass media is greater than that of face-to-face contact. (8) The effect of the mass media on certain people was found to depend on the kind of other people to whom they intended to tell what they were hearing or reading.

Lowe, Francis E. and Thomas C. McCormick. "A Study of the Influence of Formal and Informal Leaders in an Election Campaign." *Pub. Opin. Q.* 20 (Winter 1956): 651–62.

The authors assessed the number of formal and informal leaders who are identified by people seeking political information. How well do the opinions of the leaders coincide with those whom they are informing?

Method: survey; questionnaire. *Statistics*: discriminant analysis, Pearson correlation. *Pop. (N)*: 743 (643).

Findings: (1) Informal leaders were usually at higher education levels than those who sought their information. Wives usually named their husbands as their sources but husbands did not reciprocate this bias. (2) There was a considerable amount of agreement between respondents and the opinions ascribed to their information leaders, both formal and informal. (3) People tend to change in the direction that their information leaders are proposing. (4) When discrepancies between initial and final opinions existed, the highest correlations between the chosen leaders existed among apathetic groups and the lowest correlations existed for the politically most active.

Maslong, Crispin. "Images and the Mass Media." *Journalism Q.* 48 (Autumn 1971): 519–25.

"A comparison of attitudes of Filipino and Indian students in the U.S. toward the mass media supports a general hypothesis that the media are many things to many people" (p. 519).

Method: survey; questionnaire. *Statistics*: frequencies. *Pop. (N)*: 52 Indian, 47 Filipino students.

Findings: (1) The single most important source of information about Asia for both Indians and Filipinos was local newspapers (Phillipine or Indian). (2) Magazines and radio were listed as the next two most important sources of information about Asia. (3) Only Filipinos named books and television as important sources of Asian information. (4) More than half of the two groups combined indicated foreign newspapers were important sources of news about Asia. (5) Three-fourths of the Filipinos and one-half of the Indians named books and pamphlets as important foreign sources of Asian news. (6) Foreign movies were deemed by both groups as more important than local movies as sources of facts about Asia. (7) Personal contacts were considered more important by Filipinos than by Indians. (8) Filipinos and Indians rated their mass media reliable all the way down.

McClenghan, Jack S. "Effect of Endorsements in Texas Local Elections." *Journalism Q.* 50 (Summer 1973): 363–66.

McClure, Robert D. and Thomas E. Patterson. "Television News and Voter Behavior in the 1972 Presidential Election." Paper presented at annual meeting of the American Political Science Association, New Orleans, 4–8 September 1973. See abstract in Chapter 3.

McCombs, Maxwell E. "Mass Communications in Political Campaigns and Information, Gratification, and Persuasion" in P.J. Tichenor and F. Gerald Kline, eds., *Current Perspectives in Mass Communication Research.* Beverly Hills, Calif.: Sage, 1972, pp. 169–94.

McCombs, Maxwell E. "Negro Use of Television and Newspapers for Political Information, 1952–1964." *J. Broadcast.* 12 (Summer 1968): 261–66.
This paper examines Negroes' use of media: that there has been a "massive shift" of Negroes from a "low media use" pattern to a "high television use" pattern for information-seeking activity. This development is particularly clear with respect to obtaining political information.
Method: time-series analysis, 1952–56, 1960–64. *Statistics:* frequencies. *Pop. (N):* 1952, 171; 1956, 147; 1960, 172; 1964, 159.
Findings: Of the 22% of the Negro population that no longer can be classified as low media users, 20% became high television users and only 12% became high newspaper users. "In short, the data suggest that a historical period of intensive civil rights activity engendered extensive information-seeking behavior, overcoming many of the barriers posed by a lack of formal education" (p. 266).

McCombs, Maxwell E. and L.E. Mullins. "Consequences of Education: Media Exposure, Political Interest, and Information-Seeking Orientations." *Mass Comm. Rev.* 1 (August 1973): 27–31.
Through this research, the author develops a model where education, mass media (exposure and content), and political interest are ranked in terms of causality. The results indicate the following primary effect relationships: Education → Media Exposure → Political Interest → Content Orientation. Including these four variables in the study of information-seeking orientation would facilitate and clarify our understanding of individuals' behaviors in political activity which ranges from alienation to high political interest.
Method: survey; questionnaire. *Statistics:* cross-tabulations. *Pop. (N):* 816 UCLA students.
Findings: (1) The cross-lagged correlation coefficients clearly support the hypothesis that media exposure leads to political interest, not vice versa (p. 28). (2) The "extra" media use associated with high political interest consisted disproportionately of exposure to national and international news, analysis of social issues, and editorials (p. 29). (3) General exposure to the media, political interest, and content orientation are functionally interrelated (p. 30). (4) The relationships between media exposure, media content orientation, and political interest are independent of their joint relationships with education (p. 30).

McLeod, Jack M. "Political Conflict and Information Seeking." Paper presented at American Psychological Association Convention, Chicago, 1965.

McLeod, Jack M., Ramona R. Rush, and Karl H. Freiderich. "The Mass Media and Political Information in Quito, Ecuador." *Pub. Opin. Q.* 32 (Winter 1968–69): 575–87.

The authors examine the relationship between media exposure and amount of political knowledge.

Method: survey; questionnaire. *Statistics*: frequencies. *Pop. (N)*: 200 adults.

Findings: (1) National and international political knowledge are highly correlated and each of these is strongly associated with a current relevant news story. (2) The awareness of a problem and the offering of a solution to that problem are not strongly correlated with each other or with national, international, or current news knowledge. (3) Radio is used by 90% of the sample. (4) No generalized pattern of media exposure was found. (5) Magazine and television exposure show stronger associations with knowledge than does newspaper use. (6) Parents who believe that children should participate in family decisions and political discussions have higher levels of media possession and use.

Mendelsohn, Harold. "Broadcast vs. Personal Sources of Information in Emergent Public Crisis: The Presidential Assassination." *J. Broadcast.* 8 (Spring 1964): 147–56.

The author discusses the need for news to be broadcast immediately after it happens, with particular attention to a Colorado study of the dissemination of the news event of Kennedy's assassination. The study indicates an extension of Katz's two-step flow hypothesis to include the use of mass media sources for verification of news events.

Conclusions: (1) 75% of people interviewed in state of Colorado (200 S's) agreed with the statement "In these times it is absolutely necessary that we constantly keep up with all the news as soon as it happens." (2) "Because the public needs to be informed of major news events as soon as possible, it is in continuous touch with sources of immediate news. (3) Factors such as time of day, social status, and usual patterns of attending the mass media influence how and where various subpublics learn of an emergent crisis. (4) By virtue of its reliable performance in past crises plus its easy accessibility nearly everywhere, radio can be expected to be the major first source of information about most emergent crises. (5) In times of very serious crisis, the public as a whole does not appear to pass through the two-step process as described by Elihu Katz. Instead, most people hear about such an event directly from the mass media. A majority then turns to another source to verify what they have learned originally" (pp. 155–56).

Mendelsohn, Harold. "Comment on Spitzer's 'Mass Media vs. Personal Sources of Information about the Presidential Assassination: A Comparison of Six Investigations.'" *J. Broadcast.* 9 (Winter 1964–65): 51–54.

This rebuttal to Spitzer's article suggests that Professor Spitzer is incorrect in many of his "conclusions."

Conclusions: More credible conclusions which should have been reached by Spitzer (according to Mendelsohn) are: (1) Of the six studies of information sources, one major national study indicates that the American public learned of the assassination with equal frequency from personal and mass media sources. (2) "Three localized studies suggest that selected populations sharing characteristics appropriate to upper education were more likely to hear of the tragic event via personal contact. (3) One state-wide study showed that when a major event coincides with a relatively high degree of normal media attendance, the mass media will become the prime source of information. (4) Together, the six studies suggest that the determination of whether personal or mass media sources will become primary in times of major public crises depends on a 'mix' of time of day, locale, 'normal' media attendance habits for that time of day, and the occupational and social statuses of various sub-publics" (pp. 53–54).

Mendelsohn, Harold. "Some Reasons Why Information Campaigns Can Succeed." *Pub. Opin. Q.* 37 (Spring 1973): 50–61.

The author builds a case by using case studies on how information campaigns can succeed as a result of collaboration between social scientists and communication practitioners. By giving reference to such campaigns as the "National Drivers' Test" and "Cancion de la Rasa," the author shows how this collaboration has worked. The author contends that given that the mass media alone cannot produce attitude change, and that the audience is generally apathetic, information campaigns can succeed if the appropriate targets, themes, appeals, and media vehicles are determined. "Finally, it should be noted that information campaigns can succeed if, in their evaluation, as much attention is paid to delineating specific elements of success as has been allotted to demonstrating failure" (p. 61).

Merton, Robert K. "Patterns of Influence," in P.F. Lazarsfeld and F.N. Stanton, *Communication Research 1949*. New York: Harper and Brothers, 1949.

Mills, J., E. Aronson, and H. Robinson, "Selectivity in Exposure to Information." *J. Abnorm. Soc. Psychol.* 59 (September 1959): 250–53.

This study was performed to test Leon Festinger's Cognitive Dissonance Theory. The situation implemented two types of examination for different groups; one exam carries more weight than the other.

Method: experiment. *Statistics*: means, *t*-tests. *Pop. (N)*: 712 students in an introductory psychology course.

Findings: (1) Persons tend to seek out information that supports their choice and to avoid discrepant information. (2) Persons seek more information about the alternative they have chosen. The latter statement differed from the original dissonance theory in that the importance of the decision did not influence selectivity (p. 253).

Nafziger, Ralph O., Warren C. Engstrom, and Malcolm S. MacLean, Jr. "The Mass Media and an Informed Public." *Pub. Opin. Q.* 15 (Spring 1951): 105–14.

The public opinion polls taken in 1948 indicated that written materials, books, newspapers, and magazines were the most significant areas related to public information on current affairs, magazines being the most salient. Radio and movie-going provided a small relation to being informed except among rural farmers. In this study, it was revealed that men were more informed about political figures than were women.

Method: survey; questionnaire. *Statistics*: frequencies. *Pop. (N)*: metropolitan audience, 299; small city audience, 335; rural, 466.

Findings: (1) Though Molotov had been receiving considerable attention in newspapers, magazines, and radio newscasts, about three-fourths of the metropolitan and rural groups and more than half of the small city people could not identify him (p. 107). (2) Those people who were avid readers of the news in their newspapers tended to be better informed than those who were light readers (p. 108). (3) The newspapers appear to be more helpful in the identification of political personalities than those in the arts (p. 109). (4) Radio listening and information are somewhat negatively related among the small city and metropolitan adults, but affected the information level of farmers (p. 109). (5) In the small city, those who listened most to radio were least informed (p. 109). (6) In every case, there was a sizable positive correlation between the number of magazines read and information level (p. 110). (7) In the metropolitan areas, going to the movies and amount of information were apparently unrelated. (8) Books reached a small segment of the population

(p. 111). (9) Nowhere were there strong relationships between political alignment and information levels; the nonvoter was least informed.

Nafziger, Ralph O., Malcolm MacLean, Jr., and Warren Engstrom. "Who Reads What in Newspapers?" *Int. J. Opin. Attitude Res.* 5 (Winter 1951): 519–40.

Office of Social Research, Columbia Broadcasting System. *Bandwagon: A Review of the Literature.* New York: Office of Social Research, 1964.

O'Keefe, Garrett J. and H.T. Spetnagel. "Patterns of College Undergraduate Use of Selected Media." *Journalism Q.* 50 (Autumn 1973): 543–48.

This is a recent study of Colorado College undergraduate media use. The author believes that it is important to study adolescent-adult media use, because 18–21-year-old individuals are now eligible to vote. The results of this study indicate that newspapers were the greatest source of information on voting rights. It also confirmed past studies that concluded that television was considered a credible source of international information, and newspapers were the most used sources for local information.

Method: survey; questionnaire. *Statistics:* t-test, F-test. *Pop. (N):* 815 Colorado undergraduates.

Findings: (1) "Time spent watching television among the undergraduates was markedly lower than reported in studies of children, adolescents, and older adults. Respondents reported a mean viewing time of 4.31" (p. 545). City newspapers were read 3.67 times a week; magazines, 2.50 times per month. (2) "Males indicated higher attendance to television and newspapers than did females, but slightly less attendance to radio, news magazines and movies" (p. 545). (3) Television viewing and newspaper reading increased consistently from the 17–18-year-old bracket through the 23- and 24-year-old plus category. (4) Newspapers scored highest as the source of detailed information about international and local news events. The most listed medium for information on voting rights was likewise newspapers (43.6%), followed far behind by television (13.4%), another person (11.4%), and radio (9.6%). (5) "In general, studies in the media use area have been limited by looking at one medium over a number of demographic characteristics, or by looking at a number of media over one or two demographic characteristics. Moreover, practically none have studied interaction between various demographic and socio-psychological characteristics as determinants of media use. It seems that any meaningful inferences about the roles media serve for various individuals must result from multi-variable studies which allow analysis of such interactions" (p. 548).

Patterson, Thomas E. and Robert McClure. "Political Advertising: Voter Reaction." Paper presented at the annual meeting of the American Association for Public Opinion Research, Asheville, N.C., 1973.

Prisuta, Robert H. "Mass Media Exposure and Political Behavior." *Educ. Broadcast. Rev.* 7 (June 1973): 167–73.

Rarick, Galen R. "Political Persuasion: The Newspaper and the Sexes." *Journalism Q.* 47 (Summer 1970): 360–64. Evidence is presented which indicates that women read more newspaper content concerning home and family than do men, but they are less influenced by newspapers on these matters. Similarly, men give more attention to newspaper content concerning matters far removed from the home, but they are less influenced on these issues.

Method: survey; questionnaire. *Statistics:* percentage. *Pop. (N):* 1 = 189 Oregon voters, 2 = 402 newspaper subscribers.

Findings: (1) These data support the hypothesis that women attach greater importance to issues the nearer they are to home. (2) Data from two Oregon studies support the proposition that in their newspaper reading, women tend to be home and family oriented whereas men give greater attention to matters outside the home. (3) Data support the view that the editorial is a more efficacious persuader of women than of men on issues far removed from the home, but has greater influence over men in domestic matters. (4) Regardless of sex, 42.2% of the respondents said they would take the advice of the newspaper in a local bond election. Only 32.8% said the newspaper's advice is heeded in presidential elections.

Rhine, Ramon J. "The 1964 Presidential Election and Curves of Information-Seeking and Avoidance." *J. Pers. Soc. Psychol.* 5 (April 1967): 416–23.

Rhine attempts to replicate Leon Festinger's study of cognitive dissonance using the 1964 presidential election as the basic situation. The findings indicated a partial confirmation of Festinger's Inverted U Theory of information seeking and avoiding which indicated a significant difference due to avoiding dissonant information, but not due to seeking consonant information.

Method: experiments; questionnaire. *Statistics*: analysis of variance. *Pop. (N)*: 161 undergraduates.

Findings: Goldwater voters exhibited greater seeking and avoiding than Johnson voters under the conditions of this experiment. Goldwater voters may have been more committed to their views than the Johnson voters.

Riggs, Frank L. "The Changing Role of Radio." *J. Broadcast.* 8 (Fall 1964): 321–39.

The content of radio broadcasts has been adapted throughout the years to meet the needs of its audience. Today radio fulfills a need which could not be filled by the other media.

Conclusions: (1) Radio has become a source of news and information. Dr. E. Dichter states that "the public has considerable confidence in what it hears via radio." This confidence "results from the strong impression that this news comes from authoritative sources, and because of the speed of transmission tends to create the feeling that there is less opportunity to edit, distort or otherwise modify the news" (p. 335). (2) Radio satisfies the audience's need for companionship. (3) The latest trend in radio broadcasting is the programming of talk shows and the reduction of musical programs. (4) Radio is rapidly becoming a service medium.

Robinson, John P. "Mass Communication and Information Diffusion " in F. Gerald Kline and Phillip J. Tichenor, eds., *Current Perspectives in Mass Communication Research*. Beverly Hills and London: Sage Publications, 1972, pp. 71–93.

This article is a general review of the research of mass communication and its role in the diffusion of information. Contrary to past conclusions that media have little influence on public opinion, various studies indicate that in different situations, media have successfully diffused information to the public.

Conclusions: (1) Public dissatisfaction with the handling of the Viet Nam war, growing distrust of the institutions in society, and improving racial attitudes now current in our society may also be seen as directly following from the dominant messages emanating from the media (p. 73). (2) Strong linkages have been found between media use and information. Briefly stated, heavy users of print media are better informed than light users or non-users (p. 75). (3) "Research indicates that the extent of the audience member's exposure to formal education is the most powerful factor intervening between media usage and information level" (p. 75). (4) "The mass media largely function to increase those already existing gaps in information that separate the college graduate from the rest of society and hence may have been responsible for creating even wider divisions of opinion in our society than might have been the case without media" (p. 83). (5) The evidence is persuasive and pervasive that persons already well informed are more motivated to become better informed through the mass media than persons less well informed (p. 87). (6) Exactly what information excites discussion, what norms and circumstances allow information transmission in ordinary conversation, how information gets distorted in interpersonal transmissions, or how lengthy or persuasive the claims of information are in these processes have only been vaguely touched in information diffusion research (p. 89).

Rogers, Everett M. *Diffusion of Innovations.* New York: Free Press, 1962.

Rogers, Everett M. and Floyd Shoemaker. *Communication of Innovations.* New York: Free Press, 1971.

Rosengren, Karl E. "News Diffusion: An Overview." *Journalism Q.* 50 (Spring 1973): 83–91.

This study is essentially an analysis of news diffusion studies. It demonstrates that there are relationships between importance, rate, and amount of diffusion, and the role played by media and personal communication.

Conclusions: (1) The more important the event, the higher the rate and amount of diffusion. (2) The higher the rate and amount of diffusion the less the proportion that has learned news from the press and the higher the proportion that has learned news from personal communication. (3) There seems to be practically no relationship between rate and amount of diffusion and the proportion that learned the news from personal communication. (4) The higher the proportion that first learns news from personal communication, the lower the proportion that learns it from the newspaper. (5) The more important the event, the larger the proportion that has learned the news from personal communication. (6) The larger the proportion that learns the news from television, the smaller the proportion that learns it from radio (although this relationship did not reach statistical significance).

Roucek, Joseph S. "The Influence of Television on American Politics." *Politico* 28 (March 1963): 124–34.

In this article the author tries to assess the most important implication that the event of television may have on American political life. The author cites previous studies to support his major contention.

Conclusions: (1) On several grounds, "published reports of de facto selectivity fall somewhat short of representing ideal proof that people do in fact tend to expose themselves to those mass communications which are in accord with their existing attitudes" (p. 202). (2) Available evidence fails to indicate the presence of a general preference for supportive information. (3) Factors which significantly affect voluntary exposure to information are education and social class, perceived utility of the information (information that is expected to serve a practical purpose is preferred to less useful information), past history of exposure on the issue (when subjects of three studies were exposed initially to biased or one-sided information, they later preferred information favoring the opposite position, regardless of whether it attacked or supported their own position).

Rowe, Ronald Roger. "Selective Factors Influencing Voter Response to a School Bond Issue." Doctoral dissertation, U.S. International University, 1971.

Rubin, B. *Political Television.* Belmont, Calif.: Wadsworth, 1967.

Scammon, Richard and Ben Wattenberg. *The Real Majority.* New York: Coward-McCann, 1970.

Schramm, Wilbur and Donald F. Roberts, eds. *The Process and Effects of Mass Communication,* rev. ed. Urbana: University of Illinois Press, 1971.

Sears, David O. and Jonathan L. Freedman. "Selective Exposure to Information: A Critical Review." *Pub. Opin. Q.* 31 (Summer 1967): 194–213.

Sears, D.O., J.L. Freedman, and E.F. O'Connor. "The Effects of Anticipated Debate and Commitment on the Polarization of Audience Opinion." *Pub. Opin. Q.* 28 (Winter 1964): 615–27.

The authors test the validity of previous research concerning early commitment of viewers to candidates. Exposure to debates appears to strengthen the existing opinions of viewers regardless of the impact of the two debaters' presentations. The results of this experiment indicated that anticipating a debate polarized the opinions of highly committed subjects and moderated the opinions of weakly committed subjects. *Method*: experiment; questionnaire. *Statistics*: chi-square and F-test. *Pop. (N)*: 156 introductory psychology students at UCLA.

Findings: (1) The highly committed debate condition was most polarized and the low commitment debate condition least polarized. (2) Anticipating two speeches had no major systematic effect on polarization, whereas anticipating a debate polarized the opinions of highly committed subjects and moderated the opinions of weakly committed subjects. (3) Selective exposure and selective retention do not seem to operate in any simple sense with regard to debates. There is substantial evidence for the operation of selective evaluation of debaters' performances and arguments (p. 626).

Sheinkopf, Kenneth G., Charles K. Atkin, and Lawrence Bowen. "How Political Party Workers Respond to Political Advertising." *Journalism Q.* 50 (Summer 1973): 334–39.

A study of the reactions of individual party workers to campaign advertisements indicates "that party activists are heavily exposed to political advertising for each candidate, using the material as a source of encouragement and substantive intelligence about the campaign" (p. 339).

Method: survey; questionnaire. *Statistics*: frequencies, chi-square. *Pop. (N)*: 375 Wisconsin party workers, 262 Wisconsin voters.

Findings: (1) "The campaign workers paid considerable attention to the newspaper and television advertising of both candidates, with viewing and reading levels significantly greater than for the voting public" (p. 335). Two-thirds of the activists vs. one-quarter of the voters paid close attention to television spot ads, and most workers gave more attention to political spots than conventional commercials. (2) The party workers more actively sought out the television commercials for positive reasons rather than passively yielding. (3) Although most workers gave equal attention to each candidate's advertising, those who gave closer attention to one set of ads tended to exercise a selective bias in favor of their candidate. (4) While allowing themselves to be exposed to the opponent's ads, the party workers did demonstrate a defensive reaction to the content of the messages. (5) 63% of the party activists reported that they learned something about their candidate's gubernatorial qualifications and 50% said they became better acquainted with him as a person as a result of the ads. The advertisements also encouraged the workers, as 73% felt that their candidate's ads helped to keep up their campaign morale and 74% said that their confidence of doing well in the election was bolstered. (6) The television ads were a useful information source for subsequent persuasion activities for 65% of the party volunteers.

Sheinkopf, Kenneth G. and M. Timothy O'Keefe. "The Eagleton Affair: A Study of News Diffusion." Paper presented to the Mass Communication Division of the International Communication Association, Montreal, 25–28 April 1973.

A study of normal media exposure patterns and variables affecting their disruption (using the Eagleton withdrawal as the disruptive event) found that source disruption did occur among the audience.

Method: survey; questionnaire. *Statistics*: frequencies. *Pop. (N)*: 162 Florida residents.

Findings: (1) Of those persons able to recall when they first heard the news, 60% said they learned Monday evening soon after the announcement was made; 32% reported hearing the following morning, with the remainder learning throughout Tuesday. (2) 36% of the respondents said they heard the announcement of Eagleton's withdrawal through television; 21% through radio; 16% from the newspaper; 3% through more than one source; 24% were unable to recall specifically which source was first used. (3) The disruption in normal media usage was found to be significant at the .01 level.

Sherrod, Drury R. "Selective Perception of Political Candidates." *Pub. Opin. Q.* 35 (Winter 1971): 554–62.

Singer, Benjamin. "Mass Society, Mass Media and the Transformation of Minority Identity." *Br. J. Sociol.* 24 (June 1973): 140–50.

Mass society theorists such as Le Bon, Cooley, and Mills in the past accepted the conclusion that the role of mass media and the masses has been a homogenizing force, pacifying them, and causing a crisis in identity. This article discusses other studies and events that indicate an opposite effect, that mass media become a process of transformation, especially for minority group identities. This case of transformation includes such media influence as causing revolutionary changes (black revolution), generation of new identity (blacks fitting into the American mainstream), and promotion of differentiation.

Conclusions: (1) "One of the unforeseen consequences of the communication explosion led by television has been the potential for revolutionizing minority groups. Although mass media may have a conformative potential for majority groups, it possesses a transformative function for minority group identities. With future developments of multi-channel cable vision and other 'individualized' media, an accentuation of this process may occur" (p. 141). (2) In reference to ghetto environments, Singer notes: "The process, however, begins with demographic changes; following this, poverty becomes compressed, community institutions falter as neighborhood transience and fear reduce interpersonal contact; activities become transferred indoors where the television set helps incorporate the individual into the larger network" (p. 142). (3) Mass media portray the urban community as more dangerous than it really is, with the result that the white community continues to move to the suburbs. (4) "As urban interaction goes down, the Negro becomes more insular, spends more time indoors and more of his knowledge of the world will be gained 'symbolically,' i.e., through mass media" (p. 144). (5) He cites Greenberg's studies on how blacks use television more than whites, and rely on it more as a source of information. (6) "Television makes minority groups lose their minority weakness and perceive their strength through numbers in other cities and to become bolder as lines of communication open up" (p. 146). (7) Television contributes to greater black militancy.

Spitzer, Stephan P. "Mass Media vs. Personal Sources of Information About the Presidential Assassination: A Comparison of Six Investigations." *J. Broadcast.* 9 (Winter 1964–65): 45–50.

A brief review of six recent journal articles on the effects of broadcasting vs. personal sources in the diffusion of the news of the presidential assassination indicated that five studies reported personal sources as the most frequent source of news; one study reported radio as the initial primary source of news.

Conclusions: (1) In all but one study, that of Mendelsohn, interpersonal channels were the primary source of the news about Kennedy's assassination. As a general rule, radio as a source was second and television was third. (2) "While mass media of communication may be largely responsible for transmitting information about commonplace or even mildly unusual news stories, person to person message transmission becomes of primary importance in situations of the magnitude of a presidential assassination" (p. 48).

Starck, Kenneth. "Values and Information Source Preferences." *J. Comm.* 23 (March 1973): 74–85.

The results of this study on the relationship between an individual's information and value systems confirm the hypothesis that interpersonal sources are more important than impersonal sources in providing information.

Method: survey; questionnaire. *Statistics*: frequencies. *Pop. (N)*: 204 *S*'s from Illinois.

Findings: (1) Interpersonal information sources were regarded as most important in helping the respondents achieve value-prescribed goals. (2) 54% of the respondents indicated they preferred either relatives and family (35%) or friends and acquaintances (19%) as sources of information. (3) As for the media, percentages of respondent preferences were books, 12.7%; newspapers, 8.3%; television, 7.4%; and magazines 6.4%. Five respondents (2.5%) chose public events as the most preferred information source. None of the 204 respondents chose radio as his first choice. (4) Print media were preferred over the electronic media 66.6 to 17.6%. (5) Respondents indicated that they attached differing degrees of importance to the various information sources in helping them to achieve value-prescribed goals. Certain value items did seem to make a difference in preferences for certain sources of information, although results were too sparse to delineate overall value systems.

Stempel, Guido H., III. "Selectivity in Readership of Political News." *Pub. Opin. Q.* 25 (Fall 1961): 400–404.

This study of selectivity in readership of political news in a campus election revealed the existence of selectivity to a significant degree, but at the same time, nearly half of the readers of campus newspapers read equal amounts about the two candidates.

Method: survey; questionnaire. *Statistics*: frequencies. *Pop. (N)*: 205 Central Michigan University students.

Findings: (1) Readership of four articles by those who indicated a choice of candidate: 31% read more about the candidate of their choice, 1% read more about the opposition candidate, 49% read equal amounts about both candidates, 19% read nothing about either candidate. (2) Selectivity operated primarily in the decision to read or not to read rather than in the decision on how much to read. (3) The person who had read any of the story was as likely to read all the story about the opposing candidate as he was to read all the story about his candidate. (4) Considering those who read the stories, the average number of paragraphs read in each story was virtually the same for Jones voters and Toffolo voters.

Tichenor, P.J., G.A. Donohue and C.N. Olien. "Mass Media Flow and Differential Growth in Knowledge." *Pub. Opin. Q.* 34 (Summer 1970): 159–70.

The authors discuss studies that confirm the "knowledge gap" hypothesis which states that increasing flow of news on a topic leads to greater acquisition of knowledge about that topic among the more highly educated members of society. These studies are confirmed for printed media, but have not been extensively studied with television. The authors believe that is is possible for television to supply the knowledge to the poorly educated population that would equalize the impact of information.

Conclusions: (1) Education is a powerful correlate of acquisition of knowledge about public affairs and science from mass media (p. 160). (2) A widening knowledge gap may be occurring in developing nations as a result of the system for delivering information to people (p. 161). (3) Respondents with more education learned of the events more rapidly than did those with less education, and a larger proportion of persons with more education were aware of the events two days after they had occurred. Within this time span, the gap in awareness between socioeconomic groups actually widened (p. 163). (4) The knowledge difference between educational levels is greater in the community with no newspaper strike than in the community where the newspaper had been on strike the previous week (p. 167). (5) In Minneapolis-St. Paul, the correlation between education and understanding was higher among "more publicized" articles than less publicized ones (p. 169). (6) The mass media seem to have a function similar to that of other social institutions—reinforcing or increasing existing inequities (p. 170).

Tichenor, P.J., J.M. Rodenkirchen, C.N. Olien, and G.A. Donohue. "Community Issues, Conflict, and Public Affairs Knowledge," in Peter Clarke, ed., *New Models for Mass Communication Research.* Beverly Hills, Calif.: Sage, 1973, pp. 45–80.

Trenaman, Joseph and Denis McQuail. "The Effects of Television and Other Media," in Joseph Trenaman and Denis McQuail, *Television and the Political Image.* London: Methuen, 1961, pp. 182–206.

In the course of an election, significant changes take place. Even though these may be considered marginal, they touch every member of the electorate. McQuail and Trenaman try to discover what is responsible for these changes. They indicate that television is a major factor in enlarging political knowledge.

Method: survey; questionnaire. *Statistics*: correlations. *Pop. (N)*: 661, 180 changers.

Findings: "As a result of this outpouring of political persuasion, people saw more clearly not only what the main policies of the party were; they gained a better understanding of the nature of the parties, of their attitudes to the public and to public programs. And yet, of all the channels through which this information was conveyed, only television produced a direct and progressive effect" (p. 190). They also reached the conclusion that within the frame of reference set up in their research, political change was neither related to degree of exposure nor to any particular programs or argument put forward by the parties. The individual elector "is looking for a whole, coherent policy, for a general picture of what the party as a whole stands for, and it is this general impression, and not particular items of policy, that weigh most with him" (p. 205). This article also discusses the importance of individual judgment, why the campaigns have no direct effect on attitudes, and some of the reasons newspapers and television have less effect.

Troldahl, Verling C. "A Field Test of a Modified 'Two-Step Flow of Communication' Model." *Pub. Opin. Q.* 30 (Winter 1966): 609–23.

This study tends to refute some of the assertions made in the Katz and Lazarsfeld "Two-Step Flow of Communication Model" and to accept some new assertions made by the author concerning the model. The author believes that there is a one-step flow of information from the media to the receiver, and a two-step flow of influence on beliefs, attitudes, and behavior. If the media that he is exposed to are inconsistent with his own beliefs, he will seek out the opinion leader.

Method: survey; questionnaire. *Statistics*: frequencies, cross-tabulations. *Pop. (N)*: 318 *Bulletin* subscribers in Boston.

Findings: (1) Among opinion leaders, exposure to mediated communication did not produce a statistically significant awareness effect. Among the followers, exposure produced a significant awareness effect. (2) Exposure to media did induce some belief changes in followers, but not in opinion leaders. (3) The mediated communication may have influenced some followers in this study, while others were influenced by face-to-face communication. (4) Troldahl predicted that followers who were exposed to media messages that were inconsistent with their predispositions would initiate the second step flow of communication. There was a tentative support for this prediction.

Wade, Serena and Wilbur Schramm. "The Mass Media as Sources of Public Affairs, Science, and Health Knowledge." *Pub. Opin. Q.* 32 (Summer 1969): 197–209.

This article relates patterns of information-seeking to levels of public knowledge in public affairs, science, and health.

Method: secondary analysis of national sample surveys.

Conclusions: (1) For a majority of the public, television is the chief source of information during national election campaigns. (2) Print media are more likely to be major sources of information for highly educated groups, whites, males, professionals, white-collar workers, and high-income groups than for others. (3) Newspapers are dominant in providing current knowledge of science. (4) Print media (newspaper and magazine) are main providers of health information. (5) The more education a person has, the less likely he is to turn to television for health information. (6) Print users, on the average, had more specific information than persons whose chief source was one of the broadcast media. (7) Whether a person reads about elections or views campaign programs on television seems to be associated with different amounts of knowledge only among those with high school education or less.

Wamsley, Gary L. and Richard A. Pride. "Television Network News: Re-Thinking the Iceberg Problem." *West. Polit. Q.* 25 (September 1972): 343–50.

The authors contend that "the need is clear to view television news with a new scholarly skepticism for it may hold a far more important place in the flow of political information than social scientists have assumed up to now" (p. 450).

Conclusions: (1) In comparison to other mass media, television network news is oligopolistic in character, television is identified as the most important source of campaign information by the greatest number of Americans, television is accorded more trust by the public, it is more difficult for the television viewer to avoid being confronted with, and absorbing some information from, television news, television leaves more room for definition or interpretation by the viewer, television's insatiable appetite for action shapes all of television news, television does very little with background and analyses of news stories it presents, the pictures of television disrupt the usual journalistic style of presenting salient important facts first and then elaborating on them (the interpretation of reality is left up to the viewer), and television news cannot be reviewed by the viewer in case of misunderstanding, etc. (2) Exposure entailing low ego-involvement means that perceptual defenses are weak; this opens the possibility of alterations in perceptions with a potential change in behavior and a later change in attitudes. (3) Blumler and McQuail found that attitude change was a function of exposure when viewer motivation was low; the "toleration viewer," one who merely likes to have the set on, was most likely to change his attitude. (4) The key to change lies in repetition and positive gratification. It is possible for a relative acceleration of this process to take place as a news viewer, to take a hypothetical example, is nightly exposed to news that puts the conduct of the Viet Nam war in an unfavorable light. This portrayal of reality is reinforced by repetition and the gratifying aspects of the semi-entertainment nature of television. Attitudes may change later after a perceptual shift. (5) Preliminary research into the context of television news conducted by authors at Vanderbilt University makes it at least feasible to suggest that while there is little or no direct advocacy for changing the status quo, it is not safe to conclude that the total effect on the political system is supportive or reinforcing.

Warren, Donald I. "Mass Media and Racial Crisis: A Study of the New Bethel Church Incident in Detroit." *J. Soc. Iss.* 28, 1 (1972): 111–32.

The author indicates in his study that media can increase polarization among races through its biased coverage of an event. The author calls for an increase in balance of reporting accurate information by the media to counteract the basic distrust that the black community has in the media and the great reliance on the media by the white community.

Method: survey; questionnaire. *Statistics*: frequencies. *Pop. (N)*: 1130 black and white Detroit residents.

Findings: (1) Black respondents relied on newspapers for information half as often as whites. (2) Word of mouth was the primary source of information 12% of the time for whites but 18.2% of the time for blacks. (3) The total word-of-mouth reliance is 29.3% for black college-educated respondents compared to 9.6% for whites. (4) Blacks appear to be subject to persuasion by newspapers and to reject television-based information. (5) Whites show the highest acceptance of the mass media thesis of court actions for the two situations where television and newspapers are the major information sources. (6) There is a general trend toward word-of-mouth information sources to lead to the lowering of polarization scores between early and late interviews. The newspaper without television combination shows two instances of sharp polarization. The television-newspaper combination showed the least depolarization trend of all mass media combinations, with television-no newspapers having a somewhat similar pattern.

Westley, Bruce H., and Lionel C. Barrow, Jr. *Exploring the News: A Comparative Study of the Teaching Effectiveness of Radio and Television.* Research Bulletin No. 12. Madison: University of Wisconsin Television Laboratory, 1959.

Westley, Bruce H. and Lionel C. Barrow, Jr. "An Investigation of News-Seeking Behavior." *Journalism Q.* 36 (Fall 1959): 431–38.

This study presents a rationale for the existence of an attribute called "news-seeking." The data from this study provide evidence that this attribute is more or less independent of intelligence and capable of predicting certain kinds of communication-reception behavior.

Method: survey; questionnaire. *Statistics*: Guttmann scale; frequencies; analysis of variance. *Pop. (N)*: 228 Wisconsin pupils.

Findings: (1) Percentage distribution of daily news intake: 55% reported attending to news on television every day, 28% by radio and 20% in newspapers; only 9% reported that they read news in news magazines every week. (2) Neither of the indices of news-seeking behavior produced significant relationships with immediate recall of factual information. The other two main variables, medium and intelligence, did produce significant differences. (3) The analysis of variance based on delayed-recall data revealed that the intelligence variable was significant, but the radio-vs.-television variable was not. (4) Both indices of news-seeking behavior produced significant differences in delayed recall. (5) Subjects learned more information initially from television than from radio, but the difference washed out 6–10 weeks later. The more intelligent subjects learned more than the less intelligent and they retained more 6–10 weeks later. (6) It is possible to think of the news-seeking attribute as "a persistent tendency to place a positive value on information that is potentially relevant to the individual's orientation to his surroundings" (p. 437).

Wiebe, G.D. "Responses to the Televised Kefauver Hearings: Some Social-Psychological Implications." *Pub. Opin. Q.* 16 (Summer 1952): 179–200.

An investigation into the impact of the Kefauver hearings on the thinking and behavior of a sample of New York citizens reveals that although the problem was perceived by the citizens, the hearings did not stimulate a majority of them to engage in constructive problem-solving behavior.

Method: survey questionnaire. *Statistics*: frequencies. *Pop. (N)*: 260 New York adults.

Findings: (1) A unanimous concern with a social problem (government corruption) was observed. (2) In regard to behavioral intentions, only 25% of the responses appeared to qualify as "problem-solving" in the sense that they might be expected to contribute to the solution of the problem. (3) What enrolled party members felt like doing more frequently fell into the classification of "problem-solving" (35% against 14% for nonparty members). (4) Party members more frequently reported that they had actually done something (25% against 11% for nonparty members).

Witt, William. "Multivariate Analysis of News Flow in a Conservation Issue." *Journalism Q.* 49 (Spring 1972): 91–97.

This study analyzed the selective use of news in promoting a shoreline issue in Wisconsin. The results indicated a selective exposure to news information was made by communities.
Method: survey; questionnaire; content analysis. *Statistics*: multiple regression analysis, *t*-test. *Pop. (N)*: 71 counties in Wisconsin, editors of 39 newspapers.
Findings: (1) "This study suggests that social systems, being made up of many audiences, also tend to become selectively exposed, because gatekeepers are themselves secondary audiences, responding to feedback from their own audiences" (p. 91). (2) "This study suggests that a greater amount of news concerning adoption of a proposal will be formed where the proposal is closer to enactment in the political process" (p. 91). (3) "News flow is of particular interest because it suggests that conditions and events in social systems, such as counties, may indeed be related, perhaps reciprocally, to the flow of news on these conditions and events" (p. 95). (4) "In general, it seems that mass communication may be accountable for some social effects in particular directions, where social systems are disposed to act in those directions, and effects may occur through interactive processes in which mass communications is both agent and recipient of change" (p. 96).

Wright, Charles R. "Evaluating Mass Media Campaigns." *Int. Soc. Sci. Bull.* 7, 3 (1955): 417–30.
This paper discusses several possible intended and unanticipated effects of campaigns. Three major research procedures for detecting effects—experiments, surveys, and panels—are described. The evaluation of campaign effectiveness is considered in terms of three formal dimensions: audience response, audience coverage, and process of influence. The methods of research in these areas are described and problems noted. No specific hypothesis is advanced in this study. This paper provides a brief, non-technical discussion of the application of some of these general research procedures to the special problems in evaluating mass media campaigns.

Wright, Charles R. *Mass Communication: A Sociological Perspective.* New York: Random House, 1959.

5

Media Use
and
Political Processes

Mass media exposure and use have been linked frequently to particular patterns of political action. In previous chapters we have considered many of these relationships. Research findings have linked media variables to levels of political knowledge, forms of campaign activity, discussion of political affairs, and so on. In considering these relationships, we have not explored their implications for the development of political institutions. Some of these implications may appear obvious: for example, effective political socialization which involves mass media use should enable us to maintain a democratic political system. However, such an assumption may prove simplistic or invalid. Political theorists have long been suspicious of the way in which the mass media might influence trends in political behavior. It will be necessary for future mass communication research to go beyond establishing that the media *can* influence political action, and to find out *how* they do so.

We cannot assume that the mass media are improving the political process by reinforcing certain activities and discouraging others. Researchers must discover how media use is linked to trends in political attitudes and actions, and then they must consider the implications of these trends for the overall political system. This task will be difficult because it requires conceptualization of two types of social process: mass communication use processes and political processes. This chapter is concerned with the areas where these two processes overlap.

In Chapter 4, we suggested an outline of a transactional model of mass communication. In this chapter, we will develop a model of the political system which is compatible with the transactional model. In doing so, we will review previous efforts at conceptualizing political processes. The influence of mass communication in each of these models will be considered. After this review, we will examine a model of the political system derived from Gabriel Almond and Bingham Powell (1966) and discuss its compatibility with the transactional model and with some of the most recent research on uses and gratifications. The implications of certain media uses and gratifications will be explored using the Almond-Powell model.

From this discussion we shall deduce several parameters for future theories. Theories constructed using these parameters would necessarily integrate mass communication uses with the study of political processes. An approach to theory construction which already fits within our parameters is agenda-setting research. In our next chapter we will discuss agenda-setting research as a possible model for other political communication research.

Mass Communication Institutions in Political Theory

Political theorists have considered mass communication to be part of the political system, but its role has traditionally been conceived of as secondary. The media were not thought to be part of any process which shaped political structures.[1] At best (or worst), they merely reinforced trends of political change which were instigated by a political elite or by the leaders of important social groups. New political institutions were shaped by leaders in face-to-face interaction and then the mass media were used to elicit support for these institutions. Thus one important role of the media was legitimation of political institutions and the actions of political leaders. This legitimation was usually conceived to take place by a one-way communication process in which political innovations were diffused to the population. History records in some detail the face-to-face interactions which shaped the American Constitution, but it accords less attention to the role of the media in disseminating and developing popular support for this document. Though some historians have rewritten this historic episode to include the influence of economic variables, less effort has been made to consider the role of mass communication variables.[2] This omission is curious when we note that many of the leaders of the American Revolution (such as Thomas Paine and Benjamin Franklin) were effective propagandists. Political theorists appear to have assumed that such men engaged in one-way communication which immediately effected support for their actions. Little detailed consideration has been given to the role of the partisan revolutionary press in shaping the social movements which precipitated the American Revolution and which later forged the basis for our present political institutions.

Our contention is that an adequate model of mass communication can greatly increase the usefulness of political history and theory. Much of this history and theory relies implicitly on models of the mass communication process whose weaknesses we examined in Chapter 4. The hypodermic needle model has enjoyed particular popularity and to a lesser extent, simplistic, one-way diffusion models have been used. As a result, our understanding of political processes is inadequate. Theorists have come to opposite conclusions about the political fate of this nation on the basis of similar evidence, in part because they have used different implicit models of the mass communication process.[3] Let us review the conclusions of some of these theorists, paying particular attention to the limitations of the models of the mass communication process which underlie them.

Mass Society Theory

Kornhauser[4] has provided an extended discussion of mass society theory, which sought to explain nineteenth-century revolutions and twentieth-century totalitarianism. Mass society theorists blamed certain changes in the social order for these political catastrophes. They were particularly alarmed by the collective actions of individuals whose only social bond appeared to be affiliation with the same charismatic leaders. These individuals appeared to have abandoned traditional social roles. They were thought to be motivated by frustration and anxiety produced by the necessity of coping with a complex urban environment. Individuals were thought to be atomized, broken apart from one another.

A conception of the process of mass communication is implicit in Kornhauser's descriptions of mass society. Atomized individuals were directly reached by charismatic leaders through print and broadcast media. Because they lacked traditional roles and social relationships which could have stabilized their behavior, masses of individuals were easily motivated to follow leaders' instructions, even when these instructions defied existing norms or values. But political elites had to take account of the masses. Unlike traditional societies in which elites simply imposed their demands, in the mass society elites were thought to be governed in large part by public opinion.

Mass society theorists painted a grim picture of the future, in which members of elite groups would manipulate confused and anxious masses, creating public opinion which subsequently manipulated them. Democratic political institutions would inevitably be destroyed even though leaders might pay lip-service to democratic values. Power would be gained and held through proper control of the mass media. Eventually, elites would institute totalitarian states in which the mass media would be used to dominate public opinion completely.[5]

The model of mass communication implicit in most mass society theory is a variant of the hypodermic needle model. Communication flows from elites directly to the masses and it can have immediate, dramatic effects. However, if this communication is improperly controlled it can have unexpected consequences: public opinion may turn from support of one elite to another which has made more effective use of the media. There is constant danger that the propaganda of one elite will prove to be so devastatingly effective that all competition from other elites is eliminated. The rise of the Nazis in Germany or the Bolsheviks in Russia was seen as an example of this process. So long as the power of the mass media was diffused among several elites, a weak form of democracy might be maintained, but if this power should pass into the hands of a single elite, democracy would inevitably yield to totalitarianism. So long as competing elites "injected" the masses with conflicting beliefs and values, a semblance of a free society might be maintained. But if the "injections" came from a single source, society-wide thought control was possible.

Mass society theorists pointed to certain patterns of media use which they found especially disturbing. These patterns included use of mass media for entertainment, use of the media for reassurance and guidance, and use of the media to replace personal relationships.[6] The use of media for entertainment was thought to distract individuals from reports of political events. The media were viewed as the new opiate of the masses which prevented individuals from noticing the way in which ruthless members of elite groups were exploiting them. The use of the media for reassurance and guidance could lead individuals to become dependent upon media sources for vital information, with no way of personally verifying its truth. Media personalities could persuade them to act in ways which were socially destructive. Leaders could broadcast reassuring messages which were untrue.

Finally, use of the mass media to replace personal relationships made it likely that individuals would project traditional interpersonal roles onto media figures. Persons who were separated from their family or who lacked friends might visualize media personalities as filling these roles. Forms of information and influence which would otherwise come from personal relationships would now come from the mass media.

Elitist Theory

Though the description of social processes by mass society theorists is in error,[7] their descriptions of existing political structures were frequently accurate. Perhaps the most useful aspect of their work was the concern which they focused on the centralization of authority. This concern has been elaborated and consolidated in elitist theory. In *Power Elite*, C. Wright Mills[8] presented an extended description of the form which centralization has taken. One does not have to agree that conspiracy provides the dynamic force toward centralization to recognize that at least some of Mills' descriptions of social structures are partially accurate. It is important to note that when social organizations become centralized effective control is transferred to a few individuals. Whatever social forces produce centralization, it is a fact of modern political life that the day-to-day decision-making power over a wide range of actions of most individuals is held by a relatively small number of persons.

This situation may not be incompatible with democracy as long as the majority of individuals responsibly and voluntarily accept legitimate directions of their leaders while exercising the right to reject demands which they believe are illegitimate. This view of democracy assumes that our political system is at least partially based on the ability of the majority to make occasional critical judgments about their leaders. Mass society and elitist theorists predicted that powerful leaders easily distort this ability to make judgments by clever manipulations. Some studies of the effects of political advertising partially support this position (see Patterson and McClure, 1973). But it is equally plausible to argue that the ability to make critical judgments is less subject to manipulation because it is grounded in a political process in which mass communication plays an important role. For example, regular access to conflicting sources of communication, together with the development of media use patterns which enable effective use of these sources, may provide a basis for critical judgments. If such a political process exists, mass communication could play an important role in preserving modern democracies.[9] Further research is necessary to delineate the role of mass communication. The arguments of elitist theorists cannot be accepted in lieu of such research.

Pluralistic Theory

A second school of political theorists has argued that political power is divided among many diverse and conflicting groups.[10] These groups encourage the participation of individuals and translate this participation into political power. Voluntary interest groups such as labor unions, professional societies, or religious organizations were said to comprise a broadly based social structure which intervened between political elites and the masses. David Truman [11] has described a pluralistic social structure:

> This structure—which in simplest terms includes at least the great array of interest or pressure groups, corporations, trade unions, churches and professional societies, the major media of communication, the political parties, and, in a sense, the principal state and local governments—this

pluralistic structure is a central fact of the distribution of power in the society. (pp. 56–57)

Thus, in Truman's view, the mass media affect politics through their role as pluralistic interest groups. The various media presumably constitute separate groups that balance the power of other groups and are capable of forming alliances to achieve political objectives. This view of the media may adequately conceptualize the traditional role of newspapers in politics, but it does not adequately account for the present role of the media. As the press has become increasingly commercialized, journalists have tended to reduce their direct participation in political matters. Urban dailies, especially those which lack competition, tend to maintain political neutrality as a means of securing the largest possible circulations. The centralized, national network structure of television militates against direct involvement in local or state politics. The media are often too constrained by professional values, commercial concerns, and bureaucratic structure to function as freely as other interest groups in the pursuit of their own political objectives.[12]

Other researchers have argued that mass media serve pluralistic groups by aiding these groups in political socialization and providing information for group leaders. According to this view, the political influence of the mass media is indirect, dependent upon how pluralistic groups and their leaders choose to make use of the media. Studies published by Lazarsfeld et al. (1944) and Berelson et al. (1954) have provided much empirical support for this position. In Chapter 10 of their book, Berelson et al. argue that a "division of labor" exists with regard to media use during political campaigns. The majority of the public does not use the media in any systematic way for political purposes during a campaign. Most voters were found to be apathetic, ignorant, and prejudiced about political matters in general and voting in particular. They showed little inclination to follow the campaign on radio or in the newspapers. Group leaders tended to make greater use of the mass media for political purposes. If especially important information was communicated by the media, group leaders were likely to pass it along. Agger and Ostrom (1956) reported evidence of a similar political process operating in a small community.

Berelson et al. offered a theory to explain why, although individuals can act in politically irresponsible ways, the political system continues to function effectively. In their scheme, social groups stabilize the political process. Political apathy on the part of the majority is not only acceptable but necessary in a democracy. If everyone were politically involved, partisanship might make people inflexible, unwilling to accept actions by leaders which compromised their ideological views. Groups encourage the apathetic to vote as their friends do, not on the basis of ideological beliefs. Groups shield the uninformed from barrages of campaign propaganda. They encourage traditional political prejudices and prevent voters from being reached and manipulated by demagogues.

A model of mass communication used by Berelson et al. is the two-step flow model. In Chapter 4, we discussed the limitations of this model: it exaggerates the influence of groups and cannot account for many patterns of media use which researchers have found. In particular, the use of television appears to deviate greatly from two-step flow notions. For example, Patterson and McClure (1973) found that politically apathetic individuals do attend to political advertisements on television. This use of the media may directly influence beliefs about candidates' stands on issues.

In our discussion of the transactional model we argued that groups may encourage the development of particular media use patterns but that they probably do not effectively mediate particular messages from the media.

Political Activity and Apathy

Much recent research in political science has been concerned with explaining political participation or inactivity.[13] This research synthesizes the work of mass society, elitist, and pluralistic theorists into an explanation of political behavior. These researchers avoid making assumptions about what constitutes a good or bad political system and focus on explaining what they consider interesting and important variables. They derive variables from all of the earlier schools of thought and then use these variables to construct explanations of why some persons become politically active while others remain inactive. Variables derived from mass society and elitist theory include anomie and alienation. Variables derived from pluralistic theory include reference group values and reference group involvement.

In addition to suggesting variables, mass society and pluralistic theories are used to derive predictions which link demographic variables to political action. For example, both mass society and pluralistic theories predict that socioeconomic status and education should be positively correlated with participation. For mass society theorists this correlation is evidence that an apathetic mass is dominated by a politically active elite. For pluralists it reflects a necessary division of political labor in social groups.

William Erbe (1964) has provided a systematic examination of the relationships among three independent variables—socioeconomic status, reference group involvement, and alienation—and one dependent variable, political participation. His study replicates most of the findings of previous research. Socioeconomic status, organizational involvement, and low alienation were all positively correlated with political participation. He notes that while socioeconomic status and organizational involvement remained highly correlated with political activity when the other two independent variables were controlled statistically, the correlation with alienation was sharply reduced. Erbe explains this finding by arguing that alienation may be a consequence of low social status and low organizational involvement. Thus direct relationships found between alienation and political activity may be spurious. Erbe does point out that studies using other measures of alienation might produce different results.

Erbe's findings provide greater support for pluralistic theory than for mass society theory. Involvement in organizations apparently can produce increasing levels of political participation. This means that one organization can socialize individuals to become active in other organizations. Presumably this effect could "snowball" as more and more individuals are socialized, providing an ever larger pool of possible recruits for other groups. If alienation is simply a consequence of low involvement, it can be gradually overcome by the proliferation of social groups which encourage increased social action.

Further confirmation of Erbe's findings can be found in a study by Olsen (1972), who found that participation in nonpolitical social organizations explained a moderate amount of variance in voting turnout even when several demographic and mass media exposure variables were controlled. Findings like those of Erbe lend encouragement to the view that the key to maintaining a democratic society is to be found in policies which encourage the development of a wide variety of social groups. Participation in these groups will ensure that individuals will become involved in political affairs. Social factors that encourage alienation may be overcome.

Alienation

Alienated persons are those who cannot understand social institutions and, in particular, their own relationships to those institutions. Consequently, they experience frustration and anxiety whenever they attempt to engage in political action. These persons should tend to withdraw from all political action and develop attitudes which rationalize or reinforce this withdrawal.

Research on political participation has produced conflicting results. Mass society theory predicts that alienation will be negatively correlated with political activity. While some research results such as Erbe's support these notions, these results vary according to how the variables are defined and measured. Dwight Dean (1961) found that when four separate measures of alienation were intercorrelated with four different measures of political apathy, the highest intercorrelation was .19. Although many of the correlations are statistically significant, Dean argued that they are not practically significant. Levin and Eden (1962) provided case studies of three elections in which alienation may have produced votes for certain candidates, thus influencing election outcomes. It can be argued that alienation actually encourages certain forms of voting behavior.

Marvin Olsen (1969) attempted to resolve apparent inconsistencies in research by dividing existing measures of alienation into two categories. He labels these categories attitudes of incapability and attitudes of discontent. He posits that the first type of alienation arises because an individual is born into a subordinate, confusing social position. The second type of alienation is chosen by individuals who do not experience incapability in their everyday lives but who are dissatisfied with a social order which unduly subjugates others. He predicted that the first type of alienation would be significantly correlated with low socioeconomic status and low political activity, while attitudes of discontent would be positively correlated with higher socio-economic status and political activity. Some evidence was found for the first two predictions. Although socioeconomic status was slightly correlated with attitudes of discontent, these attitudes were not consistently related to any level of political activity.

One inconsistency which appears in some studies of political alienation is that alienation is found to be negatively correlated with traditional, institutionalized forms of political action, but it is often positively correlated with involvement in nontraditional social movements. Von Eschen, Kirk, and Pinard (1969, p. 316) report that alienated whites were more likely than nonalienated whites to join the civil rights movement. Rex Hopper[14] presents a theoretical framework which assumes that revolutionary move-ments must mobilize the discontented and alienated to be successful. Thus it may be necessary to separate observations of political action into catego-ries of traditional and radical action. Most research which has studied the relationship between alienation and political activity has been concerned with traditional political action. The studies by Erbe and Olsen are examples of such research.

Other research has found alienation positively related to traditional political activities such as voting. Joel Aberbach (1969) provides a critical review of the use of the concept of alienation in empirical studies of political participation. He points out that most measures of alienation are composite indices made up of several subscales. The relationship of the subscales to various dependent variables is rarely investigated. Researchers simply assume that some combination of attitudes like powerlessness, meaninglessness, or distrust will produce specific political behaviors. Aberbach analyzed Survey Research Center data from the 1964 election and found that of several measures of alienation, only political distrust was positively related to voting for Goldwater. However, this relationship held only for those persons who considered themselves politically powerful. Aberbach's research suggests that relationships between alienation and political behavior should be studied cautiously. He suggests that these relationships may fluctuate greatly from one election situation to another. Eckhardt and Hendershot (1967) found alienated individuals interested and involved in local politics but they tended to overestimate their political strength. Levin and Eden (1962) proposed a political strategy for mobilizing alienated voters. Thus some forms of alienation may increase rather than decrease the likelihood that certain types of political action will occur in certain election situations.

Media Use and Political Activity

Few firm conclusions can be drawn from research which has attempted to predict political activity or apathy. Only socioeconomic status and education have shown consistent positive relationships with a variety of political actions.[15] Other variables like reference group involvement or alienation have proved less useful predictors of political action. This research has provided little basis for theory building beyond generating some interesting empirical generalizations. Other researchers have attempted to link mass communication variables with other predictors of political activity. In some cases their work has resulted in improved explanations of such activity.

Katz and Foulkes (1962) clarified the links between mass media use and alienation. They pointed out that a variety of research has indicated that alienated individuals make greater use of the mass media. These individuals appear to be using the media to compensate for their lack of contact with other persons. This use of media can further alienate them by providing them with interests and concerns which have no social value or it can reintegrate them by arousing interest in other people and concern about social institutions (pp. 381–82). It is important to study the types of media content which alienated persons use and the function of this content for them rather than just the amount of exposure to media. In terms of the transactional model discussed in the previous chapter, alienation can be viewed either as causing certain types of media use or as a consequence of certain media uses. Media use may function to increase or attenuate alienation; alienation, in turn, influences political action.

This model of the interrelationship among media use, alienation, and political action is obviously too simplistic to explain much variation in any of these variables, yet it illustrates a useful approach to theory construction. Media uses or gratifications can be causally linked to specific predispositions toward political action. These predispositions can be used to explain specific actions. In this approach, media use is not directly linked to political action as in the hypodermic model. Instead, it contributes to a process in which various types of political predispositions are formed, which ultimately influence political action. The process can be influenced by other social or psychological variables. Research must specify the particular conditions which encourage or attenuate such a process.

Several studies illustrate how this approach could be implemented. McLeod, Ward, and Tancill (1965) studied the relationship between media use and alienation. Unlike some previous researchers, they did not find simple media exposure related to alienation or activity. Correlations between measures of exposure and alienation were generally statistically insignificant. Instead, they found that specific uses of media and gratifications derived from media were linked to alienation. Alienated persons expressed less interest in informational headlines and were less likely say they read newspapers for information. Alienated individuals were more likely to read newspaper content that excited or distracted them (vicarious gratification). This research suggests the existence of a process in which alienation causes specific uses of newspaper content and these uses produce further alienation.

McLeod et al. found correlations between education and media use to be the reverse of those between alienation and media use. This finding suggests that education may operate as a contingent condition which either accentuates or attenuates the relationship between media use and alienation. If so, the greatest evidence for the process suggested above should be found among people with little formal education. Such evidence was provided by Becker and Preston (1969). In their secondary analysis of Survey Research Center data on the 1964 election they found that education, income, and media use independently explained significant amounts of variance in several political attitude and activity variables. Bennett and Klecka (1970) analyzed Survey Research Center data from three elections (1964, 1966, 1968) and found that education was consistently the best predictor of political activity when compared to occupation and income. However, alienation was not considered in this study.

Other studies provide additional evidence of the link between media use and political involvement. Utilizing survey data from five nations, Burstein (1972) found media use and organizational involvement to be the most useful predictors of political participation. Eulau and Schneider (1956) found that persons more "related" to the political process were more exposed to the mass media. Jackson (1971) attributed increased political activity by young blacks to media use and communication with peer groups.

Not all research has found media use related to political action. Chaffee, Ward, and Tipton (1970) demonstrated that an apparent association between active election campaign behavior and mass communication variables was spurious. Lang and Lang (1956) argue that viewing the 1952 national political conventions on television may have reduced rather than encouraged participation in the election.

These findings may be best interpreted by referring to the transactional model. Highly educated individuals tend to learn specific uses of the mass media, especially how to use media to seek information. Chaffee, McLeod, and Atkin (1971) demonstrated that pluralistic families were more likely to encourage information-seeking patterns. Chaffee, McLeod, and Wackman (1966) linked these patterns to political activity. These patterns of media use are likely to persist even when the individual develops attitudes which would otherwise attenuate information seeking. For example, college students who become disillusioned with government are more likely to continue to seek information about government than will alienated individuals who failed to complete high school. For the dropouts, information seeking is a more arduous task which is likely to be abandoned at the first sign that it will prove unrewarding.

The research summarized above provides evidence of the usefulness of the approach being developed here, but it cannot answer the research questions being raised. Data were typically collected at a single point in time so the existence of a process cannot be determined. Variables like education and income were treated as independent variables, not as contingent conditions affecting relationships between media use and political attitudes or actions.

A study by Veikko Pietila (1970) builds on the McLeod et al. findings and provides additional support for our approach. Rather surprisingly, Pietila found insignificant correlations between use of the media for information or vicarious gratification and people's perceptions of the media as unreliable or self-contradictory (a measure of alienation from the media). Similarly, when alienation from society was measured using the Srole Alienation Scale, it was found to be insignificantly correlated with media use. However, the direction of the correlations obtained were consistent with those found by McLeod et al. Alienated individuals were less likely to use the content of radio, television, or newspapers for information seeking and more likely to seek vicarious gratification.

Pietila attempts to account for his null findings by suggesting that a process may underlie the relationship between media use and alienation. This process may result in a curvilinear relationship which is misinterpreted as a zero correlation when analyzed using product-moment correlation coefficients. Pietila argues that persons who are only slightly alienated may actually be more likely to seek information. For them, alienation provides motivation to become more informed. He draws on a conceptualization of alienation provided by Eric Allerdt in which four levels of alienation are distinguished. The first and simplest level of alienation consists of dissatisfaction with situational definitions. The individual feels out of touch with individuals or groups because he is continually frustrated in everyday interactions or because he rejects the way in which the mass media portray everyday life situations. This form of alienation may lead to more severe forms of alienation which include dissatisfaction with social roles, societal norms, and societal values. Pietila argues that there is a linear process in which one form of alienation leads to another. He believes that alienation related to concern about situational definitions will be most likely to provoke increased use of the media for informational purposes. This form of alienation can occur when an individual observes persons on television who behave very differently from himself. It can be resolved by seeking more information about this behavior. Similarly, a national event may provoke interest because it violates the individual's conceptions of how to act in situations. For example, the release of the White House tapes by Nixon aroused public indignation because they revealed behavior which contradicted many individuals' definition of action appropriate for certain situations. Thus the release of the tapes may have triggered a mild form of alienation among persons who previously were strong Nixon supporters. This alienation might have led them to seek information about Watergate which they previously avoided. As a result, they may have become increasingly alienated from the Nixon administration.

Pietila cannot test this conceptualization of a process linking media use and alienation. Like McLeod et al., he has drawn his data from a cross-sectional sample. He does provide an indirect test by demonstrating that when alienated persons do use the media for information reasons, they use the media more for delayed reward information material than nonalienated persons. In addition, they are more likely to regularly follow news and current events programs on radio and television than nonalienated persons.

If Pietila's theory is correct, it suggests some strengths and weaknesses of the mass media. The media would be best suited to resolving mild forms of alienation by presenting useful information. On the other hand, the media could do little to resolve extreme alienation but could intensify it still further by providing a means of escape or withdrawal which prevents individuals from coping directly with the estrangement they feel.

A recent study by Blumler and McLeod (1974) provides an additional basis for extending our approach. Blumler and McLeod link social structural variables, media use, and political activity. In doing so they begin to identify a political process in which media uses and gratifications play an important role. They describe a wide range of variables which may be related to media use. Their research seeks to construct a consistent explanation of political actions in terms of this set of variables using regression analysis. In particular, attention is given to the role of the mass media in explaining whether or not an individual decides to vote in an election.

Blumler and McLeod report data from the British general election of 1970. They found that mass communication variables explained significant amounts of variance in voting turnout among young voters even when social structural variables like socioeconomic status, education, sex, marital status, and age were controlled. Several variables influenced the voting turnout effects produced by mass communication. These included political party affiliation, time at which the decision for whom to vote is made, and age of the voter. Mass communication most affected young voters who had not chosen a candidate before an initial set of interviews was conducted. Some evidence was found that viewing of campaign programming on television encouraged family discussions. These two factors apparently combined to mobilize individuals to vote. The researchers speculate that mass communication may have "set agendas" for family discussion, thus indirectly influencing voter turnout. This form of media influence could occur only in those homes where family discussion took place frequently.

Perhaps the most intriguing finding in this study was that precampaign Labor supporters were especially likely to form negative assessments of the campaign. These assessments apparently reduced the likelihood that an individual would vote even though he had intended to vote before the campaign began. On the other hand, Labor supporters who originally intended to abstain but formed favorable impressions of the campaign were more likely to vote for Labor. The approach we suggested above is supported by these findings. For some Labor supporters, campaign information may have produced a mild form of alienation. This alienation from their party intensified during the campaign as the situational definitions of Labor supporters continued to be frustrated and resulted in their failure to vote. This interpretation receives its strongest support from the finding that the individuals who formed the most negative evaluations of the campaign were also well informed. These individuals apparently failed to vote because of alienation engendered by active participation in the campaign process. There was evidence that this participation (as measured by viewing of Labor campaign broadcasts on television) fell off sharply late in the campaign. An indication that this alienation was not severe is that most of these nonvoters were willing to label themselves Labor supporters in a survey taken after the election.

Additional research will be necessary to evaluate this interpretation. Ideally, measurement of individuals' evaluations of a campaign should precede voting if this measure is used as a predictor of voting. In this study it was measured after voting was completed. Perhaps individuals who decided not to vote for other reasons rationalized their decision by blaming the way in which the campaign was conducted. In addition, an effort should be made to isolate those campaign messages which are most likely to create positive or negative impressions about an entire campaign. It may be that for some individuals, news about certain events creates impressions which persist throughout an entire campaign and ultimately influences voting behavior. It is these impressions which in effect become "themes" of the campaign, dominating an individual's perception of information about issues, policies, and candidates. For example, it is reasonable to speculate that in 1968 the reporting of the demonstrations at the Chicago Democratic convention may have strongly influenced some people's perceptions of information throughout the campaign. News coverage of the event may have alienated some members of the public, producing increased attention to the campaign, especially to the issue of law and order, and perhaps an increased willingness among traditional Democrats to believe the promises of Nixon. Ironically, this possible media effect is the opposite of what media professionals intended because their commentary was frequently critical of police actions.

John P. Robinson (1970) noted in an analysis of Survey Research Center data for the 1968 election that there may have been an erosion of support for Humphrey among voters who felt that not enough force was used against demonstrators. He points out that the law and order issue was more important than the Chicago incident in drawing support to Nixon. However, this issue might not have aroused public concern if the Chicago events had not "set the stage" for it. In dealing with an event like this it would be necessary first to determine who was most influenced toward a state of alienation, and then to attempt to isolate social conditions and mass communication variables which may have affected or will now affect these individuals. From such data, a theory could be constructed which attempts to conceptualize the underlying process.

In the theory and research reviewed above, many variables were considered and various models of the relationships between these variables were described. We argued that there has been a trend away from attributing negative direct "effects" to mass communication variables. The media should not be viewed as enabling charismatic leaders to instantaneously mobilize masses to political action. Acting alone, the media cannot "brainwash" the masses to support authoritarian leaders. On the other hand, the media do play an important role in political processes which cannot be explained away by such pluralistic theory variables as reference group involvement or reference group values. People do not necessarily vote as their friends or families do. Nor is their vote always intended to serve the interests and values of the group to which they belong. Pluralistic variables may prove to be important conditions affecting political communication processes but they do not preclude mass communication from being influential.

This review of research demonstrates that mass communication "effects" must be studied carefully if they are to be correctly interpreted. Hitler's successful use of radio does not prove that mass communication always subverts democratic political processes. Nor did the 1940 American presidential election studies prove that pluralistic groups control the political process with minimal help from mass communication. It is necessary to search beyond the most immediately discernible variable relationships to select those which provide more comprehensive, dynamic explanations of political action.

We have argued that more useful explanations can be created by linking specific uses of mass media to processes in which certain predispositions to political action are formed. In our discussion, we focused attention on a particular predisposition—alienation. Much research using this variable has proved disappointing. Conflicting results have been obtained. However, these results may be attributable to the way in which alienation was measured and to the methods used to analyze relationships between alienation and other variables. We favored the definition of alienation derived from Eric Allerdt by Veikko Pietila. In our view, this definition has the advantage of focusing attention on the social process which gives rise to alienation. This process can be linked to specific uses of the mass media and to specific political actions.

Political Systems Approaches

Our discussion so far provides evidence that mass communication may be influential in a variety of political processes. This evidence is scattered and inconsistent. No systematic explanation of the role of mass communication in politics can be constructed from it. Without such an explanation, few guidelines can be given for future research which are more than simple speculation. Such an explanation can be and should be constructed from the findings of future research. As this explanation is developed, it should permit research efforts to become more efficient. Meanwhile our review of the literature permits us to specify some requirements for future theory construction.

The first requirement of theory construction is that it should attempt to conceptualize the various political processes identified by research as being interrelated with one another to form an overarching political system. This does not mean that political processes should not be conceptualized separately. On the contrary, most empirical research will be guided by such models. But a continuing effort must be made to integrate the various models. The consequences of one process may become the contingent conditions which determine the outcome of a second process. The outcomes of individual processes may appear to be encouraging and yet the consequences for the system as a whole may be dysfunctional. Only when the system is conceptualized as a whole is it possible to evaluate the consequences of its component processes.

Strengths and Weaknesses of a Systems Approach

Systems terminology and conceptualizations derived from general systems theory are currently being applied in many social science disciplines. What we are proposing may not appear particularly innovative to readers unfamiliar with the many variants of systems theory. To differentiate the approach we are advocating here from conceptualizations that have already been popularized requires some knowledge of the literature on systems theory and of the criticisms which it contains.[16] We agree with many of the criticisms which have been made of general systems theory and of its numerous applications in various disciplines. In formulating our position we have attempted to avoid some of the major weaknesses of systems theories. Briefly summarized these weaknesses include:

1. A tendency to provide only a means of organizing descriptions of past or present social structures while failing to explain why these structures appeared or how they function on a day-to-day basis. No basis for predicting future operation of the system is provided.

2. A tendency to accept an implicit, homeostatic explanation for all changes in social structures. That is, theorists tend to assume that any structural change which occurs is necessary to restore the "balance" of the system, returning the system to its "normal" state.

3. A tendency to make predictions about the future of social systems by finding analogies between social systems and mechanical or biological systems. Systems theorists can be accused of promoting a new form of positivistic organicism because some early theory equated the functioning of various types of systems.

4. A tendency to focus on the individual structures that make up a system rather than on the dynamic interaction between structures.

5. A tendency to spawn "grand theories" of social structures which cannot be empirically tested. Acceptance of such theories has tended to correlate with the reputation of the theorist, not with the amount of empirical research done to evaluate the theory.

6. A tendency to produce overly simple representations of reality and to assume that linear models, which include only a few variables, could summarize valid, universal laws of human behavior.

This list is a sample of problems endemic to a systems approach. Our concern has been to outline an approach which is sensitive to these criticisms and adjusts for some of them.

We believe that one key to constructing useful systems models in the social sciences is to focus on processes rather than on particular social structures. A social process is made up of a specific set of actions at a particular time. But a list of these actions is about as useful to understanding a social process as a list of the parts of a dead cell is to understanding how living tissue functions. Hence our concern in much of this book is with models of processes, not with lists of structures. A concern about process should direct the theorist toward seeking to explain how and why patterns of action are created, maintained, and altered, interrelating and changing over time.

The construction and evaluation of models of isolated social processes may be a necessary step toward construction of a useful social system model. Frequently, however, such models are constructed only to serve the immediate, practical purposes of the researcher. They are not constructed with a view toward eventual inclusion in a model of a system. Such models may not prove of long-range use. Our view is that a properly formulated systems approach can guide construction of useful models of social processes, which contribute to an eventual model of the whole system.[17]

The immediate purpose to be served by systems models is *not* to provide precise or universal explanations of social action. While these are reasonable long-range objectives, any attempt to achieve them now appears doomed to fail. Social system models which purport to serve these objectives can be justifiably subjected to criticisms like those listed above. Since little is known about individual social processes, any system model must be grounded on a host of assumptions about such processes. Such models will necessarily be perceived as unduly abstract, unrealistic, or even fraudulent to those individuals who fail to understand or who reject the assumptions which underlie the models.

The most practical purpose to be served by system models today is to coordinate the study of social processes. As our review of the literature makes apparent, the study of social processes is proceeding in many directions, guided by a variety of conceptualizations and serving diverse objectives. We make no further claims for the particular system model we shall introduce here. The model is intended to guide the study of social processes in the direction that we have deduced is likely to prove fruitful. Readers who reject our model are urged to substitute one of their own. In our view, the study of social processes will not realize its potential for building theory until many different systems models are created or until those system models which are implicit in existing studies are explicitly acknowledged and elaborated.

The Almond and Powell Approach

A system model introduced by Gabriel Almond and Bingham Powell (1966) is the starting point for our model construction. We shall accept some of their definitions but significantly alter other parts of their approach. Like

Almond and Powell we limit our model to the *political* system. It is not a model of the entire social system. We accept their definition of a political system as including "all the interactions which affect the use or threat of use of legitimate physical coercion" (p. 18). Almond and Powell present an extended explanation for this definition. We accept their conclusion that it is the relationship to coercion that is the distinctive quality of the political system. In some societies, the political system is integrated into other parts of the society, so that legitimate use of physical coercion is exercised by leaders of families, religious organizations, business groups, and so on. In most modern societies, specialized social structures have been created which tend to monopolize the use of coercion.

Almond and Powell provide standard definitions of other key concepts (pp. 21–22). Political systems are defined as made up of subsystems which consist of structures made up of sets of related roles. The basic units of the political system are roles which consist of "that particular part of the activity of individuals which is involved in political processes."

In our view the basic definitions provided by Almond and Powell are too static. The focus on roles, structures, and subsystems diverts attention toward relatively static, easily observable activities. This approach is in contradiction to the objective which Almond and Powell set for themselves: to take a major analytical step by building political development explicitly into their approach (p. 13). They have attempted to accomplish their aim by focusing on what they term the "conversion processes" of the political system. Borrowing from David Easton's work, they depict day-to-day operation of the political system as consisting of inputs (demands and supports) which are converted into outputs (taxes, regulations, allocations, affirmations of values) by conversion processes. They list six conversion processes: interest articulation (formulation of demands), interest aggregation (combining of articulated demands), rule making, rule application, rule adjudication, and communication. Figure 4 is a diagram of the Almond and Powell model.[18]

Almond and Powell argue that political systems change in response to

Figure 4

ALMOND AND POWELL MODEL OF THE POLITICAL SYSTEM

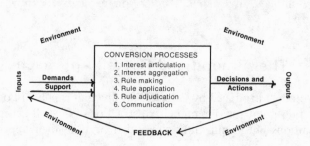

four types of problems: state building, nation building, participation, and distribution. State building refers to attempts by an elite to gain control of a society. Nation building refers to the problem of developing a political system to which members are loyal and committed. Participation problems arise because groups seek to exercise decision-making power. Distribution problems result from pressures to use the coercive power of the political system to redistribute wealth.

Much of the Almond and Powell book consists of an analysis of examples drawn from studies of political systems in many nations. Essentially, the authors evaluate how the conversion processes operate in different systems and then look at how well these systems have coped with the four problems. This leads them to conclusions about the capabilities of various political systems based on the ease or difficulty with which these systems cope with problems.

The authors conclude that three criteria of system development characterize systems that have high capability for dealing with problems. These criteria are subsystem autonomy, structural differentiation, and cultural secularization. In their view, modern, well-developed political systems tend to exhibit these characteristics. Such systems have specialized structures to handle conversion processes (structural differentiation); individuals who are increasingly rational, analytic, and empirical in their political action (cultural secularization); and specialized, independent subsystems which deal directly with specific problems (subsystem autonomy). The authors are careful to point out that development can go backward as well as forward but that historical trends have favored increased capability (p. 25).

We find several flaws in this view of political systems and the way in which the authors apply it. In some respects the authors have created a taxonomy and then selected examples to fit it. They cannot claim to have evaluated their model empirically. They have demonstrated that their model is a cogent, plausible way of "rereading history." Conversion processes by definition always have specific consequences. More "modern" systems tend to be more capable. Everything hangs together logically. But how useful is this model for explaining current political events or predicting the future of specific political systems? The authors argue that just as useful predictions about the future career of a high school graduate can be based on "a few very strong relationships between fundamental variables. . . . We may be able to go a long way toward predicting the limitations, potentialities and pressures shaping the future of a political system if we can find a few very strong relationships"; they hold that "the utility of the developmental approach, as it has been formulated above, is that it rests upon the initial designation of several such fundamental variables . . . " (p. 323).

This claim is too ambitious. The authors have no proof that they have actually designated the fundamental variables. At best, their work is suggestive of how these variables might be measured and the resulting data analyzed. Just such problems of conceptualization, measurement and analysis plague research in educational counseling which attempts to make predictions about students' careers. It is extremely risky to generalize from strong relationships which are found to hold for a population to predictions about a specific individual. The controversy over using I.Q. scores as a basis for predictions of academic success is a good example of a fundamental variable that has been conceptualized even though its measurement and application are in dispute. Similarly, it is difficult to make predictions about an individual nation on the basis of generalizations which are valid for groups of nations.

A New Political System Model

We shall refine the Almond and Powell model by differentiating three types of processes which make up the political system: public, elite, and shared processes. Public processes involve actions by private individuals but do not involve elite action. Similarly, elite processes consist primarily of elite actions. Shared processes involve both public and elite action. A system model which deals with the relationships among these processes is diagrammed in Figure 5.

Each of our three types is made up of social processes and communication processes, interlinked to generate output which then constitutes input for other types of processes. Public processes include interest articulation or alienation, interest aggregation or disintegration, political socialization, and media uses and gratifications having political consequences. Elite processes include rule making, rule application, rule adjudication, and internal promotional communication processes aimed exclusively at other elites. Shared processes include election, public opinion formation, and public affairs information dissemination. Future research can generate explanations of many other processes which fall into these three categories.

Public processes generate output in the form of demands and supports which are communicated in some way to serve as input to elite processes and shared processes (represented by arrows in Figure 5). Elite processes generate decisions and actions which impose legitimate constraints on action. These decisions and actions can be communicated to provide direct input to shared processes. Certain shared processes can also exercise legitimate coercion, as when election results compel incumbents to surrender their public offices. Images and experiences of the way in which legitimate coercion is exercised become input to both public processes and elite processes.

We have discussed many of the processes which make up this model

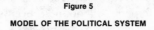

Figure 5

MODEL OF THE POLITICAL SYSTEM

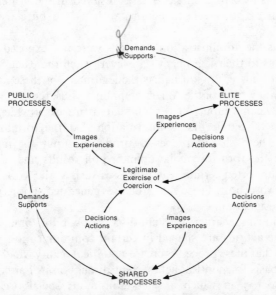

in previous chapters. Public processes were discussed in Chapter 2, Chapter 4, and in this chapter. Shared processes have been discussed in Chapters 3 and 6. We have not discussed elite processes. Discussions of such processes can be found in the political science literature. One reason for our omission of these processes is the lack of empirical studies which document how media influence elite processes. There is much speculation in this area. It is possible to argue that media directly influence the decisions of judges and even presidents. No empirical studies exist to document the extent of this influence. Thus our model indicates a large gap in the literature on political communication. If our model proves useful, filling this gap should provide a more comprehensive understanding of media's role in the political system.

The operation of our model can be illustrated using events which occurred during the Watergate affair. This discussion is not intended as proof of the validity of this model. Rather, it demonstrates how the model might facilitate the formulation of a comprehensive explanation of a series of apparently discrete events. Watergate was initiated by elite actions which members of the Nixon administration felt constituted a legitimate exercise of coercion. One explanation that has emerged to account for their actions is that these actions were a response to what the administration perceived as a direct threat to their ability to govern. This threat was generated by events such as the massive public demonstrations against the Viet Nam war, actions by small groups of individuals who destroyed draft board files, and the publication of the Pentagon Papers. All of these events can be conceived of as outcomes of various public and shared processes which then became input to elite processes. These elite processes resulted in the Watergate burglary itself as well as other related actions such as the burglary of Ellsberg's psychiatrist's office.

As long as the administration's actions were not exposed few questions were raised as to their legitimacy. However, when these actions were investigated and discussed by journalists the legitimacy of these actions came to be questioned by most of the American public. Thus, the exercise of coercion by an elite became input for certain shared processes which involved the transmission of public affairs information and the formation of public opinion.[19] These shared processes produced input to public and elite processes in the form of public opinion poll results and election results. This input supported certain elite processes such as the work by the staff of the Special Prosecutor. These elite processes generated actions which resulted in Nixon's resignation.

In the following chapter, we shall discuss how public images and experiences of elite actions are shaped in certain communication processes. We have argued that these processes create a political reality which is used by the public as a basis for political action. Our discussion is limited to American society, a society in which a semiautonomous social organization, the profession of journalism, has assumed increasing responsibility for providing surveillance and interpretation of the manner in which legitimate coercion is exercised. The influence of this organization may lie in an ability to shape agendas of both public and elite audiences so that certain political processes are transformed.

This model is highly speculative. It represents our best effort at reconstructing existing theory and data into a logically consistent, potentially heuristic framework. The model can guide research by directing attention toward certain processes and particular variables within processes. Communication variables are assigned high priority. Processes are to be studied in the context of an entire system. The output of certain processes becomes input for others. In certain processes elites and the public interact to exercise coercion, as when the public makes election choices based on information supplied by elites. In many cases links between processes are made by some form of communication. In all processes, information about the exercise of coercion supplied by journalists becomes input. Public demands and supports must be communicated in some way to be input to elite processes. Sometimes this is accomplished through physical confrontation. More typically, it is done using some form of mass communication.

The model we have created assumes a particular level of social organization. It is a model which may be applicable only to the American political system. In nations where subsystems are not autonomous or in which structural differentiation has not occurred, there may be no advantage to differentiating public and elite processes. There may be only a set of shared processes which serve all of the functions. For example, in traditional, patriarchal societies the "public" may interact daily with the village headman who serves as the "elite." There is no need to examine a public opinion formation process in this setting. The public accepts the traditional view of political reality which has been accepted for generations. Actions of the elite are not interpreted by journalists. Mass media play no role in communicating images of political reality. In other societies, certain public processes may produce a form of "mob rule" in which the public directly exercises the right to coerce action instead of indirectly influencing how coercion is exercised by the input provided to elite processes.

Thus, our model provides a plausible way of viewing the interrelationships which exist between actions and events which take place at different levels of the social order. Mass communication plays vital roles in initiating and sustaining various social processes at all levels of the social system.[20] Frequently, it is the mass media that are responsible for taking the output of one process and providing it as input for another process as when public opinion poll results are transmitted to elites and serve as input to their decision making.

Our model is not a developmental model in the broadest sense. It should, however, enable prediction of future developments within the narrow range of societies to which it is applicable. Alteration of the basic structure of this model may extend its usefulness to a wider range of societies.

Notes

1. For example, Robert Lane treats the mass media as one of several social institutions which influence American political life. He argues for a two-step flow view of mass communication effects upon politics. Mass communication is not viewed as an essential part of political processes but as an external agent having some influence upon some processes under certain conditions. The mass media are but one of many social institutions which encourage participation in politics (*Political Life* [New York: Free Press, 1959], pp. 275–98). Seymour Lipset acknowledges that mass media may have certain effects which enhance or threaten democratic political processes but he does not view the media as a part of these processes. He suggests (p. 44) that the mass media may encourage political extremism in developing countries by informing the poor of alternate life styles. Once informed of this better way of life, extremist political organizations act to achieve it. Lipset focuses on the role of such organizations in politics (*Political Man: The Social Bases of Politics* [Garden City, N.Y.: Anchor Books, 1963]). Andrew S. McFarland

(*Power and Leadership in Pluralist Systems* [Stanford, Calif.: Stanford University Press, 1969]) has dealt at length with the way in which leaders exercise political power in pluralist political systems but gives little attention to the role of mass communication in the creation and maintenance of this power. Like Lipset, he considers only the role of social groups and psychological variables in this process. He describes one route to political power as the "charisma-paradigm" model. "Thus, in times of value strain, a charismatic hero may appear whose psychological processes are paralleled by his public actions, perhaps through a widely appealing resoltuion of a personal identity crisis that provides the critical decisions and values for a new social identity, thereby leading to social change through the establishment of new social structures infused with new ideology" (p. 225). Implicit in this view of leadership is the use of mass communication to communicate the leader's public actions but no recognition of how the leader might be shaped by his association with the media.

2. Philip Davidson's book *Propaganda and the American Revolution* (Chapel Hill: University of North Carolina Press, 1941) provides a description of colonial propaganda during the Revolutionary War. While he attempts to explain the social origins of propaganda and the media used to transmit it, he does not discuss the communication process which produced acceptance of the propaganda. He does not systematically explain why propaganda proved influential at particular points in time. Other historians tend to treat communication variables in a similar, primarily descriptive fashion. For example, George Trevelyan (*The American Revolution* [New York: David McKay, 1941], pp. 259–93) describes the revolutionary "talk" that preceded and was apparently influential upon the revolution. However, he does not explain the communication process that translated "talk" into action. Esmond Wright (*Causes and Consequences of the American Revolution* [Chicago: Quadrangle Books, 1966]) has collected articles which discuss a wide variety of interpretations of the American Revolution. None of these interpretations discusses communication processes, even though propagandists and various forms of mass media are mentioned. By contrast, other social processes are frequently discussed as basic to the Revolution. For example, Charles Beard, in *An Economic Interpretation of the Constitution of the United States* (New York: Macmillan, 1913), has argued that economic variables caused the Constitution to be written in a particular way.

3. For example, Berelson, Lazarsfeld, and McPhee were not disturbed to find that only a small minority are moved to participate in politics by the mass media. They argue, "How could a mass democracy work if all the people were deeply involved in politics? Lack of interest by some people is not without its benefits, too. True, the highly interested voters vote more, and know more about the campaign, and read and listen more, and participate more; however, they are also less open to persuasion and less likely to change. Extreme interest goes with extreme partisanship." They are optimistic about the ability of social groups to provide the stability necessary to preserve democracy. In addition, these groups make possible a two-step flow of political information down to the apathetic masses. The optimism of these researchers stems in part from their confidence in the two-step flow notion (Peter Bachrach, ed., *Political Elites in a Democracy* [New York: Atherton Press, 1971], p. 38). On the other hand, C. Wright Mills finds the same political apathy deeply disturbing. "The new Little Man seems to have no firm roots, no sure loyalties to sustain his life and give it a center. . . . Perhaps because he does not know where he is going, he is paralyzed with fear. This is especially a feature of his political life, where the paralysis results in the most profound apathy of modern times." Mills goes on to argue, "This isolated position makes him excellent material for synthetic

molding at the hands of popular culture—print, film, radio, and television. As a metropolitan dweller, he is especially open to the focused onslaught of all the manufactured loyalties and distractions that are contrived and urgently pressed upon those who live in worlds they never made." The implicit model of the mass communication process in Mills' thought is the hypodermic needle model. Political apathy is induced and sustained in part by the distractions injected by the mass media. This apathy is a sign that democracy is doomed (*White Collar* [New York: Oxford University Press, 1956], p. xvi).

4. William Kornhauser, in *The Politics of Mass Society* (Glencoe, Ill.: Free Press, 1959), not only reviews mass society theory but also considers traditional, pluralistic, and totalitarian theory.

5. See the quote by C. Wright Mills in note 3. Another view is provided by Walter Lippmann, who expresses the concern that modern democracies will not survive. "The people have imposed a veto upon the judgements of informed and responsible officials and at the critical junctures prevailing public opinion has been destructively wrong." The result has been "a practical failure to govern," which may lead to "counterrevolutionary measures for the establishment of strong government" (*Essays in the Public Philosophy* [New York: Mentor, 1956], pp. 43–53). Kornhauser argues that "mass society possesses only weak defenses against mass-oriented elites who seek to abrogate all restraints on power and raise up new kinds of totalistic ideologies. ... Totalitarian elites strive to create masses as well as to mobilize existing masses. People cannot be mobilized against the established order until they first have been divorced from prevailing codes are relations. Only then are they available for 'activist modes of intervention' in the political process" (op. cit., p. 121).

6. David Riesman describes the use of mass media by "other-directed" individuals by noting, "The child must look early to his mass-media tutors for instruction in the techniques of getting directions for one's life as well as for specific tricks of the trade ... I ... am interested in showing how popular culture is exploited for group-adjustment purposes not only in the form of manifestly didactic literature and services but also in fictional guise. There is nothing new in the observation that people who would rather not admit their need for help, or who prefer to spice it with fun, look to the movies and other popular media as sources of enlightenment" (*The Lonely Crowd* [New Haven: Yale University Press, 1961], pp. 149–50). C. Wright Mills has argued, "The world created by the mass media contains very little discussion of political meanings, not to speak of their dramatization, or sharp demands and expectations. Instead, the media plug for ruling political symbols and personalities; but in their attempts to enforce conventional attachment to them, they standardize and reiterate until these symbols and personalities become completely banal. ... The explicit political content is, after all, a very small portion of their managed time and space. This badly handled content must compete with a whole machinery of amusement, within a marketing context of distrust. The most skilled media men and the highest paid talent are devoted to the glamorous worlds of sport and leisure. These competing worlds, which in their modern scale are only 30 years old, divert attention from politics by providing a set of continuing interest in mythic figures and fast-moving stereotypes" (1956, pp. 334–36). Several similar arguments concerning media use and impact can be found in B. Rosenberg and D.M. White, eds., *Mass Culture* (Glencoe, Ill.: Free Press, 1957). See especially articles by Bogart, Lazarsfeld and Merton, and Van Den Hagg.

7. For an extended discussion of the inconsistencies and inaccuracies of mass society theory, see Raymond A. Bauer and Alice H. Bauer, "America, 'Mass Society' and 'Mass Media,'" *Journal of Social Issues* 16 (1960): 3–66. The Bauers conclude,

"Basically the so-called 'theory of mass society' is a statement of alienation from our own society. A vast portion of the 'data' on which this view of mass society ought to be based is absent, contradictory, or completely ambiguous. Furthermore, when an argument, speculation, or 'theory' which is essentially two-edged is introduced, only that edge which cuts in the pessimistic direction is employed" (p. 64).

8. C. Wright Mills, *Power Elite* (New York: Oxford University Press, 1956).

9. It is important to note that this mass communication role is substantially different from the role assigned by mass society and elitist theorists. They concluded that conflicting judgments were produced because elites transmitted conflicting messages. In our view, mass media can lay a basis for critical judgments even when competing elites do not exist or where competition between elites has been formalized so that limits are placed on propaganda. What is crucial is that individuals learn to carry on certain transactions with media and not simply accept every message as true. This ability to carry on certain transactions should be learned in political processes.

10. Arnold Rose presented a systematic discussion of pluralistic views in *The Power Structure* (New York: Oxford University Press, 1967). Rose concludes "There is a power structure in every organized activity of American life and at every level—national, regional, state and local.... There are varying degrees of relationship and agreement among these varied power structures. They are certainly not unified into a simple power structure, even within the categories of the economic and the political.... Nor are they usually counterveiling, because each operates primarily within its own sphere of influence" (pp. 483–84). Our discussion of pluralistic theory is limited in scope. We have not considered recent variants of this theory, which include cultural pluralism, social pluralism, and interest group liberalism. Our intention is to demonstrate how the role of mass media has traditionally been conceptualized by pluralistic thinkers. We regret that political scientists may find our discussion somewhat dated.

11. David Truman, "The American System in Crisis," in Peter Bachrach, ed., *Political Elites in a Democracy* (New York: Atherton Press, 1971).

12. Joseph Lyford discussed factors constraining the performance of the news media in "The Pacification of the Press" in Michael Emery and Ted Smythe, eds., *Readings in Mass Communication* (Dubuque, Iowa: Wm. C. Brown, 1974). He writes, "A significant consequence of the industrialization of the mass media has been their pacification.... The extent to which these people (media managers) are able to 'manage' the news is questionable. Although they have the power to make the spot decisions on the selection and treatment of specific news items, their choice is limited by the fact that they have to pick and choose their material from a flow of signals largely generated by people who have nothing to do with the journalism profession" (pp. 417–19).

13. For example, Lester Milbrath lists 283 references in the bibliography to his book *Political Participation* (Chicago: Rand McNally, 1965).

14. Rex Hopper, "The Revolutionary Process," *Social Forces* 28:3 (1950): 270–79.

15. A recent exhaustive analysis of Survey Research Center data for elections in 1964, 1966, and 1968 found that social status and education are consistent, useful predictors of a wide variety of political action. See Bennett and Klecka (1970).

16. Several references which provide a useful introduction to systems theory approaches are Walter Buckley, *Sociology and Modern Systems Theory* (Englewood Cliffs, N.J.: Prentice-Hall, 1967); David Easton, *A Systems Analysis of Political Life* (New York: Wiley, 1965); Carl G. Hempel, "The Logic of Functional Analysis," in L. Cross, ed., *Symposium on Sociological Theory* (New York: Harper & Row, 1959); N.J.

Demerath, III, and Richard A. Peterson, eds., *Systems, Change and Conflict* (New York: Free Press, 1967); Ithiel de Sola Pool, "Communication Systems," in I. Pool and W. Schramm, *Handbook of Communication* (Chicago: Rand McNally, 1973).

17. In Chapter 7 we provide a more detailed defense of our position. We argue that theory construction normally advances by relatively small steps, not by gigantic, intuitive leaps. Each step is based on a body of empirical research that evaluates previous steps. Construction of models of processes is a middle step which can eventually permit construction of useful social system models.

18. This diagram is our representation. Almond and Powell provide no visual representation of their model.

19. In a recent paper we discussed how public opinion was formed during the Watergate affair. See Dennis K. Davis, Sidney Kraus, and Jae-won Lee, "Opinion Formation Process During the Resignation and Pardon of Richard Nixon: A Pilot Study of Critical Events Analysis." Paper presented to World Association for Public Opinion Research Congress, Montreux, Switzerland, September 1975.

20. In a recent paper we outlined a research approach which is consistent with this model. We argued that it will be useful to structure research to analyze social processes which underlie the creation, transmission, and reception of information about critical events. Such research should provide data which permit evaluation of many of the links between social processes which we have described here. See Sidney Kraus and Dennis K. Davis, in collaboration with Gladys Engel Lang and Kurt Lang, "Critical Event Analysis," in S.H. Chaffee, ed., *Political Communication: Issues and Strategies for Research* (Beverly Hills, Calif.: Sage, 1975).

Abstracts and Bibliography

Aberbach, Joel. "Alienation and Political Behavior." *Am. Polit. Sci. Rev.* 63 (March 1969): 86–99.

Agger, Robert E. and Vincent Ostrom. "The Political Structure of a Small Community," in David Reisman, "Political Communication and Social Structure in the United States." *Pub. Opin. Q.* 20 (1956): 81–89.
The study consists of a survey made of a randomly selected sample of 260 persons in a community of about 3000 to determine the ordering of a community. Five role aggregates are defined in the community: advisors, talkers, listeners, workers, and nonparticipants.
Method: survey; questionnaire. *Statistics*: frequency distributions. *Pop. (N)*: 260. *Findings*: People at all levels in the power structure are involved in political policy and decision making. The various role-playing aggregates differed from each other in terms of social and demographic characteristics. They were viewed and treated separately by both the top leadership and businessmen. *Advisors* are articulate, high-status people, who participate in many community activities and have sophisticated concerns with community politics. *Talkers* constitute the largest single aggregate of political participants and, as with the Advisors, can be expected to articulate demands in relation to the top leadership. *Listeners* are somewhat politically passive, as represented by meeting-going and failure to keep up with local news. Advisors and Talkers read newspapers more often than Listeners. *Workers* belong to fewer

organizations than Listeners but are somewhat more active in local elections. *Nonparticipants* constitute 51% of the population. They play no active political roles. Fewer of them read the local newspaper.

Almond, Gabriel and G. Bingham Powell. *Comparative Politics: A Developmental Approach.* Boston: Little, Brown, 1966.

Becker, Jerome D. and Ivan L. Preston. "Media Usage and Political Activity." *Journalism Q.* 46 (Spring 1969): 129–34.

Becker and Preston present a secondary analysis of the relationship between the use of four mass media to follow the 1964 election campaign and political activity. Their analysis indicates that a high level of media use was associated with some types of political activity, such as concern for election outcome, interest in the campaign, voting in 1964, and attempts at personal persuasion. Various political activities covary with media usage. *Method*: survey; questionnaire. *Statistics*: frequencies; Kandall's tau; Goodman and Kruskal's gamma. *Pop. (N)*: 1571, national cross section of voting-age citizens, Survey Research Center.

Findings: (1) Media use was more highly associated with interest than with concern. (2) 15% of the respondents "didn't care at all" about the election and 15% "didn't care very much" about the election, but this is less likely to be true at high levels of media use. (3) For those who attended the campaign in all four media, only 8% had no concern for the outcome, and only 12% indicated they did not care very much. (4) An index of political efficacy was highest when levels of media use, education, and income were highest. Education had a considerably higher association with political efficacy than did media use. (5) The higher the mass media use, education, and income, the greater the voter percentage. But media use had a much stronger relationship with 1964 voting than with previous elections, with the reverse true for education. Income was more strongly associated with 1964 voting than with any other political activity variable. (6) Of those failing to vote, 9% used four media, while 27, 34, 22, and 8% used three, two, one, and no media respectively. (7) The activities of writing public officials and expressing an opinion, as well as trying to persuade persons to vote for a particular candidate, tended to be performed by persons on higher levels of media use, education, and income. (8) Media use had the strongest association with the respondents' concern for the election, interest in the campaign, voting in 1964, and attempts at personal persuasion. Education had the highest relationship with the time of voting choice and tendency to write letters. Income had the second strongest association with time of voting choice and with voting in 1964.

Bennett, Stephen E. and William R. Klecka. "Social Status and Political Participation: A Multivariate Analysis of Predictive Power." *Midwest J. Polit. Sci.* 14 (August 1970): 355–82.

Berelson, Bernard, Paul F. Lazarsfeld, and William McPhee. *Voting: A Study of Opinion Formation in a Presidential Campaign.* Chicago: University of Chicago Press, 1954.

Blumler, J.G. and J.M. McLeod. "Communication and Voter Turnout in Britain," in T. Legatt, ed., *Sociological Theory and Survey Research.* Beverly Hills, Calif.: Sage, 1974, pp. 265–312.

Burstein, Paul. "Social Structure and Individual Political Participation in Five Countries." *Am. J. Sociol.* 77 (May 1972): 1087–1110.

This is a summary research involving the construction and testing of a causal model of individual political participation. Survey data from the United States, Great Britain, West Germany, Italy, and Mexico are utilized.

Hypotheses: (1) "The degree of political participation of an individual will vary directly and strongly with the number and kind of his organizational and media

ties into society; (2) An individual's attributes will affect his political participation insofar as they affect his organizational and media ties into society" (p. 1106).
Method: survey; questionnaire. *Statistics*: zero-order correlations, path analysis.
Pop. (N): National samples of adults from five countries.
Findings: (1) The following hypotheses were supported by the data: the best predictors of political participation are media and organizational involvement, followed by SES, followed by ascribed attributes; the best predictor of media and organizational involvement is SES, followed by ascribed attributes; socioeconomic status will predict participation; ascribed attributes will predict SES better than they will predict media and organizational involvement, and media and organizational involvement better than participation. This is generally supported throughout the study. (2) "An individual's political participation can be predicted by locating him in his social structure, even crudely, and prior variables operate through their influence on his social location" (p. 1103). (3) Though status, sex, race, etc., have widely different strengths of relations with other variables in the system, the path coefficients of media and organizational involvement with participation are very similar from country to country. (4) The best predictors of level of political participation are measures of various types of communication among people. (5) Participation is most greatly affected by a changing structure of relations among people and such changes are much easier to implement than economic development. Thus it is likely that people will come to participate in politics before they acquire the perspective and resources to participate along democratic lines.

Chaffee, Steven H., Jack M. McLeod, and Charles K. Atkin. "Parental Influences on Adolescent Media Use." *Am. Behav. Sci.* 14, 3 (January-February 1971): 323–40. See abstract in Chapter 2.

Chaffee, Steven H., Jack M. McLeod, and Daniel B. Wackman. "Family Communication and Political Socialization." Paper presented at the annual meeting of the Association for Education in Journalism, Iowa City, August 1966. See abstract in Chapter 2.

Chaffee, Steven H., L. Scott Ward, and Leonard P. Tipton. "Mass Communication and Political Socialization." *Journalism Q.* 47 (Winter 1970): 647–59. See abstract in Chapter 2.

Dean, Dwight G. "Alienation: Its Meaning and Measurement." *Am. Sociol. Rev.* 26 (October 1961): 753–58.

The concept of alienation is considered here as having three major components: powerlessness, normlessness, and social isolation. There is a low but statistically significant negative correlation between the three components of alienation and occupational prestige, education, income, and rural background. There is a small positive correlation between alienation and advancing age.
Method: survey; questionnaire. *Statistics*: zero-order correlation coefficients. *Pop. (N)*: select sample of four political wards in Columbus, O., random sample of precincts and individuals in wards, respondent rate of 39%. 384 usable returns.
Findings: The correlation coefficients are uniformly of such a low magnitude that it would not be feasible to predict the degree of alienation from the score of any of the five social correlates measured.

Eckhardt, Kenneth and Gerry Hendershot. "Transformation of Alienation into Public Opinion." *Sociol. Q.* 8 (Autumn 1967): 459–67.

Erbe, William. "Social Involvement and Political Activity: A Replication and Elaboration." *Am. Sociol. Rev.* 29 (April 1964): 198–215.

Eulau, Heinz and Peter Schneider. "Dimensions of Political Involvement." *Pub. Opin. Q.* 20 (Spring 1956): 128–42.

The authors present an analysis of the interrelations of selected dimensions of

political involvement, in particular "efficacy" and "responsibility."
Method: survey; questionnaire. *Statistics*: cross-tabulation, frequency distributions.
Pop. (N): national, area probability, Survey Research Center, $n = 1,146$.
Findings: Those more highly related to the political process are more sensitive to differences between the parties, more issue-oriented, more concerned about the outcome of the election, more partisan on issues, more partisan in their choice of candidates, more likely to have strong party identifications, more interested in the campaign, know more, are more frequently exposed to the mass media, and are more likely to vote and otherwise participate in the campaign than the less politically related.

Jackson, John S. "The Political Behavior and Socio-economic Backgrounds of Black Students: The Antecedents of Protest." *Midwest J. Polit. Sci.* 15, 4 (November 1971): 661–86.
Jackson describes the political activities of black college students in the South, including protest and conventional political behavior. Data were drawn from three prominent Negro colleges. Rates of involvement were compared with the Matthews and Prothro survey taken in 1962. The study also seeks to explain this behavior in terms of the background characteristics (variables).
Method: survey; questionnaire. *Statistics*: chi-square, gamma correlation, frequency distributions. *Pop. (N)*: Students at Tennessee State University, Texas A & M, and Fisk University; 448 students in selected classes were asked to complete questionnaire.
Findings: Political activity, including both protest activities and normal political channels, has increased 46% in southern black students over the last nine years. The levels of activity are highest among urban and middle-class blacks. The author attributes the increase in political activity to media use and peer groups. "Young blacks in the urban environment currently are surrounded with many stimuli which push them in the direction of increased protest participation, and the most notable of these influences are the mass media and their peer groups (pp. 675–76). The emphasis in the sampling procedure was to have the data drawn from as heterogeneous a population as possible.

Katz, Elihu and David Foulkes. "On the Use of the Mass Media as 'Escape': Clarification of a Concept." *Pub. Opin. Q.* 26 (Fall 1962): 377–88.
In a literature review, the authors examine the limited applications of the concept of escape and argue that the ultimate referent of the term "escape" should have to do with the consequences of media use.
Conclusions: (1) Past "studies present impressive evidence that alienation or deprivation are associated with increased exposure to particular media or particular kinds of media content" (p. 381). (2) Media may be sought for the purpose of strengthening one's position in his immediate network of social relations. (3) Media may be both sought and used not only to compensate for abortive or ineffectual social relations but also to maintain extant and effective ones. (4) Mass media may serve as a facade for individual retreat, but may also be used to keep oneself close to desired others. (5) " 'Escape drives' do not invariably lead to 'escapist exposure patterns' " (p. 387). (6) "Escape content" does not function as escape for all who are exposed.

Lang, Kurt and Gladys Engel Lang. "Political Participation and the Television Perspective." *Soc. Probl.* 4, 2 (October 1956): 107–16.
The authors study the effect on political participation of large-scale political telecasts. They state that "the opportunity to observe does not suffice to transform members of the mass audience into members of an active public. While it may arouse interest in viewing similar telecasts, it does not necessarily stimulate—and may even discourage —active political participation." (p. 115).

Method: survey; questionnaire. *Statistics*: frequencies. *Pop. (N)*: South Chicago, quota sample drawn from five census tracts, $n = 47$.

Findings: The task for the viewer was a reduction of the situation. The reduction took several forms: reduction of meaningful events; simplification of the race; inattentiveness to the activities of "managers"; inattentiveness to "pressures" on delegates. "TV treatment of certain episodes and personalities did stress—intentionally or unintentionally—particular interpretations which may have been accepted by viewers holding different points of view" (p. 814).

Lazarsfeld, Paul F., Bernard Berelson, and Hazel Gaudet. *The People's Choice*. New York: Columbia University Press, 1944.

Levin, Murray B. and Murray Eden. "Political Strategy for the Alienated Voter." *Pub. Opin. Q.* 26 (Spring 1962): 47–57.

The authors argue that new methods of securing voters are necessary for the candidate who is forced to campaign in a community where many alienated voters reside; these strategies should appeal to feelings of powerlessness and meaninglessness. They describe a theoretical framework which can be used to derive such strategies.

Conclusions: (1) The rational citizen votes for the party he believes will provide him with the most benefits during the coming election period. To do this, he compares the benefits he believes he would have received had the "outs" been in power with the benefits received from the "ins." (2) "The standard cliches and the traditional vote-getting techniques will not work for the alienated" (p. 55). (3) The alternatives available to the alienated voter are abstention or voting for the lesser evil. (4) The alienated voter tends to vote against the candidate who appears to be more experienced, well-known, professional, political, dishonest, and heavily financed. The alienated voter will respond, if he responds at all, to the candidate who gives him a sense of power or leads him to believe that the election is meaningful. (5) A candidate can use two methods to appeal to feelings of powerlessness: he can try to enhance feelings of powerlessness by emphasizing the unchecked tyranny of the incumbents and suggest that their hegemony is the cause of the citizen's powerlessness or he can offer the alienated voter a way out by identifying himself with the alienated voter by stressing his own powerlessness. (6) The candidate can use three strategic methods to appeal to feelings of meaninglessness in the alienated voter: he can offer the alienated voter information he did not expect to receive; he can make an appeal of frankness (e.g., tell the alienated voter many facts of political life which are usually censored); or he can indicate that he cares about the voter.

McLeod, Jack, Scott Ward, and Karen Tancill. "Alienation and Uses of the Mass Media." *Pub. Opin. Q.* 29 (Winter 1965): 584–94.

From past research in this area, media were considered a means of escape and gratification for the alienated individual. This study replicates this research, correlating alienation and education with mass media use. The results showed "little evidence that alienated adults spent more time with mass media generally" (p. 593). Education correlated positively with print media time and negatively with electronic media. The use of newspapers was somewhat related to alienation.

Method: survey; questionnaires. *Statistics*: correlations. *Pop. (N)*: Madison, Wisc., 180 adults selected in a random sample which oversampled an urban renewal section of the city.

Findings: (1) "Little support is given the prediction that alienation will be positively correlated with time spent using the mass media" (p. 586). (2) "The only significant correlation shown indicates that the more alienated are less apt than other respondents to read books. The prediction that the alienated would give special attention to the 'fantasy-oriented' media is given some rather weak support" (p. 587). (3) "Education appears to bear a stronger relationship to time spent with the media" (p. 587). (4) There were significant negative correlations of education with television and radio time (refer to Table 1). (5) "The data ... show that alienation is associated with lower interest in 'nonsensational' headlines." The prediction that "a positive association of alienation and interest in 'sensational' headlines was not supported" (p. 589). (6) "The data indicate that the more alienated the respondent, the less likely he was to think informational reasons applied to him and the more likely was his acceptance of vicarious reasons as gratifications connected with his newspaper reading" (p. 590). (7) The information seekers spend more time with the newspaper than do the vicarious seekers (p. 591). (8) "Alienation does, then, show promise as an explanatory factor in the use of the newspaper. While the correlations shown are not high, they are as high as those of education with these same media-use variables and considerably higher than those of other demographic variables customarily used in media studies" (p. 593).

Olsen, Marvin E. "Social Participation and Voting Turnout: A Multivariate Analysis." *Am. Sociol. Rev.* 37 (June 1972): 317–33.

Social participation theory argues that involvement by individuals in nonpolitical social organizations, such as voluntary associations, community affairs, and churches, will in turn mobilize them to become politically active. Survey data from an Indianapolis study supported this hypothesis. "The relationship between social participation and voting remains moderately strong after the compounding variables of age, education, political contacts through the mass media and political parties, and political orientations such as political interest and party identification are all held constant" (p. 317).

Method: survey; questionnaire. *Statistics*: frequency distributions, eta, beta, and multiple regression coefficients. *Pop. (N)*: Indianapolis urbanized area, probability sample with quotas, $n = 750$ adults.

Findings: (1) Participation in voluntary associations correlates with voting turnout at mean eta $= .31$. The only exception is labor unions. (2) Participation in community events and church activities are also both related to voting, with mean etas for both of .29. (3) Measures of informal interaction with friends and neighbors correlate only weakly with voting, and both relationships become nonsignificant with the above measures of participation in a more formal setting held constant. (4) Among respondents belonging to one or more voluntary associations who voted in the 1964 and 1966 elections, almost all belonged to these organizations before the election. This provides a basis for arguing causal direction. (5) Among the other voting correlations examined in this study, the factors of age; education; political contacts via the mass media, partisan mailings, and party workers; and political orientations such as party identification and interest in politics, all remain significantly related to voting turnout when simultaneously controlled.

Olsen, Marvin E. "Two Categories of Political Alienation." *Soc. Forces* 47 (March 1969): 288–99.

This study separates political alienation into two broad categories: attitudes of discontentment and attitudes of incapability. The former include attitudes of dissimilarity, dissatisfaction, and disillusionment; the latter include attitudes of guidelessness, powerlessness, and meaninglessness. This conceptualization of alienation is evaluated, revealing that both categories inversely correlate with education, occupation, and income. These categories also correlate with activities of political behavior (mass media exposure, political discussion, voting participation, and political involvement). Results indicate moderate association of attitudes of incapability with lack of participation in political activities.

Method: survey; questionnaire. *Statistics*: means, zero-order correlations, eta coefficients, frequency distributions, multiple classification analysis. *Pop. (N)*:

154 upper- and lower-middle-class adults were "systematically selected" from two census tracts in Ann Arbor, Mich.

Findings: (1) 35.3% expressed some attitudes of discontentment toward politics. (2) Incapability and discontentment toward politics are partially interrelated, but do represent distinct categories of estranged attitudes (p. 293). (3) In general, political activity correlated negatively with alienation (see Table 2, p. 297). (4) Media exposure increased with decreased alienation. (5) "Overall, we might conclude that attitudes of incapability toward politics are moderately associated with lack of participation in political activities, but that attitudes of political discontentment have very little effect on a person's political actions" (p. 297). (6) "Over 80 percent of the respondents who were high on incapability but low on discontentment chose the Democratic candidate in both elections, while only about one-fourth of those respondents low in incapability but high on discontentment voted Democratic" (p. 298).

Patterson, Thomas E. and Robert McClure. "Political Advertising: Voter Reaction." Paper presented at the annual meeting of the American Association for Public Opinion Research, Asheville, N.C., 1973. See abstract in Chapter 3.

Pietila, Veikko. "Alienation and Use of the Mass Media." *ACTA, Sociol.* 13, 4 (1970): 237–52.

From a survey in Finland of areas that had a newspaper strike and a television strike, people were interviewed to determine correlations between alienation and media use. Alienated people utilized the media differently, depending on whether their use was for informational purposes or vicarious reasons. The author believes that alienation should be studied as a process. He hypothesizes that in the early stages of alienation, the need for information increases and an individual seeks out various sources of information. When this does not alleviate his feeling of helplessness, he begins to avoid the information and withdraws. There would then be high media use in the early stages of alienation and a decrease in media use in the later stages.

Method: survey; questionnaire. *Statistics*: means, Pearson correlation. *Pop. (N)*: Five Finnish towns, respondents with telephones chosen from sample interviewed in a previous study.

Findings: (1) The results of the Srole Alienation Scale and the use of mass media did not correlate significantly. The use of mass media seemed to be independent of alienation. (2) There was some support for McLeod, Ward, and Tancill's study which concluded that alienated individuals use each medium for vicarious reasons more than nonalienated, who in turn use the media more for informational reasons (p. 241). (3) It is the author's opinion that mass media contribute to uncertainty in cases of situation definitions. Difficulties in this area bring about temporary alienation (p. 241). (4) "In those cases where alienated individuals read the local paper more for informational than for vicarious reasons, they generally read more delayed reward information material than do nonalienated individuals of the same group" (p. 242). (5) "Similarly, when alienated individuals do use the radio or television more for informational than for vicarious reasons, they tend to follow news and current event programs more regularly than nonalienated individuals of the same group" (p. 242). (6) There was some confirmation for the assumption that "when an individual is alienated, but his use of the media is more heavily loaded for informational than for vicarious gratification, he is in the stage of compensatory adaptation (his need for information is great). Similarly, when he shows alienation and uses the media more for vicarious than for informational purposes, he is in the stage of withdrawal and his need for information has decreased (he is trying to restrict his information intake)" (p. 248).

Robinson, John P. "Public Reaction to Political Protest: Chicago 1968." *Pub. Opin. Q.* 34 (Spring 1970): 1–9.

The study examines two main questions: Who comprised the minority sympathetic to the demonstrators? How did attitudes toward the protestors and the police affect presidential voting behavior in November 1968?

Method: survey; questionnaire. *Statistics*: frequency distributions. *Pop. (N)*: national sample of 1005 drawn by Survey Research Center.

Findings: (1) Only 57% of the under-30 college graduates felt police had used too much force. (2) It is apparent that law and order and Viet Nam were much more influential determinants of 1968 voting behavior than Chicago. (3) Only the college-educated segment of the under-30 sample yield a majority in sympathy with the demonstrators. (4) 63% of entire black population was in sympathy with demonstrators. (5) "Somewhat more Humphrey voters (33%) were sympathetic to the demonstrators than Nixon voters (22%), but the most important gulf was between the regular party voters and those who eventually voted for Wallace" (p. 7). (6) Partial explanation for black-white differences was greater trust by blacks in the accounts of the news media (especially TV) (p. 6).

Von Eschen, D., J. Kirk, and M. Pinard. "The Conditions of Direct Action in a Democratic Society." *West. Polit. Q.* 22 (June 1964): 309–25.

6

Construction of Political Reality in Society

We turn now to consider media's role in reflecting *political reality*. To what extent do the mass media "hold the mirror up to nature"? Many of us have experienced situations in which we were involved in acts subsequently reported in the media. We may have been elated or dismayed with the reporting of those acts. In some instances the reports attributed to us favorable qualities which we felt we did not deserve; sometimes negative or misleading comments were presented and we were angered and frustrated.

The political arena, often unclearly represented by the mass media during campaigns, contains many examples of politicians' disenchantment with the press. Richard Nixon was so upset with the press that upon losing the California gubernatorial race in 1962 he told them that they wouldn't have Nixon "to kick around anymore." A little more than a decade later, his press representatives and presidential staff were suggesting during the Watergate crisis that the press was "hounding Nixon out of office." In a similar vein, press disclosures (during the 1968 presidential campaign) about Spiro Agnew's performance in Maryland prompted the following reply by Agnew:

> You know, when a man's reputation is bandied about by a large newspaper in the last few days of the campaign, and he has no newspaper of his own to answer the libel, the whole thing becomes more than a little unfair. So I say to the *New York Times*: act with decency, act like men, act with intellectual honesty—and for heaven's sake let in the fresh air.[1]

Historians will record these accusations of press unfairness, bias, and distortion in the light of findings by Congress and the courts and the pressures of public opinion.

The problem of press coverage of political candidates and issues and its influence upon the public is complex and not easily resolved. It includes the issues of press responsibility and credibility, distortion and bias, the proper role of editorials and editorializing, and the nature of political reality.

Philosophers have wrestled with propositions about reality and truth, but they have not sufficiently considered the social processes which "create reality" as shaped and perceived by individuals and institutions. Among these processes are the mass media processes. As we have already seen, the mass media *alter* "reality" in many ways. Errors of fact appearing in the media and intentional bias distort or change our notions of "what really happened" in a given situation. The media often reshape events, causing perceptions among the media's audience members to differ from those held by "on-the-scene" participants and observers of those events.

Despite the oft-repeated phrase, "One picture is worth a thousand words," a picture may be no less a distortion of "reality" than are words. Lang and Lang (1953) suggested that the televised coverage of an event as perceived by viewers "overshadows the 'true' picture of the event, namely the impression obtained by someone physically present at the scene of the event." Further, they argue that "the spectator's interpretation of his own experience may be reinterpreted when he finds the event in which he participated discussed by friends, newspapermen and radio commentators" (p. 3).

Thus, in many crucial and diverse ways, the mass media "create reality" —defining activities and events, molding and shaping a variety of images for us.

Theoretical Frameworks

Research so far provides five perspectives on the role of media in the construction of political reality in society. These five perspectives may be labeled image, communicational reality, status-conferral function of the mass media, pseudo-events, and agenda-setting function of the mass media.

We will briefly review the first four of these perspectives and then concentrate on the last, agenda-setting.

Image

Kenneth Boulding's contribution to analyzing political reality is anchored in his proposition that *"behavior depends on the image."*[2] In his view, messages change images, which in turn account for changes in individual behavior patterns. Social construction of reality is a result of the process of image formation, stimulated by messages transmitted by communication networks. From this view of the social process, he abstracts the political process by examining how public decisions are made and who makes them. Essentially, it is an examination of power roles in society and the process used in filling those roles.

Boulding views the political process (which, in our discussion, corresponds with political reality) as "a process of mutual modification of images through the processes of feedback and communication" (p. 102). Hence political behavior is a response to political images. Political reality is defined by political messages which alter political images and ultimately result in changes in political behavior. Boulding's image model, therefore, operationalizes "reality" in a nonstatic perceptual framework based on an interaction of several processes—message dissemination, image alteration, and behavior change. What we call "real" and "true" is what we hold as an image gained through these processes. Boulding concludes his theoretical position by asserting that "we can never examine the correspondence of the image with reality, whether in the field of value or in the field of fact" (pp. 174–75).

A crucial element in image formation is the role of communication networks, especially the mass media, which in effect stimulate us to perceive a certain "reality."

Communicational Reality

The concept of communicational reality has been advanced by Lee Thayer.[3] It describes reality as a function of human communication behavior. Reality is structured through communication acts (talking, listening, and thinking). Thayer believes that "whatever one or more men can and do talk about, but which is not amenable to direct sensory contact by them, has no reality beyond what can be and is said about it" (p. 54).

Mass media create communication reality by shaping the conceptual environment in which humans communicate. Extending Thayer's notions, political reality is formed by mass communication reports which are talked about, altered, and interpreted by citizens in a society. The totality of this process constitutes reality.

Status-Conferral Function of the Mass Media

By giving attention to certain people, their acts, and various issues, the mass media may *confer status*. This status-conferral function—one of three social functions of the mass media posited by Lazarsfeld and Merton[4] just prior to the mass diffusion of television sets in America—serves to *legitimize* the actions and opinions of those who receive favorable publicity. However, Lazarsfeld and Merton felt that mere *attention*, not only media support, conferred status. They viewed mass media audiences as subscribing to the belief that "if you really matter, you will be at the focus of mass attention and, if you *are* at the focus of mass attention, then surely you must really matter" (p. 498).

As we will note later, status conferral occurs when the mass media endorse political candidates. Editorials, which are perhaps at the pinnacle of the status-conferring process, not only legitimize candidates, they select from among the "status group" the few who will be given "elite status."

Pseudo-Events

If, because of media's conferral of status, an individual is deemed by the public as "special"—noteworthy and important—is it not compelling for those in or seeking elected office to pursue opportunities for such "recognition"? By creating and staging events which capture the attention of news directors, reporters, editors, and commentators, they may obtain status conferral.

If we assume, and there is evidence to suggest that we should, that status conferral is correlated with name recognition and that name recognition is at least a necessary condition for election to office, should not candidates hire public relations specialists, stage events, and woo media personnel?

If the status-conferral function of the media operates as has been suggested, if events can be created to seize that confirmation, and if publics believe and act in accordance with these actions, have we not shaped reality?

We are, through these processes, "manufacturing" reality, creating a preference, in Boorstin's terms, for what we see instead of what is really there. Boorstin, in his excellent book on pseudo-events, argues that

> we seem to have discovered the processes by which fame is manufactured. Now, at least in the United States, a man's name can become a household word overnight. . . . Discovering that we [consumers of the media] and our servants [media producers] can so quickly and so effectively give a man "fame," we have willingly been misled into believing that fame—well-knowness—is still a hallmark of greatness . . . mistaking our powers for our necessities, we have filled our world with artificial fame.[5]

Boorstin defines a pseudo-event as a "happening" which has four characteristics (p. 11). First, it is not spontaneous; it is "planned, planted or incited." Second, its primary purpose is that of "being reported or reproduced." The question of its reality is less important than its newsworthiness. Third, the pseudo-event is ambiguous in its correspondence to reality. Last, it is self-serving; "it is intended to be a self-fulfilling prophecy."

Clearly, the mass media in their totality, irrespective of motives and intentions, create "realities" about people and events. The extent to which these "realities" are accepted, acted upon, and sustained in society is difficult to assess empirically. Common sense tells us that much of what Boulding, Thayer, Lazarsfeld and Merton, and Boorstin claim and imply about media's role in constructing reality is true. It remains for the social science community to piece out mass media processes, examine their influence on social and political behavior, and empirically verify these "commonsense" effects.

In that regard an interesting area of political communication research has recently emerged, representing a fifth perspective. It is called the agenda-setting function of the media. We will discuss this research area in some detail and then we will consider the implications of the "construction of reality" for the political system.

Agenda-Setting

Television, newspapers, radio, and film seem to have enormous power in shaping public opinion of issues confronting society. By just paying attention to some issues while ignoring others, the mass media, deliberately or otherwise, may set priorities of concern within various sectors of the public.

Recently, this power ascribed to the media has been the focus of much research. Its foremost investigators, Maxwell McCombs and his associates, have conducted a number of studies examining this influential press power. They have suggested that

> while behavioral scientists have not discovered that media have all the power ascribed to them by popular conventional wisdom, they recently are finding considerable evidence that editors and broadcasters play an important part in shaping our social reality as they go about their day-to-day task of choosing and displaying news. Audiences not only learn about public issues and other matters through the media, they also learn how much importance to attach to an issue or topic from the emphasis placed on it by the mass media. For example, in reflecting what candidates are saying during a campaign, the mass media apparently determine the important issues. In other words, the media set the "agenda" of the campaign.
>
> This impact of mass media—the ability to effect cognitive change among individuals—has been labeled the *agenda-setting function* of mass communication. Here may lie the most important effect of modern mass communication, the ability of media to structure our world for us. (McCombs and Shaw, 1974, p. 1)

Agenda-setting as a phenomenon of press influence is usually measured by comparing what the media report with the saliency of that report among individuals in various parts of the public. The first measure is obtained through quantitative content analysis; the second is pursued through audience self-reports of one kind or another. For example, during a defined period of time in an election, the researcher will collect news program videotapes and/or newspapers. He will code the various political contents in these media and determine the frequency of their occurrence. These political topics are rank-ordered. In the same time period, or as close to it as possible, a field survey is conducted with a sample of the electorate. Media exposure measures and measures of political topic saliences are calculated. These are also rank-ordered and then correlated with the ranked political topics of the media content analysis. The higher the correlation between the media topics and the audience topics the greater the effect of agenda-setting.

> The concept of agenda-setting asserts that media content sets personal agendas. In other words, the media are regarded as the cause of certain audience beliefs and behavior. However, most of the evidence to date for agenda-setting has been based on static correlations. While the consistent high correlations between media content and personal agendas are encouraging and supportive of the concept, stronger evidence taking into account the actual direction of effect is needed. (McCombs and Shaw, 1974, p. 25)

The researcher typically has little or no control over the way the media choose to report an election, nor can he control how individuals will perceive and use media reports. However, by measuring these variables over a period of time such as an election campaign, he can link them to certain election outcomes so that highly plausible causal inferences can be made.

In this way, agenda-setting research provides a useful model for future political communication research. It illustrates how significant communication variables can be operationalized and linked to concrete political processes such as election campaigns. It demonstrates the importance of a good research design in making causal inferences about naturally occurring events. Our review of agenda-setting research will attempt to elucidate the underlying model and thereby guide research in other areas of political communication.

The chief disadvantage of the agenda-setting concept is that it is not grounded in a body of well-elaborated theory. The choice of variables to be operationalized is typically guided by intuition derived from practical experience with the events being studied, not by parameters chosen a priori. Few predictions can be made about relationships between variables being added to a study. *Post hoc* explanations for empirical relationships are derived and then evaluated in later research. This approach to theory construction is valid, and in the case of agenda-setting research it has been useful. Its utility may be increased by efforts to codify existing findings so that a more abstract theoretical framework can be constructed. McCombs and Shaw (1974) attempt such codification. But while codification of findings may increase the usefulness of the agenda-setting concept, it will not provide guidelines for creating models for political communication research in other areas.

Thus it is not possible to look to agenda-setting research for a guide to theory construction in other areas. However, the empirical generalizations provided by agenda-setting research are especially useful when they are viewed as describing processes which ameliorate stress in a political system. We will advance this view of agenda-setting research in our conclusions to this chapter.

Research on Agenda-Setting

Agenda-setting as a research concept in the social and behavioral sciences is a recent development. In most newly emerging areas of study in mass communications, there is a preoccupation with identifying historical roots. This is understandable since a link with past scholarly efforts often provides a foundation for present endeavors. Several contemporary scholars, most notably Jack McLeod and Maxwell McCombs and their associates, have rendered a plausible epistemological explanation of the agenda-setting concept. Though McLeod, Becker, and Byrnes (1974) elaborate agenda-setting's historical development using empirical voting studies and McCombs and Shaw (1972) recognize agenda-setting elements appearing in nineteenth-century American presidents' attitudes toward the press, the earliest agreed-upon "root" appears in Walter Lippmann's book *Public Opinion*, which was published in 1922.

Lippmann's introductory chapter, "The World Outside and the Pictures in Our Heads," suggests several factors of press/audience relationships bearing upon agenda-setting. His concluding remarks in that chapter are worth quoting here:

I argue that representative government, either in what is ordinarily called politics, or in industry, cannot be worked successfully, no matter what the basis of election, unless there is an independent, expert organization for making the unseen facts intelligible to those who have to make the decisions. I attempt, therefore, to argue that the serious acceptance of the principle that personal representation must be supplemented by representation of the unseen facts would alone permit a satisfactory decentralization, and allow us to escape from the intolerable and unworkable fiction that each of us must acquire a competent opinion about all public affairs. It is argued that the problem of the press is confused because the critics and the apologists expect the press to realize this fiction, expect it to make up for all that was not foreseen in the theory of democracy, and that the readers expect this miracle to be performed at no cost or trouble to themselves. The newspapers are regarded by democrats as a panacea for their own defects, whereas analysis of the nature of news and of the economic basis of journalism seems to show that the newspapers necessarily and inevitably reflect, and therefore, in greater or lesser measure, intensify, the defective organization of public opinion. My conclusion is that public opinions must be organized for the press if they are to be sound, not by the press as is the case today. (p. 19)

Three years after Lippmann's remarks Robert Ezra Park suggested elements of agenda-setting in his discussion of the news-gathering process.[6] But perhaps the most cogent agenda-setting comment was first developed by Bernard Cohen (1963) when he advanced the idea

that the press is significantly more than a purveyor of information and opinion. It may not be successful much of the time in telling people what to think, but it is stunningly successful in telling its readers what to think *about*. And it follows from this that the world looks different to different people, depending not only on their personal interests, but also on the map that is drawn for them by the writers, editors, and publishers of the papers they read.... The editor may believe he is only printing the things that people want to read, but he is thereby putting a claim on their attention, powerfully determining what they will be thinking about, and talking about, until the next wave laps their shore. (p. 13)

The first formal empirical test of the agenda-setting hypothesis appeared in the early 1970s. McCombs and Shaw (1972) hypothesized that "*the mass media set the agenda for each political campaign, influencing the salience of attitudes toward the political issues*" (p. 177). They investigated this notion of press power with a sample of Chapel Hill, North Carolina, voters during the 1968 presidential campaign. It was found that voters share the "media's composite definition of what is important" (p. 184).

Before this study, Jack McLeod (1965), a leading communication researcher and director of the University of Wisconsin's respected Mass Communication Research Center, provided direct empirical evidence for the hypothesis in a study of the 1964 presidential campaign. His content analysis of two newspapers revealed sharp differences in media reports of two issues—federal spending policies and control of nuclear weapons. His findings suggest that it is important to control for party affiliation. Although Democrats were more concerned with nuclear testing and Republicans concentrated on the spending issue, within each party the respondents' ranking of the issues correlated with their choice of newspaper: readers exposed to the newspaper espousing nuclear control ranked that issue higher than the spending issue, while the reverse was found for the other paper.

These two pace-setting studies are illustrative of reviews and other studies on agenda-setting (see McCombs and Weaver, 1973; Funkhouser, 1973;

Kline, 1973; McLeod, Becker, and Byrnes, 1973, 1974; Weaver, McCombs, and Spellman, 1975; and McCombs and Shaw, 1972).

To help guide research on agenda-setting, McCombs and his associates distributed a preliminary analysis of suggested agenda-setting hypotheses in 1973. These *Working Papers on Agenda-Setting* provided suggestions on methodology and tentatively reported some specific findings.

In studying potential first-time voters, McCombs found that similarity between their agendas of national issues and the news media's agenda varied directly with the amount of their exposure to the media. Among these young voters, McCombs' data revealed an interesting relationship between the mass media and interpersonal communication. For those whose interpersonal discussion on issues was low, the correlation with the media's agenda was high. This inverse relationship suggests that the impact of media agenda declines as discussion increases.

McCombs was also concerned about the young voter's need to understand the physical and psychological environment and the relationship between that need and the agenda-setting function of the media. He utilized *the need for orientation* model to describe that need in terms of *relevance* and *uncertainty*. [7] Apparently, young voters who were registered (high political relevance) showed the highest agreement with the agenda set by a newspaper. Further, those who were politically committed (partisans) showed low uncertainty and high correlations with the media agenda whereas those who were uncommitted (independents) recorded high uncertainty and low correlations with the media agenda.

Eugene Shaw, in the *Working Papers*, investigated agenda-setting effects of the newspaper's front page compared to the entire newspaper. Almost the same correlations were found for the agendas of respondents (a small sample of Durham, North Carolina, registered voters) when compared to issues on the front page and to the total news coverage in the newspaper. Though this study must be viewed as suggestive and not definitive, an interesting path to pursue is prompted by the contention that "front-page effects can be extrapolated to broadcast news effects and total coverage effects identified with specifically print effects [sic]." Two other studies in the *Working Papers* also suggest that the agenda-setting function hypothesis is worth further testing.

Testing Agenda-Setting Hypotheses

Testing agenda-setting hypotheses appears on the surface to be a relatively easy process, but that simplicity is misleading. The conceptual framework within which these hypotheses are tested requires a fair amount of specificity coupled with precise operational definitions.

Three issue salience conceptual frameworks for testing agenda-setting hypotheses have been advanced by McLeod, Becker, and Byrnes (1973): *individual issue salience, community issue salience,* and *perceived issue salience.* The first of these, they suggest, is *intra*personal, stemming from Lippmann and extended empirically by McCombs and Shaw (1972). The second concept is centered in *inter*personal interaction and is derived from Park. The third conceptual scheme lies

> midway between *intra*personal and *inter*personal concepts. . . . The agenda-setting hypothesis implies that the media can change the views of social reality of its individual audience members by indicating which issues are being discussed by the candidates, by friends in the future, or those that will be used by other voters in their decisions about the candidates, and therefore be the key issues in the campaign. (p. 8)

Recognizing that determining which conceptualization is most useful for predicting political behavior outcomes is an empirical question, they suggest that researchers be precise in their selection of variables.

A crucial question must be answered before the agenda-setting hypotheses can be confirmed or rejected for political communication: Is there a direct influence from mass media political reports upon the perceptions and behaviors of voters attending to those reports? To date the evidence in favor of or against the hypothesis is tenuous. McCombs argues that there *is* an agenda-setting effect of the mass media. He states, "Yes, there is something out there which supports the hypotheses. What is needed is a clear delineation in careful terms: when it is there and when it is not."[8] McLeod et al. (1974), on the other hand, offer a word of caution: "Our results provide a strong warning against the uncritical acceptance of agenda-setting as a broad and unqualified media effect."

Differences in these two evaluations may be attributed to conceptual and methodological applications of their respective research. McLeod's conceptual framework places the measurement of the dependent variable in the category of *perceived issue salience,* anchored in the interpersonal environment of the individual. Respondents are asked to *rank* issues submitted to them by indicating "which issue has been most important so far." McComb's conceptual scheme locates the dependent variable in the *individual issue salience* category and is operationalized with this *open-ended* question: "What are you *most* concerned about these days? That is, regardless of what politicians say, what are the two or three *main* things which you think the government *should* concentrate on doing something about?"

There are three striking differences between their approaches which may account for the conflicting findings. One difference is that McCombs used one-newspaper settings, whereas McLeod studied competitive papers. A second difference is that the McCombs and McLeod groups aggregate their data differently. A third difference between the two approaches is a result of the way in which the dependent variable (issue salience) is measured. McLeod "anticipated" that the two newspapers would give different attention to the issues selected for ranking by respondents. McCombs elected to let the respondents decide both the issues and the rankings. Both methods are defensible and examples of each are plentiful in the social science literature. An empirical test of the methodology is necessary in order to resolve which method more validly measures the behavior. At this juncture, we are in no position to make judgments about the validity of such measurements in agenda-setting research. We must point out, however, that these methodological problems must be addressed before definitive statements can be made about the agenda-setting hypothesis. Elaboration of this problem appears in Chapter 7.

Despite these problems, agenda-setting and related research offer some useful insight in assessing press influences. Berelson, Lazarsfeld, and McPhee (1954) studied the 1948 presidential campaign and found that those respondents who were most exposed to the media more accurately identified campaign themes than those who were least exposed. Similarly, Lipset et al. (1954), examining data from the 1952 congressional races, concluded that political messages primarily affected the saliency of issues among the electorate. They suggest that short-term exposure to political messages probably does not affect voters' attitudes greatly, but it can affect the way they perceive the electoral contest.

Additional evidence that "something is out there" comes from studies by RePass (1971) and Cobb and Elder (1971). RePass reviews studies on voting behavior and suggests that researchers have underestimated the influence of voters' perception of issues in predicting their voting decisions. He concludes that the distinction between a party-affiliated voter and a nonaffiliated voter is less than previously thought; rather, the presentation of issues and candidate information has the greater influence. Here we find another indication that party influence is diminishing and issue salience is increasing as a factor of influence on voters. The media's presentation of issues is likely to be as influential on voting behavior as party identification, or more so.

Systemic versus Institutional Agendas

Cobb and Elder expand our notions about agenda-setting to include the variable of political participation. Analyzing the potential political power of the agenda-setting hypothesis, they propose that it affects people who participate in political activities. This group is a minority which generally tends to select out of political information that which reinforces their individual preconceived notions.

Agenda-setting has also been divided into two categories of "agenda" by Cobb and Elder. The *systemic agenda* refers to a general set of political controversies that fall within the range of legitimate concerns meriting the attention of the public. *Institutional agenda* denotes a set of concrete items scheduled for active and serious consideration by a particular institutional decision-making body. By setting this type of agenda, media can play an important role in elevating issues to the systemic agenda and increasing their chances of recurring on institutional agendas. This view suggests that agenda-setting is not a sketchy, peripheral influence, but a constant and acceptable method of presentation for political information.

Against the two types of agenda-setting, institutional and systemic, the validity of the concept can be examined. Institutional agendas include topics and how they are put forth to the public. Systemic agendas are more abstract in nature, legitimizing either a political group or issue to effect a change in accordance with the dictates of a particular action. Both agendas contain bias. Institutional agendas often maintain the status quo and make it difficult to bring new issues to the attention of the decision-making body. Systemic agendas are often ensnared by their own publicity; the issue is often dependent upon the party supporting it, which is, in turn, scrutinized for public acceptability. This associative requirement may result in the value of the issue being ignored in favor of determining the integrity of those who seek to present it to the general public. Both types of agenda become interrelated through the use of media. Media may be utilized to elevate an institutional issue to the systemic agenda; if publicized as a controversy an issue has a greater chance of being accepted by individuals and subsequently promoted by groups. Thus any attempt at influence or persuasion tends to have its greatest impact concerning controversial issues: controversy has the greatest effect and captures the attention of the largest amount of people. In the opposite direction, public acceptance of an issue as "legitimate" on the systemic level increases the likelihood of its appearance on an institutional agenda. It is due to this interdependent relationship between the two agenda forms that media play such a dominant role. Media, it is suggested, afford the means by which issues may be presented and may become the most important force in the creation of opinion concerning a certain political idea or issue.

Contingent Conditions
That Affect Agenda-Setting

The correlation of media's presentation of issues with issues the electorate feel are important may be a function of contingent conditions. Dependent variables such as political use of television, interpersonal discussion, news interest, election interest, and the like, may account for much of the agenda-setting effect. There is evidence to suggest that the relationship between media content and audience issue salience may be attenuated or extended by these contingent conditions.

McCombs and Weaver (1973) were able to isolate agenda-setting effects by comparing their respondents' interest in the election and voting choice. Those who were highly interested and not sure about their voting decision "fit" the agenda-setting model, while others did not. Thus level of interest and vote choice certainly may be contingent conditions that affect agenda-setting.

Although the usefulness of agenda-setting findings is improved by isolating contingent conditions, sometimes the findings are in opposition. McCombs, Shaw, and Shaw (1972) found that, among other contingent conditions, *low* levels of interpersonal discussion accounted for the agenda-setting effect; Mullins (1973) countered that *high* interpersonal discussion and other conditions were responsible for the effect.

The agenda-setting perspective assumes direct effects from exposure to the mass media. However, not everyone is assumed to be equally susceptible to influence. Only individuals in certain contingent social conditions are viewed as open to media influence. A rephrasing of the hypothesis may eventually read as follows: The mass media influence the salience of events in the public mind when certain contingent conditions are present. The precise nature of these conditions is presently being extrapolated by combining agenda-setting research with research on uses and gratifications of the mass media. Much remains to be accomplished, then, before research will be able to answer our previously posed query about the validity of agenda-setting measures.

Who Sets the Agenda?

Moving from an examination of direct effects to isolation of contingent conditions is a necessary step to improvement of agenda-setting research, but it is not sufficient. Agenda-setting researchers need to resolve the problem of causation: Is the agenda set by the media, or is it set by media's perceptions of audience priorities? Since most studies utilize static designs, taking measurements at a single point in time, it is not possible to determine causal direction, but only to establish the existence of covariation.[9]

McLeod et al. (1974) raise this question of the *direction* of causal influence in agenda-setting studies by examining the studies of Funkhouser (1973), Kline (1973), and Tipton, Haney, Basehart, and Elliott (1973). These three studies with designs measuring audience variables and media content over a specified time period provided useful information but were not able to answer the causation question. Funkhouser and Kline found correspondence between the two "agendas." Funkhouser studied media's coverage of fourteen issues over seven years. Kline investigated the 1972 campaign. McLeod et al. correctly observed, "As in the case with the Funkhouser data, the graphs of the Kline data appear to show some issues where the peaks of attention precede public endorsement and other issues on which the reverse holds" (p. 136). Tipton et al. used cross-lagged correlational analysis over a three-month time period to study statewide elections in Kentucky, but they were unable to show precise causal direction of agenda-setting effects.

Most researchers agree that the strategy with the most promising payoff in agenda-setting research is the current trend in specifying the contingent conditions affecting agenda-setting. That strategy coupled with at least two separate media/audience agenda measurements over a specified time period promises interesting and useful additions to the literature.

Maxwell McCombs, whose prolific contributions to the agenda-setting literature are widely known, has recognized the tenuousness of the agenda-setting function of the mass media:

> No one contends that the agenda-setting function of the press is a universal influence affecting all persons on all topics at all times. Considering the dominant theme of daytime TV commercials, if agenda-setting were a universal influence, the American housewives would speak of little but the brightness of their laundry.[10]

So far we have looked at the agenda-setting hypothesis that the media's attention to certain issues is correlated with voter-audience concerns about those issues, resulting in the subtle, indirect formation of political cognitions which ultimately affect attitudes. In earlier chapters, we considered aspects of editorials and polls, media practices which are intended to directly influence attitudes. Next we consider editorial endorsement and its influence on voters and point out the relationship between these practices and the agenda-setting function of the press.

Editorial Influence

Editorial support and endorsement may be considered part of the process of structuring reality for voters. We make a distinction between editorials and editorializing. When the media, especially newspapers, support an issue or a candidate in an *editorial*—usually located on a page devoted to analysis and opinion—they are promulgating that, *in their view*, the issue should be supported or the candidate should be elected. When newspapers report on issues and candidates in their pages devoted to news coverage and that coverage is slanted they are *editorializing*—either omitting relevant information or emphasizing certain information in terms of their preconceived positions. Editorials, then, are statements of *preference*; editorializing involves acts of *bias*. We concede that these distinctions may be somewhat simplistic, missing nuances of reportorial practices and intentions. Further, these definitions may not at times be mutually exclusive, contaminating certain considerations of press practice in political communication. Nevertheless, for our discussion, they provide us with convenient "categories" for reviewing studies and linking findings to aspects of press influence.

Editorial endorsements of candidates have been the subject of much research on press influence.[11] The most recent study as of this writing is Robinson's "The Press as King Maker" (1974). Robinson's analysis of five presidential campaigns, from 1956 through 1972, supports the influence of editorials on voters' selection of the president. Robinson used data (national probability samples) gathered by the Center for Political Studies of the University of Michigan in their ongoing analyses of election behavior. American adults were asked in 1968 to name the newspaper they usually read for information about the campaign and in 1972 what their perceptions were of their newspaper's stand on candidates. Adults' responses were checked against the actual presidential endorsement of the newspapers. Robinson's findings were eye-opening, considering the attention paid to television as a potent force in elections. *Newspaper editorial endorsements predicted five of six presidential elections.* Only the close Kennedy-Nixon race in 1960 did not fit the pattern. We are tempted to recall the 1960 presidential debates, which may explain the exception to Robinson's findings since none of the other campaigns included such an innovation. But even without the perfect fit, his results are not to be taken lightly. His conclusion that a positive linkage exists between newspaper endorsements and presidential voting behavior was well supported. The finding persisted through a number of statistical manipulations controlling for party identification, eleven other predictors of voting behavior, and regional interaction effects.

Other studies tend to confirm Robinson's results. Examination of the link between editorials and California election results from 1948 to 1962 revealed that endorsements had a great deal of influence. Gregg (1965) found that California voters relied on newspaper endorsements for their voting decisions, especially in local elections.

The manner in which a newspaper presents its editorial support was investigated by McCombs (1967). He suggests that the influence of newspaper editorial endorsement is greater when few other determinants affect the voter's decision. The greater the disagreement among the variables that shape the ballot decision, the greater is the influence of an editorial endorsement. Spector (1970) concurred with these findings, proposing that the newspaper is a prime mover in setting "territorial agenda." The newspaper, he argues, plays a great part in determining what most people will be talking about, what most people will think the facts are, and what most people will regard as the right way to handle certain problems.

Several studies compare editorial endorsements and bias. Newspapers will often choose those news items that are favorable to their endorsed candidates, emphasizing them while playing-down unfavorable reports (Repass and Chaffee, 1968; Lee, 1972–73). The media, particularly newspapers, are aware of their readers' political bias, which helps explain the "legitimacy" of adopting a public persona.

Hooper (1969) indicates that while political party factors are overwhelmingly significant in the outcome of an election, the distinctions made between the separate stands taken by Democrats and Republicans are exposed primarily through newspaper endorsements.

In 1954, Klein and Maccoby found that in the eight newspapers studied, there existed biased coverage of the candidates favored and endorsed in the 1952 campaign. Martin, O'Keefe, and Nayman (1972) postulate that editors, to a certain extent, perceive the position of their readers and that these perceptions influence them.

One study found that relatively little if any bias can be attributed to the media's coverage of the 1972 campaign. Evarts and Stempel (1974) examined campaign coverage by the three television networks, the three news magazines, and six major newspapers by sampling twenty-five days of media reports between Labor Day and the day before the election. They concluded:

> For the networks, the so-called liberal bias that has been talked about so much simply was not evident. The widely-voiced assumption that CBS might be more favorable to the Democrats than were the other networks was not the case. For newspapers, there seemed to be no relation between editorial position and the direction of coverage. In short, in an election campaign in which not too many things went well, the performance of these major media seemed to have been noteworthy. (p. 676)

Roshwalb and Resnicoff (1971) in a study on the impact of endorsements by leading political figures and by opinion polls suggest that these events have their greatest effect on last-minute voter decisions, though these did not determine the election outcome.

A study of newspaper editorials in the 1968 presidential election showed that voters were motivated primarily by foreign affairs issues—in particular, the Viet Nam war (Myers, 1970). The media helped to create a controversy through its agenda on the war issue; the "hawk" and "dove" positions stirred interest, while a growing disenchantment and sense of the futility of the war among several correspondents and editors gave credibility to endorsements urging our withdrawal. The influence of endorsement was inextricably bound to other media machinations: the news broadcasts depicting both the horror and futility of the war, and the total media coverage given to the dissent concerning the war.

A recent study compared newspaper endorsement of candidates and the news treatment of public opinion polls. Wilhoit and Auh (1974) supported the hypothesis that "an editorially endorsed candidate would be given more favorable coverage in public opinion poll news than the editorially opposed candidate" (p. 658). Least bias about political candidates in the reporting of public opinion polls was found when competing newspapers displayed editorial opposition.

Finally, it should be noted that editorial influence upon the public is not endemic to the American society alone. The results of several field studies in Switzerland and West Germany examined by Noelle-Neumann (1973) suggest that

> the thesis that mass media do not change attitudes but only reinforce them cannot be upheld under conditions of consonance and cumulation. Our data point in this direction. It is true there exists a tendency to protect attitudes through selective perception. Yet the more selective perception is being restricted—by consonance of reporting and editorial comment, reinforced by cumulation of periodical repetition in the media—the more attitudes can be influenced or molded by the mass media. (p. 594)

Editorial endorsements appear to have effects on opinion and apparently alter and shape political reality. The implications of these effects, of agenda-setting, and of the perspectives discussed earlier in this chapter are outlined below.

Implications for the Political System

We have now summarized research that gives perspective on the role of media in the social processes by which political reality is constructed. We reviewed several perspectives but focused on agenda-setting and the empirical research findings that support this perspective. The implications of these media phenomena for the political system in this country rest upon two basic propositions:

1. There is both qualitative (judgmental opinion) and empirical evidence to posit that the mass media shape and alter political reality.
2. Political behaviors of politicians and the electorate are, at least in part, a result of the political reality projected by the mass media.

We label these as propositions since they are theorems which must be accepted or denied based on the *aggregation* of data, both empirical and qualitative. From the empirical data set we found evidence of media's role in projecting and shaping political reports which have been acted upon by the electorate. From the qualitative set we noted characteristics of the mass media which make our propositions appear logical.

Given these propositions, then, were they to be affirmed, what are the implications for the political system? We leave to others most of the moral and ethical implications involved in media's role in the construction of political reality; to consider them is beyond our present task and competence. Rather, we will comment on how two democratic political values are affected by media's participation in the process.

These values are the amelioration of stress in the political system and the participation of the citizenry in the construction of political reality. The mass media contribute positively to the former, while several undesirable consequences emerge from media's role in the latter. We have only begun to examine the media's role. The five perspectives reviewed here provide limited insight. As these perspectives are elaborated, particularly those grounded in empirical research, our understanding of the process may guide important policy decisions.

Notes

1. From Governor Agnew's speech at Staunton, Virginia, 29 October 1968. The statement was included as part of an advertisement in the *New York Times*, 4 November 1968.
2. Kenneth Boulding, *The Image* (Ann Arbor: University of Michigan Press, 1961), p. 6.
3. Lee Thayer, "Communication—*Sine Qua Non* of the Behavioral Sciences," in D.L. Arm, ed., *Vistas In Science* (Albuquerque: University of New Mexico Press, 1968), pp. 48–77.
4. P. Lazarsfeld and Robert Merton, "Mass Communication, Popular Taste and Organized Social Action," in W. Schramm, ed., *Mass Communication*, 2d ed. (Urbana: University of Illinois Press, 1960), pp. 492–512.
5. D.J. Boorstin, *The Image: A Guide To Pseudo-Events in America* (New York: Harper & Row, 1961), p. 47.
6. Robert E. Park, *The City* (Chicago: University of Chicago Press, 1925).
7. The model of need for orientation is grounded in Tolman's concept of cognitive mapping. Each individual *needs* to "map" his world, to orient himself so that he may understand his total environment. See E.C. Tolman, *Purposive Behavior in Animals and Men* (New York: Appleton-Century, 1932). *Relevance* and *uncertainty* as factors in the model were found in several studies. See Westley and Barrow, 1959; Wade and Schramm, 1969; Chaffee et al., 1969; and Donohew and Palmgreen, 1971.
8. Telephone conversation, Maxwell McCombs-Sidney Kraus, 17 June 1975.

9. McCombs informs us "that cross-lagged correlations showing a causal relationship between media agendas and voter agendas now exist for the Charlotte Voter Study in D.L. Shaw and M.E. McCombs, eds., *Mass Media and the Rise of Public Issues*, book manuscript in preparation" (letter to the authors, 29 September 1975).
10. Maxwell McCombs, "Agenda-Setting: A New Perspective on Mass Communication," keynote address for conference on Perspectives in Mass Communication, Mohawk Valley Community College, Utica, N. Y., 1–3 April, 1975.
11. We have selected a sample of studies for our discussion in this section. Other studies are listed in the bibliography.

Abstracts and Bibliography

Abelson, Robert P. "Computers, Polls, and Public Opinion—Some Puzzles and Paradoxes." *Transaction* 5 (September 1968): 20–27.
Reviews several past applications of computers to the study of public opinion. Outlines six questions about the feasibility of computer projects: the validity question; the obsolescence question; the completeness question; the relative-importance question; the quantitative question; and the marketing question. The proposal involved two steps: assemble from archives covering the previous decade a massive public opinion data bank; and predict the consequences of a potential emphasis by the Democratic candidate on a number of issues.
Finding: "There will always be margin for error in computer prognosis of public opinion, particularly . . . prognosis that try to project too far forward in time."
Abrams, Mark. "Opinion Polls and Party Propaganda." *Pub. Opin. Q.* 28 (Spring 1964): 13–19.
A discussion of the information learned from political surveys, its effects on party propaganda, and its effects on the quality and character of democratic politics in Britain. Some lessons learned from political surveys include the following: there is no simple and complete alignment of social class and political faith; each party can rely on the unwavering support of approximately one-third of the electorate; the remaining uncommitted one-third of the electorate do not form a homogeneous group; of the uncommitted, no more than half usually vote, they will usually vote on the basis of direct personal dissatisfaction, and their votes will be of campaign consequence only in those constituencies where the committed stalwarts of the two political parties are evenly matched in numerical strength; the supporters of the two parties differ on very few issues. The effects of survey information on party propaganda include the following: in the battle for votes, the attack is concentrated on the uncommitted; there is the professionalization of local propaganda under close and detailed guidance from the party's central office; the propaganda battle must be fought on mundane issues (since uncommitted electorate is not attracted to ideological ideals); each party must prove that it alone has the skills, brains, competence, and talent to carry out programs effectively; the party is personified in the personality and appearance of the party leader because the uncommitted electors' interest in party politics is slight; to be effective, advertising to the uncommitted electors must be sustained over a long period. The effects of survey information on the quality of democratic politics include the following: the waging of political warfare becomes costly, and consequently the parties turn to external economic interests for funds; the definition of politics is widened, and consequently the number

of participants in everyday political discussions is increased; the voter is often deprived of a genuine choice between the two parties.

American Institute for Political Communication. *Media and Non-Media Effects on the Formation of Public Opinion.* Washington, D.C.: American Institute for Political Communication, 1969.

A special report based on one of five surveys carried out during 1968 in the Milwaukee metropolitan area in connection with an in-depth study of voter behavior under campaign conditions. Mass media were rated first, after the candidate himself, among the organizations and groups as a source of influence. This study was designed to shed light on the specific effect of media and nonmedia influences on the mass mind. *Method*: survey; questionnaire. *Statistics*: percentages. *Pop. (N)*: 300 residents of a general public panel; 26 for a leadership panel.

The two panels agree on the salience of the major issues in the 1968 presidential campaign. They also agree on the basis of comparative ratings—that issues, personality factors, and candidate attributes are more influential than groups or organizations (including the media) in determining political behavior (p. 21).

Anderson, Patrick. "Issues vs. Image." *New Republic* 158 (27 April 1968): 32–35.

The author reviews two books that have conflicting views on the function of television and political use. *The Image Candidates: American Politics in the Age of Television* by Gene Wykoff promotes image making of a candidate on TV as a key factor in candidate popularity and describes ways in which it is done. In *The Scheer Campaign* Serge Lang suggests that candidates should use TV to promote key issues and not be concerned with promoting their image. TV should be used to take hard political questions to the people for decision. Promoting the issues will draw more votes. The author believes that future use of TV for political purposes will be primarily for promoting the issues and not the image.

Arrendell, Charles. "Predicting the Completeness of Newspaper Election Coverage." *Journalism Q.* 49 (Summer 1972): 290–95.

"The original questions were these: which known facts about Texas daily newspapers are related to the amount of coverage those newspapers gave to the Democratic and Republican campaigns for the presidency in 1968? And how much of the variation in the campaign coverage score can be explained by these factors? Number of days published, size of average weekday news hole and wire services subscribed to were found to be related to the campaign coverage score and together explained 47.3% of the variation in the coverage score."

Method: survey; questionnaire. *Statistics*: correlations, multiple regression. *Pop. (N)*: 30 different newspapers and 292 campaign events.

Completeness of coverage findings: The 1960 Danielson and Adams study reported sample newspaper presented to the average newspaper reader "60% of the events of the campaign." The 1968 sample presented to the average newspaper reader 47.2% events of the campaign. Factors affecting completeness of coverage: 6 known factors about newspapers were quantified and used as predictor variables in the multiple regression analysis (news services subscribed to, size of average weekday news hole, number of days the newspaper was published per week, time of publication, ownership status, and political interest).

Atkin, Charles K. "How Imbalanced Campaign Coverage Affects Audience Exposure Patterns." *Journalism Q.* 48 (Summer 1971): 235–44.

Explores news exposure patterns of partisan and undecided readers under varying availability conditions.

Method: experiment; survey; questionnaire. *Statistics*: analysis of variance, frequencies. *Pop. (N)*: (1) 82 students from University of Wisconsin, (2) 122 Madison residents. *Findings*: (1) Republicans and Democrats can overcome a low availability situation by actively seeking out articles that support their position. (2) Respondents who attended different amounts of partisan information did selectively expose themselves at a 79% rate to supportive material. (3) Neutrals on a given topic pay less attention to mass media information dealing with the issue than partisans. (4) Relative availability of news items about two candidates has a clear effect on the exposure preferences of individuals with no preexisting opinions; controlling most other factors, people tended to choose neutral information in proportion to the amount of space and favorability it received. For messages that are supportive or discrepant of an individual's partisan predispositions, the level of availability seems to have a much weaker influence.

Atkin, Charles K. "The Impact of Political Poll Reports on Candidate and Issue Preferences." *Journalism Q.* 46 (Autumn 1964): 515–21.

Experimenting with a student primary election, this study confirmed that voters' exposure to political poll reports representing a reference public can be used as a reference point for individuals' opinions and choice of candidates and issues. The voter does not have to perceive an absolute majority in order to be influenced in his opinion and position, as in the "bandwagon approach." "If a voter feels the electorate is a positive and relevant standard on a particular political question he may alter his candidate or issue images in the direction indicated by the relative majority" (p. 516).

Method: survey; questionnaire. *Statistics*: analysis of variance and chi-square. *Pop. (N)*: 101 undergraduates at the University of Wisconsin.

Findings: (1) Over the five concepts, 33% of the experimental subjects became more favorable toward the concept supported by a relative majority, whereas 11% shifted to unfavorable. (2) The findings seem to indicate that knowledge of the preferences of a highly valued reference public may be an important factor in the decision-making process of some voters.

Atkin, Charles K. "Some Effects of Public Opinion Polls on Voter Images and Intentions." Paper presented at Association for Education in Journalism Convention, Lawrence, Kans., August 1968.

Atwood, L. Erwin. "How Newsmen and Readers Perceive Each Others' Story Preferences." *Journalism Q.* 47 (Summer 1970): 296–302.

Q-analysis shows that among newsmen, desk-bound editors are least able to predict subscriber preferences, but on the whole, newsmen and readers show high agreement in their preferences. Newspapermen (including editors) and subscribers sorted newspaper stories according to preference.

Method: *Q*-analysis. *Pop. (N)*: 13 newspaper personnel, 19 men and 21 women subscribers.

Findings: (1) Impact was the preferred news element and conflict was the second most preferred element. (2) Differences among preference types centered on the oddity element. (3) Prominence was found to be a determinant of story selection in the editor condition but not in the subscriber condition. (4) For both staffers and subscribers, news selection patterns seem relatively homogeneous. (5) Staffers who were poorest in predicting audience preferences held desk jobs. (6) Among the newspaper subscribers, age, sex, place of residence, and occupation did not appear to be consistently related to preference type.

Barber, James D. *Citizen Politics: An Introduction to Political Behavior*, 2d ed. Chicago: Markham, 1972.

Benham, Thomas W. "Polling for a Presidential Candidate: Some Observations on the 1964 Campaign." *Pub. Opin. Q.* 29 (Summer 1965): 185–99.

The author discusses the results of a polling method used to measure the impact of a political campaign. The panel technique with 4 waves of interviewing was used to provide the Republican party various types of information. The results revealed voters' familiarity with the candidates, their change in candidate choice, their image of the candidates, their perceptions of candidate stance on issues, response to TV commercials, and the background of Republican defectors. The author attempted to measure reactions to candidates and to issues, examine the key voter groups in population, and provide basic information on campaign events, changes, and movements.

Method: survey; questionnaire. *Statistics*: frequencies. *Pop. (N)*: sample of adults, nationwide.

Findings: (1) Johnson had greater familiarity with the public than did Goldwater—an obvious advantage of a candidate who is already in office. (2) In the 1964 campaign, only about 1 voter in 5 changed his candidate choice between August and Election Day, which implies that most persuasive actions take place many months before Election Day. (3) Throughout the campaign, Goldwater supporters were infected with defeatism. (4) The 1964 campaign put great emphasis on TV commercials and programs but did not change opinions of voters because opinions were already crystallized. (5) Goldwater's use of TV increased voters' familiarity with him. (6) 29% who saw a Goldwater half-hour show felt they knew a great deal about what he stood for, as opposed to 17% who had seen Goldwater TV commercials. (7) TV commercials had a remarkable effect in Republican appeals for funds to finance their candidate.

Berelson, Bernard. "Communications and Public Opinion," in Wilbur Schramm, ed., *Communications in Modern Society*. Urbana: University of Illinois Press, 1948, pp. 167–85. See abstract in Chapter 2.

Berelson, Bernard, Paul F. Lazarsfeld, and William McPhee. *Voting: A Study of Opinion Formation in a Presidential Campaign*. Chicago: University of Chicago Press, 1954.

Berg, Stephen R. "News Media Content vs. Audience Priorities on Public Affairs." Unpublished master's thesis, University of North Carolina, 1971.

Blumler, Jay G. "Producers' Attitudes Towards Television Coverage of an Election Campaign: A Case Study." *Sociol. Rev. monogr.* 13 (January 1969): 85–115. See abstract in Chapter 4.

Bogart, Leo, B. Stuart Tolley, and Frank Orenstein. "What One Little Ad Can Do." *J. Advert. Res.* 10 (August 1970): 3–14.

Boorstin, Daniel J. *The Image: A Guide to Pseudo-Events in America*. New York: Harper & Row, 1961.

Bowers, Thomas A. "An Analysis of Information Content in Newspaper Political Advertising in Selected Senatorial, Gubernatorial, and Congressional Campaigns of 1970." Unpublished doctoral dissertation, Indiana University, 1971.

Bowers, Thomas A. "Issues and Personality Information in Newspaper Political Advertising." *Journalism Q.* 49 (Autumn 1972): 446–53.

Bowers, Thomas A. "Newspaper Political Advertising and the Agenda-Setting Function." *Journalism Q.* 50 (Autumn 1973): 543–48.

The author's examination of the agenda-setting function of the mass media suggests the following alternative (to McCombs and Shaw data) explanation: voters, indirectly through the candidate, set the agenda of the media, instead of the media directly setting the agenda of the voters, though this relationship might be true only in the short-term campaign situation.

Method: content analysis. *Statistics*: rank order correlations (Spearman's rho). *Pop. (N)*: 5 issues from 46 newspapers (representing 23 states).

Findings: (1) Rank order correlation between voter emphasis and advertising emphasis was +.97 for all candidates. By party affiliation, the correlation was +.93

for Republicans and +.87 for Democrats. By contest, the correlation was +.93 for senatorial candidates, +.95 for gubernatorial candidates, and +.92 for candidates for the House. (2) The concept of the agenda-setting function should be expanded to include three different agendas: those of the candidate, the media, and the voters.

Bowes, John E. "A Discussion of Four Papers: Political Communication." Paper presented to the Association for Education in Journalism, Fort Collins, Colo., August 1973.

Two of these studies capitalize on techniques discussed at the symposium on advanced methodology for communication research held during the 1972 AEJ convention; the other two attack the manifold problems of agenda-setting. "These studies show a breaking with traditional lines of persuasion based on political research."

Findings: Bowes gives a brief description of these four papers' findings. He concentrates on methodological concerns and issues for future research.

Buckalew, James K. "The Television News Editor as a Gatekeeper." Unpublished doctoral dissertation, University of Iowa, 1967.

"Campaign '72: Political Advertising: Making It Look Like News." *Congr. Q. Weekly Rep.* 30 (4 November 1972): 2900–2904.

Campbell, Angus, Phillip E. Converse, Warren E. Miller, and Donald Stokes. *The American Voter*. New York: Wiley, 1960.

Carter, Roy E. "Newspaper 'Gatekeepers' and the Sources of News." *Pub. Opin. Q.* 22 (Summer 1958): 133–44.

Chaffee, Steven, Keith Stamm, Jose Guerrero, and Leonard Tipton. "Experiments in Cognitive Discrepancies in Communication." *Journalism Monogr.* 14 (1969).

Clausen, Aage R. "Political Predictions and Projections. How are They Conducted? Do They Influence the Outcome of Elections?" *Grass Roots Guides on Democracy and Politics*. No. 24. Washington, Conn.: Center for Information on America, 1966.

Cleary, Robert E. "Elections and Image Building." *Today's Educ.* 60 (December 1971): 30–32, 58–59.

This article discusses image building in elections, stating that the average voter is uninterested in finding out what politicians are talking about. Thus politicians try to "sell themselves based on a public image that is appealing." The author also attributes the expense of television rather than long speeches as being a major factor in image making. He concludes that the voter should be aware of what television is doing and seek many different sources of information before deciding who to vote for.

Cobb, Roger W. and Charles D. Elder. "The Politics of Agenda Building: An Alternative Perspective for Modern Democratic Theory." *J. Polit.* 33 (November 1971): 892–915.

This article discusses the elitist theory of democracy, which concerns the distribution of decision-making and agenda-setting activities among a few elite people in power, resulting in limited political participation by the average citizen. Agendas of controversy are being set by people who have their own biases and tend to give priorities to older items. To improve our democratic processes, it is necessary that we increase popular participation in setting systemic and institutional agendas, which will promote social change, and broaden the range of recognized influences on the public policy making process. "Agenda" refers to a general set of political controversies falling within the range of legitimate concerns meriting the attention of the policy. This is called the *systemic agenda*. The *institutional agenda* denotes a set of concrete items scheduled for active and serious consideration by a particular institutional decision-making body. The article keys in on what determines the agenda for political controversy within a community, how an agenda is built, and who participates in the process of building it. The authors consider whether a greater disparity between systemic and institutional agendas causes greater intensity and frequency of conflict within the political system.

Conclusions: (1) Media can play an important role in elevating issues to the systemic agenda and increasing their chances of receiving considerations on institutional agendas. (2) Certain personages in the media can act as opinion leaders in bringing publicity to a particular issue.

Cohen, Bernard. *The Press and Foreign Policy*. Princeton: Princeton University Press, 1963.

Colldeweih, Jack Howard. "The Effects of Mass Media Consumption on Accuracy of Beliefs About the Candidates in a Local Congressional Election." Unpublished doctoral dissertation, University of Illinois, 1969.

Cook, S.W. and A.C. Welch. "Methods of Measuring the Practical Effect of Polls and Public Opinion." *J. Appl. Psychol.* 24 (August 1940): 441–54.

Crespi, Irving. "Longitudinal Versus Cross-Sectional Measures of Public Opinion on Vietnam: A Methodological Note." Unpublished paper, May 1968.

Crossley, Archibald M. and Helen M. Crossley. "Polling in 1968." *Pub. Opin. Q.* 33 (Spring 1969): 1–16.

A review of polls in the 1968 election finds ample controversy surrounding their use but also generally good performance. Pollsters came very close to predicting the division of the popular vote in an election marked by rapid shifts in opinion, and newspaper analysts did well in forecasting the electoral vote.

Danielson, Wayne A. and John B. Adams. "Completeness of Press Coverage of the 1960 Campaign." *Journalism Q.* 38 (Autumn 1961): 441–52.

This study deals with the amount of newspaper campaign coverage that was made available to the average reader during the 1960 campaign. In the United States newspapers covered between 41% and 60% of the campaign events. This percentage of coverage is explained by various factors that contribute to the news potential of the newspapers.

Method: survey; questionnaire. *Statistics*: correlation. *Pop. (N)*: 90 newspapers and campaign events of President and Vice President.

Findings: (1) On the basis of a rigorous criterion the average newspaper reader has 41% of events available to him. (2) On the basis of the easier criterion, the average reader has 60% of events available to him. (3) The following news potential factors were significantly related to completeness of coverage scores of newspapers: size of average weekday news holes—news must have paper space in order for it to appear; editorial staff size—larger staff covered more events; number of news devices; publication 7 days a week—number of days a paper is published affects its coverage score; morning publication—morning newspapers had more complete campaign coverage.

Davison, W. Phillips. "Public Opinion Research as Communication." *Pub. Opin. Q.* 36 (Fall 1972): 311–22.

"Survey research can be seen as one component of the social communication network. This perspective highlights several aspects of the role played by polls in our society. It also suggests some problems in the present and some directions for the future." This study discusses the upward and downward flow of communication and points to the lack of information concerning lateral and diagonal flows of communication in society.

Donohew, Lewis. "Newspaper Gatekeepers and Forces in the News Channel." *Pub. Opin. Q.* 31 (Spring 1967): 61–68.

Examined relationships of publisher's attitude, perceived community opinion and community conditions to behavior of newspaper gatekeepers, as indicated by news coverage of topic—Medicare issue. Kentucky newspapers were studied. Publishers were questioned as to their attitudes, perceived community attitudes and conditions. *Method*: survey; questionnaire; content analysis. *Statistics*: frequencies, correlations. *Pop. (N)*: all 17 Associated Press affiliated newspapers in Kentucky and their editors. *Findings*: (1) Publisher attitude correlated .73 with newspaper content analysis. (2) The difference in coverage scores (derived by content analysis) between newspapers whose publishers favored Medicare and those publishers who opposed it was significant at .006 level. (3) The publishers' estimates of how the community would have voted on the issue were not significantly related to any of the average scores. (4) Community conditions were not related to coverage scores.

Donohew, Lewis and Philip Palmgreen. "A Reappraisal of Dissonance and the Selective Exposure Hypothesis." *Journalism Q*. 48 (Autumn 1971): 412–20.

Erskine, Hazel. "The Polls: Opinion of the News Media." *Pub. Opin. Q*. 34 (Winter 1970–71): 630–43.
This article reviews various polls taken from the late 1930s to early 1970s which indicated the growth in popularity of TV as a source of information. According to the polls, TV climbed steadily during the 1960s and by 1968 became the most popular medium viewed by the public. The question of how Agnew's criticism of the press affected media credibility was asked, and there is some evidence indicating that the public has reached a lower opinion of the news media.
Conclusions: (1) Early in 1970, Harris reported that a majority (56%) thought Agnew was right "in criticizing the way the television networks cover the news." (2) "Before the days of Agnew, half or more in this country ordinarily rated television news fair and impartial in its coverage, depending on the way a question was worded." In December 1969, however, Gallup reported a new low of only 4 in 10 across the country who thought "the TV networks deal fairly with all sides in presenting the news dealing with political and social issues." (3) Similarly, before the Agnew broadcasts, about 5 or 6 in 10 Americans usually maintained that the press should have a free hand in its reporting of the news. In March 1970 the CBS News telephone survey reported only 42% of the U.S. public advocating freedom of press.

Erskine, Hazel Gaudet. "The Polls: The Informed Public." *Pub. Opin. Q*. 26 (Winter 1962): 669–77.
A summary including all available previously published questions asked of nationwide cross sections of the American public from 1947 to 1962 that get at what people actually know about a news item. Topics include "People in the News," "Understanding of the News," and "Exposure to News and Knowledge of Issues."

Evarts, Dru and Guido H. Stempel, III. "Coverage of the 1972 Campaign by TV, News Magazines and Major Newspapers." *Journalism Q*. 51 (Winter 1974): 645–48, 676.

Funkhouser, Ray. "The Issues of the Sixties: An Exploratory Study in the Dynamics of Public Opinion." *Pub. Opin. Q*. 37 (Spring 1973): 62–75.
"This article relates news media coverage of major issues in the 1960's to public opinion and to the realities underlying those issues. It challenges some major assumptions—for example, that the media provide a useful picture of what is 'really' going on—and discusses implications for policy makers and future research." This study seeks to relate news media coverage to public opinion and to the realities underlying the various issues of the 1960s, examining trends in each of these as a means of exploring the dynamics of public opinion.
Method: content analysis. *Data base*: three major magazines and Gallup polls.
Findings: The news media are believed by many people (including many policy makers) to be reliable information sources, but the data presented here indicate that this is

not necessarily the case. Reliance on the news media may mislead anyone who wants to know what is happening in the world and how the public really feels about it.

Gallup, George, Jr. "Polls and the Political Process—Past, Present, Future." *Pub. Opin. Q.* 29 (Winter 1965–66): 544–49.

Gallup, George, Jr., et al. *Politics and the Press.* Washington, D.C.: Acropolis, 1970.

Gerbner, George. "Toward 'Cultural Indicators': The Analysis of Mass Mediated Public Address Systems." *Audio-Visual Comm. Rev.* 17 (Summer 1969): 137–48.

The purpose of this paper is to justify development of the analysis of mass mediated public message systems and find results of practical policy significance, such as a scheme of social accounting for trends in the composition and structure of mass mediated public message systems. "The truly revolutionary significance of modern mass communications is its 'public-making' ability."

Gieber, Walter. "Across the Desk: A Study of 16 Telegraph Editors." *Journalism Q.* 33 (Fall 1956): 423–32.

This study looked at the telegraph editors of 16 afternoon newspapers in Wisconsin. Gieber sought to determine how telegraph editors decided what news to include and what news to reject. "The purpose of this study was to determine how a group of telegraph editors actually carried out the role" (p. 424).

Method: survey; questionnaire. *Statistics*: frequencies. *Pop. (N)*: 16 telegraph editors for 16 afternoon newspapers in Wisconsin.

Findings: "The telegraph editor described in this study is caught in a strait jacket of mechanical details" (p. 432). The most significant force is getting copy into the newspaper. Concerned with immediate details of his work rather than the social arena in which news is made. "As a 'gatekeeper' in the channel of telegraph news, the wire editor appears to be passive" (p. 432). Although the wire editor expresses his own opinions, these opinions generally have no effect on the selection of wire news.

Gieber, Walter. "Two Communicators of the News: A Study of the Roles of Sources and Reporters." *Soc. Forces* 39 (October 1960): 76–83.

Graber, Doris A. "Personal Qualities in Presidential Images: The Contribution of the Press." *Midwest J. Polit. Sci.* 16 (February 1972): 46–76.

A study of press data available for presidential image formation reveals that they reflect an imperfect match between press and public images.

Method: content analysis. *Statistics*: frequencies. *Pop. (N)*: 20; 1557 adults.

Findings: (1) The images of respondents who claimed to have read the papers regularly or often during the campaign were significantly closer to images presented in the newspapers than the images of those who used papers rarely or not at all. (2) The newspaper sample shows that general circulation dailies everywhere, regardless of differences in community settings and newspaper conditions, supplied their readers with similar raw materials for constructing presidential images. (3) The categories which encompassed qualities of the candidate as a man and an image rather than a political actor made up 77% of all mentions of presidential qualities (p. 53). (4) The bulk of media information stressed personal qualities. Political philosophy in general and organizational changes which a president might wish to institute in accordance with his philosophy were almost totally ignored. (5) Images drawn by and about candidates agreed substantially in emphasizing personal qualities and de-emphasizing professional capacities. (6) A comparison of the public's images with press images shows that dimensions used in the public's images were closer to observer images than to candidate images. (7) When the mood of news stories was analyzed, positive comments constituted only 37% of the total, compared to 41% for negative and 22% for normative (p. 69). (8) Candidates who are ignored by the opposition and discussed primarily by their friends are likely to present a more favorable image than their highly publicized colleagues.

Graber, Doris A. "The Press as Opinion Resource During the 1968 Presidential Campaign." *Pub. Opin. Q.* 35 (Summer 1971): 168–82.
Analyzes campaign information presented by a sample of the national press during the last four weeks of the 1968 presidential campaign by asking the following questions: Are there significant differences in news presentation across the U.S.? Was coverage partisan? How much and of what quality was information to public?
Method: content analysis. *Statistics*: frequencies, ranks. *Pop. (N)*: 3163 campaign stories in 20 selected newspapers.
Findings: (1) Everywhere, regardless of geographic, demographic, or political differences, the public received an image of the ideal president based primarily on personal qualities, with little information provided on candidate ability or political philosophy. (2) The issues were fairly uniformly presented throughout the nation. Issue coverage showed significant gaps reflecting the tendency of the press to rely on information provided by candidate himself.

Gregg, James E. "Newspaper Editorial Endorsements and California Elections, 1948–62." *Journalism Q.* 42 (Autumn 1965): 532–38.
This study of editorial endorsements of California newspapers shows that newspapers do exert an influence on the political process, which is particularly evident at the local level and on statewide ballot propositions.
Method: content analysis. *Statistics*: frequencies. *Pop. (N)*: 11 California newspapers.
Findings: (1) Approximately 90% of California's newspapers have consistent partisan endorsement records; of all California newspapers 80% are Republican in orientation, 10% are Democratic in orientation, 10% are either independent or do not make political endorsements. (2) Local endorsements are more influential than endorsements for state and national office. (3) The role of the local press is more influential in nonpartisan elections than in partisan elections. (4) State and local ballot measure endorsements are more influential than candidate endorsements. (5) The influence of newspaper editorial endorsements is greatest when few other determinants affect the voter's decision. (6) Endorsements of candidates of a party opposite that which a newspaper usually supports were more closely related to election results than endorsements of a predictable partisan nature.

Harris, Louis. "Polls and Politics in the United States." *Pub. Opin. Q.* 27 (May 1963): 3–8.
Harris discusses how polls are put to use by candidates, where this development is leading, and some of the sense and nonsense in current discussions about private political polling.
Conclusions: (1) Polls provide a candidate with a realistic appraisal of the situation. (2) Polls make the desires and feelings of people in the nation known. (3) Polls can make the candidate face issues of concern to his electorate, they can make the voice of people clearer and more articulate, they can make democracy function better.

Hooper, Michael. "Party and Newspaper Endorsement as Predictors of Voter Choice." *Journalism Q.* 46 (Summer 1969): 302–5.
"An attempt is made here to determine for Chicago and suburban Cook County how important ... party and newspaper endorsements were in the 1964 at-large election for the Illinois State House of Representatives." Analysis shows that party allegiance exhausts most of the total variance but that endorsements account for much of the within-party variance.
Method: correlation and regression analysis. *Statistics*: correlation between candidate's party and his vote is nearly perfect. *Pop. (N)*: voters in Cook County (Chicago).
Findings: Party was the overwhelming factor in this election. The major source of variation that distinguishes one Democrat from another and one Republican from

another is newspaper endorsements.

House of Representatives Communication Subcommittee. "Hearings to Examine Policy on Broadcast Editorials." *New York Times* 51 (28 June 1963). Announcement of House Subcommittee's plans to examine editorializing by radio stations.

Inoue, K. "Shinbun to Dokosho—Audience Hano nituite (Newspapers and Readers: How the Reader is Influenced)." Kansai Diagaku Keizai Seiji Kenkyusho, *Kenkyu Socho* 9 (1961): 15–150.

Katz, Elihu, Michael Gurevitch, and Hadassah Haas. "On the Use of Mass Media for Important Things." *Am. Sociol. Rev.* 38 (April 1973): 164–81.

A study of the uses made of the media in gratifying social and psychological needs indicates the "interchangeability of the media over a variety of functions." *Method*: survey; questionnaire. *Statistics*: smallest space analysis. *Pop. (N)*: 1500 Israeli adults.

Findings: "(1) For all needs examined, the non-media sources (combined) were deemed more gratifying than the mass media. Friends, holidays, lectures and work were often said to be more important sources of gratification. (2) The greater the 'distance' from a referent—social, physical or psychological—the more important the role of the media. Yet, interpersonal communication—formal and informal—competes even in areas relating to political leadership and negative reference groups. (3) Certain comparative processes—such as striving for a higher standard of living, or satisfying oneself that one's time is well spent or that one's country is a good place to live in—seem well served by the media. So are 'escapist' needs. On the whole, however, friends are more important than the mass media for needs having to do with self-gratification, even the need 'to be entertained.' (4) For individuals who say that matters of state and society are important to them, the rank-order of media usefulness in serving these needs is entirely consistent, regardless of the respondent's educational level. Newspapers are the most important medium, followed by radio, then television. Books and films fall far behind. Altogether, the centrality of the newspaper for knowledge and integration in the socio-political arena cannot be overstated" (p. 180).

Katz, Elihu and Paul F. Lazarsfeld. *Personal Influence: The Part Played by People in the Flow of Mass Communications*. Glencoe, Ill.: Free Press, 1955.

Katz, Elihu, Martin L. Levin, and Herbert Hamilton. "Traditions of Research on the Diffusion of Innovation." *Am. Sociol. Rev.* 28 (April 1963): 237–52.

Keirstead, Phillip O. "The Differences in Selection of News Items for Telecasting by Television Newscast Staff Members and a Sample of the General Public." Unpublished master's thesis, University of Iowa, 1966.

Kelley, S., Jr. "Policy Discussion in Political Campaigning," in James D. Barber, ed., *Readings in Citizen Politics*. Chicago: Markham, 1969.

Key, V.O., Jr. *Public Opinion and American Democracy*. New York: Knopf, 1961.

King, Robert and Martin Schnitzer. "Contemporary Use of Private Political Polling." *Pub. Opin. Q.* 32 (Fall 1968): 431–36.

"It is the premise of the authors of this article that confidential political polling is widely used by major political office-holders and is regarded as an important device for helping to win elections." "The trend observed in the study is unquestionably toward increased use of professional political polling." *Method*: survey; questionnaire. *Statistics*: frequencies. *Pop. (N)*: 333 governors, senators, and congressmen.

Findings: 41 out of 45 governors and senators used polls compared with 69 out of 135 congressmen. 85% of poll users engaged the services of professional pollsters. Republicans are greater users of polls than Democrats in the House. Younger candidates in particular employ polling in their campaigns and often they force older incumbents to follow suit.

Kjeldahl, Bill O., Carl W. Carmichael, and Robert J. Mertz. "Factors in a Presidential Candidate's Image." *Speech Monogr.* 38 (June 1971): 129–31.
Based on the need for research on the dimensions comprising the images of political candidates, the authors were interested in analyzing the categories of judgment that voters used to perceive their candidates. They studied the Oregon primary of 1968 and indicated that the key factors for voters' judgment were "genuineness" and leadership, based on a semantic differential they used. The study confirmed Boulding's hypothesis that image might be divisible into few dimensions, and that image has a conceptual superiority over the political science concept of power.
Method: survey; questionnaire. *Statistics*: factor analysis. *Pop. (N)*: 519 subjects including supporters of each candidate in 1968 Oregon primary.
Findings: The factors of genuineness and leadership account for over half of the total variance and the only scales that weigh consistently on the same factors for all groups of presidential candidate supporters.
Klein, Malcolm W. and Nathan Maccoby. "Newspaper Objectivity in the 1952 Campaign." *Journalism Q.* 31 (Summer 1954): 285–96.
The authors attempt to refine and augment quantitative methods of measurement and content analysis as applied to the problems of reporting and editorial objectivity and to provide indices of the 1952 campaign coverage in prominent American newspapers. This was accomplished by analyzing front-page coverage.
Method: content analysis. *Statistics*: F-tests, frequencies, means, chi-square. *Pop. (N)*: 8 papers.
Findings: There was a definite and statistically significant bias in all 8 papers favoring that candidate who was editorially supported.
Kline, F. Gerald. "Sources and Impact of Political Information in the 1972 Elections." Paper presented to the American Association for Public Opinion Research, Asheville, N. C., May 1973. See abstract in Chapter 4.
Kolehmainen, J.I. "U.S.A.N. Presidentinvaali Propagandan nako Kulmasia (Techniques of Propaganda in American Presidential Elections)." *Valtio jo Yhteisk* 16 (1956): 40–50.
Kraus, Sidney and Raymond G. Smith. "Issues and Images," in Sidney Kraus, ed., *The Great Debates*. Bloomington: Indiana University Press, 1962, pp. 289–312.
Krieghbaum, Hillier. "What About Editorials' Political Influence?" *Masthead* 8 (Spring 1956): 84.
Lang, Gladys Engel and Kurt Lang. "The Inferential Structure of Political Communications: A Study in Unwitting Bias." *Pub. Opin. Q.* 19 (Summer 1955): 168–87. See abstract in Chapter 4.
Lang, Kurt and Gladys Engel Lang. "Mass Media and Voting," in E. Burdick and A.J. Brodbeck, eds., *American Voting Behavior*. Glencoe, Ill.: Free Press, 1959.
Lang, Kurt and Gladys Engel Lang. "The Unique Perspective of Television and its Effects: A Pilot Study." *Am. Sociol. Rev.* 18 (February 1953): 3–12.
This study tends to refute the claim that the "camera does not lie." The authors suggest that the viewer can base his opinion of events on only a limited and selected amount of information that he is exposed to by television. MacArthur Day in Chicago was studied; the reactions of spectators were compared to reactions of those who viewed the event on TV. The results indicated that each type of viewer had a different perception of the event. The television perspective was different from that of any spectator in the crowd.
Method: survey; questionnaire. *Statistics*: content analysis. *Pop. (N)*: 31 participant observers in Chicago.
Findings: (1) People who went to see MacArthur publicly anticipated "mobs" and "wild crowds." (2) The pattern of expectations was shaped by the mass media. (3) Many observers wished that they had remained at home to see the parade on TV.

(4) TV is unlimited in its mobility; it can order events by using close-ups for what is deemed important and leaving the apparently unimportant for the background. (5) The descriptive accounts of the commentators determined the structure of the TV presentation. (6) Through close-ups, it was possible for each viewer to see himself in a personal relationship to the general. (7) Unseen parts of the video were open to the inferences of the viewer. (8) TV viewers perceived the MacArthur event as being a solemn one where the actual spectators were too confused to see the solemnity of the occasion, largely because the officials were too concerned with the way that the ceremony would be televised. The dissemination of an image of overwhelming public sentiment in favor of the general was incorporated into political strategy, picked up by other media, entered into gossip, and thus came to overshadow immediate reality as it might have been recorded by an observer of the scene. (9) A more careful formulation of the relations among public opinion, the mass media, and the political process is vital for the understanding of many problems in the field of politics.

Lang, Serge. *The Scheer Campaign.* New York: Benjamin, 1968.

Lee, Jae-won. "Editorial Support and Campaign News: Content Analysis by Q-Method." *Journalism Q.* 49 (Winter 1972–73): 710–16.

This study looks at 10 "prestige" newspapers, using content analysis and *Q*-factor analysis, to try to find a relationship between the newspaper's candidate support and campaign news. Candidate endorsement was found to be a strong predictor of news items selected and used.

Method: survey; questionnaire. *Statistics*: content analysis, *Q*-factor analysis. *Pop. (N)*: 10 "prestige" newspapers.

Findings: Newspapers will emphasize news items that are favorable to the candidate they endorse. Those items that are not favorable will be played down.

Lippmann, Walter. *Public Opinion.* New York: Macmillan, 1922.

Lipset, S.M., P.F. Lazarsfeld, A.H. Barton, and J. Linz. "The Psychology of Voting: An Analysis of Political Behavior," in G. Lindzey, ed., *Handbook of Social Psychology*, vol. 2. *Special Fields and Applications.* Cambridge, Mass.: Addison-Wesley, 1954, pp. 1124–75.

Lubell, Samuel. "Personalities vs. Issues," in Sidney Kraus, ed., *The Great Debates.* Bloomington: Indiana University Press, 1962, pp. 151–62.

Lyle, Jack and Richard A. Stone. "Election Coverage and Audience Reaction." University of California at Los Angeles. Santa Monica, August 1971. (mimeo)

Martin, Ralph K., Garrett J. O'Keefe, and Oguz B. Nayman. "Opinion Agreement and Accuracy Between Editors and Their Readers." *Journalism Q.* 49 (Autumn 1972): 460–68.

An examination into the relationship between editors and readers reveals that editors, to some extent, perceive position of audience and these positions influence them to a degree, but the audience still perceives newspapers as biased, generally against their own opinion.

Method: survey; questionnaire and content analysis. *Statistics*: frequencies. *Pop. (N)*: 65 editors, 34 Wisconsin papers.

Findings: (1) There is no relation between personal position of newspaper editors and the news play given a story. (2) There is some association between editors' perception of their communities' consensus opinion and the news play given a story. (3) There is little accuracy on the part of readers in perceiving the stand of their newspaper on a specific news event. (4) There is little agreement between editors and their readers on positions taken on a news event. (5) Editors think they agree more with their readers than they actually do. (6) Better educated editors perceive their audiences more accurately, while thinking they agree with them less. (7) Readers with higher income have lower agreement, accuracy, and congruency; income is associated with reader neutrality toward news topics.

McCombs, Maxwell E. "Editorial Endorsements: A Study of Influence." *Journalism Q.* 44 (Autumn 1967): 545–48.

This study discusses and tests two hypotheses: the influence of newspaper editorial endorsements is greater when few other determinants affect the voter's decision; and the greater the disagreement among the variables that typically shape the ballot decision, the greater the influence of an editorial endorsement are negatively correlated.

Method: survey; questionnaire. *Statistics*: percentages and rank order correlation. *Pop. (N)*: 61 voters randomly selected.

Findings: Correlation for the first measure—percentage of endorsed candidates or measures receiving a majority in the county is a perfect +1.0. The rank order for the second measure is .50.

McCombs, Maxwell E. and H.F. Schulte. "Expanding the Domain of the Agenda-Setting Function of Mass Communication." Prepared for presentation to the World Association for Public Opinion Research, Montreux, Switzerland, August-September 1975.

McCombs, Maxwell E. and Donald L. Shaw. "The Agenda-Setting Function of Mass Media." *Pub. Opin. Q.* 36 (Summer 1972): 176–87.

This study investigates the agenda-setting capacity of the mass media in the 1968 presidential campaign, attempting to match what voters said were key issues with content of the mass media used by them during the campaign.

Method: survey; questionnaire. *Statistics*: percentages, correlations. *Pop. (N)*: 100 Chapel Hill voters.

Findings: (1) Much campaign news was not devoted to major political issues but to analysis of the campaign itself; 35% news coverage of Wallace, 30% Humphrey coverage, and 25% Nixon coverage was analysis and estimation of chance of success (p. 180). (2) Correlation between major item emphasis on the main campaign issues carried by the media and voters' independent judgments of what were the important issues was +.967 (p. 180). (3) Between minor item emphasis on the main campaign issues voters' judgments, the correlation was +.979 (p. 181). (4) The judgment of the voters seem to reflect the composite of the mass media coverage. "This suggests that voters pay some attention to all political news regardless of whether it is from, or about, any particular favored candidate" (p. 181). (5) For major and minor news items, correlations were more often higher between voter judgment of important issues and issues reflected in all the news than were voter judgments of issues reflected in news only about their candidate or party. (6) "Considering both major and minor news coverage 18 of 24 possible comparisons show voters more in agreement with all the news rather than with news only about their own party-candidate preference" (p. 182).

McCombs, Maxwell E., Donald L. Shaw, and Eugene F. Shaw. "The News and Public Response: Three Studies of the Agenda-Setting Power of the Press." Unpublished paper presented to Association for Education in Journalism, Carbondale, Ill., August 1972.

McCombs, Maxwell E., Eugene Shaw, Donald L. Shaw, and L. Edward Mullins. *Working Papers on Agenda-Setting, Series 1.* School of Journalism, University of North Carolina, Chapel Hill, July 1973.

Maxwell E. McCombs, "Young Voters: Three Hypotheses on Agenda-Setting." The focus of this paper is on the influence of the press on the issue orientations of potential first voters. The subgroups studied are defined in terms of need for orientation and frequency of exposure to interpersonal and mass communications. Evidence was found that the strength of the agenda-setting effect varies directly with the amount of exposure to mass media.

Eugene Shaw, "Front Page Versus Total Coverage." It was hypothesized that the front page would have a disproportionate influence on respondents' choices of issues they are most concerned about. Front-page reports may have a decisive impact on the setting of issue priorities for certain types of voters: the undecided; those discussing issues outside the family; infrequent general readers of newspapers; and heavy reliers on newspapers for information. *Method*: survey; questionnaire and content analysis. *Statistics*: zero-order correlations. *Pop. (N)*: 60 registered voters. *Findings*: Support the agenda-setting hypothesis.

Donald Shaw, "The 1971 Economic Freeze: From Event to Issue." The study compares how TV and newspapers played the story of the freeze over the five-week period; uses survey data to determine how readers reacted to the sudden increase in economic news. The study found support for a relationship among major news emphasis, greater media exposure, and increase in salience of news issues "high" on the media agenda. *Hypotheses* (both confirmed): (1) Media use: the presentation of an important news story, especially news of a continuing "issue" nature, in newspapers or on television will result in increased use of newspapers or TV. The more "complex" the story, the longer will be the increased use of media. Use of newspapers is greater than television. (2) Learning the media agenda: the publication of an important news story, especially news of a continuing "issue" nature, in newspapers or on television will result in increased saliency of that news/issue to reader/viewers.

McCombs, Maxwell E. and David Weaver. "Voters' Need for Orientation and Use of Mass Media." Paper presented to the International Communication Association, Montreal, 1973.

McLeod, Jack M. "Political Conflict and Information-Seeking." Paper presented to the American Psychological Association, Chicago, 1965.

McLeod, Jack M., Lee B. Becker, and James E. Byrnes. "Another Look at the Agenda-Setting Function of the Press." *Comm. Res.* 1, 2 (April 1974): 131–66.

This paper attempts to trace the origins of the agenda-setting expectations and offers three separate dependent measures or criteria of media agenda-setting effects—community issue salience, perceived issue salience, and individual issue salience. The authors found some support for the agenda-setting hypothesis, but conditions under which the hypothesis is likely to hold need to be clarified, variables that work in complementary and contradictory function need to be identified, situations in which the media are unlikely to have an impact on the perceived issue saliences of their audience need to be isolated.

Method: survey; questionnaire and content analysis. *Statistics*: correlations. *Pop. (N)*: 389 potential voters and 2 newspapers.

McPhee, William. *Public Opinion and Congressional Elections.* New York: Free Press, 1962.

Mendelsohn, Harold A. and Irving Crespi. *Polls, Television, and the New Politics.* San Francisco: Chandler, 1970.

Milbourn, M. Thomas and Vernon A. Stone. "Source-Message Orientation and Components of Source Credibility." *Journalism Q.* 49 (Winter 1972): 663–68.

Morrison, Matthew C. "The Role of the Political Cartoonist in Image-Making." *Central States Speech J.* 20 (Winter 1969): 252–60.

The editorial cartoon delineates the features of a popular image. The treatments by selected cartoonists of Abraham Lincoln, James G. Blaine, and Robert F. Kennedy demonstrate that the cartoonist, using graphic counterparts of effective oral style, can bring obscure values and images into sharp focus.

Conclusions: "Cartooning has translated abstractions into visual symbols and given emotional impetus to values and public images that have previously been obscure."

Mosteller, Fred, Herbert Hyman, Philip J. McCarthy, Eli S. Marks, and David B. Truman. "The Pre-Election Polls of 1948: Report to the Committee on Analysis of Pre-Election Polls and Forecasts." New York: Social Science Research Council, 1949.

Mullins, L. Edward. "Agenda-Setting on the Campus: The Mass Media and the Learning of Issue Importance in the 1972 Election." Paper presented to the Association for Education in Journalism, Fort Collins, Colo., August 1973. Reprinted in Maxwell E. McCombs, Eugene Shaw, Donald L. Shaw, and L. Edward Mullins, *Working Papers on Agenda-Setting, Series 1.* School of Journalism, University of North Carolina, Chapel Hill, July 1973.

Research on the process of agenda-setting reveals that the media appear to have had a direct effect on how students perceived the importance of eight major issues in the 1972 presidential election.

Method: survey; questionnaire. *Statistics*: frequencies, correlations. *Pop. (N)*: 292 first-time student voters.

Findings: (1) A comparison of media issue emphasis shows the six media were remarkably alike during the study period; newspapers were more like each other than like TV networks. (2) Student issue ratings paralleled mass media emphasis moderately to strongly for nearly all the media.

Myers, David S. "Editorials and Foreign Affairs in the 1968 Presidential Campaign." *Journalism Q.* 47 (Spring 1970): 57–64.

The study of newspaper editorials supports the conclusion that voters in the presidential election of 1968 were motivated primarily by matters of foreign affairs, especially the issue of Viet Nam.

Method: survey; questionnaire and content analysis. *Statistics*: frequencies. *Pop. (N)*: 475 election editorials from 10 leading newspapers.

Findings: (1) Of the total number of election editorials, 29.1% were devoted entirely to foreign policy matters. (2) When the election editorials were considered in terms of printed lines, all of the newspapers showed an increase in the percentage of the space devoted to foreign affairs. (3) The partisan direction of the foreign affairs and mixed election editorial differed only slightly from that of the total number of election editorials. (4) 49.6% of all foreign affairs and mixed election editorials dealt with the Viet Nam issue. (5) Among the campaign editorial remarks, emphasis was placed on the conduct and attitudes of the candidates, the Paris peace negotiations, and a bombing halt. (6) "The sample newspapers clearly suggested that the war in Vietnam and foreign policy generally were the most crucial considerations in the 1968 presidential election" (p. 63).

Nicolai, Richard R. and Sam G. Riley. "The Gatekeeping Function From the Point of View of the PR Man." *Journalism Q.* 49 (Summer 1972): 371–73.

Noelle-Neumann, Elisabeth. "Mass Communication Media and Public Opinion." *Journalism Q.* 36 (Fall 1959): 401–10.

The author cites findings of empirical studies to show how they frequently are more enlightening than conventional sources of information. She feels the communication process in our present society cannot be analyzed or understood unless we simultaneously study, in detail and in its broad context, the whole field of social processes and structures. Noelle-Neumann surveys recent research to justify her points.

Conclusions: The effect of the mass media derives not just from their dissemination, volume, editorial style, or intellectual level and themes. The effect of the media depends on what information people accept or reject, and this is a question of the current interplay of social forces affecting the individual, his psychological needs, and his material interest.

Noelle-Neumann, Elisabeth. "Return to the Concept of the Powerful Mass Media," in H. Equchi and K. Sata, eds., *Studies of Broadcasting*, No. 9:67–112 (1973), p. 109.

Perry, Paul. "Gallup Poll Election Survey Experience, 1950 to 1960." *Pub. Opin. Q.* 26 (Summer 1962): 272–79.

RePass, David E. "Issue Salience and Party Choice." *Am. Polit. Sci. Rev.* 65 (June 1971): 389–400.

RePass presents new data concerning issue salience and party choice. Issues which were salient in 1960 and 1964 were examined. The voting public has at least a few substantive issues in mind at election time, and the voters seem to be acting more responsibly than had previously been the case.
Method: survey; questionnaire. *Statistics*: frequencies, cross-tabulations. *Pop. (N)*: Survey Research Center national samples.
Findings: (1) It is not possible to predict what issues will be salient in an election, but the public does seem to respond most to current and recurring news and events. (2) Political parties have only a limited influence on what issues become real to the public. (3) The public does perceive party differences on those issues which are salient to them. "On most issues, more than 60% of the respondents perceived party differences" (p. 394). (4) There is a strong tendency among voters toward "issue alignment" (p. 399), the tendency to name one party as the best party to handle all problems. (5) Independent voters have a relatively high degree of issue concerns. (6) When issue partisanship conflicted with party identification, the issues often overcame the long-term party loyalties; the stronger the issue partisanship, the greater its electoral effect. (7) There was a tendency for Democrats to mention pro-Democratic issues and for Republicans to mention pro-Republican issues as salient. (8) The tendency for people to believe that their party is performing in consonance with their personal viewpoints was substantiated, but a strong strain toward a correct perception of party positions was also evident.

Repass, Donald E. and Steven Chaffee. "Administrative vs. Campaign Coverage of Two Presidents in Eight Partisan Dailies." *Journalism Q.* 45 (Autumn 1968): 528–31.

Robeck, George B. and Verling C. Troldahl. "News-Selection Patterns Among Newspaper Readers." Paper presented to Association for Education in Journalism, Iowa City, August 1966.

Robinson, John P. "The Press as King Maker: What Surveys From Last Five Campaigns Show." *Journalism Q.* 51 (Winter 1974): 587–94, 606.

Roll, Charles W., Jr., and Albert H. Cantril. *Polls: Their Use and Misuse in Politics.* New York: Basic Books, 1972.

Rose, Richard. "Political Decision Making and the Polls." *Parliamentary Affairs* 15 (Spring 1962): 188–202.

This article discusses the use of polls in Britain, where they are not used enough by political parties to understand public opinion on issues for decision making. The author indicates some of the biases, partisanships, and selective perceptions involved with polling and suggests ways in which polls can be used to benefit the government. "Public opinion surveys can help bridge the differences in thinking about politics which characterize politicians and most members of the general public" (p. 196).

Roshwalb, Irving and Leonard Resnicoff. "The Impact of Endorsements and Published Polls on the 1970 New York Senatorial Election." *Pub. Opin. Q.* 35 (Fall 1971): 410–14.

A study of the impact of endorsements by leading political figures and public polls suggests that these events did affect decisions of some last-minute deciders (voters) but did not determine the outcome of this election between Buckley, Ottinger, and Goodell.

Method: survey; questionnaire. *Statistics*: frequencies. *Pop. (N)*: 1000 persons in New York.

Findings: (1) Voters for senator were twice as likely as voters for governor to have made their decision in the last week of the campaign. (2) Only 8% of Buckley voters mentioned endorsements of their candidate as "the most important reason" for their decision, while 13% of Goodell voters and 5% of Ottinger voters mentioned endorsement as the most important factor in making up their minds. (3) There was no voluntary mention of the newspaper poll as an influence on voting decisions. The publicity given the poll may, however, be the reason why 11% of late deciders said they voted for Goodell and 20% said they voted for Ottinger.

Shaw, Donald L. and Thomas A. Bowers. "Learning From Commercials: The Influence of TV Advertising on the Voter Political Agenda." Paper presented to the Association for Education in Journalism, Fort Collins, Colo., August 1973.

"This study blends results of a content analysis of the agenda of themes appearing in network commercials for Nixon and McGovern in the 1972 campaign with the agenda used by a sample of voters asked to role-play what they would tell a friend if asked to describe Nixon or McGovern. Commercials, like other sources of communication, arrive in tangled complicated news composed of many strands of incoming information."

Hypotheses: (1) High use of TV for political news is positively related to high exposure to TV political advertising, low use to low exposure. (2) High exposure to television advertising is positively related to high "affect" in describing a candidate, low exposure to low "affect." (3) High exposure to TV political advertising is positively related to the salience of issues which voters use in describing a candidate. Those highly exposed will more often use the "agenda" of issues made salient in the commercial.

Method: survey; questionnaire. *Statistics*: means, frequencies. *Pop. (N)*: 246 voters.

Findings: All major hypotheses confirmed but the relationship does not seem to be clear between the issues emphasized in commercials and actual vote choice.

Shaw, Donald L. and C. Long. "Voters and Issues: A Study of Media Agenda-Setting in the 1972 Campaign." University of North Carolina, Chapel Hill, 1975.

Sheinkopf, Kenneth G. "Issues vs. Images in the 1972 Presidential Campaign Strategies." Paper presented to the Association for Education in Journalism, Fort Collins, Colo., August 1973.

Smith, Don D. "Mass Communications and International Image Change." *J. Confl. Resol.* 17 (March 1973): 115–30.

Spector, N.J. "The Impact of the Editorial Page on a Municipal Referendum." *Journalism Q.* 47 (Winter 1970): 762–66.

Stempel, Guido, III. "A Factor Analytic Study of Reader Interest in News." *Journalism Q.* 44 (Summer 1967): 326–30.

Tannenbaum, Percy H., Bradley S. Greenberg, and Fred R. Silverman. "Candidate Images," in Sidney Kraus, ed., *The Great Debates*. Bloomington: Indiana University Press, 1962, pp. 271–88.

Tannenbaum, Percy H. and Jack M. McLeod. "Public Images of Mass Media Institutions," in *Paul Deutschmann Memorial Papers in Mass Communications Research*. Cincinnati: Scripps-Howard Research, 1963, pp. 51–69.

Tichenor, Philip J. and Daniel B. Wackman. "Mass Media and Community Public Opinion." *Am. Behav. Sci.* 16 (March-April 1973): 593–607.

This study was primarily interested in the kinds of information that local and metropolitan newspapers exposed to the public, concerning conflict issues between local and state political subsystems. They predicted that different media fulfilled different functions in the production and resolution of conflict. Their findings indicated that the local media fulfilled a maintenance-support function in the community, and metropolitan media tended to fulfill more of a conflict-reporting function. The study questioned the media function of accurately informing the public about the "real" state of public opinion. It also implied that the newspaper has more impact on public opinion than TV.

Method: survey; questionnaire. *Statistics*: chi-square. *Pop. (N)*: 125 adults from a suburb of Minneapolis.

Findings: (1) Persons who read local newspapers tended to offer more support for and greater definitional agreement with officials. (2) Level of metropolitan media use is not related to either support or definitional agreement. (3) Socioeconomic status does not account for differences in agreement with officials. (4) Knowledge of the issues increased with exposure to media. (5) Local newspaper readers with low TV use are higher on knowledge, support of officials, and definitional agreement. (6) Individuals estimated majority opinion as being congruent with their own stand on the issue.

Tipton, Leonard, Roger Haney, Jack Basehart, and William Elliott. "Media Agenda-Setting in a State Campaign." Paper presented to the Association for Education in Journalism, Fort Collins, Colo., August 1973.

Trenaman, Joseph and Denis McQuail. "Election Television—An Unknown Factor," in Joseph Trenaman and Denis McQuail, *Television and the Political Image*. London: Methuen, 1961, pp. 13–16 (a).

Trenaman, Joseph and Denis McQuail. "The Effects of Television and Other Media," in Joseph Trenaman and Denis McQuail, *Television and the Political Image*. London: Methuen, 1961, pp. 182–206(b). See abstract in Chapter 4.

Wade, Serena and Wilbur Schramm. "Mass Media as Sources of Public Affairs, Science and Health Knowledge." *Pub. Opin. Q.* 33 (1969): 197–209.

Ward, Walter. "News Values, News Situations, and News Selections." Unpublished doctoral dissertation, University of Iowa, 1967.

Weaver, David H., Maxwell E. McCombs, and Charles Spellman. "Watergate and the Media: A Case Study of Agenda-Setting." *Am. Polit. Q.* (October 1975).

Westley, Bruce H. and Lionel C. Barrow, Jr. "An Investigation of News-Seeking Behavior." *Journalism Q.* 36 (Fall 1959): 431–38.

White, David Manning. "The 'Gatekeeper': A Case Study in the Selection of News." *Journalism Q.* 27 (Fall 1950): 383–90.

This study follows a Chicago wire editor for one week, looking at the stories he published and those he rejected. The wire editor commented on all the stories he rejected. In addition he answered four questions (pp. 389–90).

Findings: The wire editor apparently chose stories based on his own prejudices and biases. If he had a choice between wire services for the same story, he chose the "conservative" story (p. 389). Other factors which appeared to influence his choices were newspaper policy, "gatekeepers" above him, and "gatekeepers" from other newspapers and other news sources (p. 389).

Whiteside, Thomas. "Corridor of Mirrors: The Television Editorial Process, Chicago." *Columbia Journalism Rev.* 7 (Winter 1968–69): 35–54.

A detailed description of CBS coverage of the 1968 Democratic National Convention in Chicago.

Conclusions: (1) Television coverage does not always present the total reality, for by focusing on one subject, it may ignore others. (2) "Individual reporters and photographers possess much greater mobility in such scenes of disorder [the protesting outside the Hilton] than do television crews, burdened with cameras, lights, and sound equipment" (p. 49). (3) "A press reporter is in a better position to isolate and record the relationship between a confrontation." "The television cameraman ... may record the police action, but his camera has no memory of what happened before he passed the camera trigger."

Wiebe, Gerhart D. "*The New York Times* and Public Opinion Research: A Criticism." *Journalism Q.* 44 (Winter 1967): 654–58.

The author gives five examples from the *Times* of faulty treatment of stories dealing with polls and opinion research. He states, "rather than helping readers toward perceptive understanding there is evidence that the *New York Times* deliberately holds public opinion research up to derision by lumping together studies that do and do not employ scientific sampling, providing the reader with no help in identifying which is which, and then stigmatizing both by pointing out discrepancies in findings." *Conclusions*: The rise of public opinion research calls upon the journalist to use the following technique: Inform the few about the many or inform the many about the many. "The principle of representative sampling which is irrelevant to the reporter in pursuit of the atypical event or the powerful person is basic to the public opinion research in pursuit of opinions and behavior that have their importance primarily in the frequency among a specified public."

Wilhoit, G. Cleveland and Taik Sup Auh. "Newspaper Endorsement and Coverage of Public Opinion Polls in 1970." *Journalism Q.* 51 (Winter 1974): 654–58.

Windlesham, Lord. "Television as an Influence on Political Opinion." *Polit. Q.* 35 (October–December 1964): 375–85.

The author discusses TV as an influence on political opinion from the standpoint that it is a medium for distribution of information. Political information is not in itself a persuasive influence, because its effect will depend on what the viewer already knows, on what he wants to hear, and on what information he is willing to retain. The important political function of TV is to bring to the surface opinions on new issues from new events or existing situations.

Conclusions: (1) Since television has become a standard convenience of everyday life, it is scarcely possible to separate the effects of its programs from other extramedia influence on behaviors and attitudes. (2) Some viewers will be more receptive than others to political information. (3) The persuasive power of television lies not so much in conversion, since for the most part the viewer is already predisposed to accept whatever information he retains, but in reinforcement. (4) The political influence of television can be seen in the reinforcement of existing opinions, in the bringing out of opinion on new issues, and in the acceleration of existing situations into issues.

Witt, William. "Multivariate Analysis of News Flow in a Conservation Issue." *Journalism Q.* 49 (Spring 1972): 91–97. See abstract in Chapter 4.

Ziff, R. "Voters' Bias in Interpreting Election Poll Predictions." *Pub. Opin. Q.* 12 (Summer 1948): 326–28.

7

Methods of Political Communication Research

We have saved for last a significant form of political communication. In a most important way, published political communication research findings themselves constitute political communication. Certainly our arguments in preceding chapters would have political consequences if they were widely accepted. The findings of the past three decades have had political consequences if only because they buttress what political and other societal leaders chose to believe about society. In this chapter we depart from a typical consideration of the role of methods in research so that we can discuss what should differentiate political communication research findings from other forms of political communication.

We will take the position that the way in which methods are applied can produce findings whose political consequences differ significantly. For this reason a perspective on methods and their role in political communication research is vital if research is to produce useful findings which have productive political consequences. This perspective on methods cannot be found in most methodology texts, which are limited to discussions of such factors as research design, measurement techniques, and data analysis procedures. Rather, methods should be viewed as sets of procedures which permit phenomena to be observed so that temporarily useful conclusions can be reached. Inherent in this definition of methods is the notion that method should not be expected to yield universal truth. Methods are justified if they serve far less ambitious goals. Methods should seek findings that are temporarily useful. From this viewpoint, the best findings are those which point beyond themselves and permit themselves to be rapidly replaced by more useful conclusions. It might be argued that our definition of methods is too pragmatic, with a concern for the usefulness rather than the validity of findings. In our view, methods are inherently pragmatic; they seek knowledge for a purpose even when the purpose is simply the intellectual curiosity of the researcher.

There is one purpose which methods should not serve. They should not be used as a means of justifying conclusions which were in effect decided upon before the research was performed. Methods serve no purpose if they are so biased that only one set of conclusions is possible. The consequences of applying methods in this way are clear—methods simply justify what the researcher wants to believe. The ill effects of applying methods in this way could be attenuated by confining all researchers to an ivory tower where they could be allowed to perpetuate their fantasies without consequences. However, to the extent that research findings are used as a basis for planning social policy, the perpetuation of one person's fantasy can have a detrimental impact on the lives of many individuals.

Stanislav Andreski [1] has written a harsh indictment of the social sciences in which he argues that many researchers use the scientific method to enhance their power just as sorcerers used their methods to gain power in medieval society. The power of the sorcerer was a function of his ability to manipulate how others perceived reality. Andreski argues that many social scientists use the scientific method to create similar self-serving misperceptions of reality. Just as sorcerers could use their methods to facilitate social control, modern social scientists can serve the state through their ability to use methods to convince people that the chosen policy is the correct course of action. Andreski has described some extreme consequences resulting from the abuse of method. While it is possible to defend the social sciences against many of his specific criticisms, and while most social scientists do not *intend* such abuse of methods, his central argument appears sound. Social science can be "corrupted" and reduced to a scientifically useless activity.

One of our purposes in this chapter is to suggest procedures which assure that method will be applied meaningfully in political communication research. For this reason we will probe the social context in which method is applied and suggest what its role in social and political decision making might be. For example, findings can be used to justify alternate strategies for conducting political campaigns, new ways of presenting political information to children, or new procedures for providing for public participation in the design and transmission of political messages.

In the first section of this chapter, we will probe the methods used to produce specific sets of findings in "classic" research. Our intention is not to criticize the researchers nor to demean their contribution to the field. Certainly we do not intend to question their professional ethics. It must be recognized that social science disciplines in general and political communication research in particular are developing disciplines. Methods which were once appropriate have become less acceptable as their flaws have become apparent. Our review of methods used in previous political communication research is intended to indicate pitfalls and shortcomings to be avoided in future research.

We will also discuss some of the possible consequences for social policy of the findings of previous research. In doing this we frequently engage in speculation. We cannot easily link specific policy decisions to specific research findings. (In our next and final chapter we have attempted such linkage since the exercise was illustrative of the major theme of this book.) We hope that most readers will find our arguments sufficiently plausible to stimulate their own thinking in this area.

We will argue that only rarely have research findings contradicted existing social policies while almost all findings more or less legitimize the commonsense beliefs on which such policies tend to be based. Why? We conclude that methods were not applied productively. For example, studies which generated and evaluated isolated bivariate empirical generalizations tended to have minimal power to "transcend" the implicit conceptual frameworks which guided them. The implicit conceptual frameworks were frequently simple elaborations of popular political, economic, or social beliefs. Research had the function of confirming what societal leaders already accepted as true while refuting the claims of troublesome social critics. The null findings concerning the influence of mass media on political behavior confirmed the wisdom of permitting mass media to develop as profit-making, privately operated industries.[2] The warnings of mass society critics could be ignored because the media could not be proven to produce the effects critics predicted.

In the second section of this chapter we will discuss the role of methods in present-day political communication research. We will point out that new, sophisticated data-gathering procedures are being utilized. Data are processed in ever larger "batches" by computer programs capable of reducing many variables measured in qualitatively different ways at different times into a form which can be understood and communicated by researchers. Research is conducted in an ever growing number of academic, private, and government research units. Researchers are guided by a multiplicity of explicit and implicit conceptual schemes. Some are engaged in "policy" research in which findings presumably translate directly into decisions, while others conduct "pure" research aimed at developing particular conceptual schemes. Current economic pressures have increased the resources available for "policy" research and reduced funding of "pure" research.

Yet despite all the trends which suggest that methods are being developed and applied in ever more useful ways, we maintain that no concerted, systematic effort is being made to assure that method will not be used only to "package" popular beliefs and "market" them. Discussions of methods in most texts fail to provide sufficient perspective. Many discussions appear to assume that modern researchers work in social situations similar to those occupied by their nineteenth-century counterparts. Texts still contain descriptions of the "hypothetical deductive method."[3] No mention is made concerning how the traditional notions of doing research have been transformed in modern applications.

In concluding this section, we argue that the most significant methodological problem facing political communication researchers is how to develop procedures which will assure that conceptual frameworks will be built and evaluated even when those frameworks contradict popular beliefs or accepted ways of doing things. Methods are flexible and cannot be expected to guarantee that only "true" findings will be produced. Researchers who work in particular social situations can be expected to occasionally conform to the pressures of those situations and produce self-serving findings. Existing procedures for replicating research findings cannot solve this problem. Nor can professional organizations begin to cope with it. It is not simply a matter of formulating a new code of ethics nor of disbanding research organizations in which social pressures exist to confirm certain beliefs. The experience of sociology in the past decade provides evidence that none of these solutions is particularly effective.[4]

In the third section, we suggest a solution to the methodological dilemma. One part of this solution lies in greater self-knowledge and self-criticism. Researchers must seek to understand their role more clearly. They should remain open to constructive criticism. Simply acknowledging the existence of the problem can help to initiate its solution. The second part of the solution is more speculative. We argue that a particular strategy for doing research, a "new method," can solve the problem. The method we describe is not really new but is rather a synthesis of what we consider to be useful aspects of existing research approaches. Our method presumes the existence of ever more sophisticated data collection and analysis techniques. It presumes that research units will grow in size and will be more closely integrated into the day-to-day operation of certain social institutions. This is not the most efficient strategy for organizing social research, nor is it the most effective strategy for producing immediately useful findings. Some would argue that it is an approach which is itself grounded in a particular view of society. Indeed it is. Our hope is that the perspective in which the method is grounded does not limit its usefulness significantly.

Methods Used in the Classic Studies

In our opinion, political communication in modern society can best be understood by examining the role it plays in various social processes. In previous chapters we defined a number of such processes. We focused attention on the relationship of mass communication variables to each of these processes. Where possible we cited studies which document the role of mass communication for each process. In the absence of data, we engaged in speculation about the existence of certain relationships. We argued that this approach clarifies and organizes previous research findings. Inevitably, we criticized studies which failed to examine the role of mass communication variables in the various processes we defined. It can be argued that we are biased in our definition of these social processes. As indicated above, other researchers have created plausible definitions for similar processes which excluded attention to mass communication variables while focusing attention on social structural variables. We consistently define processes to include a central role for mass communication variables. The usefulness of our definitions cannot be established here. Much more research is required.

No one would disagree that mass media are heavily used in our society. Elsewhere, we documented the level of certain forms of mass communication behavior. But it should be clear from previous chapters that the usefulness of mass communication behavior in explaining political behavior is a subject of some controversy. One view, perhaps the dominant view at present, argues that mass communication behavior is so constrained by other variables such as family structure or reference group affiliation that it introduces no new variation in dependent variables. Thus, while no one denies that mass communication takes place, the usefulness of studying it can be questioned. We would agree that if mass communication use serves only to transmit the influence of other variables, it should be ignored in constructing parsimonious models of social processes.

However, this conveyor-belt notion of mass communication must be established by a series of definitive studies which conclusively demonstrate that mass communication variables are not useful even when defined in a wide variety of ways, measured with many different techniques, and analyzed by available mathematical models. What we object to is a premature movement to define "parsimonious" models of social processes which relegate mass communication variables to the position of exogenous variables to be examined in a few choice anecdotes along with a host of other residual variables. Classic studies are cited frequently to justify this movement. We previously questioned the conceptualizations underlying these classic studies. In the remainder of this section we criticize the method used in the classic studies.

Our purpose is not to deny or minimize their contribution, but to consider these studies objectively. Only after the basis for their conclusions has been examined, can we decide whether findings warrant omitting mass communication variables from future research.

Studying Social Processes

In the past two decades social scientists have become increasingly aware of the difficulty of scientifically studying social processes. Such processes cannot be directly observed; their very existence must be inferred from data. Ideally, we should seek to conceptualize the various parts of a social process, construct a model of the process, collect data which measure these parts, and then put the process "back together" in the computer by assessing the relationship of the various parts of the model to each other. To the extent that our model appears to "fit" reality, that is, when greater numbers of predicted relationships are found between variables, we can have increasing confidence in the usefulness of our model. If the model can be found to "fit" other data sets which use differing measures of key variables and are representative of differing populations, our confidence in the model increases. In fitting the model to new data sets, it can be elaborated to account for new relationships.

Working researchers may find this description too idealistic. They might point out that research papers still discuss *hypotheses* rather than *models*. These *hypotheses* are rarely evaluated using more than one or two data sets. "Strings of hypotheses" are occasionally collected in some more or less logical fashion and published as a *theory*. In our view, this state of affairs stems in part from the fact that most researchers adhere to a traditional view of method. Their hypotheses still seek to capture "truth." Their theories are intended to stand as collections of universal laws. This is idealistic. We have shown that sometimes the work of these researchers can be interpreted in other ways than their own. We maintain that social processes are best studied by model construction and evaluation. Hypothesis testing can be regarded as construction and evaluation of very limited, time-bound models of processes. Viewed in this way, this approach is subject to many criticisms.[5]

Models of social processes can be very simple, perhaps predicting only two or three relationships between important variables. Our review of research has found most models of processes to be of this type. For example, parental authority patterns were found to be related to children's perceptions of authority, which in turn predicted children's political values, beliefs, and attitudes. These cognitive structures were related to political behavior. Clearly, a political socialization process is implicit in this set of relationships. Each of these relationships has been tested as a separate hypothesis by several researchers using different data sets. (See Chapter 2 for a summary of this research.) However, no research exists which tests all of these relationships simultaneously, over a period of time, with several different samples of children. This is not surprising, given the cost of making such an elaborate evaluation. But, lacking such an evaluation, the usefulness of this model remains to be demonstrated even though many tests of the separate hypotheses exist. A complete evaluation of the model might find that different relationships hold true for different samples but that the model in its entirety is useless for any particular group.

The preceding discussion indicates the nature of the criteria which we will employ in evaluating the methods used in "classic" research as well as our rationale for imposing these criteria. Certainly, none of this research was designed to meet the standards we will impose. Nevertheless, these standards should be imposed if social processes are to be studied with rigor and the consequence of biased findings is to be avoided. Although model construction and evaluation provides no guaranteed solution to this problem, it is an important first step. We will discuss other steps later in the chapter.

In proper model construction and evaluation, researchers should adhere to the following procedures:

1. Social processes should be carefully conceptualized in terms of the findings of previous research and theories which the researcher feels are important. At this stage in the development of the social sciences it may be necessary to conceptualize unwieldy, unparsimonious models of processes. Care must be given to specifying the particular social conditions that influence each process.

2. Observable parts of social processes, particularly those which are easily observed, should be operationally defined. Ideally, more than one operational definition should be formulated, so that every important variable is measured using more than one scaling technique. Contingent conditions that affect the functioning of processes should be specified, operationally defined, and measured.

3. Data which evaluate social psychological processes and organizational processes should be collected over time from a panel of the same individuals or from a series of samples drawn from the same population. Both of these over-time measurement procedures have serious drawbacks, but they are preferable to short-term, scattered studies. These data should be compared to data drawn from panels or samples representing other populations.

4. Several mathematical models should be used to determine whether the conceptual model is isomorphic ("fits") with the data. Mathematical models should be chosen on two criteria: their underlying assumptions should be satisfied by the data, and they should permit an extensive, exhaustive evaluation of all the relationships contained in the conceptual model. (For example, a regression analysis provides a more extensive evaluation of a set of relationships than does a series of product-moment correlations.)

5. Conclusions drawn from research should always be qualified in terms of the model evaluated. No model can completely represent "reality." Every model represents only a tiny portion of a "real process," and this representation is from a particular point of view and serves a specific purpose. The point of view used to generate the model and the purpose served by the model

should be explicitly described and defended. Conclusions should indicate how the model can be refined and what research should be done to evaluate this refined model. In this way, the most useful models to serve specific purposes may be generated and evaluated.

Classic Studies of Political Socialization Processes

Implicit in early studies of political socialization are models which include too few variables to be useful. In general, these studies focus on only one or two so-called socialization agents. One agent which has received great attention is the family. A large number of family variables have been found to predict politically relevant cognitive and behavioral variables. These family variables are assumed to so constrain a child's thoughts and actions that other sources of variation can be ignored. In Chapter 2, we discussed why these models should be enlarged to include mass communication variables. We found many reasons why it is plausible to predict that mass media will influence the manner in which some children are socialized. In our opinion, careful conceptualization of such models requires inclusion of mass communication variables.

Early studies of political socialization were based on the assumption that study of one or two agents could explain how political behavior developed. As this research became more sophisticated, more agents were considered until in recent studies some attention has been given to mass communication as an agent. Yet in even the more recent research, "agent" models of socialization processes are rather simple. Socialization processes tend to be conceived of as linear, universal processes. Each variable in a process is linked to every other variable by unidirectional causal relationships, forming a chain of relationships in which the first variables clearly dominate later variables. Greenstein[6] makes a similar observation: "The study of political socialization has suffered from inattention to actual sequences of socialization and from the failure to proceed in a frame of reference that takes sufficient cognizance of the general theories of human development." Four classes of variables make up the "chains" of relationships typically studied: social structural variables, socialization "agents," various intervening variables, and political belief or behavior variables. These classes of variables stand in a definite time order in relation to each other. Social structural variables occur first, followed by socialization "agents," intervening variables, and finally political belief or behavior variables. These processes are assumed to be universal in the sense that it is not necessary to define qualitatively different processes to explain the beliefs or actions of persons in various communities or subcultures. One all-encompassing model is proposed to account for all variation in dependent variables.

When political socialization research is examined in this way its flaws become immediately apparent. Many of the researchers who performed this research might respond by arguing that we have interpreted their findings too narrowly. If we read their work carefully, we find they have described complex social processes. However, these processes are alluded to in vague descriptions, while the processes actually elaborated and evaluated are those which we criticize.

The two most serious flaws in the "classic" models deserve particular attention. First, these models fail to conceptualize developmental processes in which variation introduced by early variables is significantly altered or transformed by changes in a child's abilities or social situation. Cognitive development has not been overlooked by political socialization researchers, but they tend to view such development as contributing to a long-term linear socialization process. For example, Adelson and O'Neil examine how political concepts change as children mature. In general, such studies emphasize continuity. Political concepts learned in the family are elaborated, not discarded. Little attention is given to changes in communication patterns or in mass media use habits occasioned by cognitive development. In our view an eight-year-old will have very different media use habits than a teenager. Most psychologists believe that children gradually develop new cognitive skills for handling environmental stimuli. Development of these skills radically transforms the child's relationship to his environment. For this reason, it may be more useful to define separate models for various stages of children's cognitive development, particularly as work in psychology provides better definitions of these stages.[7] Thus, one model of political socialization might be found to hold for most preadolescent children while a different model might hold for adolescents. Parents might be able to control children's political beliefs in one model, but their influence may disappear later. Ward and Wackman[8] illustrated the utility of such an approach for studying children's information processing of television commercials. Applying Piaget's theory of cognitive development, they evaluated two models of consumer socialization, each of which is most useful for explaining learning from commercials by children in a particular age range. A similar approach could be taken to examine the processing of political content.

Similarly, it may be necessary to define different models of political socialization for children in very different social situations. Chaffee[9] has discussed this possibility in summarizing his conclusions after reviewing political socialization research. He argues that different social situations may support qualitatively different "media cultures." Children in these different situations learn to use media differently. For example, Clarke found strong relationships between parents' use of newspapers and certain socialization values.[10] We developed a similar argument in Chapter 4. In our view, children learn certain quite specific uses for mass media from their interaction in situations. These differing uses later support qualitatively different political socialization processes. In one model, use of newspapers and magazines may constantly enlarge a store of political knowledge, which in turn is a basis for belief and action. In another model, vague, dramatic images recalled from television news broadcasts may buttress old political prejudices and rationalize traditional political actions. If this view is correct, great priority must be given to specifying the social conditions for which differing models are appropriate.

The second flaw in classic studies is the assumption of unidirectional causal relationships between variables. For example, structural variables like socioeconomic status and education of parents are hypothesized to cause particular family authority patterns which in turn cause societal authorities to be viewed in certain ways. The ultimate result is particular political beliefs and actions. This assumption arises because each relationship is typically evaluated separately with a single bivariate test of statistical significance. Bell[11] questioned such unidirectional studies, arguing that children influence parents. Correlations found between the behavior of parents and children are at least partially due to children. Bell is able to provide a plausible way of reinterpreting the findings of several previous studies. Correlations found between political party preferences of parents and children are not necessarily evidence of parental influence.

In our view, many relationships between variables in socialization processes are likely to be reciprocal. Sets of variables may influence other sets and in turn be influenced by them. It will be necessary to build relatively complex models to represent these relationships adequately. Evaluation of such models will require the development of new mathematical models.

The ways in which political socialization researchers have evaluated their models can also be criticized. As we have noted, concern has been centered on evaluation of bivariate relationships. A number of simple statistical tests of covariation are used, including chi square, phi, gamma, one-way analysis of variance, and of course the Pearson product-moment correlation coefficient. Usually the results of these statistical tests are reported without any attempt to assess whether relationships are spurious or significantly influenced by other variables. As a result one should be very cautious in generalizing from such findings. Observed covariation may be due to true covariation, the influence of other variables which were not controlled, systematic bias in the method used to observe the variables, or random error in the measurement operation. In addition, there is no way of estimating how long observed covariation will persist. It may disappear an hour after the researcher takes his measurements. Similarly, the failure to observe covariation may be due to any of the factors mentioned above. But only one of these factors is legitimate—absence of covariation. Covariation may return within moments after a researcher completes his measurements.

Such "tests" of hypothesized relationships can hardly be considered conclusive. Their power to force the researcher to overcome his initial bias or misconceptions is minimal. If covariation is found, it supports the researcher in his prejudices even if it is due to measurement errors. If other researchers commit similar errors in measurement (as is possible if all use the same techniques), then erroneous findings can be replicated. In this way, an entire set of findings may be in error.

We do not mean to suggest that any impact of mass communication on political behavior would have been verified empirically if measurement errors had not been a factor. To the contrary, our criticism is often applicable to studies which claim media effects on political behavior as well as to those which do not.

Classic studies of political socialization may have served to justify and preserve widely held views of political institutions. As Greenstein[12] points out, such studies had inherent conservative bias. Their intention was to examine processes of "pattern maintenance," not those of change. They directed concern toward the family and schools. These two institutions were perceived as the "bedrock" of democracy. So long as American families were nonauthoritarian, our political system was in no danger. So long as high school civics classes taught reverence for the three branches of government and the duty to vote, communism was no threat. Laws which benefited the family and education would in the long run preserve our political order.

The classic studies directed attention away from mass media. Patterns of media use could be ignored as irrelevant. No political consequences were foreseen from the particular images of politics television conveyed. No effort was made to ascertain why television content presents certain images of authority, or what use certain individuals make of these images.

It may be comforting to some to believe that we can preserve our present system of government simply by helping families and schools to continue as they are. Certainly individuals who choose to believe so can find much support for their views in previous research findings. In our view these findings must be questioned and with them the views of politics which generated them.

Classic Studies of the Electoral Process

Although classic studies of political campaigns have given attention to the role of mass communication in campaigns, we argued in Chapter 3 that this research was deficient because it did not evaluate the influence of television. Due to the recent appearance of this medium, it evaluated media impact only indirectly, and it did not take into account declines in party affiliation and in the influence of political opinion leaders.

The models used in classic studies of the electoral process include four sets of variables: social structural variables, especially group affiliation and political party membership; cognitive structure variables, especially pre-existing political beliefs and attitudes; intervening variables, especially mass media exposure; and political behavior, especially campaign activity and voting behavior. As in classic models of political socialization a universal, linear process is assumed, consisting of a chain of unidirectional bivariate relationships. A typical chain begins with group affiliation and political beliefs, leads to communication behavior, and ends with voting. Models differ in the importance assigned to social structural variables or cognitive structure variables. Some models omit one or the other of these sets of variables. As in the models of political socialization, mass communication variables are treated as intervening variables. We have pointed out (Chapter 3) that a "phenomenistic" perspective is used to conceptualize the manner in which media "intervene." Media are considered as only one of many influences. Frequently, social or cognitive structure variables are found to so constrain media impact that researchers have concluded that media influences are spurious. For example, the so-called selectivity processes are said to constrain media exposure, perception, and retention so that people see or hear only those messages which are consistent with their existing beliefs or group affiliations. Once again, a common perspective which emerges from this research is that the mass media merely transmit the influence of other variables.

Most of the criticisms which we made of political socialization models are relevant to electoral process models also. Though often preceded by lengthy discussions of relatively complex sets of relationships, the models actually evaluated by research tend to include only a few variables. "Important" relationships are tested using bivariate statistics. Statistically significant observed covariance is accepted as conclusive proof of the validity of the relationships and of the theory that predicts the relationships. Rarely are attempts made to assess possible sources of error.

Other serious questions can be raised about the usefulness of electoral process models. Differences in cognitive skills or capacities are usually not considered. It is assumed that "average" citizens participate in the electoral process with the equivalent levels of cognitive skills and equivalent abilities to process and use information. Variables like education or level of political information may measure cognitive skills indirectly, but this variable should be assessed more directly. As with political socialization research, it may be useful to construct very different models of the electoral process for persons having different levels of skills.

Lazarsfeld et al.[13] have argued that the electoral process reinforces political convictions and affiliations held before the campaign began. From this viewpoint, all campaign variables simply transmit the influence of cognitive or social structures. The electoral process simply produces increasingly strong convictions or affiliations resulting in a vote that is consistent with these. This linear process would not explain elections in which significant numbers of voters change candidates during the campaign.

It may be necessary to differentiate election campaigns in terms of characteristics which may drastically affect the electoral process. Such characteristics might include familiarity of voters with each candidate, whether more than two significant candidates are involved, whether events attract widespread attention to the campaign, and whether candidates use similar, traditional campaign strategies. Thus there may be a model of the electoral process which fits some elections but which is useless when certain deviations occur. For example, the simple linear process suggested by Lazarsfeld et al.[14] may be useful only for predicting voting behavior of white, middle-class high school graduates, when well-known candidates wage traditional campaigns which fail to attract high levels of public attention.

In certain elections, models which view media as decisive influences may be more useful. This may be true in an election in which one candidate is a "political unknown," in which events occur that draw public attention to the campaign, in which one candidate originates an innovative strategy for using mass media, or in which more than 30 percent of the voters define themselves as politically independent. For example, an unknown candidate may send out many times the number of messages his opponent sends. These messages may attract attention because they are well structured and because events that occur during the campaign arouse interest in it. As a result, significant numbers of voters may switch to the unknown candidate.

Recent research by Patterson and McClure[15] provides some support for this position. They differentiated between voters who were highly interested in the campaign and those who had little interest. They found evidence that voters with low interest used information gained from television advertisements differently than persons having high interest. The beliefs of low-interest voters were more likely to be affected by the information gained. Thus, if the circumstances of the campaign lead to significant shifts in voter interest, beliefs, and perhaps voting decisions, may be affected.

"Classic" studies of the electoral process may also have served to justify and preserve widely held views of political institutions. They are concerned with understanding a process which researchers believed ensured political stability. Just as political socialization assured the orderly transmission of democratic political beliefs and attitudes from one generation to the next, the electoral process sufficiently involved the public in the choice of leaders so that they would accept these leaders as legitimate. The electoral process also reaffirmed existing political beliefs and affiliations. It was regarded as a ritual activity which reminded people of their privileges and responsibilities as citizens. Even the apathetic were temporarily roused to minimal participation.

While the electoral process may serve these objectives, they are not always met nor are these the only or even the most important consequences of the process. As we have tried to indicate, the process is difficult to understand. Its consequences are not easily predicted. Deviations from ideal objectives are not necessarily dysfunctional. The electoral process may take different forms in elections having certain characteristics. Mass media may transform the process depending on how events are reported and on how media are used by politicians. Much more research will be required to construct useful models of the electoral process.

Classic Studies of Political Information

As was the case with early research on political socialization and the electoral process, early studies of political information tended to be based on simple, linear models. In contrast with these other two sets of studies, research on political information initially assumed that mass communication played a central, dominant role in dissemination of information. This research grew out of content analysis studies of propaganda during World War II. Researchers devoted much time and effort to the analysis of propaganda because they assumed it significantly affected mass audiences. Effective propaganda was thought capable of converting entire nations, directing them toward goals selected by a small elite. The model implicit in these notions about propaganda has been labeled the "hypodermic model." As we indicated in Chapter 4, this model assumes that mass media "inject" messages directly into individuals, inducing rapid changes in attitudes and behavior. The model was linear in the sense that propaganda messages were thought to "collect" in the individual's mind until a sufficient number produced the desired effects. It was universal in the sense that propaganda was thought to be equally effective everywhere. All individuals were expected to respond to the same propaganda stimulus in the same way. Hence the fear that Axis, Communist, or Fascist propaganda would inevitably convert the American public if it was permitted to be broadcast or published.

The hypodermic model was empirically evaluated by content analyses of propaganda. These analyses predicted that propaganda messages structured in certain ways would prove more effective. These studies could not evaluate the model because they did not actually measure changes in the attitudes or behaviors of persons exposed to propaganda. Instead, they inferred such effects from observations of the popular responses to leaders like Hitler or Roosevelt. It was not until Hovland assembled a group of researchers during World War II that direct tests were made of the effectiveness of specific messages. Using an experimental research design borrowed from psychology, Hovland et al.[16] found that certain forms of military propaganda apparently changed particular attitudes of soldiers who were required to attend to it. Hovland soon modified the hypodermic model by adding the notion of "selectivity processes,"[17] which he argued enable an individual to ignore, misinterpret, or forget messages that are inconsistent with his present attitudes.

The hypodermic model was also modified by social influence researchers,[18] who posited a two-step model of information flow in which an opinion leader elite evaluated and interpreted mass media messages before they passed them on to their followers. This model in turn was modified to the diffusion process model, which posits a process in which media communicate information but social influence is required before information will be adopted and used. Thus media are assumed to play a limited though necessary role in bringing about social change. In Chapter 4 we discussed at length our reservations concerning the two-step flow model and the diffusion process model. Clearly, sufficient research exists to label the two-step flow model relatively useless. Many hypotheses derived from the diffusion process model have been useful in understanding and controlling social change in developing nations.[19] However, the model places an emphasis on examining only the downward flow of information from centralized, government sources. It is inadequate for understanding a total process in which the public carries on transactions with mass media. These transactions are structured around sets of media use and gratification patterns which are learned in social situations. The patterns are subject to constant change, but while particular patterns persist, certain consequences can be predicted.

None of these political information models has been adequately evaluated. Research findings consist largely of statistical tests of bivariate covariation. For example, though Rogers and Shoemaker[20] are able to list hundreds of such two-variable hypothesis tests, they cite relatively few evaluations using more variables. As we argued earlier, such two-variable tests have little power to determine the actual source of observed covariation. In particular, bias introduced by measurement procedures cannot be discounted.

These political information models clearly reinforce certain widely held beliefs about political institutions. The discredited hypodermic model supported the view that the American public could be easily subverted by foreign influences. It could be used to justify curtailing freedom of the press during World War II. It argued for careful government control of information to "preserve democracy." It constituted a very elitist conception of society. Only a highly trained class of "scientists" could be trusted to detect propaganda and prevent others from being exposed to it. Visions of *1984* may have guided the work of these researchers. Yet the policy implied by their work was that centralized control of communication, which is at the heart of Orwell's nightmare, should be institutionalized.

In Chapter 4 we discussed at length the political implications of the two-step flow model. At first glance, this model is the "democratic answer" to the hypodermic needle model. It implies that the average citizen has effective protection from propaganda. Yet when examined more closely it simply substitutes one elite for another. Propaganda only reaches an interested, active political elite who, like the scientists in the hypodermic model, act as censors and prevent subversive content from reaching their followers. This model was well suited to the postwar era in which it was elaborated. Americans chose to view themselves as a pluralistic society in which everyone had an equal opportunity to gain and use political power. Only interest and a willingness to work hard were necessary. An individual began his ascent to power by leading a small group of peers. If his talent for leadership was proved here he could expect to rise to political success in any number of social organizations. In retrospect, this viewpoint ignored the many barriers that limit access to political power in our society. The 1960s were to indicate the nature of these barriers. Minorities were systematically excluded because their rights as citizens were less carefully guarded.

The fifties and sixties were also fertile ground for the diffusion process model. The policy suggestions of this model have been widely recognized and implemented. The model has been used as a guide in structuring communication to persuade individuals around the world to adopt certain innovations. Moderate success has apparently been achieved. The model has spawned strategies for overcoming the traditional beliefs and superstitions of peasants in many cultures.[21] Yet, as we have argued, the model is inadequate to the extent that it fails to conceptualize communication from "adopters." When such communication is studied it tends to be viewed in an instrumental manner; that is, researchers explore how it can be used to achieve the goals of the "change agent." Americans have been too ready to assume that the goal of transmitting technological innovations was not ultimately self-serving and too quick to use a model of the diffusion process to rationalize and justify their actions.

Conclusions

In reviewing classic studies we have attempted to illustrate several characteristics:

1. Studies were generated by conceptualizations which were congruent with widely held beliefs about political institutions.

2. Models evaluated in specific studies were too simplified to represent social processes usefully.

3. Models were not evaluated rigorously; only isolated, bivariate relationships were tested.

4. Conclusions drawn from research tended to exaggerate its usefulness.

As a result, classic research possessed minimal power to reject or modify the conceptualizations which generated it. When these conceptualizations were used to justify or plan social policies, they failed to provide a scientific basis for decision making.

Below we will review some recent political communication studies. Some of these studies are so recent we have not properly integrated them into chapters completed earlier. We have tended to consider only the strengths of each study. None of these studies is without serious flaws but each contains at least one important advance over previous research. It would be misleading to credit these methodological improvements to the authors of these studies. In most cases, they have borrowed techniques from other social science disciplines. Their contribution lies in the way they have applied these improvements to the study of political communication.

Methods in Present Political Communication Research

The field of political communication research is in a state of flux. The models and methods of the past two decades have been recognized as inadequate by many researchers. Yet no new model has acquired the widespread acceptance of previous conceptualizations. Researchers are exploring a range of alternate models. For example, a recent volume edited by Peter Clarke[22] lists nine models which have varying applicability to political communication research. Similarly, there is less consensus concerning the appropriateness of particular data collection or data analysis techniques. Although the limitations of older techniques are apparent, no new procedures have been widely adopted. Instead, various researchers have pioneered different, sometimes competing sets of procedures.

In this section we do not seek to pass judgment on present research trends. To do so would be presumptuous. None of these trends has had sufficient time to demonstrate its long-term utility, but most have produced intriguing short-term results. Nor will we attempt an exhaustive discussion of all new research approaches. Such discussions will in all likelihood fill many books in the years ahead. Instead we will discuss parts of existing studies which illustrate what we believe to be the greatest strengths of these research efforts. We do not consider failings of particular studies but in concluding this section we will indicate what we failed to find in present research.

Earlier in this chapter we outlined five procedures to be followed in doing research which constructs and evaluates models of social processes. These procedures were intended as descriptions of ideal steps to be followed and we contrasted these ideal steps with the limitations of "classic" research. Our contention was that conceptualizations of social processes cannot be tested adequately until sufficiently elaborate models of those processes are built and rigorously evaluated. Though "classic" studies failed to conduct such conclusive tests, they frequently made generalizations which implied that such tests had been made.

Our description of how conceptualizations of social processes should be tested is intended as a goal toward which researchers should strive rather than something which is presently realizable. David Heise[23] has described the difficulty of making causal inferences using existing mathematical models. In particular it is difficult to make inferences when the social processes include variables which influence each other (reciprocal causal relations).

If the goal cannot be presently achieved, what purpose can it serve? As we have illustrated above, it provides a useful standard against which to judge past and present research. It is frequently easy for researchers to forget the limitations within which they work and be tempted to make generalizations which are unwarranted. In our view such temptations must be resisted especially when data are not collected in carefully controlled situations and when researcher bias is likely to affect data collection systematically. Most political communication research is subject to these failings, particularly "policy" research.

Using the standard we propose, it should be possible for researchers to properly qualify their findings. No one can claim to have provided a definitive evaluation of a complex model. Instead, researchers can indicate how their studies have made a definitive evaluation more likely at some point in the future.

Below we will describe eight ways in which specific studies can contribute to the likelihood that definitive evaluations of models will be done. We have labeled these eight forms of contribution as follows:

1. Isolation of a few important variables.
2. Evaluation of bivariate relationships between a few important variables.
3. Evaluation of a small set of bivariate relationships which are logically related to each other.
4. Specification of contingent conditions which are necessary before a small set of bivariate relationships will be found to hold.
5. Evaluation of a small set of multivariate relationships which are logically related.
6. Specification of contingent conditions which are necessary before a small set of multivariate relationships will be found to hold.

7. Evaluation of a large set of multivariate relationships which are logically related.

8. Specification of contingent conditions which are necessary before a large set of multivariate relationships will be found to hold.

Each of these contributions facilitates other contributions which have been listed after it. For example, it is necessary to know what the most important variables are before a test of their interrelationships can be conducted. Evaluations of logically related bivariate relationships should precede evaluations of logically related multivariate relationships because the former are easier and less expensive to conduct. The difficulty and expense of the latter may be justified only after sets of bivariate relationships have been found to hold. Specification of contingent conditions has been listed after evaluation of sets of relationships. We view specification of contingent conditions as a necessary step in the research process. Sometimes these conditions can be incorporated into more complex models. In any case, they serve to delimit the boundaries of specific models, indicating where their usefulness ceases. For example, one model may fit only middle-class teenagers; another may only explain the voting behavior of well informed, politically independent voters.

The findings of the classic studies tend to fall into the first three categories of contributions. Perhaps their greatest usefulness lies in having isolated a large number of potentially important variables. In addition, they have proposed ways to measure these variables. These studies also have evaluated many bivariate relationships and in a few instances have tested small sets of logically related bivariate relationships.

We will use these eight categories of contributions to evaluate several recent studies of political communication and to reach some conclusions about the present state of political communication research. Although these studies provide some of the building blocks for future research, their long-term usefulness is limited. Care must be taken to examine these studies critically to determine whether important variables have been omitted.

We will indicate how each study can be seen to fit into an ongoing effort to conceptualize social processes using model construction and evaluation techniques. No one study can stand alone. Each has value only as part of a continuing effort by many researchers to understand the processes that involve political communication.

Contributions of Recent Research

Three recent convention papers by Thomas Patterson and Robert McClure[24] provide important contributions in categories one through four. Their research is explicitly based upon the findings of several classic studies. In one paper McClure and Patterson (1974) make direct comparisons of their findings to *The People's Choice* (1944). These researchers have been able to advance beyond the classic studies in one very important respect. They have begun to specify certain contingent conditions which are necessary before mass media variables will be found to covary with other variables. By specifying these conditions McClure and Patterson may have provided a basis for building more complex models of social processes in which mass media will be found to play a significant role.

The basic framework for the Patterson and McClure studies is deceptively simple. Using a traditional panel design, they collected survey data from more than 600 persons in Syracuse, New York. They measured four sets of variables: media use, respondent's perceptions of candidate's stand on issues (beliefs), respondent's stand on issues (attitudes), and voting intentions. They also analyzed political content in the mass media. In analyzing relationships among these variables they used a variation of a classic linear media effects model: media use causes change in perception of candidates' stands (beliefs), which causes reevaluation of candidates in light of respondents' issue positions (attitudes), which causes changes in voting intentions. If one candidate is perceived to shift away from the voter's stand while an opponent shifts closer, a change in vote intention may occur. Bivariate statistical tests were used to evaluate each causal link in this model. In contrast with much previous research, the model was found to hold. Strong evidence was found that *certain* media uses cause changes in *certain* candidate perceptions. When these changes in perception cause the voter to evaluate one candidate as closer to himself on issues, his vote intention is likely to change.

Why did the researchers find effects undetected by earlier research? The answer appears to lie in their specification of contingent conditions that are necessary before effects occur and their inclusion of an evaluation step as a necessary part of the process which produces changes in vote intentions. Persons who do not reevaluate candidates for whatever reasons (for example, because they are committed to a political party) will not be affected by the mass media. Patterson and McClure identified voter interest in politics as a contingent condition affecting covariation between high television use and changes in beliefs about candidates. Low-interest voters who had high television use changed their beliefs in ways consistent with certain political commercials. Similarly, a relationship between changes in evaluations of candidates and changes in voting intention was found when only those voters who changed their vote intention were analyzed separately. Thus, the McClure/Patterson model does not hold for persons who do not change vote intentions nor does it hold for persons highly uninterested in politics.

A major finding of their research was that television political commercials may most influence the vote intentions of low-interest voters who change vote intentions. Persons in this group are using the advertisements differently than most other individuals. They apparently have few alternate sources of political information but are willing to listen to political commercials.

The McClure and Patterson studies are by no means definitive tests of even the relatively simple causal models they have proposed. They have taken measures of their variables at only two points in time to evaluate a chain of four causal relationships. Thus measures of changes in variables must be based on only two data collection points. Such changes may fluctuate widely before, between, or after these two points. The value of these studies lies in their ability to give direction to future research, not in having "proved" the effectiveness of political commercials.

Tichenor, Rodenkirchen, Olien, and Donohue[25] evaluate a set of logically interrelated hypotheses. These hypotheses are derived from a conceptualization of a process by which decision making on controversial issues takes place within relatively small communities. Mass media, especially community newspapers, are viewed as occupying a central role in this process. This study contributes in our first four categories. Its most important contribution lies in the fourth category: once again, contingent conditions are specified which delimit the boundaries of particular models.

One of the major findings of the study was that when community newspapers provide extensive coverage of controversial issues, and where these issues are widely perceived as being controversial, poorly educated persons may tend to become as well informed about the issues as highly educated persons. This is in contradiction to a "knowledge gap" hypothesis reported by this same group of researchers earlier.[26] Thus, under certain conditions, media may equalize rather than accentuate knowledge differences. If responsible participation in decision making requires becoming informed, media may increase the number of people capable of participating well. This study also reports that interpersonal communication was higher in communities where issues were perceived as controversial and this increased interpersonal communication was also related to increased knowledge. Thus both mass and interpersonal communication may be reinforcing each other's effects, or the effect of one or the other may be spurious. The design of this study did not permit these alternate explanations to be evaluated. Again, an important value of this study lies in its specification of contingent conditions which permit isolation of significant covariation between media measures and other variables. More complex models can be based on these findings.

McLeod and Becker[27] report an attempt to use a survey panel to validate uses and gratification of media measures by determining whether such measures have the behavioral consequences attributed to them by social theorists. For example, persons who say they use newspapers to find out more about candidates should tend to know more differences between the candidates if in fact their use of media has served the purpose they intended.

McLeod and Becker are building on a research base relatively strong in comparison to other mass communication research areas. Previous findings enabled them to construct several small sets of logically related multivariate relationships and to predict contingent conditions which would affect these sets of relationships. Thus they were able to attempt contributions in categories five and six. They constructed a multivariate model in which all of the media gratifications measures were combined and used to predict eight separate effects variables. Regression analysis was used to evaluate the covariance of each of twenty-two media gratification and avoidance measures with each effect. (The use of regression analysis implies that the researchers were willing to assume that all of the relationships in their model were linear.) The relative predictive power of the entire set of gratification and avoidance measures was compared to the predictive power of a set of five media exposure measures taken at two points in time. The gratification and avoidance measures were found to be more powerful predictors, especially of effect measures at the second point in time. However, this finding may be a methodological artifact because so many gratification and avoidance measures were used relative to the number of exposure measures. (In regression analysis, predictive power of a set of variables tends to increase as you add variables.)

Previous research has shown that media gratifications and avoidance differ greatly by age group. Therefore, it was reasonable for McLeod and Becker to specify age as a contingent condition for their model. Though control of age enabled them to isolate significant relationships, they do not report whether these relationships were increased by the addition of the control variable. Other variables which were statistically controlled for in the regression analysis included political interest, political activity, alienation, education, and media dependence. All of these variables have been found to influence relationships involving uses and gratifications measures in previous studies. Controlling for them allowed McLeod and Becker to discount them as alternate explanations for the observed covariation.

These researchers also tested a somewhat more complex model in which they tried to assess whether covariance of exposure measures and gratifications measures should be added together (model 1) or multiplied (model 2) to estimate the impact of these variables upon dependent measures:

$$\text{exposure} + \text{gratification} = \text{effect} \qquad \text{(model 1)}$$

$$\text{exposure} \times \text{gratification} = \text{effect} \qquad \text{(model 2)}$$

The second model was preferred on conceptual grounds but was found to predict fewer significant effects. The first model would appear to have greater predictive power. Future research will be necessary to determine which model is actually more useful under a variety of contingent conditions.

This study is boldly innovative in a methodologically conservative discipline. It attempts to make contributions at levels beyond those attempted by even some of the best existing research. In doing so, it uses a data analysis technique (regression analysis) which places severe constraints on the form of the models evaluated. In particular, the assumption of linear relationships between variables may be suspect.

Also, the researchers have simply grouped their gratifications measures into sets and used these sets to predict many effects. In many instances only a few of the twenty-two gratification/avoidance measures may be necessary to predict a particular effect. They have left the job of pruning their models for future research. As argued above, parsimony in model construction may be too limiting a criterion to be applied at this stage in the development of the discipline.

No firm substantive conclusion can be reached on the basis of this study. McLeod and Becker have not proved that when individuals gratify certain needs using media content, they will behave in certain ways. But they have lent considerable weight to the argument that this line of research may prove fruitful, and they have set some guidelines for conducting research which will make more important contributions.

A recent study by Katz, Gurevitch, and Haas[28] has also examined media uses and gratifications. Fifteen hundred respondents answered thirty-five items that probed their perceived needs in five areas: information, emotional experience, confidence, social contact, and tension release. Respondents were asked how important various media were to them in satisfying each of these needs. The study makes contributions in categories five and six.

Findings of previous studies were replicated. Strong evidence was found that a "division of labor" exists in which different media are consistently used to serve differing needs. Newspapers were used for information about the world, books were used to increase self-knowledge, and movies were used for emotional experience. While previous studies have reported similar results, none can claim to have examined so many relationships simultaneously, using different items to link media to various needs. The test of covariance used is not a powerful one—only the group average rank orders for various media on each need item are reported—but it is the consistency of the observed covariation, not its "statistical significance," which makes it noteworthy.

The most innovative feature of this study is its use of Smallest Space Analysis (SSA), a data analysis technique that permits a set of intercorrelations to be represented as distances in an N-dimensional space. Objects which generated the intercorrelations (in this case, questionnaire items) appear as points in the space. This permits a quick visual analysis of a large number of relationships. SSA permits the researchers to reach the following conclusions: political uses of radio, television, and newspapers differ from the political uses of movies and books. Both the political and personal uses of radio and television are closely allied. Personal uses of newspapers differ from personal uses of television and radio even though political uses of these media are similar.

These conclusions describe a multivariate model of media-needs relationships which is both complex and descriptive. It is not a process model. It can provide no predictions concerning how relationships will alter in the future. Indeed, it can only note differences in use but these differences cannot be explained in any detail. However, the information provided by this model could conceivably be useful in constructing process models of various kinds. Thus a future model of political socialization might be derived partly from a knowledge that political uses of certain media are similar and thus may have similar socialization consequences.

Katz, Gurevitch, and Haas specify two important contingent conditions for their descriptive models. One is education. The less educated apparently look to electronic media like television to satisfy cognitive as well as emotional needs. The well educated are more likely to use television exclusively to serve emotional needs. The other contingent condition is nationality. The study was completed in Israel and the researchers cite many reasons why Israelis' use of media is likely to differ from media use in other nations.

This study could provide a useful design for future research. Descriptive studies of media use could be made of a variety of populations. Some of these populations could be chosen for theoretical reasons, for instance, because media use is known to be atypical in a specific group. The descriptive studies could eventually permit more useful process models to be constructed by providing insight into how individuals perceive media are serving their needs.

A study by McLeod, Becker, and Byrnes[29] reviews the agenda-setting approach and suggests areas for conceptual and methodological development. Contributions are made in categories three and four. The article makes suggestions which could enable agenda-setting research to make contributions at higher levels.

Two major points made by McLeod et al., both of which have been detailed in the preceding chapter, concern method. First, the agenda-setting process needs to be conceptualized more carefully. Second, the contingent conditions that affect this process must be carefully specified.

In our view, the suggestions made by McLeod et al. point toward the construction and evaluation of process models of agenda-setting. The authors argue that for agenda-setting to be a useful concept, it must predict behavior. In other words, agenda-setting should be viewed as one stage in a social process. But how should this process be conceptualized? In particular, what level of analysis is likely to prove most fruitful?

While the authors raise these questions skillfully, they can provide few answers. Their own research failed to locate any significant links between their measures of how individuals perceived agendas and a set of political behaviors. Links between media agendas and public perceptions of those agendas were found to be tenuous, significant only when certain contingent conditions were present.

One reason for the null findings reported by McLeod et al. may be the highly structured quasi-experimental design which they used. This design may not have been sufficiently flexible to be most useful in conducting what was essentially exploratory research. The authors appear to be attempting a definitive test of the agenda-setting approach, but their conclusions make apparent the exploratory nature of their study. A less structured design might have allowed them to use several measures of how agendas were perceived. It might have been possible for them to locate a more useful measure of this variable.

In Chapter 6, we presented our view that the agenda-setting approach is best viewed as part of a reality construction process. Agenda-setting looks at that part of the process in which media transmit certain perspectives of the world. These perspectives are accepted and used by certain individuals under certain contingent conditions. We also noted that agenda-setting researchers disagree on several methodological issues. These issues primarily concern operational definition of key variables. McCombs[30] has pioneered an approach which has produced useful results even though, as McLeod et al. (1973) point out, it may be difficult to conceptualize these results. Agenda-setting research is at an early stage of development. In our view a wide variety of operational definitions and data collection and analysis techniques should be tried. After considerable research, an attempt can be made to determine which research strategies have proved most useful.

Conclusions

The research reviewed in this section makes contributions which go beyond those of the classic studies. Signs of gradual development of research bases are apparent. In those areas of study where significant previous research has been done, such as media uses and gratifications, it is possible for researchers to build on these findings and construct small-scale multivariate models. Statistical and mathematical models borrowed from other disciplines (such as the form of regression analysis pioneered by economists) are used to evaluate these models. It is possible to assume that with time the normal course of development of this discipline will lead to the origination and evaluation of truly useful models of political communication processes.

We do not wish to be unduly pessimistic but this "normal" course of development may not suffice in the face of certain obstacles. The greatest obstacle may be the temptation to take inconclusive findings too seriously, failing to put them into proper perspective. If our analysis of recent studies is accurate, it suggests that researchers in this area have only begun to make "middle level" contributions. Because these findings are "middle level" they appear to be telling us much more than earlier research. The research reports reviewed above are filled with tables of data. The McLeod and Becker[31] paper, for example, contains fourteen tables, several of which report only the most important summary statistics from a much larger number of regression analyses. We have learned through sometimes bitter experience that the "classic" studies failed to yield "truth." Can we accept the notion that though our present research is obviously more sophisticated, it still falls short of what is needed to provide a firm basis for formulation of social policy? This does not mean that it cannot contribute to policy discussions. But it should not yet be expected to transcend popular belief in any consistent or dramatic fashion.

It is our position that political communication researchers should devote greater concern to where this area of study is going and how it is getting there. It is hard to find much current discussion of this subject in the literature. Most of the discussions which are extant, whether concerned with theory development or with research procedures, appear to be consistent with nineteenth-century "pure science" notions. Are we seeking a "pure" understanding of how political communication processes operate? Are we attempting to find something which is "out there" and which we simply need to get a conceptual and methodological "handle" on? We have rejected the view that political communication research can or should proceed from such abstract motives. We have argued that misleading conclusions can result when it does. There are pragmatic purposes to be served, decisions to be made, which ideally should be based on some knowledge, however flawed and incomplete, of how certain political communication processes operate. Yet in participating in such decision making, it is important not to forget the limitations of research findings.

In "pure science," researchers are not concerned about the implementation of their findings. The researcher bears no responsibility for the actions of the technologist who applies scientific knowledge to the solution of practical problems. This conception may be workable for the physical sciences in which the ability to carefully control variables has made it possible to find universal laws using relatively simple evaluation procedures. However, even here it is being challenged as scientific knowledge yields ever more powerful methods for shaping the environment and man himself. Scientists themselves should anticipate the policy consequences of research. The difficulty is to prevent such awareness from introducing bias which renders subsequent findings useless. In the next section we have described a research approach which we believe can guide pragmatic studies of political communication phenomena. It attempts to meet the needs which we have discussed.

A Method for Political Communication Research

The method introduced here is a synthesis of existing approaches structured to meet the following requirements:

1. It must be useful for studying social processes which may change dramatically as time passes. Relationships between variables cannot be expected to persist for very long. In fact, the very purpose of research may be to suggest how to restructure such processes so that relationships are altered.

2. It must be directed toward the ultimate building and evaluation of complex, multivariate models of social processes. Only such models hold out the possibility of transcending common sense or popular belief.

3. While directed toward model building and evaluation, it should provide findings which have some immediate application. The researcher should be able to participate in policy discussions using tentative, incomplete findings.

4. It should be capable of making efficient use of increasingly sophisticated data collection and analysis procedures. Not only should it borrow such procedures, but it should also guide the construction of procedures which are more directly suited to its purposes.

5. It should be practical in the sense that it does not risk expending great amounts of time and effort attempting to study accurately and precisely phenomena which are not well understood.

We may be too optimistic in suggesting that the method described below satisfies these requirements. Though we provide some arguments for this view, only future research using this approach will show its worth.

Four Stages of Research

Political communication research can be viewed as involving four stages: description, exploration, simple model evaluation, and complex model evaluation. Each of these stages provides elements useful for later stages. Each can answer certain practical questions. Each stage requires the develop-

ment of a more elaborate conceptual framework and the use of more sophisticated data collection and analysis procedures. Whenever a new set of political
communication phenomena is to be examined, researchers should expect
to advance deliberately through all four stages. This deliberate advancement
should be justified on the basis of findings. While movement back and forth
between two stages may prove fruitful, attempts to leap entire stages risk
failure.[32] Data collection and analysis procedures used at later stages must
be guided by more elaborate conceptual frameworks. They should not be
guided by speculation and hope. Nor is a model directly deduced from
"grand theory" sufficient. All of the variables in this model must be operationalized through descriptive and exploratory research. An attempt to
quickly evaluate a complex model using structured, powerful data analysis
procedures is likely to fail. What is worse, in failing it may generate findings
which are temporarily accepted as guides to policy decisions. When its
failings are discovered it may discredit more painstaking, less ambitious
research.

THE DESCRIPTIVE STAGE   At the first stage the researcher should
define operationally the important variables to be studied. A number of
definitions should be created for each important variable. These definitions
should rely on several different measurement techniques. For example, both
unobtrusive observation and a survey questionnaire might be used to gather
data on the same set of variables. During this stage variables should be eliminated when they cannot be measured reliably. New variables should be
created to take their place.

If this stage is neglected, research may proceed without an ability to
observe phenomena objectively. Unreliable, biased measures of variables
may be used which only find what the researcher intended to find. Also,
the researcher will have no way of knowing whether the variable being
measured is important. For example, the researcher may have an accurate,
precise measure of a variable and yet find that less than one percent of the
population vary on this characteristic. Unless the purpose of the research
warrants studying such a small proportion of the public, this information
alone should lead to abandoning the variable.

Once variables are adequately measured, researchers can answer policy
questions concerned with the prevalence of certain phenomena. For example,
they can report how many individuals behave in a particular manner,
possess certain characteristics, or express certain opinions. Occasionally
this information alone can guide important policy decisions.

THE EXPLORATORY STAGE   At the second stage the researcher
should examine a wide range of possible relationships between pairs of

variables. If strong relationships are found, their strength should be further tested by controlling (directly or statistically) for a variety of variables capable of influencing the relationship. In this respect, conventions are gradually emerging concerning the types of variable to be controlled for. For example, it is becoming a common practice to statistically control for demographic variables.

Occasionally this stage may be guided by theory. In most cases, theories provide only vague, incomplete guides in looking for covariation. They may miss important covariation which should be taken into account. In many cases, the theory which guided the descriptive stage will be found to be completely inadequate in the exploratory stage. While serving as an excellent guide to important variables, it may fail completely to anticipate covariation between the variables. Thus a thorough, rigorous exploratory stage can permit theories to be discarded. In turn, it can generate new conceptualizations by directing attention to strong relationships. If the exploratory stage fails to isolate consistent sets of strong relationships between variables, the researcher should return to the descriptive stage and generate new measures of variables.

Exploratory research can answer policy questions concerned with the existence of strong covariation. In some cases such covariance can indicate that certain changes should be made. For example, research which shows that television commercials influence the vote decisions of certain individuals may be taken to indicate that efforts should be made at least to inform these individuals of how they may be influenced. If the research finding is later found to be in error, then the effort made to inform will be of no value. Thus the cost of making certain policy decisions should be balanced against the likelihood that the finding is biased or inaccurate.

The final task of the exploratory stage is to specify systematically the range of contingent conditions which affect a set of bivariate relationships. These data can provide the basis for model construction.

SIMPLE MODEL EVALUATION   Even simple model evaluation should be grounded in a solid set of research findings. Its prime task should be to take the findings of exploratory studies and use them to construct several models which can be evaluated using one or more data analysis procedures. The purpose here is not to find the "true" model which totally explains observed relationships. Rather, it is to find the model which best fits observed relationships and which can guide future data collection and analysis. Several models may provide equally good fits to previous research. Research should be designed which can be expected to provide the most efficient test of the model(s). For example, it may not be necessary to test a model with data collected from a random sample of a population. An easily drawn selective sample may serve as well, in certain instances, to evaluate the usefulness of the model(s).

Simple model construction and analysis can produce tentative answers to social policy questions concerned with the nature of social processes. For example, models may be created of isolated stages in a process (because modeling of the process as a whole may not be possible with present methods). On the other hand, overly simple representations of entire processes may provide a few insights useful for policy decisions. In any case, great care must be taken in drawing conclusions to be used in formulating policy from findings that serve to evaluate simple models. It may be necessary to establish a set of guidelines for using such findings in this way.

The final task of simple model construction is the specification of contingent conditions which affect its usefulness. For example, if a model provides a timebound "snapshot" of a process, then time should be specified as a contingent condition. Attempts can then be made to construct models of the process at earlier or later stages in time. Eventually this work should enable the construction of a complex model of the process which encompasses all of the simple models and thus incorporates the contingent conditions as part of the model.

COMPLEX MODEL EVALUATION   Complex model evaluation should occur as the culmination of a long research effort. It should not be used to attempt an evaluation of a very complex theory which has not previously been empirically tested. Instead, it should serve to integrate and organize findings from studies which evaluate simple models. It should attempt to overcome the contingent conditions which limit the usefulness of simple models by incorporating these conditions as variables inside the model.

Data analysis procedures appropriate for complex model evaluation in the social sciences have yet to be created, though some techniques are being applied on an experimental basis. This situation should not be viewed as discouraging. We have yet to begin adequate work on simple model construction. We will not need procedures for evaluating complex models until we have generated useful sets of simple models.

As we argued earlier, complex model evaluation should provide the best means of generating useful findings for policy decisions. However, this will happen only if it is preceded by well-executed research at each prior stage. Complex model construction and evaluation can be viewed as an attempt to represent entire social processes. The representation is useful to the extent that it enables useful predictions to be made about *changes* in the relationships between variables over time. Thus it predicts not only the existence of relationships but also the way in which those relationships change. Many policy decisions could be improved if accurate predictions of changes in social processes could be made. Social planners are frequently able to manipulate at least a few of the variables in a social process. However, they may have only political doctrine, partisan claims, intuition, and popular beliefs to guide their manipulation. For example, most of the "War on Poverty" programs of the 1960s set out to manipulate variables in a wide range of social processes. The "war" was guided by an inadequate knowledge of these processes. In many cases, consequences were quite different from those intended. What appeared to be a golden opportunity to establish the usefulness of policy research instead tended to discredit such research.

Assumptions of Our Method

Two assumptions are inherent in the method we have proposed. First, model building and testing are assumed to be desirable and practical research objectives. Second, policy decisions are assumed to be best guided by research which evaluates social processes. These assumptions, in our opinion, are vital if future political communication research is to progress beyond the findings we have summarized here.

The notion that social researchers should construct and evaluate models of social processes is relatively new, particularly in the area of communication research. Very few examples exist of research which explicitly attempts model building and evaluation. Our review of current research found only simple models being evaluated, often with analysis techniques which were not particularly suited to the testing of process models. Often bivariate measures of covariance were used. At best, regression analysis or smallest space analysis was used. None of these procedures is appropriate for evaluating models in which variable relationships are expected to change over time. However, examples of research on social processes can be found in other disciplines. James Coleman[33] has provided some useful, though relatively simple, mathematical models suitable for the study of social processes. Blalock[34] has also provided models for the study of social change. It should be relatively easy for communication researchers to apply existing techniques to social processes which involve communication. Research barriers should appear only after the usefulness of these techniques has been exhausted.

Our second assumption holds that research on social processes will provide the best guide to policy decisions.[35] This assumption must be tested empirically. We have outlined our reasons for accepting this assumption. In our view, communication variables will be found to play crucial roles in a wide variety of social processes ranging from political socialization to elections. In our review of research we have found what we consider to be overwhelming evidence for this view.

Future Role of Mass Communication Research

Why is the study of communication, especially mass communication, likely to prove fruitful for social policy research? In addition to playing important roles in social processes, communication variables possess another characteristic which should make them of special interest to social planners. Unlike many social variables which are costly or difficult to manipulate, communication variables can be altered relatively easily. We live in a society which has accepted constant disruption of communication patterns as the price to be paid for new communication technology. Unlike some social variables which require decades for change to be implemented, changes in communication patterns can occur overnight. The television ratings game is testimony to the transitory nature of prime time television viewing habits.

Not only do communication variables lend themselves to social planning, but such planning may be necessary to avert crises occasioned by chaotic changes in communication patterns. Perhaps in no other aspect of human life is the development of new technology as likely to introduce sudden, potentially disruptive change during the next few decades. We have made numerous references to the disruptive impact which the introduction of television may have had in the 1950s. Socialization processes may have altered. The way in which elections take place has been transformed.

Changes in communication technology are much more likely to occur than changes in most other technologies because changes in communication devices can significantly alter the quality of daily life while consuming a minimal amount of natural resources and having only an incidental impact on the physical environment. By comparison, the automobile is a clumsy, destructive piece of technology for facilitating human contact. As we alter our lifestyle from conspicuous consumption of material goods, a logical alternative is likely to lie in the increased production and consumption of communication products. But while communication technology offers a logical alternative for the future, the social consequences of choosing this alternative are uncertain.

If our view of mass communication is useful, the development of new communication technology will offer the possibility of completely reshaping existing communication patterns. To the extent that these patterns underlie or facilitate various social processes, these processes can be altered. Thus the development of communication devices may provide a key to transforming human existence. This is a power which can be used positively or negatively. One task of communication research will be to provide a basis for deciding which communication technologies should be developed and which uses of those technologies should be encouraged.

The knowledge produced by communication research could conceivably be used by social planners at all levels in society. In our view, the ideal use of this knowledge would be made by individuals seeking to reshape their immediate social environment. Planning done at higher levels of society should be directed toward shaping flexible communication systems that have many capacities. Then, these systems could be given final form by the individuals using them. For example, a flexible cable/videocassette system would allow groups of individuals to create and exchange television programs. Each individual would be permitted to do his own programming from a large "library" of diverse program offerings. Programming choices could be made with a knowledge of the social consequences likely to follow from particular choices. Programs could be produced by small amateur groups that have designed the programs to have a particular social impact. The ideal communication system will maximize the ability of each member of the system to carry on useful transactions with the system.

The potential usefulness of future communication research is great. Our immediate task is to realize this potential by creating a discipline grounded on a sound methodological foundation with some firm directions for theory construction. The challenge of the discipline will be to keep pace with communication technology so that technical changes are used creatively and constructively. We must avoid at all costs creating a discipline which simply rationalizes existing technology or commonsense beliefs about social processes. Research on political communication should itself become a most useful form of political communication.

Notes

1. Stanislav Andreski, *Social Science as Sorcery* (New York: St. Martin's Press, 1972).
2. Paul F. Lazarsfeld, in *Qualitative Analysis: Historical and Critical Essays* (Boston: Allyn and Bacon, 1972), noted the welcome reception given early media research findings by industry executives because these findings supported them. He expressed concern about what would happen when research findings inevitably conflicted with what media professionals believed. "The reverse side of this picture is that the critic himself becomes nervous. Because he anticipates the kind of reaction which his criticism will elicit, he is somewhat hesitant to make it. This is a rather serious matter. Those of us social scientists who are especially interested in communications research depend upon the industry for much of our data. Actually most publishers and broadcasters have been very generous and cooperative in this recent period during which communications research has developed as a kind of joint enterprise between industries and universities. But we academic people always have a certain sense of tight-rope walking: at what point will the commercial partners find some necessary conclusion too hard to take and at what point will they shut us off from the indispensable sources of funds and data?" (p. 124).

3. Philip Emmert and William D. Brooks, *Methods of Research in Communication* (Boston: Houghton Mifflin, 1970), p. 12.
4. Jack Douglas recently edited an anthology which describes the experience of sociology from several perspectives. Jack Douglas, *Relevance of Sociology* (New York: Appleton-Century Crofts, 1970).
5. Another reason hypotheses are presented as theories is the constraint imposed on research by "publish or perish" norms which influence researchers to generate a few quick hypothesis tests. Once an article is published no pressure exists to replicate any other test.
   In addition, the evaluation of individual hypotheses is most appropriate when done using data collected in laboratory experiments. Ideally, such experiments permit complex natural processes to be broken up into their component parts such that each part can be considered separately under carefully controlled conditions.
6. See Chapter 2 abstracts, Greenstein, 1970, pp. 50, 975.
7. Cognitive development has not been overlooked by political socialization researchers. But they tend to view such development as contributing to a long-term linear socialization process. For example, Chapter 2 abstracts, Adelson and O'Neil, 1966, pp. 295–306, examine how political concepts change as children mature.
8. Scott Ward and Daniel Wackman, in Peter Clarke, ed., *New Models for Mass Communication and Research* (Beverly Hills, Calif.: Sage Publications, 1973), pp. 119–40.
9. Draft of political socialization chapter prepared for S. Renshon, ed., *Handbook of Political Socialization*, "Mass Communication in Political Socialization" (in press).
10. Chapter 2 abstracts, Clarke, 1965, pp. 20, 539–46.
11. Chapter 2 abstracts, Bell, 1968, pp. 6, 82–95.
12. Greenstein, 1970, p. 973.
13. See Chapter 3 abstracts of *The People's Choice; How the Voter Makes Up His Mind in a Presidential Campaign* by Paul F. Lazarsfeld, Bernard Berelson, and Hazel Gaudet (New York: Duell, Sloan and Pierce, 1944), and *Voting; A Study of Opinion Formation in a Presidential Campaign* by Bernard Berelson, Paul F. Lazarsfeld, and William N. McPhee (Chicago: University of Chicago Press, 1954).
14. Ibid.
15. Thomas E. Patterson and Robert D. McClure, "Political Advertising: Voter Reaction." Paper presented to the American Association for Public Opinion Research meeting in Asheville, N. C., May 1973.
16. Carl I. Hovland, A. A. Lumsdaine, and F. D. Sheffield, *Experiments on Mass Communication* (New York: Wiley, 1949).
17. Carl I. Hovland, Irving L. Janis, and Harold H. Kelly, *Communication and Persuasion; Psychological Studies of Opinion Change* (New Haven: Yale University Press, 1953). Though the authors do not use the term "selectivity process," they were the first to create a conceptual framework that emphasized the need to differentiate attention, comprehension, and acceptance.
18. Elihu Katz and Paul F. Lazarsfeld, *Personal Influence* (Glencoe, Ill.: Free Press, 1955).
19. Everett M. Rogers and F. Floyd Shoemaker, *Communication of Innovations* (New York: Free Press, 1972).
20. Ibid., Appendix.
21. Ibid., for descriptions of such strategies.
22. Peter Clarke, ed., *New Models for Mass Communication and Research*, Vol. II, Sage Annual Review of Communication Research (Beverly Hills, Calif.: Sage Publications, 1973).

23. David Heise, "Problems in Path Analysis and Causal Influence," Chapter 2 in Edgar Borgatta and George W. Bohrnstedt, eds., *Sociological Methodology 1969* (San Francisco: Jossey-Bass, 1969).
24. Robert D. McClure and Thomas E. Patterson. The 1973 papers are abstracted in Chapter 3. The 1974 reference is McClure and Patterson, "The People's Choice Revisited in the Age of Television," paper presented to the American Association for Public Opinion Research meeting in Lake George, N.Y., May 1974.
25. P.J. Tichenor, J.M. Rodenkirchen, C.N. Olien, and G.A. Donohue "Community Issues, Conflict and Public Affairs Knowledge," in Clarke, *New Models for Mass Communication*, Vol. II.
26. Chapter 4 abstracts, Tichenor, Donohue, and Olien, 1970.
27. Jack M. McLeod and Lee B. Becker, "Testing the Validity of Media Gratification Through Political Effects Analysis." Paper presented to the Association for Education in Journalism, San Diego, Calif., August 1974. Also in J. Blumler and E. Katz, eds., *The Uses and Gratifications Approach to Mass Communication Research* (Beverly Hills, Calif.: Sage Publications, 1974).
28. Elihu Katz, Michael Gurevitch, and Hadassah Haas, "On the Use of Mass Media for Important Things," *American Sociological Review* 38 (April 1973): 164–81.
29. Jack M. McLeod, Lee B. Becker, and James Byrnes, "Another Look at the Agenda-Setting Function of the Press," *Communication Research* 1:2 (April 1974): 131–66.
30. Maxwell E. McCombs and Donald L. Shaw, "The Agenda-Setting Function of the Mass Media," *Public Opinion Quarterly* 36 (1972): 176–87.
31. McLeod and Becker, 1974.
32. Samuel Becker provides what we consider an important caveat to this conclusion: "I would suggest that the history of knowledge shows no pattern and you err when you suggest that it does. You might come to your conclusion by looking at the failures in the history of knowledge. But if you look at the successes—the points at which clear gains were made—you would be hard put to find a consistent pattern. I would suggest that any important theoretical advance requires a logical leap which no one yet has been able to explain; it is creativity of the purest sort" (letter to the authors, 17 September 1975).
33. James Coleman, *Introduction to Mathematical Sociology* (New York: Free Press, 1964).
34. Herbert Blalock, ed., *Causal Models in the Social Sciences* (Chicago: Aldine, 1971).
35. For an excellent discussion of social science research for utilization and policy, see Paul F. Lazarsfeld and Jeffrey G. Reitz, *An Introduction to Applied Sociology* (New York: Elsevier, 1975).

8

Concluding Remarks

The purpose of this book was to examine and evaluate the empirical evidence on the impact of the mass media on political behavior. By considering the many studies in the preceding chapters, we sought to delineate the issues confronting the field as well as to explore the significance of the findings. Our specific objectives as stated in Chapter 1 were to determine what we know about the field; what we do not know; what, in our opinion, we ought to know; and how we measure, assess, and evaluate the effects of mass communication on political behavior. Chapters 2 through 6 explored the first three objectives, while Chapter 7 addressed the last of these objectives. Here we will review the current state of knowledge and the impact of the knowledge gained so far. Finally, we will conclude with a brief discussion of the transactional model—the model which we have referred to many times and which, in our opinion, augurs best for advancing our knowledge of the relationship between mass communication and political behavior.

Current State of Knowledge

For at least two decades, the classic studies in our field have permeated the scholarly literature of mass communication and political science, and have dominated interpretations of media's impact on political behavior. Throughout this book we have referred to the classic studies as pace-setting, innovative, scholarly achievements. Chapters 2 and 3, particularly, detail these studies. We have also noted several problems with them recognizable in hindsight. It should be apparent (we have explicitly stated so in several discussions), however, that our criticisms are directed more toward the persistent reliance on the findings of classic studies by researchers than they are toward the studies themselves. It is true that we have serious reservations about the classic studies' conceptualizations and methods. We have discussed these reservations at length in the preceding chapter. Several of these observations could be made only in light of the development, subsequent to these studies, of sophisticated research procedures and techniques.

Human behavior is not a static phenomenon. Neither is media technology dormant in society; it advances in both sophistication and application. Thus media and political behavior may have different relationships at different times under different conditions. Certainly, if newspapers and radio reinforced the predispositions of the electorate of 1940 and television was developing as a source of political information in the early 1950s, we should expect *some* differences in findings in 1976 from those that were reported thirty-six years earlier.

The findings of the classic studies have been the benchmarks for subsequent studies. They have been used as reference points from which variables in other studies of media's impact on political socialization, voting, political information, political alienation, and media use in campaigns have been measured, when measured at all. While many of our comments on and interpretations of particular study findings may be debatable, the epicyclic influence of classic findings upon later researchers in the field is irrefutable.

Clearly, the classic findings of mass media's impact on political behavior have been sacrosanct in the political science literature in two ways. First, new studies often extend their results, generalizing to the effects of selected communication variables by quoting the findings of classic studies. Second, where mass communication variables are empirically investigated, often they are conceptualized from the point of view generated within the classic studies in our field.

On the other side, when viewing the way mass communication researchers have made use of political science variables (such as political socialization), we found that in many studies those variables were not conceptualized as thoroughly as they had been by political scientists. In addition, studies often failed to include theory or models to guide the selection of research designs and variables in the testing of hypotheses.

Any assessment of the current state of knowledge which is derived from the findings of studies discussed in this volume must be attenuated by these research artifacts. This attenuation imposes two restrictions on our assessment. The first restriction is that we cannot be reasonably certain of what we know about mass communication and political behavior; that is, our probability estimates for given media/political behavior relationships are not reliable, because research in the two areas has been conducted as distinct and separate enterprises. Relatively few systematic approaches to research take into account variables in both fields. The second restriction is an extension of the first. Studies in both fields tend to be isolated investigations, making it difficult to perceive the cumulative body of theory which could advance our knowledge. Heinz Eulau's analysis of dilemmas in behavioral research is appropriate for this discussion. He asserts:

An empirical science is built by the slow, modest, and piecemeal cumulation of theory, methods and data. The importance of a study, no matter how big or small, must be judged in the total context of relevant research. The dilemma of behavioral research in politics [we would add mass communication as well] is not the scarcity of studies but absence of a cumulative body of theory within which new studies can be accommodated and digested so that as research proceeds, one can speak of an expansion of knowledge.[1]

As with most inquiries about phenomena, the more we know, the more we need to know. To put it another way, answers to questions often prompt new questions which need answers. But with the current state of knowledge of how the mass media affect political behavior, a more correct phrase for our assessment is: *what we know is not what we thought we knew and what we thought we knew is more persistent in the literature than what we know.*

Tracing the Influence
of the Classic Studies

What we thought we knew comes partly from the classic studies. *What we know* comes partly from our assessment of studies conducted since the classics.

What has been the influence of *what we thought we knew* on policy decisions in the United States? Assuming that we are correct in the assessment of *what we know*, what are the implications for future policy decisions? To answer these questions we must be able to demonstrate that given studies in fact have influenced policy decisions.

Tracing the influence of social science research on policy decisions of institutions is a risky business. The task is subject to errors of inference and judgment. Moreover, since the process requires the linking of study findings over a considerable time period, it is complicated with problems of determining causation. Most studies are designed to investigate given phenomena to expand our knowledge about them. In this sense, behavioral scientists are not concerned with affecting policy. Scientists concerned with policy might do a series of studies on a particular phenomenon so as to produce *alternative strategies* for policy-making bodies. Yet, lacking such data, policy makers may connect discrete studies—the findings of which appear to have support among scholars—and propose policy as a result of their evaluation. In this way, studies may be used for policy when in fact their original purpose was otherwise. It is one thing to form a commission on desegregation in education and to generate the Coleman Report.[2] It is yet another to search the literature on race attitudes, education, housing patterns, economic factors, and the like, and then propose from the findings of those studies a national policy on desegregation. Both methods to secure policy data may be subject to errors; clearly, the "Coleman" approach is more desirable than the other.

In Chapter 7 we emphasized the need to design research not to establish "universal truths" but to achieve more pragmatic purposes such as decision making. Whether the behavioral scientist is amenable or not, whether his research is intended to influence policy decisions or not, others in and out of scholarly research will most likely use his findings to affect change in policy, especially if the "evidence" appears to be widely accepted and adopted to support theory. Calling again on Eulau, but for reasons other than those he had perhaps intended, what is accepted as *theory* is most persuasive among those who conduct and use research:

> Theory found useful in one context will sooner or later fertilize investigations in other contexts. A theory's viability is best judged by its range of interdisciplinary applicability. If it contributes to the explanation of behavior in many different settings, political as well as non-political, *the knowledge gained will be the more significant.* [Italics added][3]

Despite these caveats, it would be useful to trace the influence of classic studies on mass communication and political behavior upon policy-making groups. Obviously, to trace *all* influences on *all* policy-making bodies would fill yet another book, were it possible in the first place. Instead, we will look at a single example: the influence of classic findings on political socialization on policy considerations for secondary education social studies curricula in the United States. Three comments are necessary before we proceed:

1. As noted in several discussions in this and previous chapters, the contributions of the classic voting studies have been pace-setting; our critical evaluation of them in certain contexts is not meant to detract from their overall value or earned recognition.

2. Researchers whose studies are used in the case example are to be highly commended for contributions to their fields. We included their studies to illustrate an effect of science on policy which they may not have intended.[4]

3. We are concerned here only with the findings about mass communication's role in the political socialization process. We are not concerned here with other aspects of political socialization, such as positive system support versus attention to system defects, which may affect high school civics curricula.

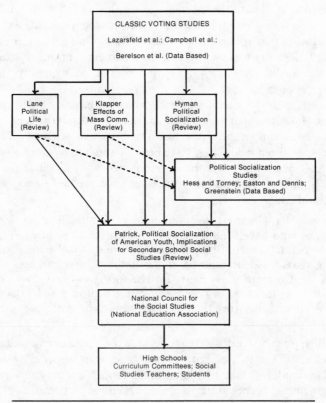

Figure 6

**A CASE EXAMPLE OF THE FLOW OF INFLUENCE OF CLASSIC STUDIES
ON POLITICAL SOCIALIZATION POLICY
CONSIDERATIONS OF SOCIAL STUDIES CURRICULA
IN SECONDARY EDUCATION IN THE UNITED STATES**

Note: Solid line indicates major influence; dashed line indicates partial influence.

Figure 6 represents the flow of influence from the classic voting studies, through reviews of studies on political behavior, mass communication behavior, and political socialization and through empirically based studies on political socialization, to policy-making groups. A review of research by Patrick[5] is the first link in the flow which is clearly in the policy domain, since the review was undertaken to affect policy.[6] The second link in the policy domain occurs between the Patrick research review and the National Council for the Social Studies, the publishers of the Bulletin.[7]

In Chapters 2 and 3 we discussed what the classic studies found on the relationship between mass communication and political socialization and the election process. Discussing the Patrick research review, we briefly linked his assessment of mass communication effects on the political socialization process to previous studies (including the "classics") and we commented then that these findings were being disseminated among educators throughout the country. We should note here that Patrick's review was, in our opinion, well done and certainly in keeping with his objectives. Once again, our criticism is not with people but with process.

We are concerned with the *substance* of the flow of influence, especially as it bears upon mass communication's role in the political socialization process. How is that role portrayed in the flow of influence represented in Figure 6? Essentially it is characterized by two conceptions of mass media effects—the media *reinforce predispositions* and consequently they have *limited effects* on behavior.

These conceptions of media's impact, which we have seriously questioned as a result of our research review and analysis, flow from the classic studies; they have been supported along the way by social scientists' reviews of studies in specialized fields; they have been assented to by empiricists studying political socialization who have determined not to include mass media variables in their studies; and they have been accepted for policy considerations with this statement:

> Those who have feared the imminence of a "Big Brother" controlled society, or who have shuddered at the prospects of a "Power Elite" with the potential to control thought through monopoly of mass communications media should be relieved at the findings of researchers about the impact of American mass media in the formation of values. The mass media tend to function as *reinforcers* of the attitudes and values already held by individuals rather than as converters to new attitudes and values. [Italics added][8]

That high school students may be studying political socialization as recommended in the Patrick report appears to us to be perfectly defensible and perhaps laudable. That as a result of the report they may *not* be studying the mass media as agents in the process of political socialization is not only unfortunate; in our opinion it would also perpetuate a tenuous conclusion about mass media effects.

Our case example is illustrative of the influence of classic studies on subsequent research and on policy-making bodies. If, as we have implied, mass media's role in the political socialization process has been misjudged, or at least underestimated, how in the future may policy groups evaluate communication studies in the face of such "overwhelming" evidence?

There are several questions which the research evaluator may ask about the inclusion or exclusion of variables, methodological procedures, and the like. But, in our view, the basic question to be asked is, *how has the communication process been conceptualized* in the study under examination? Since there are different models corresponding to different views of the process of communication, the answer to that question will at least identify the position from which the study has investigated certain phenomena. This will show whether or not the model conforms to the research evaluator's own view of the social process about which recommendations are to be made for policy decisions.

The model of the communication process utilized in many of the classic studies is best described as a communicator-dominated model—a model examining the one-way flow of influence from the communicator to the audience. Another model, which we prefer, examines influence from both the communicator and the audience. This has been termed the *transactional model*.

We will discuss this model below, since it not only applies to the process of policy making, but also concludes this book with the model we feel will most further our knowledge of mass communication and political behavior.

The Transactional Model

For several decades communication research concentrated on communicator variables. It was a natural response satisfying several societal needs to determine which kinds of communication have given effects. It was a persuasion model which fitted nicely for propaganda purposes in World War II and for achieving desired marketing results among consumers in our society.

Before World War II much of the experimental literature in communication documented strong direct effects on audiences when independent variables of the communicator and content variables were tested. Just after the war the communicator was described as the *first* element in a logical ordering of elements in the communication act. Lasswell's famous question, "*Who* says what in which channel to whom with what effect [italics added]?"[9] is a case in point, though he did not propose studying communicator variables over investigating audience variables.

Though Lazarsfeld et al. suggested that their findings of mass media effects on political behavior should be viewed as tentative, subsequent researchers clung to those findings as though they were universal truths. Moreover, the research on political effects of mass media which followed that classic study mimicked the communicator dominated model, which had been so widely accepted as the research model for inquiries in the field.

Even researchers of the superb voting studies of the Survey Research Center at the University of Michigan were persuaded that the mass media's contribution to political behavior was so slight that cursory treatment of media variables was in order. Once again, the model and results were not questioned.

The change from the communicator dominated model to a transactional model in which both the audience and the communicator is considered was slow in development. Only recently have empirical studies emerged (we have reviewed these studies in previous chapters) despite the fact that a persuasive case for such a change was advanced in the middle fifties and extended in the sixties.

In 1956 Zimmerman and Bauer[10] reported experimental results which, probably more than any other single study, altered our view of the audience as inactive. The study jarred our preconceptions of audience behavior by suggesting that audience members select new information with reference to their relationship to other future audiences. They were less likely to remember information which was in conflict with their perceptions of the future audience's views and more likely to retain information which they felt would be welcomed.

Obviously, this view of the audience was in Davison's mind when he asserted:

> The communicator's audience is not a passive recipient—it cannot be regarded as a lump of clay to be molded by the master propagandist. Rather, the audience is made up of individuals who demand something from the communication to which they are exposed, and who select those that are likely to be *useful* to them. In other words, *they must get something from the manipulator if he is to get something from them. A bargain is involved.* Sometimes, it is true, the manipulator is able to lead his audience into a bad bargain by emphasizing one need at the expense of another or by representing a change in the significant environment as greater than it actually has been. But audiences, too, can drive a hard bargain. Many communicators who have been widely disregarded or misunderstood know that to their cost. [Italics added][11]

The concept inherent in the transactional model was brilliantly advanced by Raymond A. Bauer in his article "The Obstinate Audience: The Influence Process from the Point of View of Social Communication."[12] Bauer held that of two models—the social model of communication (what we have been referring to as the communicator dominated model) and the model representing communication as a transactional process—the transactional one is better suited for communication research. He suggests that

> the social model of communication: the model held by the general public, and by social scientists when they talk about advertising and somebody else's propaganda, is one of the exploitations of man by man. It is a model of one-way influence: the communicator *does* something to the audience, while to the communicator is generally attributed considerable latitude and power to do what he pleases . . . the model which *ought* to be inferred

from the data of research is of communication as a transactional process in which two parties each expect to give and take from the deal approximately equitable values. This, although it *ought* to be the scientific model, is far from generally accepted as such.[13]

Of particular interest for us are the comments of both Davison and Bauer. Several references to audience variables appear in their articles. Davison speaks of communication content which would be *useful* to audiences. He feels that audiences *want something* from communicators. In a like fashion, Bauer uses such phrases as "seeking out information" and "man seeks and uses information."[14] These precursory phrases connect well with our previous discussions of promising areas of research—uses and gratifications and information seeking. The model's attention to audience variables also may be useful in agenda-setting research, by solving the problem of causation—whether agendas are set by communicators or audiences.

Bauer advances a most persuasive argument for applying the transactional model in social science research:

> The argument for using the transactional model for *scientific* purposes is that it opens the door more fully to exploring the intention and behavior of members of the audience and encourages inquiry into the influence of the audience on the communicator by specifically treating the process as a two-way passage. In addition to the influence of the audience on the communicator, there seems little doubt that influence also operates in the "reverse" direction. But the persistence of the one-way model of influence discourages the investigation of both directions of relationship.[15]

The argument, we feel, should be particularly pertinent for research on the effects of mass communication on political behavior.

We conclude this volume with what for us is a most comforting note. As we stated in Chapter 1, we did not want merely to review studies and leave it at that. We saw the need to develop our own assessment of the research and to comment, sometimes critically, when we felt the evidence suggested a point of view different from traditional prevailing views. Hence our discussions of the classic studies, of the Columbia and Michigan studies, and of studies on political socialization.

As we complete this book, we have received a paper from Jack M. McLeod,[16] whose research we have discussed in several chapters. His conclusions on the influence of classic studies, which stem from his extensive research with Jay G. Blumler in England, agree with the position we have advanced.

Others will, we are certain, take exception to our point of view. That is as it should be. If we have raised questions which stir social scientists—

especially mass communication and political science scholars—to debate, if not to advocate our position, we will have accomplished our mission. If we have persuaded students of political communication to search their own media and political behavior and compare their experiences with what social scientists say about them, we will indeed have been rewarded.

Notes

1. H. Eulau, *The Behavioral Persuasion in Politics* (New York: Random House, 1963), p. 116.
2. James S. Coleman, Ernest Q. Campbell, Carl F. Hobson, James McPartland, and Alexander M. Mood, *Equality of Educational Opportunity* (Washington, D.C.: U.S. Office of Education, 1966).
3. Eulau, 1963, p. 22.
4. In several studies the authors variously comment on policy matters which should be or may be considered as a result of their findings. See, for example, Fred I. Greenstein's chapter, "Postscript on the Educational Implications of Political Socialization Research," in his *Children and Politics*, rev. ed. (New Haven: Yale University Press, 1969), pp. 172–90; and R.D. Hess and J.V. Torney, *The Development of Political Attitudes in Children* (Garden City, N.Y.: Doubleday, 1967), p. 247 *passim*.
5. J.J. Patrick, *Political Socialization of American Youth: Implications for Secondary School Social Studies*, Research Bulletin No. 3 (Washington, D.C.: National Council for the Social Studies, 1967).
6. Witness this explanation of Patrick's assignment: "Mr. Patrick's paper is one of the products of the High School Curriculum Center in Government, Indiana University. This Center, established jointly in July 1966 by the Department of Government and the School of Education with a grant from the U.S. Office of Education, is writing, piloting, and evaluating new materials and methods for teaching these materials for courses in civics and government in grades nine through twelve.

   "It seemed obvious to us that any effort to write materials concerning civics and government for use in high schools without a prior examination of what students believe and understand about government as a result of earlier learning experiences would result in many frustrations and false starts. Therefore, Mr. Patrick, a research associate for the Center, undertook a review of existing research on the topic of political socialization. He made no attempt to engage in original research; *his assignment was to pull together into a single essay the research on political socialization of American youth that seemed relevant for secondary schools social studies.*

   "*Although his original purpose was merely to prepare a working paper for the use of the Center staff, the result was a document that we believe will be useful to many professional people, especially to secondary school teachers of civics and government* [italics added]." S.H. Engle and H.D. Mehlinger, Foreword, in ibid., p. v.
7. The 1967 President of the Council not only endorsed the research review, he

suggested a wider influence: "The authors of the Foreword rightly indicate that the findings surveyed in this booklet hold real implications for socio-civic education in high school. But the *studies and evidence assayed are equally important for teachers at the elementary and the college levels* who are concerned over the civic values of society [italics added]." R.E. Gross, Preface, in ibid., p. iii.

8. Ibid., pp. 46–47.

9. H.D. Lasswell, "The Structure and Function of Communication in Society," in L. Bryson, ed., *The Communication of Ideas* (New York: Institute for Religious and Social Studies, 1948). Reprinted in W. Schramm and D.F. Roberts, eds., *The Process and Effects of Mass Communication*, rev. ed. (Urbana: University of Illinois Press, 1971), p. 84.

10. C. Zimmerman and R.A. Bauer, "The Effects of an Audience on What Is Remembered," *Public Opinion Quarterly* 20 (1956): 238–48. Replication of this experiment was completed by W. Schramm and W. Danielson.

11. W.P. Davison, "On the Effect of Communication," *Public Opinion Quarterly* 23 (1959): 360. It is striking to compare Davison's comments to those of Key: "The perverse and unorthodox argument of this little book is that voters are not fools. To be sure, many individual voters act in odd ways indeed; yet, in the large, the electorate behaves about as rationally and responsively as we should expect, given the clarity of the alternatives presented to it and the character of the information available to it. In American presidential campaigns of recent decades the portrait of *the American electorate that develops from the data is not one of an electorate strait-jacketed by social determinants or moved by subconscious urges triggered by devilishly skillful propagandists. It is rather one of an electorate moved by concern about central and relevant questions of public policy, of governmental performance, and of executive personality* [italics added]." V.O. Key, *The Responsible Electorate* (Cambridge: Harvard University Press, 1966), pp. 7–8.

12. *American Psychologist* 19 (1964): 319–28. Reprinted in Schramm and Roberts, 1971, pp. 326–46.

13. Schramm and Roberts, ibid., pp. 327–28.

14. Ibid., pp. 336–37.

15. Ibid., p. 345.

16. J.M. McLeod and J.D. Brown, "Using Longitudinal Data to Identify the Political Effects of the Mass Media." Paper presented to the World Association for Public Opinion Research Congress, Montreux, Switzerland, September 1975.

Author Index

Subject Index